Themis
Bar Review

Multistate Performance Test

ISBN 978-1-949634-00-6

MULTISTATE PERFORMANCE TEST

Table of Contents

Sample answers and Drafters' Point Sheets for all MPTs found in this book are available online by clicking on the last chapters of the MPT outline.

HOW TO USE THIS BOOK

This book contains the Multistate Performance Tests (MPTs) that are assigned in your Themis Bar Review course, including those used as workshop, practice, and graded assignments. To get the most out of your PT preparation, be sure to first watch the MPT Workshop lecture series. Refer to this book when you are assigned an MPT in your course.

Note that these MPTs are reprinted as provided by the National Conference of Bar Examiners and may include typographical errors and inconsistent pagination. Therefore, we recommend that you refer to the page footers to quickly find the assigned MPT.

After you have completed an assigned MPT, you can self-grade your work by using the sample answer in the course as a guide. To view the answer, simply log in and select the applicable MPT assignment listed under Essays in Flex Study.

Additionally, sample answers and NCBE Drafters' Point Sheets for all MPTs found in this book are available online by clicking on the last chapters of the MPT outline.

Feel free to reach out directly to our experienced staff attorneys or your state directors in our online notification center, by email, or by phone.

Good luck!

Themis Bar Review

info@themisbar.com

(888) 843-6476

Outline: Introduction to the MPT

INTRODUCTION TO THE MULTISTATE PERFORMANCE TEST

Table of Contents

INTRODUCTION TO THE MULTISTATE PERFORMANCE TEST

I. INTRODUCTION

The Multistate Performance Test ("MPT") allows bar candidates an extremely short time in which to research and write a lawyer-like project. Here's the good news: you don't need to know *any* specific knowledge of the law to do well on the MPT. Everything you'll need to write a strong response is given to you by the National Conference of Bar Examiners—the issue to be addressed, the background of the issue, the facts on which the analysis will be based, and the legal authorities on which you will rely. As such, the MPT is commonly described, rightfully so, as an "open book" or "closed universe" examination. In law school parlance, the MPT may also resemble a "canned" memo project that you might have encountered during first-year legal writing, where it was your job to sift through pages and pages of factual and legal material—some relevant, some not so much—in an attempt to complete the writing assignment.

Be careful on the MPT, however. Even though you don't need to know any specific law, the MPT certainly isn't easy. On the MPT, you'll have to review and dissect more than a dozen densely filled pages of facts and legal authorities on your way to completing a polished legal document under stressful examination conditions. And you have only 90 minutes to do all of this!

But don't fret—you can easily conquer the MPT with practice. The following information is designed to help you understand the format of the MPT, to expose you to important considerations to keep in mind when preparing and outlining your response, and to give you advice and tips that you can use when you're ready to begin writing your response.

A. PURPOSE

The MPT is designed to test your ability to perform practical everyday tasks of a new lawyer, in the context of a specific problem involving a client. The MPT tests problem-solving skills through factual and legal analysis and the application of this analysis to the performance of the assigned task. Applicants perform tasks such as writing an objective memorandum or brief, a statement of the facts of a case, a witness cross-examination plan, and a closing argument, to identify just a few projects.

B. HISTORY

Having just celebrated its first decade as part of some states' bar examinations, the MPT has gained acceptance across the nation. Since it was first administered in 1997, at least 34 jurisdictions have included either one or two MPT questions in their bar examinations. In fact, 50 percent of all U.S. bar applicants take at least one MPT. If those testing in California and Pennsylvania—the two U.S. jurisdictions that develop their own performance tests—are included, more than two-thirds of all bar applicants take a performance test.

C. GRADING

The MPT is somewhat similar to traditional essay exams in that it asks for a written answer. There are some important differences, however. Because a full set of facts and a library of applicable law are provided in the testing materials, a mere recitation of the facts and the law alone won't count for much credit. Rather, examiners are looking for your ability to identify critical facts, complete a reasoned legal analysis, and organize and write an answer that reads clearly and concisely.

Moreover, the MPT tests a skill set that isn't otherwise tested on the bar examination—the ability to sort relevant and irrelevant facts, analyze the relevant law, and create a document similar to one that might be needed in practice. Because the question provides more time than a typical essay question, the MPT affords applicants with greater opportunity to show their ability to analyze and organize their answers in a compelling manner. As a result, many boards of law examiners have indicated that they find the MPT to be the most realistic test of what a new attorney might be asked to do.

MPT graders have reported that there isn't a great deal of disparity among the answers because the law is provided. Therefore, determining the relative quality of MPT answers is largely dependent on how well the applicants can apply the law to the facts and analyze the issues. The best MPT answers are typically those that most effectively use the facts.

Keep in mind that each jurisdiction determines the number of MPT's administered (either one or two) and how much weight is given to that portion of the exam in comparison to the other essays. Generally, the weight of each MPT is greater than a regular essay question, worth anywhere between 1.5 to 2.0 times a regular essay. While grading the MPT is the sole responsibility of the particular jurisdiction that adopted the MPT, the National Conference of Bar Examiners holds an MPT grading workshop for graders during the weekend following the bar examination and provides "Drafters' Point Sheets" to serve as helpful aids for jurisdictions in developing their own sample responses.

II. SKILLS REQUIRED ON THE MULTISTATE PERFORMANCE TEST

According to the National Conference of Bar Examiners, the MPT requires applicants to: (1) sort detailed factual materials and separate relevant from irrelevant facts; (2) analyze statutory, case and administrative materials for relevant principles of law; (3) apply the relevant law to the relevant facts in a manner likely to resolve a client's problem; (4) identify and resolve ethical dilemmas, when present; (5) communicate effectively in writing; (6) complete a lawyering task within time constraints.

These skills are tested by requiring applicants to perform one of a variety of lawyering tasks. Although it isn't feasible to list all possibilities, examples of tasks applicants might be instructed to complete include drafting the following: a memorandum to a supervising attorney; a letter to a client; a persuasive memorandum or brief; a statement of facts; a contract provision; a will; a counseling plan; a proposal for settlement or agreement; a discovery plan; a witness examination plan; a closing argument. These, and other possible documents, are described below in Section V.C.

A. TESTABLE AREAS

The National Conference of Bar Examiners has identified five testable areas on the MPT. Most questions will require you to tackle one or more of these skills.

1. Factual Analysis

When testing on this area, the examiners will give you one of three possible tasks: (i) Draft an opening statement for trial; (ii) Draft a closing argument for trial; or (iii) Draft jury instructions.

2. Fact Gathering

You will recognize this area because the examiners will present you with your client's case, and ask you what additional factual evidence you need to gather to improve your client's position.

3. Legal Analysis and Reasoning

You should demonstrate the ability to analyze statutory, case and administrative materials for relevant principles of law and apply them to specific factual situations. Think back to first-year legal research and writing. Legal analysis and reasoning includes the ability to: identify and formulate legal issues; identify relevant legal rules within a given set of legal materials; formulate relevant legal theories; elaborate legal theories; evaluate legal theories; and criticize and synthesize legal argumentation.

4. **Problem Solving**

You will recognize this area because it is the only MPT problem that asks you to go beyond the legal solutions to your client's problem by considering non-legal solutions.

You should demonstrate the ability to develop and evaluate strategies for solving a problem or accomplishing the objectives of your client. The problem-solving process includes the ability to identify and diagnose the problem, generate alternative solutions and strategies, and recommend a solution.

5. **Recognition and Resolution of Ethical Dilemmas**

You will recognize this area because when testing on ethical dilemmas, the examiners must include in the problem the code of ethics for lawyers in the relevant jurisdiction.

Keep in mind that not all MPTs will require you to identify and resolve ethical dilemmas. Because the MPT is considered a "closed universe" examination, if your test materials don't contain any legal authorities defining the appropriate ethical standards that exist in the jurisdiction, then you'll unlikely have to address any ethical concerns. If, on the other hand, your materials do contain applicable rules of professional conduct, whether excerpted from the relevant statute or hidden in case law, then it's a good bet that the examiners are looking for you to discuss these concerns.

B. OTHER SKILLS

In addition to the expressly identified skills noted above, the following skills are also necessary for any strong MPT response.

1. **Time Management**

Although it's not necessarily the most important substantive skill, applicants generally identify the issue of time management as one of their most problematic areas on the MPT. This shouldn't be too much of a surprise. The MPT is, for the most part, unfamiliar territory for many applicants, as they aren't exposed to examinations of this type during law school. On the MPT, you have only 90 minutes in which to read and analyze an assortment of unfamiliar materials, usually comprised of 12-25 pages of both facts and law, and to compose a sometimes similarly unfamiliar assignment.

Time management requires focus, discipline, and most importantly, the ability to separate the important from the unimportant—or, in legal terms, the relevant from the irrelevant. The MPT requires the applicant to discard certain facts and law in order to solve a problem. Compare that to law school essay examinations, where they typically contain only relevant facts, notwithstanding the occasional red herring.

2. **Ability to Follow Directions**

You must be able to follow directions. It sounds so simple, but it's often ignored in the haste to begin writing. The MPT is a task-specific assignment: you must perform the task identified to receive credit. If you are instructed to write a letter to a client in which you evaluate various courses of action and instead write a persuasive brief, you will have done nothing but demonstrate to the examiners your inability to read and follow simple directions.

3. **Writing for the Proper Audience, With the Proper Style**

Before writing your answer, you must identify who your audience is, and whether or not you are expected to be objective or subjective in your argument.

a. Audience

There are two possibilities for audience: (i) lay people (The jury or your client), or (ii) lawyers (partners in your firm, opposing counsel, or judges). When writing for lay people, do not use legal terminology. You may be asked to explain complex legal principles to lay people, but you must do it in a way that someone who does not have a legal education would understand.

b. Objective or persuasive

On every MPT, you will be required to determine if your answer is to be objective or persuasive. Obviously, your emphasis will be quite different depending on which determination you make. If you are asked to write something that will go to the court (motions, trial briefs, etc.), you should always be persuasive. If, on the other hand, you are asked to draft a memo to the senior partner of your firm, laying out the strengths and weaknesses of your case, you should write objectively.

In both persuasive and objective answers, you must discuss not only the strengths of your case, but also the weaknesses. When are writing persuasively, it is acceptable to emphasize the strengths, and explain away the weaknesses.

4. Grammar, Punctuation, and Spelling

There is an old saying: "The devil is in the details." In and of itself, writing a document with grammatical errors and poor punctuation or spelling doesn't mean you're incompetent, and it probably won't be enough to fail the MPT in the absence of other problems. But poor grammar, punctuation, and spelling can certainly leave a bad impression on the examiners about your thoroughness and meticulousness in serving your client. Remember—the examiners, by administering the MPT, are gauging your abilities to be a lawyer. Not paying attention to the rules of English probably won't serve you—or your future clients—well.

III. COMPONENTS OF THE MULTISTATE PERFORMANCE TEST

Each MPT question typically contains two parts: the File and the Library. Usually, these two sections will be separated by a cover sheet, making the determination of which is the File and which is the Library quite easy. (The File is usually the first section, and the Library the second.) Occasionally, the information that might have been separately contained in the File and Library are combined in a single File section. If this is the case, look for any legal authorities in the File. Together, the information in the File and Library should total between 12 and 24 pages.

A. FILE

1. Task Memorandum

The first document in the File is the Task Memorandum (sometimes referred to as the Call Memorandum because it contains, of course, the call of the question). This is the most important item in the MPT materials because it tells you what you're supposed to do. As it will be discussed more fully below, you must carefully review the Task Memorandum and make sure you address the specific question or questions asked, format your response exactly as required, and follow all of the directions as closely as possible. Think of the Task Memorandum, which is usually from a supervising attorney, as your work assignment or project sheet.

2. Other Information

In addition to the Task Memorandum, the File consists of source documents containing all the facts of your case. The File might include, for example, transcripts of interviews, depositions, hearings or trials, pleadings, correspondence, client documents, contracts, newspaper articles, medical records, police reports, hospital records, and lawyer's notes. Relevant as well as irrelevant facts are included. Facts are sometimes ambiguous, incomplete, or even conflicting. As in practice, a client's or supervising attorney's version of events may be incomplete or unreliable.

B. LIBRARY

The Library consists of cases, statutes, regulations, and rules, some of which may not be relevant to the assigned lawyering task. MPT's are commonly set in the fictitious state of Franklin in the fictitious Fifteenth U.S. Circuit. The legal authorities listed above are written by the examiners specifically for the test question. They follow the common tiered system for courts: the trial court is the District Court; the intermediate appellate court is the Court of Appeal; and the highest court is the Supreme Court. The states of Columbia and Olympia are also fictitious states in the Fifteenth U.S. Circuit and are occasionally used in lieu of the state of Franklin.

In some instances, the Library will also include cases, statutes, and code from real jurisdictions. Don't be thrown off by these cases and statutes from, for example, the United States Supreme Court or the U.S. Code. You are still writing a document in the fictitious state of Franklin in the fictitious Fifteenth U.S. Circuit.

When reviewing the Library, you are expected to extract the legal principles necessary to analyze the problem and perform the task. Remember: the MPT isn't a test of substantive law, and problems may arise in a variety of fields. Library materials provide the necessary substantive information to complete the task. Don't fall into the trap of relying on law that you have learned elsewhere. The general instructions to the MPT state: "What you have learned in law school and elsewhere provides the general background for analyzing the problem, the information in the File and Library provide the specific materials with which you must work." This means that you are not allowed to discuss or apply any law that is outside of what is contained in the library.

IV. OVERVIEW OF STRATEGY—*RED ROW*

Although there are no restrictions on how you apportion your time, you should be sure to allocate ample time to reading and digesting the materials and organizing your answer before you begin writing it. A good rule of thumb is to divide your time equally—45 minutes reading and organizing (which includes outlining) and 45 minutes writing your response. Below is a skeleton of the recommended strategy for approaching the MPT. Think of the mnemonic device *RED ROW*.

- ➢ **R**ead the Instructions, Task Memorandum, and Instruction Sheet
- ➢ **E**valuate task
- ➢ **D**etermine format
- ➢ **R**ead Library and File
- ➢ **O**utline response
- ➢ **W**rite your document

V. PUTTING *RED ROW* INTO PRACTICE

A. READ INSTRUCTIONS AND TASK MEMORANDUM

Before diving into the MPT question, you should quickly review the general instructions even though you'll likely be familiar with them as a result of all of your preparation. After all, the examiners can change the directions at any time, and your familiarity with the instructions on past MPT examinations will help you quickly identify any new or amended directions, if any, that you need to pay attention to.

After reviewing the instructions, carefully examine the Task Memorandum. This is the single most important page (sometimes two pages) in the File because it contains your directions, introduces your problem, and identifies your task. After reading the Task Memorandum, you'll know whether you're to write an objective memorandum, a persuasive brief, a client letter, or any one of a number of other possibilities. The information contained in the Task Memorandum provides the foundation and guidance for the rest of your time and effort on the MPT.

You should read the Task Memorandum at least twice to be certain you have identified your task and the issue or issues to be resolved. So that you don't lose sight of the issue that needs addressing, you should write the issue on the top of the Task Memorandum or on a scratch piece of paper (if your jurisdiction provides it) to remind yourself of the question that's posed as you work your way through the facts and law.

B.   EVALUATE TASK

When examining the Task Memorandum, you must read it pro-actively, with a critical eye toward solving a specific problem. You must read carefully and quickly while, at the same time, anticipating the information that may be contained in the File and Library that could help address the particular issue you have been asked to resolve. Look for key words in the question. Are you asked to *discuss, explain, describe, argue, prove, dispute, disprove, justify, analyze*? Each of these terms denotes a different approach to the question and will mean a different approach when you write your document.

Also, make sure you follow the directions contained in the Task Memorandum. While the directions may ask you to draft an objective memorandum, the Task Memorandum may give you specific instructions on how to format the document or information on what include (and not include) in the document. For instance, the Task Memorandum, even when asking you to draft an objective memorandum, may ask you to identify additional facts that would strengthen a party's position, state the most persuasive arguments that can be made to support a given position, or identify likely outcomes. Failure to address all of the questions posed to you by the Task Memorandum raises a red flag that you might not be addressing a client's concerns or objectives fully.

The Task Memorandum will indicate the document you'll have to draft. As a result of law school, you're most likely familiar with the format and structure of common legal documents.

C.   DETERMINE FORMAT

Sometimes, however, you might be asked to create a document that you might not have ever drafted or—*even worse*—ever seen. For instance, you might be asked to draft jury instructions, commentary to legislation, a premarital property agreement, or even a last will and testament. Usually, if you're asked to draft a document that examiners think would be unfamiliar to those with only three years of classroom training, they will include a separate Instruction Sheet which explains how to set out the document and gives an example of how the document should look. Even so, you should familiarize yourself with the common documents, the structure or form of the documents, the minimum components of the documents, and the legal standard (if any) to be used.

The following are some common documents that applicants have been asked to draft:

1.   Memorandum of Law

A memorandum of law is an *objective*, even-handed document in which the attorney presents all of the arguments that either side could make, assessing the relative strength of each. Attorneys and their clients rely on solid, objective memoranda of law in making key strategy decisions. Because a memorandum of law is written for those familiar with the law (usually a supervising attorney, an associate attorney or a judge), it is important that it be straightforward and even-handed. Although it's appropriate to use legal terminology in a memorandum of law, you should fully discuss or define legal terms that aren't commonly used.

2. Pleadings

The first essential element of writing a good pleading is to be clear. The next is to be brief.

a. Complaint

A complaint sets out the basic facts and legal reasons that a plaintiff believes are sufficient to support a claim against a defendant. You may be asked to draft either a civil or a criminal complaint. A complaint is *persuasive*.

b. Answer

Like a complaint, an answer is *persuasive*. An answer is the defendant's response to the plaintiff's complaint in which the defendant may deny any of plaintiff's allegations, offer any defenses, and make any counterclaims against the plaintiff, cross-claims against other defendants, or third-party claims against third parties otherwise not involved in the lawsuit.

3. Motions

A motion is a written application asking the judge to make a ruling or order on a legal issue. Motions to dismiss and motions for summary judgment are two common pretrial motions.

a. Motion to dismiss

By filing a motion to dismiss, the defendant requests the court to dismiss the lawsuit because the plaintiff isn't entitled to any legal relief. This is a *persuasive* document.

b. Motion for summary judgment

By making a motion for summary judgment, the moving party claims that all necessary factual issues are resolved or need not be tried because they are so one-sided. Like motions to dismiss, the motion must *persuade* the judge to act.

c. Motion in limine

This is *persuasive* pretrial motion that requests the court to issue an interlocutory order that prevents an opposing party from introducing or referring to potentially irrelevant, prejudicial, redundant, or otherwise inadmissible evidence until the court has ruled on its admissibility.

4. Writings to Parties

If ask to draft a correspondence, you will likely either address your client or opposing counsel.

a. Letters to client

The purpose of a client or opinion letter is to inform and advise the client about the case. The letter may respond to a particular concern raised by the client, or it may be a more general assessment of the situation. Either way, the letter is always *objective*. In addition to assessing the strengths and weaknesses of your client's legal position on a given matter, the letter may suggest strategy or request further information.

b. Letters to opposing counsel

Letters to opposing counsel include demand and negotiation letters. They are always *persuasive* documents. Writing to an opposing attorney isn't easy. You must weigh your words as carefully as any professional writer might in writing an article or essay. Your job isn't just to win court cases, it is to maintain relationships and sell your settlements so that you never even get to court. Your tone should be less formal than if you were writing to a judge, but avoid the stodgy, arrogant, or overbearing writing style.

5. Other Documents

a. Persuasive briefs

Persuasive briefs may be either trial or appellate briefs, and as the name suggests, they're *persuasive* in tone and analysis. A trial brief is designed to convince the trial judge to adopt a legal standard or to rule a certain way at trial. An appellate brief is a document submitted to an appeals court. It contains all the legal arguments as to why your client should win the case. Its purpose is to persuade the judges to rule in your client's favor.

b. Position papers

A position paper is an essay that presents an opinion about an issue. Position papers range from the simplest format of a letter to the editor through to the most complex in the form of an academic position paper (think law review article). Because position papers are most useful in contexts where detailed comprehension of one's views is important, in an attempt to cause change, they represent a *persuasive* document.

c. Statement of facts

A statement of facts is a legal document that sets forward factual information without argument. The goal of a statement of facts is to present factual information in a clear, easy to understand way. Remember to include only the legally significant facts in your statement of facts as the File will likely include information that might not be relevant to the issue. Also, make sure you include legally significant facts that both favor and hurt your client's position, although of course, you'll want to focus the statement of facts so that the positive facts are highlighted. While statements of fact are generally *objective*, they may become slightly *persuasive* by highlighting favorable facts and de-emphasizing damaging information.

d. Discovery requests

Sometimes, the examiners will ask you to draft certain discovery requests: interrogatories, requests for admissions, written deposition questions, etc. If this is the case, the examiners will likely provide an instruction sheet with examples.

e. Opening statements and closing arguments

Both opening statements and closing arguments are *persuasive* pieces while not being argumentative. An opening statement starts the trial, and it's generally the first time that the judge or jury hears from you. The opening statement is generally constructed to serve as a "road map," giving the judge or jury a preview of things to come. A closing argument is your concluding statement at trial, which reiterates the important arguments for the judge or jury. It may not contain any new information and may only use evidence introduced during trial. To draft effective and persuasive opening statements and closing arguments, you need to be a zealous advocate for your client—the more persuasive you are, the more likely you'll be forwarding your client's interests. Emphasize the strengths of your case, and don't concede weak positions.

D. READ LIBRARY AND FILE

Generally, reading the Library before you read the File is the suggested approach to attacking the testing materials. By reading the law in the Library first, your subsequent reading of the File will be formed by your knowledge of the controlling statutes and cases. If you read the File first, it may prove difficult to distinguish the relevant from the irrelevant information. You may not be able to distinguish which facts are relevant and important until you know the law and how the cases in your jurisdiction have interpreted that law. The one exception is when confronted with a problem-solving task. In that case, the file should be read first, followed by the library.

Also, keep in mind that some File and Library materials may be irrelevant; after all, one skill tested by the National Conference of Bar Examiners is your ability to sort out the irrelevancies. Keep the following considerations in mind.

1. Considerations When Reading the Library

a. Read carefully

Recall that all of the legal authorities you need are contained in the Library. Therefore, it is important that you spend an adequate amount of time reading the information in it. Some applicants make the fatal mistake of breezing through statutes or cases that contain legal rules with which they feel comfortable in law school. Remember that the examiners may have rewritten statutes and cases in whole or in part or may have created new legal authorities altogether. So, the elements of adverse possession that you learned in law school might not be the same as that followed by the Franklin courts. Thus, if you examine the issue using elements of common law adverse possession, you'll most likely fail to establish adverse possession in Franklin.

b. Note the jurisdiction and dates of the cases

Knowing the jurisdiction and dates of the cases appearing in the Library is important in jurisdictions that follow common law like Franklin. A recent decision in Franklin will be given great weight. Next in descending order would be recent precedent in jurisdictions whose law is the same as Franklin law. Least weight would be given to precedent that stems from dissimilar circumstances, older cases that have since been contradicted, or cases in jurisdictions that have dissimilar law. Don't assume that the cases in the Library are all controlling cases from the Franklin Supreme Court. They're not.

c. Cross-reference the cases

It's important to examine the cases in relation to each other. For instance, one case might be cited by another case. Recognize the significance of the referencing of one legal authority in other legal authority. Usually, a case that cites to another case in the Library will elaborate on a particular rule of law put forward in that earlier case, develop an exception to that earlier rule, or furnish you with a factual distinction from your problem. You should read cases in the Library in the order they were decided, beginning with the earliest.

d. Pay attention to footnotes

Examiners use footnotes in hopes that you will overlook the important information contained in them. After all, footnotes are in smaller print and located at the very bottom of the page. Don't fall for this trick.

e. Dissect block quotations

A block quotation, also known as a long quotation, is a quotation in a written document, usually a case, set off from the main text as a distinct paragraph or block. A block quotation is often distinguished visually using indentation on both the left and right sides. Examiners sometimes use block quotations because they want to make sure there is no ambiguity or uncertainty as to how the specific language is written. When examiners use block quotations, you'll usually incorporate some of that language in your own document because it contains elements or factors of a rule.

f. Look for commentary

Pay close attention to any "official comments" or other commentary in a statute or code provision. Examiners oftentimes include such commentary to highlight an issue, draw your attention to counterarguments, or signal a legal distinction. In the absence of any cases addressing the statute or code provision, the commentary provides an alternative mechanism on how to interpret the legislation.

g. Address all of the library materials

It should be apparent by now that not all of the legal authorities in the Library will be relevant. But that doesn't mean that you can simply ignore the case, statute or code provision. Even if the particular legal authority has no place in your document, you should still include the irrelevant authority and quickly explain why it doesn't apply to your particular situation. You don't want to spend too much time doing so—a short sentence or two will be sufficient to show the examiners that you did examine all of the library materials and you understood that it didn't apply to the situation at hand.

2. Considerations When Reading the File

One of your biggest challenges will be to identify the relevant facts from the irrelevant ones. Don't be surprised if you find yourself reading a fair amount of material that you believe will be irrelevant to your actual analysis of the problem. Following the tips below will help you find, keep and discard the appropriate facts.

a. Identify the parties

While it's self-evident to identify the parties in the File materials, it's also important to recognize their legal relationships to each other as well as to your client. By understanding how the parties are connected to one another, you'll be more aware of the legal significance of the facts contained in the File materials.

b. Stay on the issue

As noted above, you should write the issue on the top of the Task Memorandum or on a scratch piece of paper to remind yourself of the question that's posed as you work your way through the facts and law. By reading the File with the issue at the forefront of your mind, you can more easily identify the legally relevant facts from the avalanche of information given to you.

c. Attack the shorter documents first

It's not uncommon for the File materials to contain several documents of different lengths. For instance, you might have a one-page police report, a two-page interview, and a six-page deposition transcript. You should read the shorter documents first as these are likely to contain important nuggets of information that might give you a more informed reading of the longer documents.

d. Read the facts with a critical eye

As you read through the File documents, you should pay just as much attention to the information that's not included in the File as you do to the information that's included in it. Ask yourself whether additional facts would have made the issue easier to address and, further, why the examiners intentionally left out that piece of information. Knowing what's in and not in the File should help you focus your response to the issue at hand.

E. OUTLINE RESPONSE

Recall that the instructions state that the MPT "will be graded on your responsiveness to instructions regarding the task you are to complete, which are given to you in the first memorandum in the File, and on the content, thoroughness and organization of your response." You are graded on the "thoroughness and organization" of your response. Outlining your answer in advance is the key to being "thorough" and to good "organization."

Write a brief scratch-paper outline—phrases, words, ideas—that's not too long, but enough to give you a path through the document and make you feel like you know what you will do. In the outline, make sure you include the elements of the rules and the facts you'll be using to establish those elements.

F. WRITE YOUR DOCUMENT

Once you've finished your reading of the Library and File, you're ready to begin the task of writing your document. At this point, you should have half of your time remaining, or 45 minutes. Double-check the Task Memorandum once again to verify your task. Rely on your outline that you just constructed to make sure you address all of the points and included all of the legally significant facts in your document. Under the stress of exam conditions, even the most conscientious of students sometimes inadvertently miss an important argument or fact.

1. Considerations When Writing Your Document

a. Pay attention to format

Remember: the Task Memorandum will help you structure your document. If the Task Memorandum asks you to draft a client letter, then begin your document with a mock letterhead. Don't forget, also, to include the salutation (*e.g.*, "Dear Ms. Smith:"). If the Task Memorandum requires you to write a trial brief, don't forget to include the appropriate case caption. If the Task Memorandum doesn't provide you with an organizational approach, organize your document issue by issue if it is *objective*, or argument-by-argument if it is *persuasive*.

b. Pay close attention to the question asked

Once of the worse things you can do is to spend 45 minutes writing a polished document that doesn't address the issue presented to you. Not only will have you wasted half of your time, the examiners won't have known the amount of work you put into reading, analyzing and outlining the materials in the File and Library. So always verify that you're addressing the specific question or questions asked of you in the Task Memorandum.

c. Don't add or invent facts (unless asked to do so)

Again, the MPT is a "closed universe" examination. That means all of the information you need to develop your arguments and complete your document is contained in the testing materials. Therefore, you need not add facts to the File. There is one noteworthy exception, however. Sometimes, the directions on the MPT may ask you to identify additional facts that would strengthen or, alternatively, weaken a party's position. If you are to explore the effect or impact of additional "hypothetical" facts, the Task Memorandum will likely expressly indicate so.

d. Use headings

Headings guide the examiner through your document. You should use headings to make your arguments stand out to the reader. You can also use them to help you clarify and develop your analyses. For instance, if you have headings with very little discussion underneath, consider either expanding your analysis a bit more or combining the headings so that you discuss additional arguments under a broader topic heading.

e. Budget your time carefully

Forty-five minutes should be sufficient time for you to complete your document regardless of the particular assignment you're asked to draft. This assumption, however, is predicated on the fact that you've satisfactorily completed the earlier steps of RED ROW within the suggested time limits, including outlining your response. Developing a good outline on the front end will make the final 45 minutes for the writing process much easier.

f. Remember: grammar, spelling and punctuation counts

Again, the examiners are testing your ability to communicate well, both verbally and in a written format. The writing part means spelling, grammar, punctuation, capitalization and vocabulary. Even if all you want to do is spend your time in a courtroom, you'll still, at least sometimes, have to file motions and briefs that you'll end up writing or editing. Show the examiners that you'll be able to "sound" like a lawyer when you're communicating with clients or other attorneys.

g. Know your audience

Does the Task Memorandum ask you to draft a *persuasive* or *objective* document? Make sure you're clear as to the tone of your document. It will usually be guided by the party who will be reading your document in your factual situation. The goal of persuasive legal writing seems obvious enough. For instance, you might want the court—whether at the trial or appellate level—to adopt your client's position, no more, no less. The goal of objective legal writing is to provide a balanced assessment of the situation. You should make sure you examine both the strengths and weaknesses of not only your client but also the opposing party.

h. Don't forget IRAC

Good legal writing is good legal writing. What you learned in first-year legal writing is also applicable on the MPT (and the rest of the essays on the bar examination, for that matter).

i. Assume that the reader hasn't read the file or library

Your job after 90 minutes is to have produced a lawyer-like task. The fruits of your labor will be a memorandum of law, a trial brief, a set of interrogatories, or a number of other possibilities. Your final work-product should be able to stand up by itself. In other words, an outside reader—in this case, the examiner—should be able to read your document and understand the background of the case at hand, the materially significant facts involved, and the basis of the legal authorities you've used to make an argument and reach a conclusion. By assuming that the reader hasn't read the file or library, you should be more alert and aware of incorporating more facts and law into your document.

j. Citations

Although citations aren't necessary, applicants should use them when writing for an audience of lawyers or judges. After all, it's a good idea to show the examiner from where you obtained the information. This applies to materials you're referencing from both the File and Library.

k. Use common sense

Although all of the information is provided to you in the File and Library, you should let your experience of the world and your common sense guide you in interpreting these materials. Common sense is essential to solving real-world problems, and it's just as important to rely on commonsensical principles of interpretation and construction when analyzing facts and law.

l. Reach a conclusion

Lawyers are expected to reach conclusions based on a reasoned analysis. For example, either plaintiff wins or defendant wins. You're expected to reach conclusions in your document as well.

m. Practice, practice, practice

The key to success on the MPT is practice, practice, and more practice. You need to be able to put all of the above strategies to the test, and the only way to do so is to sit down and take several past MPT questions. Your goal during practice sessions is to spend the time acquainting yourself with the format of the examination and reacquainting yourself with the mechanics of legal writing and the persuasiveness and objectivity that goes along with the documents.

VI. CONCLUSION

Keep these tips in mind as you're taking the MPT:

- ➢ Budget your time.
- ➢ Focus on the call of the question.
- ➢ Be organized.
- ➢ Write clearly and concisely.
- ➢ Use the appropriate format and tone for the assigned document.
- ➢ Remember that the MPT is a test of fundamental lawyering skills rather than substantive knowledge.

Lecture Handout:
MPT Workshop

MULTISTATE PERFORMANCE TEST (MPT)
PROFESSOR PAVEL WONSOWICZ
UCLA SCHOOL OF LAW

CHAPTER 1:   THE MPT

A. Approach

What is the MPT?

What method is best to write the MPT?

What types of analyses are tested?

What writing strategies should you adopt?

How do you diagnose your writing?

B. What is the MPT?

1. **Create a _____ from materials that are provided for you.**

   o   Materials— instruction sheet, task memo, fact file, law library

2. **Skills tested**

   1) Reading comprehension (read proactively)

   2) _____

   3) Communication (you have the proper _____)

   4) Ability to follow directions

3. **Purpose—**get through the information but address only that which is required in the task memo, in 90 minutes

   o   Develop tests from the materials to analyze the facts.

   o   Find facts that prove the elements and factors.

   o   Communicate effectively.

   o   Work efficiently by focusing on one task at a time.

   o   Goal: _____ of your time analyzing; _____ of your time writing

CHAPTER 2:   MPT METHOD

A. Step #1: Read the Instruction Sheet (1 minute)

   •   Check for the following instructions:

   1. Mythical jurisdiction (usually in the state of _____); in CA usually the state of Columbia

2. Abbreviated citations allowed

3. Read the case as if it were _____.

B. **Step #2: Read the Task Memo (4 minutes)**

- Focus on:

  1. The point of view (_____ or _____)
  2. The audience (_____ or _____)
  3. The goals of the task
  4. Inclusions and exclusions (e.g., whether you need to write a statement of facts)
  5. Guidelines (if included)

  > **Exam Tip 1:** Be aware of the broad range of potential tasks. You may be asked to write a pleading, a motion, a client letter, or something different. Don't panic if you get a strange task.

C. **Step #3: Read the Library (20 minutes)**

- Skip the facts and start with the law.
- Start with _____ (if given); the cases will illuminate.
- Cases—start with the earliest case

  o Verify the jurisdiction (mandatory v. persuasive authority)

- Do not ignore _____, embedded quotes, or block quotes.

D. **Step #4: Develop a Working Outline (10 minutes)**

- Find the gray areas of the law.
- Develop tests and subtests using "if-then" propositions.

  > **Example 1:** A PT recently tested attorney work product. The analysis could be deconstructed as, "**If** anticipation of litigation, **then** substantial need and undue hardship."
  >
  > One case discussed what is a "substantial need"? = relevance and importance
  >
  > Another case discussed what is "undue?" = other sources, depositions, etc.

- Do not ignore burden of proof and policy rules.
- Read the cases while asking, "How does this fit?"

E. **Step #5: Read the File (10 minutes)**

- There may be _____ facts or even irrelevant law.
- Focus on finding facts that prove the elements or factors in your outline.

  o Be aware of facts that contradict each other or are incomplete.
  o Characterize legal relationships.

- Insert facts into your outline next to the element or factor they prove.

- Develop an _____ outline: decide the order and choose facts to prioritize.

F. **Step #6: Write (45 minutes)**

- Be responsive to tone and the assigned task.
- Be objective or persuasive as appropriate.

CHAPTER 3:   TYPES OF ANALYSES; WRITING STRATEGIES; DIAGNOSIS

A. **What Types of Analyses?**

1. **Legal Analysis**

   o Often a motion or a legal memo
   o Usually in a _____ format
   o Usually in _____ or _____ form
   o Spend time discerning why a case is present in the library.
   o Craft clear rules.
   o Focus on _____ determinative facts.

2. **Fact Analysis**

   o Often a persuasive lay scenario
   o Sometimes an _____ argument or closing argument to a jury
   o Law is often a little easier to explore the facts
   o Spend time building a narrative.

3. **Fact Gathering**

   o Looking for the ultimate fact to prove each element
   o Often an _____ scenario
   o Spend more time on "weaker" elements.

4. **Problem Solving**

   o Often a letter to a client
   o Acting as a counselor (giving advice to a lay person)
   o Do not ignore _____ facts.
   o Think in terms of client's goals and explain their options.

5. **Ethical Dilemmas**

   o Often a conflict-of-interest scenario
   o Never ignore ethical considerations.

B. **What Writing Strategies Should You Adopt?**

- Adopt the correct _____ and _____.

- Synthesize and apply.
- Focus on concepts, not case summaries.
    - Reduce a case to its core _____, _____, and _____.
- Keep factual summaries brief.
- Do not try to innovate; embrace the obvious.
- Grammar matters—write in a lawyerlike manner.
- Format matters:
    - Memo—To, From, RE:
    - Opening/Closing—"Ladies and Gentlemen of the Jury…"
    - Letter—address, date, salutation at the end
- Persuasive headings—use the "*Under the* _____ /*When these* _____ /*Then this* _____" approach.
- Make your points _____; prioritize finishing over eloquence.
- Focus on _____ facts.
    - Also note whether facts are unreliable.
- Remember, the working outlines are just for you; keep them short
- PRACTICE!

C. How to Diagnose Your Writing

1. Common Problems

- Synthesis—ask, "why is this case here?"
- Completing a sub-task (addressing only part of the task)—carefully read the task memo
- Certain type of problem—practice outside your comfort zone
- Timing—practice; divide tasks by _____

2. More Specific Diagnostic Issues

a. The "shotgunner"

- Throwing everything on paper
- To fix—work on your outline.
    - Break it down point-by-point with the model answer.

b. The "tangentializer"

- Does not respond to the question; does not see the sub-issue or focuses on irrelevant facts
- To fix—spend more time with the Task Memo to focus on sub-issues.

c. **The "objectifier"**

   ▪ Not paying attention to objective versus persuasive
   ▪ To fix—focus on _____ reasoning; think about "no bad facts"

d. **The "brainiac"**

   ▪ Goes outside the materials
   ▪ To fix—practice MPTs outside your comfort zone.

e. **The "storyteller"**

   ▪ Turns the PT into a long, fact-intensive story
   ▪ To fix—focus on giving a rule and building your application around the rule.

f. **The "legal mind"**

   ▪ Ignores _____
   ▪ To fix—focus on linking an element to a fact.

g. **The "one-trick pony"**

   ▪ Tends to do worse on one type
   ▪ To fix—practice MPTs outside your comfort zone.

3. **Other Tips**

   ○ Compare your _____ to the model answer.
   ○ Practice with time constraints—consider completing just the first 45 minutes of the MPT.
   ○ Do four to eight practice MPTs.

CHAPTER 4:   IN RE HAMMOND—LEGAL OUTLINE

> **Editor's Note 2:**   This chapter requires use of *In re Hammond*, July 2010 MPT 1. Please complete the MPT before continuing with this chapter.

A. Instruction Sheet

B. Task Memo

- Tone must be persuasive to a legal audience

- Draft "Body of the Argument only"

- Headers:

    1) _____; and

    2) _____.

- "Be sure to remain faithful to our obligation to preserve client confidences"—err on the side of _____.

- Guideline sheet for drafting persuasive briefs—use persuasive headers.

C. Law Library

   1. Franklin Rules of Professional Conduct—Rule 1.6

- ○ _____ not reveal info regarding representation
- ○ Three exceptions:

    1) Informed consent;

    2) Disclosure is impliedly authorized; or

    3) Disclosure is permitted by paragraph (b).

       - (b) – *may* be revealed to prevent, mitigate, or rectify _____ injury to the financial interests or property of another that is _____ to result or has resulted from the client's commission of a crime or fraud in furtherance of which the client has used the lawyer's services

   2. Franklin Rules of Evidence—Rule 513

- ○ Elements:

    1) Confidential

    2) _____

    3) Purpose of facilitating

    4) Legal services

- Exception—furtherance of crime/fraud: if the services were sought or obtained to enable or aid what the client knew or _____ should have known is crime/fraud
- Presumed to be _____
  - Opposing party has burden of proof by preponderance of the evidence
  - If opposing party offers sufficient evidence to raise a substantial question (probable cause OR some evidence, unclear in Franklin), must be disclosed to the court.

3. **Franklin Criminal Code**

- Arson is the building of another
- Defrauding insurer requires intent to defraud

4. *U.S. v. Robb—Federal/persuasive—pro-prosecution*

- Lawyer testifies as to former client's intent
- Policy: Oldest privilege; full and frank communication; only disrupted when necessary
- Counter: Lift veil of secrecy when purpose is to facilitate crime/fraud
- Need "some evidence"; admitted if POE that it fits crime/fraud

  - Here, "some evidence" met: midst of scheme, primary source of advice, records prove misconduct.

- More counter policy: don't want to improperly cloak evidence

CHAPTER 5:   IN RE HAMMOND—LEGAL OUTLINE (CONT.)

A. Law Library (Cont.)

1. *State v. Sawyer—Columbia/persuasive/more recent—pro-defendant*

- Mere assertion is insufficient—need _____, as it protects communications unless there is a strong factual basis for crime/fraud
- Here, inferences as to no crime/fraud are "equally strong"—may have retained due to fear of prosecution—inform choices.

B. Task Memo *with Facts*

- "Be faithful to our obligation to preserve client confidences"—err on the side of non-disclosure.

  - *In dire financial condition*
  - *Appeared nervous*
  - *Advised that if involved in any way with fire, cannot collect*
  - *Tried to create false alibi*
  - *DON'T REVEAL these facts*

C. Library *with Facts*

1. **Franklin Rules of Professional Conduct**

   o Shall not reveal info re: representation

     ▪ *Communications here concerned representation*

   o Three exceptions:

     ▪ Informed consent;

     ▪ Implied disclosure; OR

     ▪ Paragraph (b).

     ▪ *First two don't apply: client specifically requested that info not be revealed.*

   o May reveal if substantial injury to the property of another that is reasonably certain to result or has resulted from crime/fraud where client used lawyer's services

     ▪ *No _____ here: don't know cause of fire, whether he caused fire, or whether he'll file fraudulent claim.*

2. **Franklin Rules of Evidence *with Facts***

   o Elements

     1) Confidential

     2) Communication

     3) Purpose of facilitating

     4) Legal services

     ▪ *All are met: private conversation to explore financial/criminal aspects of fire*

     ▪ *Hammond requested that Walker not disclose communications*

   o Exception—crime/fraud: if sought or obtained to enable or aid what the client knew or reasonably should have known is a crime/fraud

     ▪ *Has not filed an insurance claim*

     ▪ *Not guilty of arson, as he _____*

     ▪ *No proof that client _____ the attorney for crime/fraud, as may have feared criminal charges against him*

3. ***U.S. v. Robb*—Federal/persuasive—pro-prosecution**

   o Policy: Oldest privilege; full and frank communication; only when necessary

     ▪ *Policy supports our client: needed full and frank communication to deal with possible criminal charges*

   o Need "some evidence" and then admitted if POE that it fits crime/fraud

- In *Robb*, "some evidence" met: midst of scheme, primary source of advice, records prove misconduct.
- The current facts are distinguishable:
  - *Didn't need a lawyer's help with the alleged fraudulent scheme*
  - *Fraudulent scheme hasn't come to fruition, nothing has been filed*
  - *Not even sure if fire was intentionally caused by client*

4. *State v. Sawyer*—**Columbia/persuasive/more recent—pro-defendant**

   o Mere assertion insufficient—need probable cause, as it protects communications unless strong factual basis for crime/fraud

   - *Hammond's communications need to be protected, as he was seeking attorney's advice as potential target of criminal investigation—thus, the higher probable cause standard should apply*
   - *Don't want to hurt the attorney/client relationship*

   o Here, inferences as to no crime/fraud are "equally strong"—may have retained due to fear of prosecution—inform choices.

   - *Retained due to fear of arson charges*
   - *Don't need to retain an attorney to commit this type of fraud, as merely need to file insurance paperwork; thus, didn't obtain services of attorney for crime/fraud*
   - *Sought forms before he hired the attorney*

D. **Attack Outline**

> **Note 1:** Because both cases discuss the FRE, discuss it first; then, move to the smaller Rules of Professional Conduct argument second.

1. **FRE does not support**

   o Overview of law; presumed privileged; elements
   o Should adopt probable cause standard (meets policy; similar to *Sawyer*)
   o Under probable cause, no evidence this was crime/fraud or sought counsel to further crime/fraud.
   o Even under the "some evidence" standard, the prosecutor cannot meet the burden (distinguishable from *Robb*).

2. **Rules of Professional Conduct does not support**

   o Overview of law
   o No reasonable certainty

CHAPTER 6: PHOENIX CORPORATION V. BIOGENESIS, INC.

> **Editor's Note 3:** This chapter requires use of *Phoenix Corporation v. Biogenesis, Inc.*, February 2009 MPT 1. Please complete the MPT before continuing with this chapter.

A. Instruction Sheet

B. Assignment Memo

- Tone: _____
- Audience: _____
- No statement of facts

C. Library

1. Rule 4.4 of FRPC—adopted in 2002

- IF an attorney receives a document relating to representation and knows/reasonably should know that it was sent inadvertently,
- THEN must promptly _____.
  - Comment 1: Response to *Indigo*; must be _____ and inadvertent; attorney-client privilege is irrelevant
  - Comment 2: *Indigo* was NOT adopted—must just _____
    - *Indigo* holding—notify, don't examine, await sender's instruction
  - Comment 3: rule does not apply to "no authorization" situations (different from inadvertent)
    - *Mead* gives rule—review, notify, and abide by the opposing attorney's instructions or refrain until court instruction
    - But the court did not create a rule for this

2. *Indigo v. Luna Motors*—Franklin, 1998, pro-party seeking _____

- Attorney disqualified due to _____ doc when the attorney examined it, failed to notify, used to impeach, and refused to return.
- *Klein* case: disqualification is an inherent power focusing on ethical standards
  - Paramount concern is public trust in justice and integrity.
- When privileged doc clearly inadvertently sent, should refrain, notify, and await instruction.
  - Here, attorney failed to do so.
- Disqualification proper if incurable prejudice (*Klein*)—in *Indigo*, obtained damaging admissions, can capitalize on contents at trial, and can perhaps help obtain similar evidence.

3. ***Mead v. Conley Machinery Co.*—Franklin, 1999, pro-party NOT seeking disqualification**

   o A no _____ case (not an inadvertent disclosure case)

   o Can disqualify even if there is no rule violation

   o Policy: attorney-client privilege encourages fully developed cases

   o Holding: if receives and knows, then should limit review to determining how to proceed, notify, abide or refrain until court instruction.

   o Six factors for disqualification:

     1) Knowledge of privilege

     2) Promptness of notice

     3) Extent of review

     4) Significance/curing prejudice

     5) Opposing party's fault

     6) Opposing party prejudice via disqualification

   o Application in *Mead*: no prejudice (can exclude document), harm from counsel's knowledge is speculative, and high prejudice for opposing party to lose an attorney who has developed a trial strategy.

D. **Library *with Facts***

1. **Rule 4.4 of FRPC—adopted in 2002**

   o IF an attorney receives a document relating to representation and knows or reasonably should know it was sent inadvertently

     ▪ *Client concedes it received a privileged letter*

     ▪ *But, it was not _____*

   o THEN promptly notify the sender

     • *Did not notify*

     • *But, did not get much chance to, as opponent found out same day at lunch—seems could still have given prompt notice that day*

     ▪ Comment 3: Rule 4.4 does not apply to disclosure without authorization

       • *Mead* gives the rule—review, notify, abide or refrain until court instruction

       • But court did not create rule

         • *Because this is an authorization case, Rule 4.4 does not address this issue*

         • *Is court implying no rule, or rule in Mead is OK?*

CHAPTER 7:   PHOENIX CORPORATION V. BIOGENESIS, INC. (CONT.)

A. Library *with Facts* (cont.)

1. *Indigo v. Luna Motors*—Franklin, 1998, pro-party seeking disqualification

   o Attorney disqualified due to inadvertent doc when: examined it, failed to notify, used to impeach, refused to return

   o When privileged doc clearly inadvertently sent, should refrain, notify, await instruction

      ▪ *Our case is an authorization case, not an inadvertent document case, and is therefore factually distinguishable.*

      ▪ *Rule 4.4 did not _____ Indigo.*

2. *Mead v. Conley Machinery Co.*—Franklin, 1999, pro-party NOT seeking disqualification

   o A "no authorization" case (not an inadvertent disclosure case)

      ▪ *Is case still valid if court "declined to adopt a rule" in this context? Or, was court satisfied with Mead rule so did not adopt a different rule?*

   o Can disqualify even if no ethical violation—interests of justice, including guarantee of a fair trial

      ▪ *Here, a fair trial can occur, as court can _____ the letter, and no ethical violation means limited damage to the interests of justice.*

   o If receives and knows, then should limit review to determining how to proceed, notify, abide or refrain until court instruction.

      ▪ *Reviewed the short letter, didn't have much chance to notify (few hours?), refused to return (but can refrain until court instruction)*

   o Six factors for disqualification:

      1) Knowledge of privilege

      2) Promptness of notice

      3) Extent of review

      4) Significance/curing prejudice

      5) Opposing party's fault

      6) Opposing party prejudice via disqualification

   o Application in *Mead*: no prejudice (can exclude), harm from counsel's knowledge is speculative, and high prejudice for opposing party to lose counsel who developed trial strategy

      ▪ *Against: We knew (1), didn't notify (2) (but minimal time to notify), reviewed (3) (but short letter), and opponent not at fault (5) (unauthorized)*

- *For: Under (4) minimal significance and can be cured by excluding—we didn't use this information yet in deposition and harm is speculative.*
- *For: Under (6), huge prejudice—six years of prep, trial in a month, counsel developed trial strategy, "tremendous costs" to client.*
- *Overall: Two factors in our favor, four factors against us*

B. Attack Outline

- Memo format
- Follow opponent's format?
- Structure:

    1. Concede it's protected
    2. No ethical violation under the rule (not inadvertent), *Indigo* (distinguishable and 4.4 didn't adopt it), and *Mead* (we followed its mandates and may not be good law)
    3. No disqualification, as our two factors outweigh their four

BEST OF LUCK!

[END OF HANDOUT]

Workshop MPTs

In re Hammond

THE MPT®
MULTISTATE PERFORMANCE TEST

In re Hammond

In re Hammond

FILE

LIBRARY

In re Hammond

Instructions

The back cover of each test form contains the following instructions:

> You will have 90 minutes to complete this session of the examination. This performance test is designed to evaluate your ability to handle a select number of legal authorities in the context of a factual problem involving a client.
>
> The problem is set in the fictitious state of Franklin, in the fictitious Fifteenth Circuit of the United States. Columbia and Olympia are also fictitious states in the Fifteenth Circuit. In Franklin, the trial court of general jurisdiction is the District Court, the intermediate appellate court is the Court of Appeal, and the highest court is the Supreme Court.
>
> You will have two kinds of materials with which to work: a File and a Library. The first document in the File is a memorandum containing the instructions for the task you are to complete. The other documents in the File contain factual information about your case and may include some facts that are not relevant.
>
> The Library contains the legal authorities needed to complete the task and may also include some authorities that are not relevant. Any cases may be real, modified, or written solely for the purpose of this examination. If the cases appear familiar to you, do not assume that they are precisely the same as you have read before. Read them thoroughly, as if they all were new to you. You should assume that the cases were decided in the jurisdictions and on the dates shown. In citing cases from the Library, you may use abbreviations and omit page references.
>
> Your response must be written in the answer book provided. If you are taking the examination on a laptop computer, your jurisdiction will provide you with specific instructions. In answering this performance test, you should concentrate on the materials in the File and Library. What you have learned in law school and elsewhere provides the general background for analyzing the problem; the File and Library provide the specific materials with which you must work.
>
> Although there are no restrictions on how you apportion your time, you should be sure to allocate ample time (about 45 minutes) to reading and digesting the materials and to organizing your answer before you begin writing it. You may make notes anywhere in the test materials; blank pages are provided at the end of the booklet. You may not tear pages from the question booklet.
>
> This performance test will be graded on your responsiveness to the instructions regarding the task you are to complete, which are given to you in the first memorandum in the File, and on the content, thoroughness, and organization of your response.

In re Hammond

FILE

Spencer & Takahashi S.C.
Attorneys at Law
77 Fulton Street
Gordon, Franklin 33112

DATE:	July 27, 2010
FROM:	Jane Spencer
TO:	Applicant
SUBJECT:	In re Hammond—Carol Walker Consultation

We have been retained by Carol Walker, a local attorney, in connection with her representation of William Hammond, a local businessman. Hammond owned the Hammond Container Company and the building which housed it; the building was destroyed by a suspicious fire on May 10, 2010.

Walker has been served with a subpoena duces tecum by the Gordon County District Attorney, compelling her to appear before a grand jury convened to investigate the circumstances of the fire and to testify and produce materials relating to her communications with Hammond. She does not want to have to appear before the grand jury and divulge anything related to the case. Based on my preliminary research, I believe we can successfully move to quash the subpoena. I have prepared a draft of our Motion to Quash, which I would like to file as soon as possible.

Please draft only the "Body of the Argument" for our Motion to Quash arguing that Walker may not be compelled to give the testimony or produce the materials in question, on the grounds that 1) under the Franklin Rules of Professional Conduct, she is prohibited from disclosing client communications, and 2) she has the privilege under the Franklin Rules of Evidence not to disclose confidential communications.

In drafting the body of the argument, follow our firm's briefing guidelines and be sure to remain faithful to our obligation to preserve client confidences under the Professional Rules.

Spencer & Takahashi S.C.
Attorneys at Law

MEMORANDUM   August 15, 2003

To: All Lawyers
From: Litigation Supervisor
Subject: Persuasive Briefs

_____

All persuasive briefs shall conform to the following guidelines:

[Statement of the Case]

[Statement of Facts]

Body of the Argument

The body of each argument should analyze applicable legal authority and persuasively argue how both the facts and the law support our client's position. Supporting authority should be emphasized, but contrary authority also should generally be cited, addressed in the argument, and explained or distinguished. Do not reserve arguments for reply or supplemental briefing.

The firm follows the practice of breaking the argument into its major components and writing carefully crafted subject headings that illustrate the arguments they cover. Avoid writing a brief that contains only a single broad argument heading. The argument headings should succinctly summarize the reasons the tribunal should take the position you are advocating. A heading should be a specific application of a rule of law to the facts of the case and not a bare legal or factual conclusion or a statement of an abstract principle. For example, improper: IT IS NOT IN THE CHILD'S BEST INTERESTS TO BE PLACED IN THE MOTHER'S CUSTODY. Proper: EVIDENCE THAT THE MOTHER HAS BEEN CONVICTED OF CHILD ABUSE IS SUFFICIENT TO ESTABLISH THAT IT IS NOT IN THE CHILD'S BEST INTERESTS TO BE PLACED IN THE MOTHER'S CUSTODY.

The lawyer need not prepare a table of contents, a table of cases, a summary of argument, or an index. These will be prepared, when required, after the draft is approved.

Walker & Walker, S.C.
Attorneys at Law
112 Stanton Street
Gordon, Franklin 33111

July 26, 2010

Ms. Jane Spencer
Spencer & Takahashi S.C.
77 Fulton Street
Gordon, Franklin 33112

Dear Jane:

Thank you for agreeing to represent me. A number of difficult issues have arisen in connection with the representation of one of my clients. I am writing in response to your request that I outline the facts.

I represent William Hammond, who established the Hammond Container Company about 10 years ago. Up until May 10 of this year, the company, located on South Main Street in a building owned by Hammond, manufactured disposable food containers for restaurants. On May 10, the company was put out of business when a fire destroyed the building. Hammond requested my advice as to whether he has any criminal exposure and whether he could file an insurance claim.

Thursday, I was served with a subpoena duces tecum by the District Attorney directing me to appear before a grand jury investigating the fire. Of course, I do not want to appear, and Hammond does not want me to reveal any of our communications. I would like your advice on whether I can move to quash the subpoena so that I do not have to appear. If there are grounds for a motion to quash, I would like you to draft the motion and supporting brief.

For your review, I have enclosed (1) the subpoena duces tecum; (2) a file memo summarizing my initial interview with Hammond; (3) a file memo summarizing a telephone conversation with Ray Gomez, Hammond's friend; and (4) a police incident report provided by the District Attorney.

Thank you for your attention to this matter. I look forward to meeting with you soon.

Very truly yours,

Carol Walker

Carol Walker

enc.

5

Walker & Walker, S.C.
Attorneys at Law
112 Stanton Street
Gordon, Franklin 33111

Date: May 12, 2010
From: Carol Walker
Memo to file of WILLIAM HAMMOND/HAMMOND CONTAINER COMPANY FIRE

Today I had a confidential meeting with William Hammond and agreed to represent him. On May 10, a fire destroyed a building he owned, housing the Hammond Container Company. He wanted advice as to whether he had any criminal exposure and whether he could file an insurance claim.

Hammond estimated the total value of the building as approximately $500,000, although it was encumbered by a mortgage with an outstanding balance of $425,000. The building was a total loss. It was insured in the amount of $500,000 under a policy issued by Mutual Insurance Company. Hammond claimed he was up-to-date on his premiums and said he had called Mutual for information about his coverage and the requirements for filing a claim.

Hammond said that he had been having financial difficulties in the past six months. He had lost two big accounts and did not have sufficient cash on hand to make the next payroll or mortgage payment. He said that a police officer contacted him on May 11, that he was too upset to talk at the time, and that the officer said he would contact him again soon. Hammond asked if he had to speak with the police—it seemed clear he wanted to avoid doing so—and I told him that he did not and that he should refer any questions to me. I also told him that if he was involved in any way in the fire, he could not collect on the insurance policy and could face criminal charges. I told him to contact me again within the week to allow me time to investigate the matter further.

Hammond appeared nervous during the meeting. He did not explicitly admit or deny involvement in the fire, nor did I explicitly ask about any involvement on his part. He did say that on the date of the fire he was with a friend, Ray Gomez, fishing at Coho Lake, about 60 miles from Gordon.

In re Hammond

Walker & Walker, S.C.
Attorneys at Law
112 Stanton Street
Gordon, Franklin 33111

Date: May 17, 2010
From: Carol Walker
Memo to file of WILLIAM HAMMOND/HAMMOND CONTAINER COMPANY FIRE

Today I received a telephone call from a man who identified himself as Ray Gomez. He said he had been a friend of William Hammond for several years and was calling me at Hammond's request. He said he wanted to help but didn't know what he could do. Hammond had called him on May 13 and asked him to say that the two of them were together on May 10 fishing at Coho Lake. Gomez said he was surprised at the request given that they hadn't been together that day. The police called Gomez on May 14 and asked if he was with Hammond on May 10, and he replied that he wasn't. He didn't tell the police that Hammond had called him earlier. He said he knew nothing about the fire and wanted to help Hammond, but he didn't want to get into trouble himself. When I pressed him, he said he was afraid and probably should seek legal advice. I informed him that I represented Hammond and could not represent him as well. He said he knew that and had already set up an appointment with another attorney.

GORDON POLICE DEPARTMENT INCIDENT REPORT

Date of Report: 5/16/2010   **Case No. 2010-57**

OFFENSE(S):   Suspected arson of building, 5/10/2010
ADDRESS OF INCIDENT: 20 South Main Street, Gordon
REPORTING OFFICER: Detective Frank O'Brien
SUSPECT: William Hammond, W/M, D.O.B. 11/5/1959

On 5/10/2010, a fire destroyed the building housing the Hammond Container Company.

On 5/11/2010, I contacted the owner, William Hammond, at his home at 815 Coco Lane, Gordon, at approximately 9:30 a.m. He identified himself and confirmed that he was the owner of the building destroyed in the fire. He stated he was too upset to talk, but did say he had been out of town the day of the fire with a friend and did not return to Gordon until late in the evening at which time he learned of the fire. He confirmed that the building was insured through Mutual Insurance Company but declined to talk further. I left my card and said I would re-contact him.

On 5/12/2010, I confirmed that Hammond was insured by Mutual Insurance Company for $500,000. Claim Manager Betty Anderson said that Hammond had requested claim forms and information but had not yet filed anything. She agreed to let me know when she had further contact with Hammond.

On 5/13/2010, I contacted Bob Thomas, manager of Gordon Savings & Loan, who said that six weeks ago Hammond had sought a business loan. The loan committee denied the loan after reviewing Hammond Container Company's financial condition.

On 5/14/2010, I again contacted Hammond. He identified Ray Gomez as the friend he claimed to have been with on 5/10/2010, but he referred all other questions to Attorney Carol Walker, claiming that she had advised him to do so.

Also on 5/14/2010, I contacted Gomez. He acknowledged that he knew Hammond but denied spending time with him on 5/10/2010.

On 5/15/2010, the Fire Marshal released a report finding no specific evidence of a cause but classifying the fire as suspicious and referring it to us for further investigation of arson. At this time, Hammond is a possible suspect.

cc: Gordon County District Attorney

In re Hammond

STATE OF FRANKLIN
GORDON COUNTY DISTRICT COURT

In re Grand Jury Proceeding 11-10,
Hammond Container Company

SUBPOENA DUCES TECUM

TO: Carol Walker
             Walker & Walker, S.C.
             112 Stanton Street
             Gordon, Franklin 33111

YOU ARE COMMANDED to appear in the Gordon County District Court, State of Franklin, at 9:00 a.m. on August 3, 2010, before the Grand Jury convened in that Court to investigate the circumstances of the fire on May 10, 2010, that destroyed the building that housed the Hammond Container Company, located at 20 South Main Street, Gordon, Franklin, and to testify regarding your communications with William Hammond concerning the fire, and to produce all materials constituting or reflecting such communications.

This subpoena duces tecum shall remain in effect until you are granted leave to depart by order of the Court.

Dated this __22__ day of July, 2010.

Shirley S. Grant
Shirley S. Grant
Gordon County District Attorney

9

DRAFT

In re Grand Jury Proceeding 11-10,
Hammond Container Company

MOTION TO QUASH SUBPOENA
DUCES TECUM

Carol Walker, by and through her attorney, Jane Spencer, moves to quash the subpoena served on her in this matter. In support of this motion, Attorney Walker states the following:

1. Attorney Carol Walker has been subpoenaed to testify regarding her communications with William Hammond, her current client, concerning the fire that occurred at the Hammond Container Company and to produce all materials constituting or reflecting such communications.

2. To the extent that the State seeks to compel the testimony of Attorney Walker and the production of any materials regarding her communications with her client, Mr. Hammond, Attorney Walker asserts that she may not be compelled to appear or produce materials under the Franklin Rule of Professional Conduct 1.6.

3. To the extent that the State seeks to compel the testimony of Attorney Walker and the production of any materials regarding her communications with her client, Mr. Hammond, Attorney Walker asserts that she may not be compelled to appear or produce materials under the Franklin Rules of Evidence.

4. Attorney Walker thus refuses to testify or to produce materials in accordance with the subpoena.

WHEREFORE, Attorney Walker asks this Court to quash the subpoena that seeks to compel her to testify and produce materials in this matter, and for any and all other relief appropriate.

Signed: _____
             Jane Spencer
             Attorney for Carol Walker
Date:

LIBRARY

FRANKLIN RULES OF PROFESSIONAL CONDUCT

Rule 1.6 Confidentiality of Information

(a) A lawyer shall not reveal information relating to representation of a client unless the client gives informed consent, the disclosure is impliedly authorized in order to carry out the representation, or the disclosure is permitted by paragraph (b).

(b) A lawyer may reveal information relating to the representation of a client to the extent the lawyer reasonably believes necessary:

> (1) to prevent reasonably certain death or substantial bodily harm;

> (2) . . . ;

> (3) to prevent, mitigate or rectify substantial injury to the financial interest or property of another that is reasonably certain to result or has resulted from the client's commission of a crime or fraud in furtherance of which the client has used the lawyer's services;

> . . .

FRANKLIN RULES OF EVIDENCE

Rule 513 Lawyer-Client Privilege

…

(b) General rule of privilege. A client has a privilege to refuse to disclose and to prevent any other person from disclosing a confidential communication made for the purpose of facilitating the rendition of professional legal services to the client . . . .

…

    (3) Who may claim the privilege. The privilege may be claimed by the client . . . . The person who was the lawyer . . . at the time of the communication is presumed to have authority to claim the privilege but only on behalf of the client.

…

(d) Exceptions. There is no privilege under this rule:

    (1) Furtherance of crime or fraud. If the services of the lawyer were sought or obtained to enable or aid anyone to commit or plan to commit what the client knew or reasonably should have known to be a crime or fraud.

    . . .

Official Advisory Committee Comments

. . .

[3] A communication made in confidence between a client and a lawyer is presumed to be privileged. A party claiming that such a communication is not privileged bears the burden of proof by a preponderance of the evidence. The party claiming that such a communication is privileged must nevertheless disclose the communication to the court to determine the communication's status if the party claiming that the communication is *not* privileged presents evidence sufficient to raise a substantial question about the communication's status.

    Franklin courts have not yet determined whether, to be sufficient, the evidence presented must establish probable cause to believe that the communication in question is not privileged, *see, e.g., State v. Sawyer* (Columbia Sup. Ct. 2002), or whether there must be "some evidence" to that effect, *see, e.g., United States v. Robb* (15th Cir. 1999).

FRANKLIN CRIMINAL CODE

§ 3.01 Arson of Building

Whoever, by means of fire, intentionally damages any building of another without the other's consent may, upon conviction, be imprisoned for not more than 15 years, or fined not more than $50,000, or both.

§ 3.02 Arson of Building with Intent to Defraud an Insurer

Whoever, by means of fire, intentionally damages any building with intent to defraud an insurer of that building may, upon conviction, be imprisoned for not more than 10 years, or fined not more than $10,000, or both.

. . .

§ 5.50 Fraudulent Claims

Whoever knowingly presents or causes to be presented any fraudulent claim for the payment of a loss or injury, including payment of a loss or injury under a contract of insurance, may, upon conviction, be imprisoned for not more than 5 years, or fined not more than $10,000, or both.

1

United States v. Robb

United States Court of Appeals (15th Cir. 1999)

John Robb appeals his conviction for mail fraud in the sale of stock of Coronado Gold Mines, Inc. The indictment alleged that Robb caused Coronado's stock to be sold on misrepresentations that the company was producing gold and earning money, that the price of the stock on the New York Mining Exchange was manipulated through such misrepresentations, and that the mails were used to facilitate the scheme.

Robb acquired a gold mine in Idaho that did not produce any ore that could be mined at a profit. The ore extracted contained only an average of $2.00 to $2.50 of gold per ton, with a cost of mining of at least $7 per ton. Robb claimed through advertisements and stockholder reports that the mine was yielding "ore averaging $40 of gold per ton." Robb caused Coronado's stock to be distributed to the public by high-pressure salesmanship, at prices that netted a $158,000 profit.

The sole error alleged on appeal is the district court's decision to admit the testimony of Ralph Griffin, a former attorney for Robb. At trial, Griffin's testimony for the Government showed that Robb controlled all mining operations and that Robb knew that the public information disseminated was false. Robb claims that allowing such testimony violated the attorney-client privilege. We disagree and affirm the conviction.

We have long recognized the attorney-client privilege as the oldest of the privileges for confidential communications known to the common law. It encourages full and frank communication between attorneys and clients. But because the privilege has the effect of withholding information from the fact finder, it should apply only where necessary.

The purpose of the crime-fraud exception to the attorney-client privilege is to lift the veil of secrecy from lawyer-client communications where such communications are made for the purpose of seeking or obtaining the lawyer's services to facilitate a crime or fraud.

To release an attorney from the attorney-client privilege based on the crime-fraud exception, the party seeking to overcome the privilege must do more than merely assert that the client retained the attorney to facilitate a crime or fraud. Rather, there must be some evidence supporting an inference that the client retained the attorney for such a purpose.

Once such evidence is presented, the district court must review, *in camera* (in chambers, without the parties being present), the attorney-client communications in question to determine their status. The court may properly admit the disputed communications into evidence if it finds by a preponderance of evidence that the allegedly privileged communications fall within the crime-fraud exception.

Contrary to Robb's claim, the Government satisfied the "some evidence" standard here, thereby triggering *in camera* review of the attorney-client communications and ultimately resulting in a decision that the communications were within the crime-fraud exception. The Government's evidence raised an inference that Robb retained Griffin in the midst of a fraudulent scheme; that during this time, Griffin was the primary source of legal advice to Robb, had access to all of Coronado's information, and had regular contact with Robb; and that records of the actual mining results demonstrated misrepresentations in the publicly disseminated information.

Subsequently, Robb had an opportunity to present evidence that he retained Griffin for proper purposes, but he failed to do so. Instead, the Government presented further evidence which was sufficient to enable it to carry its burden to prove by a preponderance of the evidence that Robb retained Griffin

for *improper* purposes. As a result, the district court properly ruled that the communications between Robb and Griffin were not privileged.

We understand that the modest nature of the "some evidence" standard could lead to infringement of confidentiality between attorney and client. At the same time, a higher standard could improperly cloak fraudulent or criminal activities. On balance, we are confident that the "some evidence" standard achieves an appropriate balance between the competing interests and that the district courts may be relied upon to keep the balance true.

Affirmed.

State v. Sawyer

Columbia Supreme Court (2002)

Mark Sawyer appeals his conviction after a jury trial for bribery of a public official. Sawyer claims that the trial court erred in excluding the testimony of Attorney Anthony Novak regarding Novak's conversations with his client Connor Krause, the alderman whom Sawyer was convicted of bribing. The court of appeals affirmed Sawyer's conviction. We agree with the court of appeals that the trial court properly excluded the testimony.

Sawyer owned an automobile dealership in the City of Lena, Columbia, which was located on property to which the city had taken title in order to widen the street. As first proposed, the plan required razing Sawyer's business. The plan was later changed so that Sawyer's business would be untouched. A corruption investigation of the City Council led to charges against Sawyer for bribing Krause to use his influence to change the plan.

Before trial, Sawyer subpoenaed Krause's attorney, Novak, to testify. When Novak refused to testify, Sawyer moved the court to compel him to do so, claiming that (i) Krause was currently in prison having been convicted of taking bribes while he was an alderman; (ii) Krause initially told police that Sawyer had not bribed him; (iii) Krause retained and met with Novak, his attorney;

and (iv) Krause later agreed to testify against Sawyer in exchange for a reduced prison sentence. On those facts, Sawyer argues that Krause planned to testify falsely to obtain a personal benefit; that he retained Novak to facilitate his plan; and that, as a result, Krause's communications with Novak were not privileged.

Although the attorney-client privilege has never prevented disclosing communications made to seek or obtain the attorney's services in furtherance of a crime or fraud, in Columbia the mere assertion of a crime or fraud is insufficient to overcome the presumption that such communications are privileged. Rather, the moving party must present evidence establishing probable cause to believe that the client sought or obtained the attorney's services to further a crime or fraud.

Upon presentation of such evidence, the party seeking to establish the attorney-client privilege must disclose the allegedly privileged communications to the judge for a determination of whether they fall within the crime-fraud exception. The judge's review of the communications is conducted *in camera* to determine if the moving party has established that the communications fall within the crime-fraud exception.

Some courts have required disclosure of the disputed communications to the court upon the presentation merely of "some evidence" supporting an inference that the client sought or obtained the attorney's services to further a crime or fraud. *See, e.g., United States v. Robb* (15th Cir. 1999). We believe Columbia's "probable cause" standard strikes a more appropriate balance than the "some evidence" test because it protects attorney-client communications unless there is a strong factual basis for the inference that the client retained the attorney for improper purposes.

Applying the "probable cause" standard here, the trial court concluded that Sawyer failed to present evidence establishing probable cause to believe that Krause sought or obtained Novak's services to facilitate any plan to commit perjury. We agree. While the evidence would indeed support an inference that Krause retained Novak to facilitate perjury, it supports an equally strong inference that Krause retained him to ensure that his choices were informed—and that he failed to cooperate earlier because he was afraid he might expose himself to prosecution with no countervailing benefit. A greater showing of the client's intent to retain the attorney to facilitate a crime or fraud is needed prior to invading attorney-client confidences.

Affirmed.

Phoenix Corporation v. Biogenesis, Inc.

Applicant Identification

Phoenix Corporation v. Biogenesis, Inc.

Read the instructions on the back cover.
Do not break the seal until you are told to do so.

NATIONAL CONFERENCE OF BAR EXAMINERS

INSTRUCTIONS

1. You will have 90 minutes to complete this session of the examination. This performance test is designed to evaluate your ability to handle a select number of legal authorities in the context of a factual problem involving a client.

2. The problem is set in the fictitious state of Franklin, in the fictitious Fifteenth Circuit of the United States. Columbia and Olympia are also fictitious states in the Fifteenth Circuit. In Franklin, the trial court of general jurisdiction is the District Court, the intermediate appellate court is the Court of Appeal, and the highest court is the Supreme Court.

3. You will have two kinds of materials with which to work: a File and a Library. The first document in the File is a memorandum containing the instructions for the task you are to complete. The other documents in the File contain factual information about your case and may include some facts that are not relevant.

4. The Library contains the legal authorities needed to complete the task and may also include some authorities that are not relevant. Any cases may be real, modified, or written solely for the purpose of this examination. If the cases appear familiar to you, do not assume that they are precisely the same as you have read before. Read them thoroughly, as if they all were new to you. You should assume that the cases were decided in the jurisdictions and on the dates shown. In citing cases from the Library, you may use abbreviations and omit page references.

5. Your response must be written in the answer book provided. If you are taking this examination on a laptop computer, your jurisdiction will provide you with specific instructions. In answering this performance test, you should concentrate on the materials in the File and Library. What you have learned in law school and elsewhere provides the general background for analyzing the problem; the File and Library provide the specific materials with which you must work.

6. Although there are no restrictions on how you apportion your time, you should be sure to allocate ample time (about 45 minutes) to reading and digesting the materials and to organizing your answer before you begin writing it. You may make notes anywhere in the test materials; blank pages are provided at the end of the booklet. You may not tear pages from the question booklet.

7. This performance test will be graded on your responsiveness to the instructions regarding the task you are to complete, which are given to you in the first memorandum in the File, and on the content, thoroughness, and organization of your response.

Contents

POINT SHEET

FILE

To:	Applicant
From:	Ann Buckner
Date:	February 24, 2009
Subject:	*Phoenix Corporation v. Biogenesis, Inc.*

Yesterday, we were retained by the law firm of Amberg & Lewis LLP to consult on a motion for disqualification filed against it.

Amberg & Lewis represents Biogenesis, Inc., in a breach-of-contract action brought by Phoenix Corporation seeking $80 million in damages. The lawsuit has been winding its way through state court for almost six years. Phoenix is represented by the Collins Law Firm. There have been extensive discovery, motion practice, and several interlocutory appeals over the years, but the matter is now set for jury trial in a month and is expected to last six weeks. Two weeks ago, however, Phoenix filed a disqualification motion after Amberg & Lewis obtained one of Phoenix's attorney-client privileged documents—a letter from Phoenix's former president to one of its attorneys. Yesterday, I interviewed Carole Ravel, an Amberg & Lewis partner. During the interview, I learned some background facts; I also obtained a copy of the letter and Phoenix's brief in support of its disqualification motion.

Please prepare a memorandum evaluating the merits of Phoenix's argument for Amberg & Lewis's disqualification, bringing to bear the applicable legal authorities and the relevant facts as described to me by Ms. Ravel. Do not draft a separate statement of facts, but instead use the facts as appropriate in conducting your evaluation.

Buckner:	Good to see you, Carole.
Ravel:	Good to see you too, Ann. Thanks for seeing me on such short notice.
Buckner:	My pleasure. What's the problem?
Ravel:	The problem is a motion for disqualification. Here's the supporting brief.
Buckner:	Thanks. Let me take a quick look. I'm unacquainted with the science, but the law is familiar. How can I help?
Ravel:	To be candid, we've made a few mistakes, and I thought it would be prudent to consult with someone like you with substantial experience in representing lawyers in professional liability and ethics matters.
Buckner:	Tell me what happened.
Ravel:	Sure. Six years ago, Phoenix Corporation sued Biogenesis for breach of contract in state court, seeking about $80 million in damages. Phoenix is a medical research company; the Collins Law Firm represents it. Our client Biogenesis is one of the largest biotechnology companies in the world. Phoenix claims that Biogenesis breached a contract they entered into in 1978. There's a lot about this case that's enormously complicated and technical—all that science that you said you're unacquainted with—but the dispute is fairly simple. Under the agreement, Phoenix granted a license to Biogenesis to use a process that Phoenix invented for genetically engineering human proteins. In exchange, Biogenesis was obliged to pay Phoenix royalties on sales of certain categories of pharmaceuticals that were made using the licensed engineering process. Here is the dispute: While Biogenesis has taken the position that its royalty obligation is limited to the categories of pharmaceuticals specified, Phoenix claims that it extends to other categories of pharmaceuticals as well. If the jury agrees with Biogenesis, it owes nothing more. If the jury agrees with Phoenix, Biogenesis owes about $80 million beyond what it has already paid in royalties.
Buckner:	That's how the brief sums it up, too.

2

Ravel:	Right. The factual background and procedural history set out in the brief are accurate—but of course we disagree with Phoenix's argument about Biogenesis's royalty obligation.
Buckner:	Fine. But what about this Phoenix letter that's allegedly protected by the attorney-client privilege?
Ravel:	Here it is, a letter to Peter Horvitz, a Collins partner, from Gordon Schetina, who was then Phoenix's president.
Buckner:	Thanks. It certainly looks privileged.
Ravel:	It is. I can't deny it. But it's important. Let me go back to the 1978 agreement. Discovery in Phoenix's breach-of-contract action has established to our satisfaction that, by their conduct from 1978 to 1998, Biogenesis and Phoenix revealed that they understood that Biogenesis's royalty obligation was limited to the categories of pharmaceuticals specified in the agreement. During that period, Biogenesis made a lot of money and paid Phoenix a great deal in royalties. It was only in 1998 that Phoenix began to claim that Biogenesis's royalty obligation extended to other categories of pharmaceuticals —when it saw how much more in royalties it could obtain and became greedy to get them.
Buckner:	And the Schetina letter . . .
Ravel:	And the Schetina letter amounts to an admission by Phoenix that Biogenesis was correct in its understanding of its limited royalty obligation.
Buckner:	So how did you get it?
Ravel:	Phoenix's lawyers assume that the Schetina letter was disclosed to us inadvertently during discovery, but they're wrong. The letter arrived on February 2, 2009, by itself, in an envelope with the Collins Law Firm's return address. My assistant opened the envelope and discovered the letter all by itself, with a note reading "From a 'friend' at the Collins Law Firm."
Buckner:	Do you know who the "friend" was?
Ravel:	No. But it's not hard to guess. Collins is in the process of laying off staff in an effort to increase profits. The letter was obviously sent by a disgruntled employee.
Buckner:	That makes sense. But what happened next?

Ravel:	When the letter arrived, my team and I were in full trial-preparation mode. Of course, I recognized that the letter appeared privileged on its face; it's a classic confidential communication from a client to an attorney. In our eyes, the letter was a smoking gun. It made our case and we wanted to use it.
Buckner:	So what happened?
Ravel:	We were pretty sure that we were within the ethical rules. But that same day, two of the associates on my team went out for lunch. As they were discussing the impact of the Schetina letter in what turned out to be too much detail, a man at a neighboring table asked whether they knew who he was. They said no, and the man said he was Peter Horvitz and stormed out. Horvitz called me within minutes, and he was furious. He demanded return of the letter and I refused. A few days later, he filed the disqualification motion.
Buckner:	I see. And precisely what is it you'd like us to do for you?
Ravel:	Ann, I'd like you to evaluate the merits of Phoenix's argument that we should be disqualified. Trial is only a month away, and Biogenesis would have to incur tremendous costs if it were forced to substitute new attorneys if we were disqualified. And let's be candid, we've been charged with a violation of an ethical obligation and might face some exposure as a consequence.
Buckner:	I understand, Carole. Let me do some research, and I'll get back to you.
Ravel:	Thanks so much.

PHOENIX CORPORATION
1500 Rosa Road
Lakewood City, Franklin 33905

January 2, 1998

CONFIDENTIAL

Peter Horvitz, Esq.
Collins Law Firm
9700 Laurel Boulevard
Lakewood City, Franklin 33905

Dear Peter:

I am writing with some questions I'd like you to consider before our meeting next Tuesday so that I can get your legal advice on a matter I think is important. I have always understood our agreement with Biogenesis to require it to pay royalties on specified categories of pharmaceuticals. I learned recently how much money Biogenesis is making from other categories of pharmaceuticals. Why can't we get a share of that? Can't we interpret the agreement to require Biogenesis to pay royalties on other categories, not only the specified ones? Let me know your thoughts when we meet.

Very truly yours,

Gordon Schetina

Gordon Schetina

President

IN THE DISTRICT COURT OF THE STATE OF FRANKLIN
FOR THE COUNTY OF LANCASTER

PHOENIX CORPORATION,   )

)

     Plaintiff,   )

)

     v.   )

)

BIOGENESIS, INC.,   )

)

     Defendant.   )

_____)

No. Civ. 041033

PLAINTIFF'S BRIEF IN SUPPORT OF MOTION TO DISQUALIFY COUNSEL FOR DEFENDANT

I.   Introduction

The rule governing this motion is plain: A trial court may—and, indeed, must—disqualify an attorney who has violated an ethical obligation by his or her handling of an opposing party's attorney-client privileged material and has thereby threatened that party with incurable prejudice. Just as plain is the result that the rule compels here: Defendant's attorneys obtained one of plaintiff's attorney-client privileged documents evidently by inadvertent disclosure. In violation of their ethical obligation, they chose to examine the document, failed to notify plaintiff's attorneys, and then refused to return the document at the latter's demand. By acting as they did, they have threatened plaintiff with incurable prejudice. Since this Court cannot otherwise prevent this prejudice, it must disqualify them to guarantee plaintiff a fair trial.

II.   Factual Background and Procedural History

In 1977, Phoenix Corporation, a medical research company, invented a process for genetically engineering human proteins—a process essential to the development of entirely new categories of pharmaceuticals capable of managing or curing the most serious conditions and diseases afflicting human beings, including diabetes and cancer.

In 1978, Phoenix entered into an agreement with Biogenesis, Inc., one of the pioneers in the field of biotechnology: Phoenix licensed its invention to Biogenesis, and Biogenesis obligated itself to pay Phoenix royalties on its sales of various categories of pharmaceuticals.

Between 1979 and 1997, Biogenesis produced dozens of pharmaceuticals and generated billions of dollars in revenue as a result of their sale. To be sure, Biogenesis paid Phoenix substantial royalties—but, as it turns out, far less than it was obligated to.

In 1998, Phoenix learned that Biogenesis had not been paying royalties on its sales of all the categories of pharmaceuticals in question, but only categories specified in the 1978 agreement. For the first time, Biogenesis stated its position that the agreement so limited its obligation. Phoenix rejected any such limitation.

Between 1999 and 2002, Phoenix attempted to resolve its dispute with Biogenesis. Each and every one of its efforts, however, proved unsuccessful.

In 2003, Phoenix brought this action against Biogenesis for breach of the 1978 agreement, seeking $80 million in damages for royalties Biogenesis owed but failed to pay. Between 2003 and 2009, Phoenix and Biogenesis have been engaged in extensive discovery and motion practice and in several interlocutory appeals as they have prepared for a jury trial, set to begin on March 30, 2009, and expected to last six weeks.

On February 2, 2009, Phoenix learned, fortuitously, that Biogenesis's attorneys, Amberg & Lewis LLP, had obtained a document evidently through inadvertent disclosure by Phoenix's attorneys, the Collins Law Firm, in the course of discovery. On its face, the document showed itself to be protected by the attorney-client privilege, reflecting a confidential communication from Phoenix, by its then president Gordon Schetina, to one of its attorneys, Peter Horvitz, seeking legal advice, and clearly the document was not intended for the Amberg firm. Nevertheless, the Amberg firm failed to notify Collins about its receipt of the Schetina letter. As soon as it learned what had transpired, Collins instructed the Amberg firm to return the letter, but the Amberg firm refused.

III.   Argument

A.   This Court Should Disqualify Amberg & Lewis from Representing Biogenesis Because It Has Violated an Ethical Obligation Threatening Phoenix with Incurable Prejudice in Its Handling of Phoenix's Attorney-Client Privileged Document.

The law applicable to Phoenix's motion to disqualify Amberg & Lewis from representing Biogenesis in this action is clear.

A trial court may, in the exercise of its inherent power, disqualify an attorney in the interests of justice. *Indigo v. Luna Motors Corp.* (Fr. Ct. App. 1998). The court may—and, indeed, must—disqualify an attorney who has violated an ethical obligation by his or her handling of an opposing party's attorney-client privileged material and has thereby threatened that party with incurable prejudice. *Id.* Although the party represented by the disqualified attorney may be said to enjoy an "important right" to representation by an attorney of its own choosing, any such "right" "must yield to ethical considerations that affect the fundamental principles of our judicial process." *Id.* As the court said, "The paramount concern, however, must be to preserve public trust in the scrupulous administration of justice and the integrity of the bar." *Id.*

As will be demonstrated, the law compels the disqualification of Amberg & Lewis.

1.   Phoenix's Document Is Protected by the Attorney-Client Privilege.

To begin with, the Schetina letter is protected by the attorney-client privilege. Under Franklin Evidence Code § 954, the "client . . . has a privilege to refuse to disclose, and to prevent another from disclosing, a confidential communication between client and attorney. . . ." On its face, the Schetina letter reflects a confidential communication from Phoenix's then president, Schetina, to one of its attorneys, Horvitz, seeking legal advice.

2.   Amberg & Lewis Has Violated an Ethical Obligation.

Next, Amberg & Lewis has violated an ethical obligation by handling the Schetina letter as it did. In the face of the inadvertent disclosure of attorney-client privileged material, such as evidently occurred in this case, the ethical obligation is plain under Franklin Rule of Professional Conduct 4.4: "An attorney who receives a document relating to the representation of the attorney's client and knows or reasonably should know that the document was inadvertently sent shall promptly notify the sender."

Because on its face the Schetina letter reflects a confidential communication from Phoenix's then president, Schetina, to its attorney, Horvitz, seeking legal advice, and is therefore protected by the attorney-client privilege, Amberg & Lewis should surely have known that the letter was not intended for it. The Amberg firm was at the very least obligated to notify Collins that it had received the letter. It should also have refrained from examining the letter, and should have abided by our instructions. On each point, the Amberg firm acted to the contrary, choosing to examine the letter, failing to notify Collins, and then refusing to return it at Collins's demand.

8

Even if it should turn out that Amberg & Lewis obtained the Schetina letter as a result of unauthorized disclosure as opposed to inadvertent disclosure, the outcome would be the same. In *Mead v. Conley Machinery Co.* (Fr. Ct. App. 1999) the Court of Appeal imposed an ethical obligation similar to that of Rule 4.4 to govern cases of unauthorized disclosure. It follows that the misconduct of the Amberg firm, as described above, would amount to an ethical violation if the letter's disclosure were unauthorized and not inadvertent.

3. Amberg & Lewis Has Threatened Phoenix with Incurable Prejudice.

Finally, by its unethical actions, Amberg & Lewis has threatened Phoenix with incurable prejudice. The Schetina letter could well prejudice the jury in the midst of a long and complex trial, especially if it were cleverly exploited by Biogenesis. Whether or not any *direct* harm could be prevented by the exclusion of the letter from evidence—which Phoenix intends to seek in the coming days—the *indirect* harm that might arise from its use in trial preparation cannot be dealt with so simply: The bell has been rung, and can hardly be unrung, except by disqualification of Amberg & Lewis—an action that is necessary in order to guarantee Phoenix a fair trial.

Even if it should turn out that Amberg & Lewis obtained the Schetina letter by *unauthorized* disclosure as opposed to *inadvertent* disclosure, the result would not change. It is true that in *Mead v. Conley Machinery Co.*, the Court of Appeal suggested in a footnote that, in cases of unauthorized disclosure, the "threat of 'incurable prejudice'. . . is neither a necessary nor a sufficient condition for disqualification." But that suggestion is mere dictum, inasmuch as *Mead* did not involve the threat of *any* prejudice, incurable or otherwise.

IV. Conclusion

For the reasons stated above, this Court should grant Phoenix's motion and disqualify Amberg & Lewis from representing Biogenesis in this action.

Respectfully submitted,

Date: February 9, 2009

Kimberly Block

Kimberly Block
COLLINS LAW FIRM LLP
Attorneys for Plaintiff Phoenix Corporation

10

LIBRARY

RULE 4.4 OF THE FRANKLIN RULES OF PROFESSIONAL CONDUCT

Rule 4.4. Inadvertent disclosure of attorney-client document

An attorney who receives a document relating to the representation of the attorney's client and knows or reasonably should know that the document was inadvertently sent shall promptly notify the sender.

HISTORY

Adopted by the Franklin Supreme Court, effective July 1, 2002.

COMMENT

[1] Rule 4.4, which was adopted by the Franklin Supreme Court in 2002 in response to *Indigo v. Luna Motors Corp.* (Fr. Ct. App. 1998), recognizes that attorneys sometimes receive documents that were mistakenly sent or produced by opposing parties or their attorneys. If an attorney knows or reasonably should know that such a document was sent inadvertently, then this rule requires the attorney, whether or not the document is protected by the attorney-client privilege, to promptly notify the sender in order to permit that person to take protective measures.

[2] Rule 4.4 provides that if an attorney receives a document the attorney should know was sent inadvertently, he or she must promptly notify the sender, but need do no more. *Indigo v. Luna Motors Corp.*, which predated this rule, concluded that the receiving attorney not only had to notify the sender (as this rule would later require), albeit only as to a document protected by the attorney-client privilege, but also had to resist the temptation to examine the document, and had to await the sender's instructions about what to do. In so concluding, *Indigo v. Luna Motors Corp.* conflicted with this rule and, ultimately, with the intent of the Franklin Supreme Court in adopting it.

[3] Rule 4.4 does not address an attorney's receipt of a document sent without authorization, as was the case in *Mead v. Conley Machinery Co.* (Fr. Ct. App. 1999). Neither does any other rule.

Mead v. Conley Machinery Co., which also predated this rule, concluded that the receiving attorney should review the document—there, an attorney-client privileged document—only to the extent necessary to determine how to proceed, notify the opposing attorney, and either abide by the opposing attorney's instructions or refrain from using the document until a court disposed of the matter. The Franklin Supreme Court, however, has declined to adopt a rule imposing any ethical obligation in cases of unauthorized disclosure.

Indigo v. Luna Motors Corp.
Franklin Court of Appeal (1998)

The issue in this permissible interlocutory appeal is whether the trial court abused its discretion by disqualifying plaintiff's attorney for improper use of attorney-client privileged documents disclosed to her inadvertently. We hold that it did not. Accordingly, we affirm.

I

Plaintiff Ferdinand Indigo sued Luna Motors Corporation for damages after he sustained serious injuries when his Luna sport utility vehicle rolled over as he was driving.

In the course of routine document production, Luna's attorney's paralegal inadvertently gave Joyce Corrigan, Indigo's attorney, a document drafted by Luna's attorney and memorializing a conference between the attorney and a high-ranking Luna executive, Raymond Fogel, stamped "attorney-client privileged," in which they discussed the strengths and weaknesses of Luna's technical evidence. As soon as Corrigan received the document, which is referred to as the "technical evidence document," she examined it closely; as a result, she knew that it had been given to her inadvertently. Notwithstanding her knowledge, she failed to notify Luna's attorney. She subsequently used the document for impeachment purposes during Fogel's deposition, eliciting damaging admissions. Luna's attorney objected to Corrigan's use of the document, accused her of invading the attorney-client privilege,

and demanded the document's return, but Corrigan refused.

In response, Luna filed a motion to disqualify Corrigan. After a hearing, the trial court granted the motion. The court determined that the technical evidence document was protected by the attorney-client privilege, that Corrigan violated her ethical obligation by handling it as she did, and that disqualification was the appropriate remedy. Indigo appealed.

II

It has long been settled in Franklin that a trial court may, in the exercise of its inherent power, disqualify an attorney in the interests of justice. *See, e.g., In re Klein* (Fr. Ct. App. 1947). Ultimately, disqualification involves a conflict between a client's right to an attorney of his or her choice and the need to maintain ethical standards of professional responsibility. The paramount concern, however, must be to preserve public trust in the scrupulous administration of justice and the integrity of the bar. The important right to an attorney of one's choice must yield to ethical considerations that affect the fundamental principles of our judicial process.

Appellate courts review a trial court's ruling on disqualification for abuse of discretion. A court abuses its discretion when it acts arbitrarily or without reason. As will appear, we discern no arbitrary or unreasonable action here.

A

Indigo's first claim is that the trial court erred in determining that Corrigan violated an ethical obligation by handling the technical evidence document as she did.

From the Franklin Rules of Professional Conduct and related case law, we derive the following, albeit implicit, standard: An attorney who receives materials that on their face appear to be subject to the attorney-client privilege, under circumstances in which it is clear they were not intended for the receiving attorney, should refrain from examining the materials, notify the sending attorney, and await the instructions of the attorney who sent them.

Under this standard, Corrigan plainly violated an ethical obligation. She received the technical evidence document; the document appeared on its face to be subject to the attorney-client privilege, as it was stamped "attorney-client privileged"; the circumstances were clear that the document was not intended for her; nevertheless, she examined the document, failed to notify Luna's attorney, and refused to return it at the latter's demand.

B

Indigo's second claim is that the trial court erred in determining that disqualification of Corrigan was the appropriate remedy in light of her violation of her ethical obligation.

The trial court predicated Corrigan's disqualification on the threat of incurable prejudice to Luna. Such a threat has long been recognized as a sufficient basis for disqualification. *See, e.g., In re Klein.* We find it more than sufficient here. Corrigan used the technical evidence document during the deposition of Luna executive Fogel, eliciting damaging admissions. Even if Corrigan were prohibited from using the document at trial, she could not effectively be prevented from capitalizing on its contents in preparing for trial and perhaps obtaining evidence of similar force and effect.

III

The trial court concluded that disqualification was necessary to ensure a fair trial. It did not abuse its discretion in doing so.

Affirmed.

Mead v. Conley Machinery Co.
Franklin Court of Appeal (1999)

The issue in this permissible interlocutory appeal is whether the trial court abused its discretion by disqualifying plaintiff's attorney on the ground that the attorney improperly used attorney-client privileged documents disclosed to him without authorization. *Cf. Indigo v. Luna Motors Corp.* (Fr. Ct. App. 1998) (inadvertent disclosure). We hold that it did and reverse.

I

Dolores Mead, a former financial consultant for Conley Machinery Company, sued Conley for breach of contract. Without authorization, she obtained attorney-client privileged documents belonging to Conley and gave them to her attorney, William Masterson, who used them in deposing Conley's president over Conley's objection.

Conley immediately moved to disqualify Masterson. After an evidentiary hearing, the trial court granted the motion. Mead appealed.

II

In determining whether the trial court abused its discretion by disqualifying Masterson, we ask whether it acted arbitrarily or without reason. *Indigo.*

III

At the threshold, Mead argues that the trial court had no authority to disqualify Masterson because he did not violate any specific rule among the Franklin Rules of Professional Conduct. It is true that Masterson did not violate any specific rule— but it is *not* true that the court was without authority to disqualify him. With or without a violation of a specific rule, a court may, in the exercise of its inherent power, disqualify an attorney in the interests of justice, including where necessary to guarantee a fair trial. *Indigo.*

IV

Without doubt, there are situations in which an attorney who has been privy to his or her adversary's privileged documents without authorization must be disqualified, even though the attorney was not involved in obtaining the documents. By protecting attorney-client communications, the attorney-client privilege encourages parties to fully develop cases for trial, increasing the chances of an informed and correct resolution.

To safeguard the attorney-client privilege and the litigation process itself, we believe that the following standard must govern: An attorney who receives, on an unauthorized basis, materials of an adverse party that he or she knows to be attorney-client privileged should, upon recognizing the privileged nature of the materials, either refrain from reviewing such materials or review them only to the extent required to determine how to proceed; he or she should notify the adversary's attorney that he or she has such materials and should either follow instructions from the adversary's attorney with respect to the disposition of the materials or refrain from using the materials until a definitive resolution of the proper disposition of the materials is obtained from a court.

Violation of this standard, however, amounts to only one of the facts and circumstances that a trial court must consider in deciding whether to order disqualification. The court must also consider all of the other relevant facts and circumstances to determine whether the interests of justice require disqualification. Specifically, in the exercise of its discretion, a trial court should consider these factors: (1) the attorney's actual or constructive knowledge of the material's attorney-client privileged status; (2) the promptness with which the attorney notified the opposing side that he or she had received such material; (3) the extent to which the attorney reviewed the material; (4) the significance of the material, i.e., the extent to which its disclosure may prejudice the party moving for disqualification, and the extent to which its return or other measure may prevent or cure that prejudice; (5) the extent to which the party moving for disqualification may be at fault for the unauthorized disclosure; and (6) the extent to which the party opposing disqualification would suffer prejudice from the disqualification of his or her attorney.[1]

Some of these factors weigh in favor of Masterson's disqualification. For example, Masterson should have known after the most cursory review that the documents in question were protected by the attorney-client privilege. Nevertheless, he did not notify Conley upon receiving them. Also, it appears that he thoroughly reviewed them, as he directly referenced specific portions in his response to Conley's disqualification motion. Finally, Conley was not at fault, since Mead copied them covertly.

Other factors, however, weigh against Masterson's disqualification. The information in the documents in question would not significantly prejudice Conley, reflecting little more than a paraphrase of a handful of Mead's allegations. The court may exclude the documents from evidence and thereby prevent any prejudice to Conley—all without disqualifying Masterson. Exclusion would prevent ringing for the jury any bell that could not be unrung. To be sure, it would not erase the documents from Masterson's mind, but any harm arising from their presence in Masterson's memory would be minimal and, indeed, speculative. In contrast, Mead would suffer serious hardship if Masterson were disqualified at this time, after he has determined trial strategy, worked extensively on trial preparation, and readied the matter for trial. In these circumstances, disqualification may confer an enormous, and unmerited, strategic advantage upon Conley.

In conclusion, because the factors against Masterson's disqualification substantially outweigh those in its favor, the trial court abused its discretion in disqualifying him.

Reversed.

---

[1] In *Indigo v. Luna Motors Corp.*, we recently considered the issue of disqualification in the context of *inadvertent* disclosure of a document protected by the attorney-client privilege as opposed to *unauthorized* disclosure. The analysis set out in the text above renders explicit what was implicit in *Indigo*, and is generally applicable to disqualification for inadvertent disclosure as well as unauthorized disclosure. Although we found the threat of "incurable prejudice" decisive in *Indigo*, it is neither a necessary nor a sufficient condition for disqualification.

Monroe v. Franklin Flags
Amumsement Park

THE MPT

MULTISTATE PERFORMANCE TEST

July 2013
MPT-1

Monroe v. Franklin Flags

Amusement Park

www.ncbex.org

National Conference of Bar Examiners
302 South Bedford Street | Madison, WI 53703-3622
Phone: 608-280-8550 | Fax: 608-280-8552 | TDD: 608-661-1275
e-mail: contact@ncbex.org

Monroe v. Franklin Flags Amusement Park

Contents

Instructions

MPT-1: *Monroe v. Franklin Flags Amusement Park*

FILE

LIBRARY

The back cover of each test booklet contains the following instructions:

You will be instructed when to begin and when to stop this test. Do not break the seal on this booklet until you are told to begin. This test is designed to evaluate your ability to handle a select number of legal authorities in the context of a factual problem involving a client.

The problem is set in the fictitious state of Franklin, in the fictitious Fifteenth Circuit of the United States. Columbia and Olympia are also fictitious states in the Fifteenth Circuit. In Franklin, the trial court of general jurisdiction is the District Court, the intermediate appellate court is the Court of Appeal, and the highest court is the Supreme Court.

You will have two kinds of materials with which to work: a File and a Library. The first document in the File is a memorandum containing the instructions for the task you are to complete. The other documents in the File contain factual information about your case and may include some facts that are not relevant.

The Library contains the legal authorities needed to complete the task and may also include some authorities that are not relevant. Any cases may be real, modified, or written solely for the purpose of this examination. If the cases appear familiar to you, do not assume that they are precisely the same as you have read before. Read them thoroughly, as if they all were new to you. You should assume that the cases were decided in the jurisdictions and on the dates shown. In citing cases from the Library, you may use abbreviations and omit page references.

Your response must be written in the answer book provided. If you are using a laptop computer to answer the questions, your jurisdiction will provide you with specific instructions. In answering this performance test, you should concentrate on the materials in the File and Library. What you have learned in law school and elsewhere provides the general background for analyzing the problem; the File and Library provide the specific materials with which you must work.

Although there are no restrictions on how you apportion your time, you should allocate approximately half your time to reading and digesting the materials and to organizing your answer before you begin writing it. You may make notes anywhere in the test materials; blank pages are provided at the end of the booklet. You may not tear pages from the question booklet.

This performance test will be graded on your responsiveness to the instructions regarding the task you are to complete, which are given to you in the first memorandum in the File, and on the content, thoroughness, and organization of your response.

July 2013 MPT

 *FILE*

MPT-1: *Monroe v. Franklin Flags Amusement Park*

Teasdale, Gottlieb & Lasparri, P.C.

111 S. Jefferson Street
Cooper City, Franklin 33812

TO:	Examinee
FROM:	Rick Lasparri
DATE:	July 30, 2013
RE:	Monroe v. Franklin Flags Amusement Park

We are defending our client, Franklin Flags Amusement Park, against a negligence claim made by Vera Monroe, who seeks damages for multiple injuries she suffered at the client's amusement park.

Last Halloween, Ms. Monroe went through the Haunted House attraction at the amusement park, on the attraction's first day of operation. The Haunted House attraction consists of a building, made to replicate a haunted house, and a mock graveyard. Ms. Monroe claims that, as a result of the Park's negligence, she suffered injuries, for which she is claiming damages of $250,000.

Ms. Monroe has made three separate claims of injury due to negligence: 1) she was injured when, frightened by a staff member in costume in one of the rooms of the attraction, she ran into a wall and broke her nose; 2) after exiting the building, and while going through the mock graveyard, she slipped on the muddy path and injured her ankle; and 3) after exiting the graveyard and the attraction, she was again frightened on the way to the parking lot by a staff member in costume, fell, and broke her wrist.

We have concluded discovery and will now move for summary judgment. I am attaching relevant excerpts from the deposition transcripts and case law.

Please prepare the argument section of our brief in support of our motion for summary judgment. Do not prepare a statement of facts, but incorporate relevant facts into your argument. Do not concern yourself with issues of the plaintiff's comparative negligence or damages. Be sure to follow the attached guidelines for the preparation of persuasive briefs.

Teasdale, Gottlieb & Lasparri, P.C.

TO: All Attorneys
FROM: Firm
DATE: June 6, 2012
RE: Guidelines for Persuasive Briefs in Trial Courts

The following guidelines apply to persuasive briefs filed in support of motions for summary judgment in trial courts.

I. Caption

[omitted]

II. Statement of Facts

[omitted]

III. Legal Argument

The body of each argument should analyze applicable legal authority and persuasively argue that both the facts and the law support our position. Supporting authority should be emphasized, but contrary authority should also be cited, addressed in the argument, and explained or distinguished. <u>Courts are not persuaded by exaggerated, unsupported arguments.</u>

We follow the practice of breaking the argument into its major components and writing carefully crafted subject headings that summarize the arguments each covers. A brief should not contain a single broad argument heading. The argument headings should be complete sentences that succinctly summarize the reasons the tribunal should take the position you are advocating. A heading should be a specific application of a rule of law to the facts of the case and not a bare legal or factual conclusion or a statement of an abstract principle. Examples:

<u>Improper</u>: The Applicable Standard of Care

<u>Proper</u>: Because the applicable standard of care in a professional negligence case is not within the realm of common knowledge, the plaintiff must introduce expert testimony to establish the standard of care allegedly violated by the defendant.

Do not prepare a table of contents, a table of cases, a statement of the case, or an index; these will be prepared, as required, after the draft is approved.

Excerpts of Deposition Transcript of Vera Monroe

Present: Ms. Vera Monroe, Plaintiff; F.J. Wahl, Esq., counsel for Plaintiff; R. Lasparri, Esq., counsel for Defendant

Direct Examination (by Ms. Wahl):

*　　　*　　　*

Ms. Wahl: What did you do last Halloween evening—that would be October 31, 2012?

Ms. Monroe: My husband and I went to the Franklin Flags Amusement Park, around 8:00 p.m. We figured it would be great fun, it being Halloween and all.

Ms. Wahl: Had you been there before?

Ms. Monroe: Oh yes, many, many times.

Ms. Wahl: And what did you do when you got there?

Ms. Monroe: We first went to the go-kart ride, then had a bite to eat at one of the food stands, and then went into the Haunted House they had set up there.

Ms. Wahl: Had you been in that attraction before?

Ms. Monroe: No, we had never seen it there before.

[Discussion off the record]

Mr. Lasparri: We will stipulate that the Haunted House attraction was first opened to the public on that date, October 31, 2012.

Ms. Wahl: What happened when you entered?

Ms. Monroe: Well, you go into this house, which has all these rooms with spooky stuff—spiderwebs and howling sounds and stuff like that. It was kind of scary, and every time something would appear, like an image of a ghost, or a guy dressed like a vampire lying in a coffin, I would let out a little scream, which amused my husband no end. Then we went into this room—it turned out to be the last one before the exit—it was real dark—just a couple of dim lightbulbs and the illuminated "exit" sign—and this woman dressed up as a zombie jumped out of some hiding place, yelling at the top of her lungs, and I just lost it.

Ms. Wahl: What do you mean by that?

Ms. Monroe: Well, she scared me to death—I wasn't expecting anything like that, because none of the other characters had come right up to us like that. So I let out a real shriek and just ran away from her. I took four or five steps, running like crazy, ran into the wall face-first, and knocked myself silly. It turned out I had a broken nose, and it was bleeding, although I didn't know it at the time. I screamed for my husband, and he grabbed my arm, and I said, "Get me out of here!" So he led me to the exit door and we got out of there.

Ms. Wahl: Did anybody from the park try to help you?

Ms. Monroe: No, this zombie person just kept coming toward us, so we wanted to get out of there as quickly as we could.

Ms. Wahl: Go on, what happened then?

Ms. Monroe: Well, we went out the door, and there was this kind of pathway outside through a mock graveyard. The ground was really muddy, and in my panic, I slipped on the mud and fell down, twisting my ankle.

Ms. Wahl: Was anybody from the park around?

Ms. Monroe: No, the mock graveyard was completely deserted.

Ms. Wahl: And what happened then?

Ms. Monroe: My husband helped me up and supported me, because now I was limping. The graveyard was enclosed by a fence with a gate that led back onto the park grounds. We left the graveyard through the gate, and we were outside heading for the parking lot and our car when another guy in a bizarre outfit and a hockey mask, holding what looked like a chain saw, jumped out from behind the outside of the fence. He so startled us that my husband let go of me, and I fell and felt a crack in my wrist.

Ms. Wahl: Why were you startled at that point?

Ms. Monroe: Once we were out of the graveyard and back on the park grounds, I thought that whatever they might do to scare people was behind us. I was breathing a sigh of relief that we were out of the Haunted House attraction. I mean it was an entirely different situation—there was nothing scary, like in the Haunted House, and I figured we were back to normal surroundings. So the appearance of this guy with a chain saw was completely unexpected and unnerving and really frightening.

Ms. Wahl: What happened next?

Ms. Monroe: My husband picked me up and helped me to our car—I was a wreck, crying and in a lot of pain. We went to the emergency room of Franklin General Hospital, and they told me I had a broken nose, a sprained ankle, and a broken wrist. I needed surgery to repair my wrist.

Ms. Wahl: Mr. Lasparri, we will introduce documentary and expert evidence as to the extent of Ms. Monroe's injuries.

*   *   *

Cross-examination (by Mr. Lasparri):

*   *   *

Mr. Lasparri: Ms. Monroe, when you entered the Haunted House attraction at the park, what did you expect?

Ms. Monroe: To have a good time.

Mr. Lasparri: Did you expect to be frightened or scared once you were inside?

Ms. Monroe: Well, I guess, sure, that's part of the fun on Halloween, isn't it? But there's being frightened for the fun of it, and then there's being terrified.

Mr. Lasparri: When you were injured inside the room, did you or your husband ask for help?

Ms. Monroe: No, we wanted to get out of there as quickly as possible. Besides, there was no one to ask.

Mr. Lasparri: You said that the person dressed up as a zombie kept coming toward you. Did you or your husband ask her for help?

Ms. Monroe: No, she was the reason I ran into that wall!

Mr. Lasparri: Do you know why she kept approaching you?

Ms. Monroe: I assume it was to keep playing the part of a scary zombie and frighten us—she was saying something to us, but I was crying and screaming and didn't hear what she was saying.

Mr. Lasparri: You said there was no one else present in the graveyard other than your husband and yourself when you slipped and fell there. Did you ask for help after you left the graveyard?

Ms. Monroe: No, the only person we saw after we left the graveyard was that creep with the chain saw. My husband yelled at him to get away from us, and he backed off.

Then, as I said, my husband helped me up and supported me as we went right to our car and to the emergency room of the nearest hospital.

* * *

Mr. Lasparri: Was the graveyard illuminated?

Ms. Monroe: There were little lights along the pathway.

Mr. Lasparri: How about outside the graveyard fence?

Ms. Monroe: That was lit by lampposts, like the rest of the park, and we could see okay.

* * *

Mr. Lasparri: Do you remember what the weather was like in the days preceding Halloween?

Ms. Monroe: Yes, I remember it had been really raining a lot, without letup, for the previous three days.

* * *

Mr. Lasparri: Do you normally celebrate Halloween?

Ms. Monroe: Sure, we do it every year and, up to now, we've really enjoyed it—you know, seeing people dressed up in costumes and having fun trick-or-treating and trying to scare people and stuff like that.

* * *

Excerpts of Deposition Transcript of Mike Matson

Present: Mr. Mike Matson, called by Defendant; F.J. Wahl, Esq., counsel for Plaintiff; R. Lasparri, Esq., counsel for Defendant

Direct Examination (by Mr. Lasparri):

Mr. Lasparri: Please state your name, occupation, and employer.

Mr. Matson: My name is Mike Matson, and I am General Manager of the Franklin Flags Amusement Park.

Mr. Lasparri: Can you describe the Haunted House attraction at the park?

Mr. Matson: It's a new attraction which we opened this last Halloween. It's a house with a series of rooms with scary interiors, suitable for a haunted house—things like spiderwebs and moving images of ghosts and moaning sounds played over the loudspeakers. It's dimly lit, of course, and we also have people playing the part of zombies and goblins and vampires and devils and stuff like that, who are supposed to scare the patrons who go through the attraction.

Mr. Lasparri: Once a patron exits from the house itself, is that the end of the attraction?

Mr. Matson: No, we rigged it up so that there's a mock graveyard that people have to walk through to exit the attraction, and it's very spooky too; it continues the effect.

Mr. Lasparri: And once a patron exits from the graveyard, is that the end of the attraction?

Mr. Matson: Well, we thought it would be fun if, once people thought they were out of the house and the graveyard, and thought they were safe, we would play one more trick to frighten them. So we set it up so that the graveyard was enclosed with a fence, and when you went through the gate to leave, we'd have a staff member dressed up like a character from a horror movie wielding a fake chain saw jump out from behind the outside of the fence for one last "boo," so to speak.

*   *   *

Mr. Lasparri: What steps do you take to ensure the safety of your patrons in the Haunted House attraction?

Mr. Matson: Well, we have several individuals stationed around the various points of the attraction to keep an eye on everyone. For example, we have at least one staff

Monroe v. Franklin Flags Amusement Park

	member in every room of the house in case a patron gets into some sort of trouble or needs help. And we have a doctor present at the park at all times.
Mr. Lasparri:	Did you have a staff person stationed in the last room of the house?
Mr. Matson:	Yes, that function was filled by the individual playing the part of a zombie in that room.
Mr. Lasparri:	What about in the mock graveyard?
Mr. Matson:	We don't have anyone there, because there's nothing going on there except that patrons are walking through it.
Mr. Lasparri:	And what about outside the exit from the graveyard?
Mr. Matson:	Again, the employee with the fake chain saw has that responsibility. All our employees are instructed to offer assistance to patrons, and to call the doctor if there's a medical emergency.

*   *   *

<u>Cross-examination</u> (by Ms. Wahl):

*   *   *

Ms. Wahl:	Mr. Matson, can you describe the grounds of the park—more particularly, what are they made of—are they paved, dirt, what?
Mr. Matson:	The overwhelming bulk of the park—where people walk—is paved. We have some landscaping, trees and flower beds and such, which are of course planted in earth covered in grass or flowers, but they are fenced in because we don't want people trampling them.
Ms. Wahl:	Was any part of the mock graveyard outside the house paved—the path, for instance?
Mr. Matson:	No, it was all left as natural earth, you know, for purposes of verisimilitude— you know, realism.

*   *   *

Ms. Wahl:	Aside from the person with the mock chain saw, were there any other employees on the grounds outside the Haunted House attraction who were in costume and instructed to frighten patrons?
Mr. Matson:	No.

Excerpts of Deposition Transcript of Camille Brewster

Present: Ms. Camille Brewster, called by Defendant; F.J. Wahl, Esq., counsel for Plaintiff; R. Lasparri, Esq., counsel for Defendant

Direct Examination (by Mr. Lasparri):

Mr. Lasparri: Please state your name, occupation, and employer.

Ms. Brewster: Camille Brewster. I work for Franklin Flags Amusement Park as a staff member.

Mr. Lasparri: And what are your duties as a staff member?

Ms. Brewster: To do pretty much whatever my boss tells me to do.

Mr. Lasparri: What duties were assigned to you last Halloween?

Ms. Brewster: We had opened this new attraction, the Haunted House, and I was made up to play a zombie. I was told to hide in the last room of the house, and when people came through, to jump out and try to scare them.

Mr. Lasparri: Were you given any guidelines as to what you could and could not do?

Ms. Brewster: We were told that we couldn't touch or make any physical contact with the patrons and to make sure people were having fun in the spirit of Halloween. That was about it.

Mr. Lasparri: And as a general matter, what instructions are you given should a patron need help of any sort?

Ms. Brewster: To help them—and if there's some medical emergency, we're supposed to call the doctor who's on duty in the main office.

Mr. Lasparri: Do you remember any untoward incidents that occurred last Halloween?

Ms. Brewster: Well, there was only one, involving a couple that came through. I did what I had been doing all night—jumping out at people and scaring them. But the woman just seemed to freak out. She let out a shriek and turned and ran away from me like a bolt of lightning. She ran right into the wall—there was an awful crack—and fell down.

Mr. Lasparri: What did you do then?

Ms. Brewster: Her husband was helping her get up, and I went toward them to see if I could help them and said, "Are you okay?", but they just rushed out of the exit door, and that was the last I saw of them.

*   *   *

<u>Cross-examination</u> (by Ms. Wahl):

Ms. Wahl: Ms. Brewster, how old are you?

Ms. Brewster: Seventeen.

Ms. Wahl: Do you have any training in first aid of any sort?

Ms. Brewster: Well, I do have a junior lifeguard certificate that I got at summer camp two years ago, which included basic first aid stuff like bandaging and all that.

Ms. Wahl: You said that if patrons needed help, you were instructed to help them or call a doctor for a medical emergency. Were you given any more explicit or specific instructions as to what to do in such a case?

Ms. Brewster: No, not really, just to do whatever is necessary to help them.

July 2013 MPT

 *LIBRARY*

MPT-1: *Monroe v. Franklin Flags Amusement Park*

Larson v. Franklin High Boosters Club, Inc.

Franklin Supreme Court (2002)

Two years ago, the Franklin High Boosters Club decided to run a fund-raiser for the school's cheerleading team on Halloween. They rented a local warehouse and constructed what they called a "House of Horrors" inside. The "House of Horrors" included a path to follow with various stops in rooms along the way. At each stop, the room was appropriately decorated so that some mock "horror" awaited those who entered—including individuals playing headless ghosts, zombies, vampires, werewolves, Frankenstein monsters, and the like. These roles were played by members of the club, made up and dressed appropriately. They were instructed to play the parts to the hilt. Their aim, simply put, was to scare the customers, who had each paid $20 for the privilege of being frightened.

The fund-raiser netted $4,800 for the club and would have been an unqualified success but for one incident. John Larson, a 72-year-old gentleman, entered the "House of Horrors" with his two grandchildren. At one of the stops, when one of the "vampires" came at him suddenly, Larson, startled, reeled backward, tripped over his own feet, and fell, breaking his arm and dislocating his shoulder. He sued the club for negligence, seeking recompense for his medical expenses and pain and suffering.

The trial court granted the club's motion for summary judgment, and the court of appeal affirmed. For the reasons stated below, we reverse and remand.

A court will grant a motion for summary judgment when there is no genuine dispute of material fact and the moving party is entitled to judgment as a matter of law. A "material fact" for summary judgment purposes is a fact that would influence the outcome of the controversy.

Larson cites *Dozer v. Swift* (Fr. Ct. App. 1994) as establishing the standard for liability for negligence in cases of this sort. In *Dozer*, the defendant was a coworker of the plaintiff. The defendant knew that the plaintiff was of a frail constitution and had arachnophobia—an inordinate fear of spiders. Solely to play a prank on the plaintiff, the defendant obtained a number of live but harmless spiders and dropped them over the wall of the plaintiff's cubicle while the plaintiff was sitting at his desk eating lunch. The plaintiff, in utter

15

panic, fell backward from his desk chair and sustained a serious head injury. The defendant was found liable in negligence.

As the courts below correctly held, Larson's reliance on *Dozer* is misplaced. The first question is whether there is a duty. In all tort cases, the duty is to act reasonably under the circumstances and not to put others in positions of risk. In *Dozer*, the defendant did not live up to that duty and therefore negligently caused the injury to the plaintiff, for which the defendant bore liability.

But to say that individuals have a duty to act reasonably under the circumstances—that is, to avoid risk—is only the starting point of a negligence analysis. Once the court has determined that there is a duty, it must next determine 1) *what* duty was imposed on the defendant under the *particular circumstances* at issue, 2) whether there was a breach of that duty that resulted in injury or loss, and 3) whether the risk which resulted in the injury or loss was encompassed within the scope of the protection extended by the imposition of that duty.

The question of the defendant's duty is not whether the plaintiff was subjectively aware of the risk. Rather, the question is whether the defendant acted unreasonably under the circumstances vis-à-vis the plaintiff.[1]

As the courts below also correctly held, the particular circumstances here differ from those in *Dozer*, because they occurred in a different setting. Therefore, the duty that the defendant owed to the plaintiff here must be analyzed in those particular circumstances.

Patrons at an event which is designed to be frightening are expected to be surprised, startled, and scared by the exhibits; the operator does not have a duty to guard against patrons reacting in bizarre, frightened, or unpredictable ways. Patrons obviously have knowledge that they can anticipate being confronted by exhibits designed to startle and instill fear. They must realize that the very purpose of the attraction is to cause them to react in bizarre, frightened, or unpredictable ways. Under other circumstances, presenting a frightening or threatening act might be a violation of a general duty not to scare others.

---

[1] It is well settled that assumption of the risk is no longer a valid defense under Franklin law. The plaintiff's knowledge and conduct may be considered in determining whether, under the particular circumstances at issue, the defendant breached a duty to the plaintiff. If the defendant is found to have breached that duty, then the plaintiff's knowledge and conduct are considered to determine the extent of the plaintiff's comparative negligence.

Monroe v. Franklin Flags Amusement Park

Dozer. For example, being accosted by a supposed "vampire" in the middle of a shopping mall on a normal weekday in July might indeed be a violation of the general duty. But in this setting, on Halloween, the circumstances are different.

Larson, by voluntarily entering a self-described "House of Horrors" on Halloween, accepted the rules of the game. Hence, Larson's claim—that the club was negligent in its very act of admitting him to the "House of Horrors" because the establishment of the exhibit itself, with features designed to frighten patrons, breached the club's duty to act reasonably—must fail.

The courts below ended their analysis on that point and granted and affirmed the club's motion for summary judgment. But therein lies their error, for the proper analysis does not end there. Here, the further question is what additional duty is owed by a party which invites a patron for business purposes—in this case, what is the duty of the proprietor or operator of an amusement attraction to his patron who is an invitee. The operator impliedly represents that he has used reasonable care in inspecting and maintaining the premises and equipment furnished by him, and that they are reasonably safe for the purposes intended. The operator is not bound to protect patrons from every conceivable danger, only from unreasonably dangerous conditions. More specifically, such proprietors and operators have an obligation to ensure that there are not only adequate physical facilities but also adequate personnel and supervision for patrons entering the establishment.

Larson claims that the record shows that there is a question whether such adequate personnel and supervision existed here—most particularly, whether the role-playing individuals who were part of the experience in the "House of Horrors" were adequately instructed should some unfortunate event occur which injured a patron. Larson raised that question in his brief opposing the Club's motion for summary judgment, but neither the trial court nor the court of appeal addressed that claim. We cannot, on the record presented, determine if such adequate personnel, supervision, and instruction existed.

Accordingly, a genuine dispute of material fact exists which precludes granting the Club's motion for summary judgment.

Reversed and remanded.

This is an appeal from a judgment of negligence against defendant Shadowland Amusements, entered by the Franklin District Court and affirmed by the Franklin Court of Appeal. On May 22, 2005, plaintiff Evelyn Costello had entered a "haunted house" at Shadowland's amusement park and gone into a room which was only dimly lit. In this room, the operators of the amusement park had projected ghoulish apparitions on the wall using laser holograms for realistic effect. Startled by these apparitions, Costello backed up and tripped over a bench that Shadowland had placed in the middle of the room, injuring herself. She sued for damages for both medical expenses and pain and suffering.

Defendant Shadowland cites our decision in *Parker v. Muir* (Fr. Sup. Ct. 2005) as a defense. There, plaintiff Parker sued defendant Muir for negligence, claiming damages for injuries she suffered as a result of her patronage of Muir's cornfield maze. The maze consisted of five miles of paths cut into the cornfield. Parker accompanied the youth group from her church to the maze. She had specifically suggested that the group go to the maze on their outing because she had

been through the maze "at least twice" before, by her own admission. While venturing through the maze, she mentioned to the group that the paths were very rocky and that they should be careful. However, she tripped over a large rock in the path, fell, and broke her wrist. She sued Muir for negligence. The record showed that for the entire season during which the maze was open, this was the only reported accident.

As we noted in *Parker*, Franklin law provides that the owner or custodian of property is answerable for damage occasioned by its dangerous condition, but only upon a showing that the owner knew (or, in the exercise of reasonable care, should have known) of the dangerous condition, that the damage could have been prevented by the exercise of reasonable care, and that the owner failed to exercise such reasonable care. We also noted that the fact that an accident occurred as a result of a dangerous condition does not elevate the condition to one that is unreasonably dangerous. The past accident history of the condition in question and the degree to which the danger may be observed by a potential victim are factors to be taken into consideration in the determination of whether a condition is unreasonably dangerous. Further, the condition must be of such a nature as to constitute a danger that would reasonably be expected to cause injury to a prudent person using ordinary care under the circumstances.

In *Parker*, we concluded that the mere presence of rocks on a path through a cornfield did not meet the standard for imposing liability. The plaintiff there knew of the condition from her prior trips through the maze. She warned the members of her group about it. She voluntarily entered the maze with that knowledge. No prudent person in such circumstances, using ordinary care, would incur injury. Indeed, any reasonable person would not be surprised to find rocks in a dirt path. The otherwise unblemished safety record of the maze prior to the accident bore out this conclusion.

Here, defendant Shadowland's reliance on *Parker* is misplaced. As we noted in *Larson v. Franklin High Boosters Club, Inc.* (Fr. Sup. Ct. 2002), every individual has a duty to act reasonably and not to put others in positions of risk. Shadowland did not act reasonably here. It was obviously aware of the dim lighting, the placement of the bench

(it had itself put it there), and the hazard the bench might present. This dim lighting combined with the bench placement was a dangerous condition, one of which visitors were unaware, and the injury which resulted was one that Shadowland could have prevented using reasonable care. Shadowland did unreasonably put plaintiff Costello at risk and is therefore liable for Costello's injuries.

Affirmed.

19

20

Palindrome Recording Contract

July 2013
MPT-2

Palindrome

Recording Contract

www.ncbex.org

National Conference of Bar Examiners
302 South Bedford Street | Madison, WI 53703-3622
Phone: 608-280-8550 | Fax: 608-280-8552 | TDD: 608-661-1275
e-mail: contact@ncbex.org

Contents

i

Instructions

The back cover of each test booklet contains the following instructions:

You will be instructed when to begin and when to stop this test. Do not break the seal on this booklet until you are told to begin. This test is designed to evaluate your ability to handle a select number of legal authorities in the context of a factual problem involving a client.

The problem is set in the fictitious state of Franklin, in the fictitious Fifteenth Circuit of the United States. Columbia and Olympia are also fictitious states in the Fifteenth Circuit. In Franklin, the trial court of general jurisdiction is the District Court, the intermediate appellate court is the Court of Appeal, and the highest court is the Supreme Court.

You will have two kinds of materials with which to work: a File and a Library. The first document in the File is a memorandum containing the instructions for the task you are to complete. The other documents in the File contain factual information about your case and may include some facts that are not relevant.

The Library contains the legal authorities needed to complete the task and may also include some authorities that are not relevant. Any cases may be real, modified, or written solely for the purpose of this examination. If the cases appear familiar to you, do not assume that they are precisely the same as you have read before. Read them thoroughly, as if they all were new to you. You should assume that the cases were decided in the jurisdictions and on the dates shown. In citing cases from the Library, you may use abbreviations and omit page references.

Your response must be written in the answer book provided. If you are using a laptop computer to answer the questions, your jurisdiction will provide you with specific instructions. In answering this performance test, you should concentrate on the materials in the File and Library. What you have learned in law school and elsewhere provides the general background for analyzing the problem; the File and Library provide the specific materials with which you must work.

Although there are no restrictions on how you apportion your time, you should allocate approximately half your time to reading and digesting the materials and to organizing your answer before you begin writing it. You may make notes anywhere in the test materials; blank pages are provided at the end of the booklet. You may not tear pages from the question booklet.

This performance test will be graded on your responsiveness to the instructions regarding the task you are to complete, which are given to you in the first memorandum in the File, and on the content, thoroughness, and organization of your response.

July 2013 MPT

FILE

MPT-2: *Palindrome Recording Contract*

TO: Examinee
FROM: Levi Morris
DATE: July 30, 2013
RE: Palindrome Recording Contract

We have been retained to represent the members of the rock band Palindrome. The band has had considerable success in the tri-state area of Franklin, Columbia, and Olympia and has received an offer from Polyphon, an independent record label, which wants to sign the band to a long-term recording contract.

The contract submitted by Polyphon is complex and voluminous (it runs over 50 pages of single-spaced type). The band has asked us to negotiate the contract with the record label. There are some key provisions that we must redraft to meet the band's contractual desires. We can then present the redrafted contract to Polyphon, as a step in negotiating with the label. I am attaching the provisions from the contract Polyphon submitted that I would like you to look at. I have also attached other material to give you some background and from which you may glean the band's wishes and the applicable law. For your purposes, assume that the agreement among the various band members is a binding contract and that they have formed a valid partnership.

Please draft a memorandum in which you identify those contract provisions that need to be redrafted to meet the band's wishes and to comply with the law. For each provision that you identify,

1. redraft the provision, indicating your changes from the original text, and

2. explain the reasons for your redraft, including the legal reasons (if any) for changing the provision, to guide me in conducting the negotiations over these points.

Levi Morris: Otto, it's good to see you. How are things going?

Otto Smyth: Great, really great. As I told you over the phone, we've got a mega-offer from Polyphon to sign with them, and the band asked me to take the lead in negotiating.

Morris: Excellent. What's Polyphon's offer?

Smyth: We've had a few offers in the past, but from labels that wanted to take everything we had. We really want to sign with an independent label, because they treat artists like us better, and Polyphon has a reputation for treating artists reasonably and being willing to negotiate terms. They sent our manager this huge contract—here's a copy. We'll need your help to deal with them.

Morris: That's what we're here for. Bring me up-to-date on what's happening with the band.

Smyth: Well, as you may know, about nine months ago, Al, our bass player, was injured by a drunk driver. He's okay now, thank goodness. Abby, our lead guitarist, and Coco, our drummer, are still going strong, and, as leader of the group, I'm still playing rhythm guitar, singing lead vocals, and doing all the songwriting. Our fan base really has grown here in the tri-state area, and that must've gotten the attention of the label, because they really came after us hard.

Morris: How do the members of the band get on as far as business arrangements go?

Smyth: We're fine together—when we first formed 10 years ago or so, we made an agreement among ourselves which I cobbled up out of a music book I read. Here's a copy. We do business as a partnership under the name Palindrome Partners, and everything we make has to go through the partnership into a partnership bank account. We then divide up the money in accordance with our partnership agreement.

Morris: Thanks. We'll look the agreement over. Let's turn to the label's offer, and—first things first—how's the money?

[*Discussion of financial terms of advance and royalties offered by label omitted.*]

Morris: Now, what else do you want us to negotiate with them?

Smyth: Well, I'm not really sure what's in there—I really don't understand this legal stuff. But we're all pretty much in agreement over some things that are important to us. First, we don't want to be tied up with the label for too long unless they really do a good job for us—maybe for three albums at most, and only for four years.

Second, our artistic integrity is really important—we've got to make all the artistic decisions about the songs that go into our albums, and the recordings, and the producer we want, and what gets released.

Third, since Al nearly died because of that drunk driver, we've become fanatic about drugs and booze—we've sworn off, and we owe it to him to get the message out. We'd hate it if our music didn't get that message across, or worse, if people thought we were the stereotypical drink-and-dope rockers, or if our songs were used in, like, a beer commercial. I never want to see a picture of me in some magazine holding a bottle.

Morris: Understood—we'll try to make sure that you have the right to approve of marketing and promotional efforts. You know, my daughter loves your band and wears a Palindrome T-shirt she got at one of your concerts.

Smyth: Yeah, we make a nice amount from our merchandise sales. At every show we do, and on our website, we sell T-shirts, baseball caps, tank tops, stuff like that.

Morris: Who makes them for you?

Smyth: Our manager found the various manufacturers. We're really careful to treat our fans well and give them good value for their money, using top-quality materials, making sure the merchandise is high quality—like the T-shirts, we could use some cheap cotton blends and make a few bucks more, but instead we always use those thicker Ts, with high-quality fabric. We think that if we treat our fans well, they'll stay loyal to us.

You know, we've been together for almost 10 years now, and we've always been careful of the Palindrome name and what it means to our fans. We've worked really hard to build it up to where it is now, and it means a lot to us. We put our name on every piece of merchandise we have. Our manager even got a registered trademark for us in our name, and she tells us that all of our merchandise deals are nonexclusive, which means we can license our name to more than one manufacturer. And we want to keep it that way. It's really important to us to keep control of everything that has to do with our merchandise, and the money it brings in, because it's a real source of income for us.

We understand that Polyphon is offering us a higher royalty rate for our records in exchange for a piece of our merchandise action, and that's OK with us—we'd be willing

25

to give them a quarter of the revenue for the stuff they produce and sell—but we've got to keep that trademark, and we've got to be able to use it ourselves without cutting Polyphon in on money from products it doesn't make or sell.

Morris: So you wouldn't mind licensing your trademark to Polyphon?

Smyth: Not as long as we own it, can still do our own thing with it, and can control what they do with it.

Morris: We'll see to that. We don't have to itemize the things they can produce; we just have to be sure that you can approve of what they make and the quality of it as well.

[*Discussion of other points omitted.*]

AGREEMENT AMONG MEMBERS OF PALINDROME

AGREEMENT, by and between Otto Smyth, Abby Thornton, Coco Hart, and Al Laurence (collectively, "the Band"), all citizens of the United States of America and the State of Franklin, as follows:

WHEREAS, the individual members of the Band have formed a musical group known professionally as Palindrome; and

WHEREAS, the individual members of the Band wish to set forth the terms of their affiliation;

NOW, THEREFORE, the individual members of the Band agree as follows:

1.   All property created by the Band as a collective entity (including both intellectual and material property) shall be jointly owned by all members of the Band. All income earned by the Band as a collective entity for its collective efforts or from that collective property (e.g., from recordings made as a musical group) will be divided equally among the individual members of the Band. Should any individual member of the Band voluntarily or involuntarily withdraw from the Band, that member will receive his or her proportionate share of income earned by the Band as a collective entity from undertakings made before that member's withdrawal from the Band.

2.   All actions taken for the Band as an entity will require the unanimous approval of all the individual members of the Band.

3.   The Band shall form a partnership and do business under the name Palindrome Partners.

Signed this 15th day of March, 2003.

Otto Smyth
Otto Smyth

Abby Thornton
Abby Thornton

Coco Hart
Coco Hart

Al Laurence
Al Laurence

Excerpts from Contract Presented by Polyphon

1. DEFINITIONS

"Album" shall mean a sufficient number of Masters embodying Artist's performances to comprise one (1) or more compact discs, or the equivalent, of not less than forty-five (45) minutes of playing time and containing at least ten (10) different Masters.

"Artist" or "you" shall mean each member of the band Palindrome, individually, and the band collectively.

"Contract Period" shall mean the term set forth in Paragraph 3.03.

"Master" shall mean any sound recording of a single musical composition, irrespective of length, that is intended to be embodied on or in an Album.

*   *   *

3. TERM AND DELIVERY OBLIGATIONS

3.01 During each Contract Period, you will deliver to Polyphon commercially satisfactory Masters. Such Masters will embody the featured vocal performances of Artist of contemporary selections that have not been previously recorded by Artist, and each Master will contain the performances of all members of Artist.

3.02 During each Contract Period, you will perform for the recording of Masters and you will deliver to Polyphon those Masters (the "Recording Commitment") necessary to meet the following schedule:

Contract Period	Recording Commitment
Initial Contract Period	one (1) Album
Each Option Period	one (1) Album

3.03 The initial Contract Period will begin on the date of this Agreement and will run for one year. You hereby grant Polyphon eight (8) separate options, each to extend the term of this Agreement for one additional Contract Period of one year per option ("Option Period"). In the event that you do not fulfill your Recording Commitment for the initial Contract Period or any Option Period, that period will continue to run and the next Option Period will not begin until the Recording Commitment in question has been fulfilled.

4. APPROVALS

4.01 Polyphon shall, in its sole discretion, make the final determination of the Masters to be included in each Album, and shall have the sole authority to assign one or more producers who shall collaborate with you on the production of each Master and each Album.

*   *   *

8. MERCHANDISE, MARKETING, AND OTHER RIGHTS

8.01 Artist warrants that it owns the federally registered trademark PALINDROME (Reg. No. 5,423,888) and hereby transfers all right, title, and interest in that trademark to Polyphon. Polyphon may use the trademark on such products as, in its sole discretion, it sees fit to produce or license, and all income from such use shall be Polyphon's alone.

8.02 Artist hereby authorizes Polyphon, in its sole discretion, to use Artist's, and each member of Artist's, name, image, and likeness in connection with any marketing or promotional efforts and to use the Masters in conjunction with the advertising, promotion, or sale of any goods or services.

July 2013 MPT

▶ *LIBRARY*

MPT-2: *Palindrome Recording Contract*

Franklin Statute re Personal Services Contracts

Franklin Labor Code § 2855

(a) Except as otherwise provided in subsection (b), a contract to render personal service may not be enforced against the employee or person contracting to render the service beyond five years from the commencement of service under it. If the employee or person contracting to render the service voluntarily continues to serve under it beyond that time, the contract may be referred to as affording a presumptive measure of the compensation due the employee or person rendering the service.

(b) Notwithstanding subsection (a), a contract to render personal service in the production of phonorecords in which sounds are first fixed may not be enforced against the employee or person contracting to render the service beyond 10 years from the commencement of service under it. For purposes of this subsection, a "phonorecord" shall mean all forms of audio-only reproduction, now or hereafter known, manufactured and distributed for home use.

Panama Hats of Franklin, Inc. v. Elson Enterprises, LLC

United States District Court (District of Franklin, 2004)

Panama Hats of Franklin, Inc., manufactures hats which it sells to the public. In 2000, it entered into an agreement with the Allied Hat Co., which owned a federally registered trademark in the word "Napoleon" for a style of men's hat. Other than the financial terms, the only operative term of that agreement reads as follows: "Allied owns the federally registered trademark 'Napoleon' for men's hats (Reg. No. 3,455,879). Allied hereby transfers that trademark to Panama for the monetary consideration set forth below." The agreement did not make any other transfer of tangible or intangible property, good will, or business assets to Panama. Two years later, Allied went out of business—all its other assets have been liquidated, and it no longer has any legal (or other) existence.

In 2003, Elson Enterprises, LLC, a company unrelated to Panama or Allied, began manufacturing a style of men's hat, which it marketed as the "Napoleon" style. Panama had never used the mark, but it sued Elson, claiming that it owned the federally registered trademark in the word "Napoleon" for hats by virtue of the assignment from Allied and that Elson had infringed that mark. Elson now moves for summary judgment, claiming that Panama has no interest in that trademark and so has no basis for a claim of trademark infringement against Elson.

The purpose of a trademark is clear from the definition of the term in the federal trademark statute: "The term 'trademark' includes any word, name, symbol, or device, or any combination thereof — (1) used by a person . . . to identify and distinguish his or her goods, including a unique product, from those manufactured or sold by others and to indicate the source of the goods, even if that source is unknown." 15 U.S.C. § 1127. Some examples of well-known trademarks are Coca-Cola, Exxon, and Sony.

From this it is apparent that the trademark cannot be divorced from the goods themselves—as the trademark is the assurance to the consumer of the source of the goods, the trademark cannot exist independently of the goods. Hence, if one company purchases the assets of another and becomes the manufacturer of the goods previously manufactured by the purchased company, the trademark that was associated with those goods may now become the property of, and be associated with, the new manufacturer of the goods, for the trademark is now the new manufacturer's indication of source. Short of a transfer of other assets of a business with the trademark, a trademark cannot be transferred without, at the very least, a simultaneous transfer of the good will associated with the mark, for that good will has developed from the actual product itself and so binds the trademark to the goods or services with which it is associated. In essence, the mark cannot exist in a vacuum, to be bought and sold as a freestanding property. This policy is made explicit in the federal trademark statute: "A registered mark . . . shall be assignable *with the good will of the business in which the mark is used, or with that part of the good will of the business connected with the use of and symbolized by the mark.*" 15 U.S.C. § 1060(a)(1) (emphasis added).

In the parlance of the trademark law, the sale of a trademark without any other asset of the business—without, at the very least, the good will associated with the trademark —is termed an "assignment in gross" or a "naked" assignment of the trademark. Given the policy considerations set forth above, without the necessary inclusion of the assets of the business or the good will associated with the mark, the law holds that a "naked"

"assignment in gross" of a trademark is not valid. Further, such a "naked" "assignment in gross" may cause the assignor to lose all rights in the trademark and leave the trademark open for acquisition by the first subsequent user of the mark in commerce.

Because the purported assignment of the federally registered trademark "Napoleon" from Allied to Panama was just such a "naked" "assignment in gross" of the mark, it has no validity—the purported assignment conveyed no rights. Because the assignment was invalid, the mark was free for anyone to acquire, and anyone could acquire the right to the mark by using the mark in commerce, which is precisely what Elson did. (Panama never used the mark.) Therefore, Elson did not infringe on any rights of Panama because Panama had no rights in the "Napoleon" trademark. Elson's motion for summary judgment is granted.

35

M&P Sportswear, Inc. v. Tops Clothing Co.

United States District Court (District of Franklin, 2001)

The facts giving rise to this lawsuit for trademark infringement, stripped to their essentials, are these: M&P Sportswear designs T-shirts and other items of apparel, and is the owner of the federally registered trademark "Go Baby," which it uses as the brand name of a line of T-shirts. Tops Clothing is an offshore manufacturer of clothing. In 1998, Tops entered into an agreement with M&P, under which M&P licensed the use of its "Go Baby" trademark to Tops. The agreement provided that Tops would pay a specified licensing fee to M&P, which would entitle Tops to manufacture, import into the United States, and sell T-shirts under the "Go Baby" brand. The agreement contained no other substantive provisions, and Tops immediately began the manufacture, importation, and sale of the T-shirts. Tops made the requisite licensing payments to M&P.

In 2000, M&P representatives purchased samples of Tops's "Go Baby" T-shirts at a "99-cent" store in Franklin City; this was the first sample of the Tops T-shirts M&P had obtained. M&P's representatives found that the T-shirts were, in their opinion, of the poorest quality imaginable—according to the deposition testimony of one of M&P's principals, "they were so thin and cheaply made that they would dissolve in a rainstorm." M&P then sent a purported "notice of termination" of the trademark license agreement to Tops (this notwithstanding that the license agreement did not make any specific provision for termination). When Tops continued to manufacture, import, and sell the branded T-shirts, M&P brought this action for trademark infringement against it. Tops now seeks summary judgment against M&P, on the ground that, as the license agreement contained no provisions for quality control, M&P no longer has any rights in the "Go Baby" trademark.

It is a basic tenet of trademark law that a trademark is an indication of the source or origin of goods or services to the public, enabling the public to expect that the goods or services bearing the trademark will comport with a certain uniform standard of quality, whatever that quality may be. A trademark carries with it a message that the trademark owner is controlling the nature and

36

quality of the goods or services sold under the mark. Thus, not only does a trademark owner have the *right* to control quality—when it licenses, it has the *duty* to control quality.

Accordingly, it is also a basic tenet of the trademark law that any trademark proprietor who licenses the trademark to another must assure, in the license agreement, that the goods or services offered by the licensee meet the standards of quality of the trademarked goods established by the trademark proprietor. Failure to do so causes the mark to lose its significance as an indication of origin. Indeed, many Circuits have held that such action may be seen as an abandonment of the mark itself; the federal trademark act provides, "A mark shall be deemed 'abandoned' if either of the following occurs: . . . (2) when any course of conduct of the owner, including acts of omission as well as commission, causes the mark . . . to lose its significance as a mark." Uncontrolled licensing as a course of conduct is inherently deceptive, constitutes abandonment of all rights in the trademark, and results in cancellation of its registration.

Here, M&P made no quality-control provision whatsoever in its license agreement. Accordingly, by failing to assure the public of any standard of quality of the goods and services manufactured and sold under the mark, M&P has lost its rights to the mark.

Tops's motion for summary judgment is granted.

February 2018 MPTs
State of Franklin v. Clegane
In re Hastings

THE MPT
MULTISTATE PERFORMANCE TEST

February 2018
MPTs

www.ncbex.org

National Conference of Bar Examiners
302 South Bedford Street | Madison, WI 53703-3622
Phone: 608-280-8550 | Fax: 608-280-8552 | TDD: 608-661-1275
e-mail: contact@ncbex.org

Contents

MPT-1: *State of Franklin v. Clegane*

FILE

LIBRARY

MPT-2: *In re Hastings*

FILE

LIBRARY

Preface

The Multistate Performance Test (MPT) is developed by the National Conference of Bar Examiners (NCBE). This publication includes the items and Point Sheets from the February 2018 MPT. The instructions for the test appear on page iii.

The MPT Point Sheets describe the factual and legal points encompassed within the lawyering tasks to be completed. They outline the possible issues and points that might be addressed by an examinee. They are provided to the user jurisdictions to assist graders in grading the examination by identifying the issues and suggesting the resolution of the problems contemplated by the drafters.

For more information about the MPT, including a list of skills tested, visit the NCBE website at www.ncbex.org.

Description of the MPT

The MPT consists of two 90-minute items and is a component of the Uniform Bar Examination (UBE). It is administered by user jurisdictions as part of the bar examination on the Tuesday before the last Wednesday in February and July of each year. User jurisdictions may select one or both items to include as part of their bar examinations. (Jurisdictions that administer the UBE use two MPTs.)

The materials for each MPT include a File and a Library. The File consists of source documents containing all the facts of the case. The specific assignment the examinee is to complete is described in a memorandum from a supervising attorney. The File might also include transcripts of interviews, depositions, hearings or trials, pleadings, correspondence, client documents, contracts, newspaper articles, medical records, police reports, or lawyer's notes. Relevant as well as irrelevant facts are included. Facts are sometimes ambiguous, incomplete, or even conflicting. As in practice, a client's or a supervising attorney's version of events may be incomplete or unreliable. Examinees are expected to recognize when facts are inconsistent or missing and are expected to identify potential sources of additional facts.

The Library may contain cases, statutes, regulations, or rules, some of which may not be relevant to the assigned lawyering task. The examinee is expected to extract from the Library the legal principles necessary to analyze the problem and perform the task. The MPT is not a test of substantive law; the Library materials provide sufficient substantive information to complete the task.

The MPT is designed to test an examinee's ability to use fundamental lawyering skills in a realistic situation and complete a task that a beginning lawyer should be able to accomplish. The MPT is not a test of substantive knowledge. Rather, it is designed to evaluate six fundamental skills lawyers are expected to demonstrate regardless of the area of law in which the skills are applied. The MPT requires examinees to (1) sort detailed factual materials and separate relevant from irrelevant facts; (2) analyze statutory, case, and administrative materials for applicable principles of law; (3) apply the relevant law to the relevant facts in a manner likely to resolve a client's problem; (4) identify and resolve ethical dilemmas, when present; (5) communicate effectively in writing; and (6) complete a lawyering task within time constraints. These skills are tested by requiring examinees to perform one or more of a variety of lawyering tasks. For example, examinees might be instructed to complete any of the following: a memorandum to a supervising attorney, a letter to a client, a persuasive memorandum or brief, a statement of facts, a contract provision, a will, a counseling plan, a proposal for settlement or agreement, a discovery plan, a witness examination plan, or a closing argument.

Instructions

The back cover of each test booklet contains the following instructions:

You will be instructed when to begin and when to stop this test. Do not break the seal on this booklet until you are told to begin. This test is designed to evaluate your ability to handle a select number of legal authorities in the context of a factual problem involving a client.

The problem is set in the fictitious state of Franklin, in the fictitious Fifteenth Circuit of the United States. Columbia and Olympia are also fictitious states in the Fifteenth Circuit. In Franklin, the trial court of general jurisdiction is the District Court, the intermediate appellate court is the Court of Appeal, and the highest court is the Supreme Court.

You will have two kinds of materials with which to work: a File and a Library. The first document in the File is a memorandum containing the instructions for the task you are to complete. The other documents in the File contain factual information about your case and may include some facts that are not relevant.

The Library contains the legal authorities needed to complete the task and may also include some authorities that are not relevant. Any cases may be real, modified, or written solely for the purpose of this examination. If the cases appear familiar to you, do not assume that they are precisely the same as you have read before. Read them thoroughly, as if they all were new to you. You should assume that the cases were decided in the jurisdictions and on the dates shown. In citing cases from the Library, you may use abbreviations and omit page references.

Your response must be written in the answer book provided. If you are using a laptop computer to answer the questions, your jurisdiction will provide you with specific instructions. In answering this performance test, you should concentrate on the materials in the File and Library. What you have learned in law school and elsewhere provides the general background for analyzing the problem; the File and Library provide the specific materials with which you must work.

Although there are no restrictions on how you apportion your time, you should allocate approximately half your time to reading and digesting the materials and to organizing your answer before you begin writing it. You may make notes anywhere in the test materials; blank pages are provided at the end of the booklet. You may not tear pages from the question booklet.

Do not include your actual name anywhere in the work product required by the task memorandum.

This performance test will be graded on your responsiveness to the instructions regarding the task you are to complete, which are given to you in the first memorandum in the File, and on the content, thoroughness, and organization of your response.

February 2018
MPT-1 File:
State of Franklin v. Clegane

Selmer & Pierce LLP
Attorneys at Law
412 Valmont Place
Franklin City, Franklin 33703

MEMORANDUM

To: Examinee
From: Anna Pierce
Date: February 27, 2018
Re: State of Franklin v. Clegane

We represent Sarah Karth. Sarah Karth's sister, Valerie Karth, was physically injured and incapacitated last summer when an unsupervised teenager set off fireworks at a neighborhood Fourth of July party. The teenager, a minor, was also injured. Valerie Karth was struck by the fireworks and also suffered economic injury because sparks from the fireworks started a fire that burned her garage to the ground.

The man who sold the fireworks to the teenager, Greg Clegane, was convicted of the felony of unlawful sale of fireworks to a minor. Clegane's sentencing hearing is in two weeks. Sarah Karth wishes to read victim-impact statements at the sentencing hearing both on her own behalf and on Valerie's behalf. She has also submitted a request that Clegane pay restitution for the losses she and her sister have sustained because of his actions.

Last week the prosecution notified Sarah that Clegane's counsel has filed a motion to (1) exclude the proposed victim-impact statements at the sentencing hearing, arguing that Sarah and Valerie are not victims within the meaning of the Franklin Crime Victims' Rights Act (FCVRA); and (2) deny their restitution requests. A copy of Clegane's motion is attached.

I intend to file a brief in opposition to this motion on behalf of Sarah asking that the court include Sarah's and Valerie's victim-impact statements and order Clegane to pay restitution to both of them. Please draft the argument section of our brief. In drafting your argument, be sure to follow the attached guidelines. Make the most persuasive argument possible under the FCVRA and relevant case law.

Selmer & Pierce LLP

OFFICE MEMORANDUM

To: Associates
From: Managing Partner
Date: July 8, 2012
Re: Guidelines for Persuasive Briefs in Trial Courts

The following guidelines apply to persuasive briefs filed in support of motions in trial courts.

I. Captions

[omitted]

II. Statement of Facts

[omitted]

III. Legal Argument

Your legal argument should make your points clearly and succinctly, citing relevant authority for each legal proposition. Do not restate the facts as a whole at the beginning of your legal argument. Instead, integrate the facts into your legal argument in a way that makes the strongest case for our client.

Use headings to separate the sections of your argument. Your headings should not state abstract conclusions, but rather integrate factual detail into legal propositions to make them more persuasive. An ineffective heading states only: "The court should not admit evidence of the victim's character." An effective heading states: "The court should refuse to admit evidence of the defendant's character for violence because the defendant has not raised a claim of self- defense."

In the body of your argument, analyze applicable legal authority and persuasively argue how both the facts and the law support our client's position. Supporting authority should be emphasized, but contrary authority should also be cited, addressed in the argument, and explained or distinguished.

Finally, anticipate and accommodate any weaknesses in your case in the body of your argument. If possible, structure your argument in such a way as to highlight your argument's strengths and minimize its weaknesses. Make concessions if necessary, but only on points that do not involve essential elements of your claim or defense.

The Franklin City Post

Illegal Fireworks Injure Two and Destroy Garage

July 5, 2017

FRANKLIN CITY, Franklin—The quiet neighborhood of Fair Oaks became a nightmare of exploding shells after a 17-year-old set off illegal, professional-grade fireworks during a Fourth of July celebration in a friend's backyard. The fireworks, called Little Devil Shards, sent exploding shells spraying through the yard, striking and injuring a bystander and setting a nearby garage on fire. The minor was also seriously injured.

The minor set off the fireworks to surprise his friends, Franklin City Detective Ralph Guerra said early this morning. It appears that the minor obtained the fireworks the day before the party from Greg Clegane, the proprietor of Starburst Fireworks, which sells fireworks and other party supplies from a storefront in the Third Ward of Franklin City. Clegane has three similar retail operations spread throughout the eastern part of the state. The sale of such powerful fireworks to a minor is a felony in Franklin, punishable by up to five years in prison and a $50,000 fine. The minor's name has not been released. He is a Franklin City resident.

Lena Harley, a local resident, saw the minor igniting the fireworks in the middle of a crowd of guests at the party. She watched as a spray of sparks and exploding shells flew through the air. "It was like a war zone," said Harley.

The victims were transported to an area hospital. Several shells also struck a neighbor's garage, setting it afire. The garage was totally destroyed before firefighters could control the blaze.

Franklin City police are encouraging anyone with information about the incident to contact them.

(Franklin City Associated Press contributed to this report.)

Excerpt from Transcript of Client Interview with Sarah Karth

February 26, 2018

Att'y Pierce: Good afternoon, Ms. Karth.

Sarah Karth: Good afternoon.

Pierce: Can you describe what brings you to the office today?

Karth: Yes. Are you familiar with the fireworks incident over in Fair Oaks last summer?

Pierce: I remember hearing about it on the news right after it happened.

Karth: My sister, Valerie Karth, was one of the people injured that day. Her house is next door to the yard where the fireworks went off, and she was attending the party. Sparks from the fireworks caused her garage to burn down.

I was at the criminal trial of Greg Clegane, who was convicted of the felony of selling dangerous fireworks to a minor. During the trial, the arresting officer testified that Clegane admitted selling the fireworks and that the boy had told him, "I can't wait to show these to my friends—I'm going to give everyone a big surprise." Clegane told the officer that the minor "looked like he was at least in his twenties" and that the boy's statements "didn't raise any red flags."

I want to read victim-impact statements at Clegane's sentencing hearing, one on my own behalf and one on my sister Valerie's. I also want restitution on behalf of both Valerie and myself. Last week, I heard from the prosecutor's office that Clegane's lawyer had filed a motion asking the court to keep me from making the statements and seeking restitution.

Pierce: What do you want to say? What are you asking for?

Karth: I want to make it clear to the judge, and to Clegane, that his illegal sale of dangerous fireworks to a 17-year-old had very personal and life-altering consequences for me and my family.

Pierce: Tell me more.

Karth: Clegane needs to understand that his actions have irrevocably affected our lives and that I am also a victim of his crime. I want to look him in the eyes and tell him that. I want the court to understand how Clegane's actions have ruined my sister's life. Valerie was attending the party when the fireworks went off. She was hit by fireworks and was rushed to the hospital for emergency care. Valerie was seriously injured and was in a coma for several months. She has just come out of the coma and is still incapacitated. She remains in stable condition in the hospital but cannot come to court.

Pierce: What else do you want to tell the court about Valerie?

Karth: Valerie has always loved life and lived it to the fullest. She is bright, athletic, independent, and strong. She was the first person in our family to graduate from college. She is a rock. She is someone whom you can count on and trust. My father died five years ago, and my mother has been so traumatized by Valerie's injuries that she is too frail to participate in any court proceedings.

Pierce: And what about restitution for Valerie?

Karth: Valerie's out-of-pocket medical expenses so far total $22,000—we've got the bills and receipts to prove it. Her medical providers have concluded that she will incur at least an additional $40,000 in out-of-pocket medical expenses. By the time she is able to return to work, she will have lost $120,000 in salary. The fireworks also destroyed her garage; rebuilding it has cost $17,000.

Pierce: And you want to make a victim-impact statement on your own behalf?

Karth: Yes, I truly believe that I am also a victim of Clegane's crime. Valerie and I are very close and always have been. I'm 35 and she is two years older. The day she was injured was the worst and most shocking day of my life. I spent endless days in the hospital waiting for her to come out of the coma. If not for Clegane, that teenager could not have caused me the trauma that he did. I want the court to give Clegane the maximum sentence possible—five years—so that he knows how many people his actions have harmed and will be held accountable. People think that fireworks are no big deal, but this reckless sale of fireworks has really devastated my family.

Pierce: And are you requesting restitution on your own behalf?

Karth: Yes, I have incurred $1,500 in out-of-pocket medical bills myself as a result of Clegane's criminal behavior. I've been so depressed and distraught about Valerie's future and how she will be taken care of that I've been seeing a therapist twice a month for the past six months. My insurance has a high deductible, so I've had to bear the cost of the therapist myself. I think Clegane should pay that cost, not me. We've suffered enough.

STATE OF FRANKLIN
DISTRICT COURT OF GLENN COUNTY

STATE of FRANKLIN,

      Plaintiff,

v.

GREG CLEGANE,

      Defendant.

Case No. 2017-CR-238

DEFENDANT'S MOTION TO EXCLUDE VICTIM STATEMENTS
AND DENY RESTITUTION

Defendant Greg Clegane hereby moves the Court to deny the request of Sarah Karth (acting on behalf of Valerie Karth and in her own capacity) to make victim-impact statements at Defendant's sentencing hearing in this case. In addition, Defendant requests that the Court deny the Karths' requests for restitution. In support of this motion, Defendant states:

1. After a jury trial on February 2, 2018, Defendant was convicted of the felony crime of unlawful sale of fireworks to a minor, Franklin Criminal Code § 305. Sentencing is scheduled for March 14, 2018.

2. Pursuant to the Franklin Crime Victims' Rights Act (FCVRA) §§ 55 and 56, Ms. Karth has submitted proposed victim-impact statements regarding injuries she and Valerie Karth suffered as a result of fireworks that were set off at a party in Franklin City on July 4, 2017.

3. It is undisputed that Defendant was not present on that occasion and had no part in the decision to ignite fireworks in an unsafe manner.

4. The fireworks were ignited by a 17-year-old male, who was using them contrary to the instructions on the fireworks' packaging.

5. At the time Defendant sold said fireworks, he had no reason to believe that the 17-year- old was not an adult, or that the fireworks would be ignited under unsafe conditions.

6. Defendant's only connection to the injuries suffered by the Karths is that the minor who set off the fireworks had bought them from Defendant. The Karths do not qualify as crime victims under the FCVRA because they were not "directly and proximately harmed as a result of

the commission" of the offense of which Defendant stands convicted: the sale of fireworks to a minor. Fr. Crm. Code § 305.

7.   In addition, because the Karths cannot be deemed crime victims under FCVRA § 55(b), the Court must deny their restitution requests. *See* FCVRA § 56.

8.   Even assuming that the Karths could be considered crime victims under the statute, the restitution they seek is not supported by the evidence and is excessive, and Defendant does not have the resources to pay the amounts requested. FCVRA § 56(d).

WHEREFORE Defendant asks the Court to deny the victim-impact statements and restitution requests made by the Karths and to grant such other relief as the Court deems just and proper.

Karen Pine

Filed: February 19, 2018

Karen Pine
LAW OFFICES OF PINE, BRYCE & DIAL, LLP
Attorney for Defendant Greg Clegane

February 2018
MPT-1 Library:
State of Franklin v. Clegane

Excerpts from the Franklin Crime Victims' Rights Act

§ 55. Rights of Crime Victims

(a) A crime victim has the following rights:

(1) The right to be reasonably protected from the accused.

(2) The right to reasonable, accurate, and timely notice of any public court proceeding, or any parole proceeding, involving the crime, or of any release or escape of the accused.

(3) The right not to be excluded from any such public court proceeding, unless the court, after receiving clear and convincing evidence, determines that testimony by the victim would be materially altered if the victim heard other testimony at that proceeding.

(4) The right to be reasonably heard at any public proceeding in the district court involving release, plea, or sentencing, or at any parole proceeding.

(5) The reasonable right to confer with the prosecution in the case.

(6) The right to full and timely restitution under section 56 of this Act.

(7) The right to proceedings free from unreasonable delay.

(8) The right to be treated with fairness and with respect for the victim's dignity and privacy.

(9) The right to be informed in a timely manner of any plea bargain or deferred prosecution agreement.

(b) Definitions—Crime Victim

(1) In general—As used in this Act, the term "crime victim" means a person directly and proximately harmed as a result of the commission of a Franklin criminal offense.

(2) Minors and certain other victims—In the case of a crime victim who is under 18 years of age, incompetent, incapacitated, or deceased, the legal guardians of the crime victim or the representatives of the crime victim's estate, family members, or any other persons appointed as suitable by the court may assume the crime victim's rights under this Act, but in no event shall the defendant be named as such guardian or representative.

§ 56. Restitution

(a) The court, when sentencing a defendant convicted of an offense, shall order that the defendant make restitution to any victim of such offense.

(b) The order may require that such defendant

    (1) in the case of an offense resulting in damage to or loss or destruction of property of a victim of the offense,

        (A) return the property to its owner or someone designated by the owner; or

        (B) if return of the property under subparagraph (A) is impossible, impractical, or inadequate, pay an amount equal to the repair or replacement cost of the property.

    (2) in the case of an offense resulting in physical, psychiatric, or psychological injury to a victim,

        (A) pay an amount equal to the cost of necessary medical and related professional services and devices relating to physical, psychiatric, and psychological care, including nonmedical care and treatment;

        (B) pay an amount equal to the cost of necessary physical and occupational therapy and rehabilitation; and

        (C) reimburse the victim for income lost by such victim as a result of such offense.

(c) A defendant is presumed to have the ability to pay restitution unless the defendant establishes the inability to pay by a preponderance of the evidence.

(d) In determining the amount of restitution, the court shall consider (1) public policy that favors requiring criminals to compensate for damage and injury to their victims; (2) the financial burden placed on the victim and those who provide services to the victim as a result of the criminal conduct of the defendant; and (3) the financial resources of the defendant and the nature of the burden the payment of restitution will impose on dependents of the defendant.

State v. Jones
Franklin Court of Appeal (2006)

The issue in this appeal is whether the trial court erred when it held that the girlfriend of the defendant's cocaine customer was not a "victim" entitled to provide a victim-impact statement at sentencing pursuant to the Franklin Crime Victims' Rights Act (FCVRA). We affirm.

For approximately two years between 2004 and 2006, defendant Iggy Jones was engaged in a conspiracy with others to manufacture and distribute cocaine. Based on information conveyed to an undercover law enforcement officer, the police executed a search warrant of the defendant's home, discovering the remnants of a cocaine manufacturing operation and related paraphernalia. Jones was arrested and subsequently pled guilty to conspiracy to possess cocaine with intent to distribute in violation of the Franklin Criminal Code.

After Jones pled guilty, Gina Nocona, the former girlfriend of one of the defendant's regular cocaine customers, filed a motion claiming that she was a "victim" under the FCVRA and therefore entitled to make a victim-impact statement at Jones's sentencing hearing. She claimed that her former boyfriend, a cocaine user who regularly bought drugs from Jones, "physically, mentally, and emotionally abused" her and that her former boyfriend's "poor judgment was in large part attributable to the drugs Jones had illegally sold him." Nocona asserted that her boyfriend's behavior typically became abusive only when he was under the influence of cocaine. The trial court denied Nocona's motion, ruling that Nocona did not have standing as a "victim" under the FCVRA. Nocona appealed.

Often crime victims do not feel that their voices are heard or that their concerns are properly considered in the judicial process. The Franklin legislature attempted to address these concerns when it passed the FCVRA in 2004. Among the rights this statute specifically gives victims is the right to "be reasonably heard at any public proceeding in the district court involving . . . sentencing." FCVRA § 55(a)(4). Only a "crime victim" is afforded these rights. The FCVRA defines "crime victim" as "a person directly and proximately harmed as a result of the commission of a Franklin criminal offense." *Id.* § 55(b)(1).

In applying this definition, Franklin courts have held that a purported "crime victim" under the FCVRA must demonstrate (1) that the defendant's conduct was a cause in fact of the victim's injuries and (2) that the purported victim was proximately harmed by that conduct.

In *State v. Hackett* (Fr. Ct. App. 2003), the Franklin Court of Appeal interpreted "cause in fact" and affirmed the trial court's order that defendant George Hackett, who pled guilty to aiding and abetting methamphetamine manufacture, pay restitution to an insurance company for property damage. The damage had been caused when one of Hackett's codefendants started a fire by placing a jar of chemicals used to manufacture methamphetamine on a hot plate. The court found that Hackett had procured the supplies his codefendants used to manufacture methamphetamine, and that he had "knowledge and understanding of the scope and structure of the enterprise and of the activities of his codefendants." The court held that even though there were "multiple links in the causal chain," Hackett's conduct was a cause in fact of the resulting property damage.

In the current case, the facts do not support the same conclusion. Nocona asserts that her former boyfriend was abusive only when he was under the influence of cocaine. If true, such a statement might meet the cause-in-fact prong of the standard, although the court acknowledges that the contention raises complex questions relating to the causes of domestic violence. Nocona offered no expert testimony to support her assertion regarding causation.

Nocona's motion also fails the second prong of the definition of a crime victim under the FCVRA, which requires that this court determine whether the defendant's criminal act proximately harmed Nocona. The concept of foreseeability is at the heart of "proximate harm." The closer the relationship between the actions of the defendant and the harm sustained, the more likely that a court will find that proximate harm exists. *See State v. Thomas* (Fr. Ct. App. 2002).

Nocona is unable to demonstrate that her alleged injuries were a foreseeable consequence of the defendant's drug conspiracy. She has not provided the court with evidence that the drug conspiracy led to her injuries or that the defendant knew about the impact of the drugs on Nocona's former boyfriend. Moreover, while we deplore the many undesirable social effects of drug trafficking, we do not think that the asserted abusive conduct of Nocona's boyfriend toward Nocona falls within the range of reasonably foreseeable harms resulting from the defendant's conspiracy. Nocona is not a "victim" under the FCVRA because she is not a person "directly and proximately harmed" by the criminal act committed by the defendant.

Affirmed.

State v. Berg
Franklin Court of Appeal (2012)

The defendant, Leon Berg, contends that the trial court violated his constitutional rights and the Franklin Crime Victims' Rights Act (FCVRA) in allowing the parents of Carly Appleton to make victim-impact statements at his sentencing hearing. We find that the trial court did not err, and affirm.

The defendant's girlfriend, Sheila Greene, was driving herself and Berg back from Franklin Beach to Franklin State College (FSC) in Berg's car. They offered a ride to Carly Appleton, another FSC student. Greene and Appleton were 19 years old; Berg was 22. The drinking age in Franklin is 21. They stopped at a gas station, where Berg bought a quart of vodka and a six-pack of beer. Berg and Greene drank some of the vodka and then got back into the car. Appleton did not drink anything. Berg knew that Greene had been previously arrested and fined for driving under the influence, but he allowed her to drive anyway. In fact, Berg admitted that he handed Greene a beer while she was driving. Not long after, Greene, driving considerably over the speed limit, crashed the car into a tree. Berg sustained minor injuries; Greene was killed instantly; Appleton died at the hospital four hours later. Greene's postmortem blood alcohol level was well over the legal limit for operating a motor vehicle in Franklin.

Berg pleaded guilty to the felony crime of providing alcohol to a minor resulting in death. Berg was sentenced to six months in prison followed by two years of extended supervision. Appleton's parents each petitioned the court to make victim-impact statements at Berg's sentencing hearing as representatives of their daughter, who they claimed was a victim of the defendant's offense.

We begin with an analysis of who constitutes a "victim" within the meaning of the FCVRA, which defines a "victim" as one who has been "directly and proximately harmed" by a Franklin criminal offense. § 55(b)(1). The FCVRA provides a victim with the right to "be reasonably heard at any public proceeding in the district court involving . . . sentencing." § 55(a)(4). The legislative history of the statute indicates that the term "crime victim" should be interpreted "broadly." (Citation omitted.)

Carly Appleton's life was tragically cut short as a result of the drunk driving and the car crash that occurred. It seems obvious to this court that the defendant's actions caused Greene's intoxication, which affected her ability to handle the car in the conditions leading to the crash.

But for the defendant's buying alcohol and furnishing it to Greene, the Appletons' daughter would still be alive. Thus, there is a direct causal connection between Berg's conduct and Appleton's death. This satisfies the condition that the defendant's action be a cause in fact of the person's injury. *See State v. Jones* (Fr. Ct. App. 2006).

This court must also decide whether Berg's crime proximately harmed Carly Appleton for purposes of the FCVRA. The concept of "proximate harm" is a limitation that courts place upon an actor's responsibility for the consequences of the actor's conduct; it is a means by which courts limit the scope of the actor's liability. The concept reflects ideas of what justice demands or what a court finds administratively possible and convenient. Foreseeability is at the heart of determining if an actor's conduct proximately harmed a victim. *See Jones*. In determining whether the harm was foreseeable, the court looks to whether the resulting harm was within the zone of risks resulting from the defendant's conduct for which the defendant should be found liable.

We conclude that, on these facts, it was reasonably foreseeable to Berg that if he bought alcohol and distributed it to his girlfriend, who he was aware had a history of driving drunk, then his girlfriend might drive drunk, and that her drunk driving might lead to a car crash. There is a natural and continuous sequence of events without which Appleton's death would not have occurred. In other words, there is an intuitive relationship between Berg's conduct and the resulting harm. Berg could reasonably have foreseen that he, Greene, or Carly Appleton could be seriously injured or killed as a result of Greene's drunk driving. Thus, the harm to Appleton that resulted was within the risk of Berg's actions. The loss suffered by Appleton clearly falls within the scope of Berg's conduct. Accordingly, we find that Carly Appleton was a crime victim under the FCVRA.

The trial court correctly allowed Appleton's parents to make victim-impact statements at the defendant's sentencing hearing, as they were the approved representatives of their daughter, *see* § 55(b)(2), who the trial court found was a "crime victim" under the FCVRA.

Affirmed.

State v. Humphrey
Franklin Court of Appeal (2008)

Two issues are raised in this appeal: (1) whether the trial court erred in finding that a mother, acting as the representative for her two sons, whose father had been killed, was qualified to seek restitution on behalf of her sons under the Franklin Crime Victims' Rights Act (FCVRA); and (2) whether the court erred in ordering the defendant to pay restitution under FCVRA § 56. The trial court held that the mother was an appropriate representative for the sons, who were "victims" entitled to restitution from the defendant for the loss of child-support income. We affirm with respect to the first issue and remand for further proceedings on the second.

On April 12, 2006, defendant Ted Humphrey was driving home from a party. He was texting while driving and lost control of his car. The car then skidded into the adjacent bicycle lane and hit Connor Benton, who was riding his bike home from work. Although Humphrey was able to stop his car and call 911, the first responders were unable to revive Benton, who had suffered a traumatic head injury. Humphrey was unharmed.

Humphrey was charged with one count of involuntary manslaughter, to which he pled guilty on October 30, 2006. Connor Benton's ex-wife, Kate Gove, sought restitution from Humphrey for the loss of child-support income on behalf of her two minor sons, then ages 6 and 10. Gove appeared at the defendant's sentencing hearing and testified that Connor Benton had provided critical financial support to her family before his death. The court sentenced Humphrey to 18 months in prison and ordered restitution for the lost child support provided by Connor Benton, citing the FCVRA. The defendant appeals from that decision.

One purpose of the FCVRA is to force offenders to pay full restitution to the identifiable victims of their crimes. The act applies to any "crime victim" and defines that term as "a person directly and proximately harmed as a result of the commission of a Franklin criminal offense." FCVRA § 55(b)(1). The act goes on to provide that "[i]n the case of a crime victim who is under 18 years of age, incompetent, incapacitated, or deceased, the legal guardians of the crime victim or the representatives of the crime victim's estate, family members, or any other persons appointed as suitable by the court may assume the crime victim's rights . . . . " *Id.* § 55(b)(2). It is undisputed that Gove, as the mother of Benton's minor children, is their appropriate representative under the Act.

We find that Benton's two young sons are "crime victims" in part because of the loss of financial support from their father. The FCVRA requires only that a person be "directly and proximately harmed" by an offense. The term "harm" embraces physical, financial, and psychological damage. *See* FCVRA § 56(b)(2).

We now turn to whether the court properly ordered the defendant to pay restitution in the amount of $15,200. Section 56(c) of the FCVRA creates a rebuttable presumption that the defendant is financially capable of paying restitution and places the burden of rebutting the presumption on the defendant.

The defendant did not present any evidence to establish that he was incapable of paying restitution. Apparently relying on § 56, the court ordered $15,200 in restitution for the value of lost child support without any inquiry into the defendant's financial situation and without any findings to justify the restitution order. On appeal, the defendant argues that the restitution statute requires the court to make express findings justifying a restitution order. The defendant's reading of the statute is correct. Section 56(d) identifies three factors that the court must take into account in determining the amount of restitution: (1) public policy that favors requiring criminals to compensate for damage and injury to their victims; (2) the financial burden placed on the victim and those who provide services to the victim as a result of the criminal conduct of the defendant; and (3) the financial resources of the defendant.

Before imposing restitution, the sentencing judge must make a "serious inquiry" into all three factors. *See State v. Schmidt* (Fr. Sup. Ct. 2003). While the statute places the burden of proof on the defendant to show inability to pay, the court should inquire into the additional factors. This case will be remanded with instructions to the trial court to conduct that inquiry.

Affirmed in part and remanded for further findings consistent with this opinion.

February 2018
MPT-2 File:
In re Hastings

Belford & Swan S.C.
Attorneys at Law
6701 San Jacinto Avenue, Suite 290
Marin City, Franklin 33075

MEMORANDUM

To: Examinee
From: Emily Swan
Date: February 27, 2018
Re: Danielle Hastings inquiry

A friend of mine from college, Danielle Hastings, has asked me to look into a legal matter for her. Danielle currently serves on the board of directors for Municipal Utility District No. 12 (MUD 12). MUDs are local government entities, authorized by the Franklin constitution, that provide public water, sewer, drainage, and other services to suburban neighborhoods not served by a city.

Danielle has always been civic-minded, and she is very involved in her community. In addition to being a director for MUD 12, she volunteers at the local library and is a volleyball coach at the local YMCA. She is interested in getting involved in election and voting activities in her community. There are two election-related positions available in her voting precinct: county election judge and precinct chair.

Both positions sound interesting to Danielle. She is not sure which position she would want. Before making any decision, she needs our advice as to whether she is allowed to serve as a county election judge or precinct chair while at the same time remaining a MUD 12 director. I have attached several opinions by the Attorney General of Franklin, which discuss the applicable law.

Please draft a memorandum to me analyzing whether Danielle can apply for and hold the county election judge position or the precinct chair position while simultaneously serving as a member of the board of directors for MUD 12. Address the question for both the county election judge and precinct chair positions. Make sure to discuss all legal issues relating to each position. Do not prepare a separate statement of facts, but be sure to incorporate the relevant facts and legal authorities into your analysis.

In re Hastings

Transcript of Client Interview with Danielle Hastings
February 26, 2018

Att'y Swan:	Hi, Danielle, it's great to see you. Gosh, it's been a while!
Danielle Hastings:	Yes, it has. I think the last time we ran into each other was a couple of years ago at our college class reunion.
Swan:	How is everything going? I got your phone message indicating that you wanted my advice on a legal problem, but you didn't say what the problem was.
Hastings:	Well, as I think I mentioned at our class reunion, in addition to my day job as a graphic artist, I'm also a member of the board of directors for Municipal Utility District No. 12, which provides water, sewer, and drainage services to my neighborhood, Eagle Springs.
Swan:	Yes, I remember your saying you were active on a MUD board in your community. How is that going?
Hastings:	Everything is fine. And I love the work I do as a MUD director. But I'm always looking for opportunities to get involved in my community, and frankly, I have higher political ambitions. Recently, I heard about two open positions that sound really interesting and would further my political career.
Swan:	Tell me more.
Hastings:	Well, a friend of mine who's active in local politics and highly involved in our political party mentioned that there is an open position for county election judge, which would involve supervising elections in my precinct. He also said that our political party is looking for precinct chairs to help reach out to voters and educate them about the candidates in our political party who are running for office.
Swan:	What's the process for becoming an election judge or precinct chair?
Hastings:	The county election judge is an appointed position, but the precinct chair is an elected position within the political party, which means that I would have to run as a candidate for precinct chair and be elected to the position.
Swan:	And both of these positions are for the voting precinct that you live in?
Hastings:	Yes. My precinct includes Eagle Springs as well as a handful of adjacent neighborhoods.

Swan:	What else do you know about the two positions?
Hastings:	Well, I've printed out some information from the Marin County website that compares the two positions. [Printout from website attached.] It's my understanding that if I'm appointed as a county election judge, then I would be the chief election judge for my precinct since the governor is from my political party.
Swan:	Do you have a preference between the two positions?
Hastings:	No, both sound very interesting, and either position would provide an opportunity to get more involved in the election process, which is something that I've been wanting to do. If you tell me that I can hold either position while remaining on the MUD board, then I would have to decide which of the new positions to pursue. On the other hand, if you tell me that I can't hold either of the positions while simultaneously serving on the MUD board, then I won't need to choose because my decision will be made for me.
Swan:	Tell me more about the MUD board. I think that it is important to understand what you do as a MUD director in order to evaluate whether you could hold the position of county election judge or precinct chair while simultaneously serving on the MUD board.
Hastings:	As you know, MUDs provide public water, sewer, drainage, and other basic services to suburban residents who are not served by a city. MUD 12 provides these services to residents of Eagle Springs, about 1,500 homes in all. Basically, the MUD owns, operates, and maintains all the facilities necessary to supply water to Eagle Springs residents, collect and treat wastewater from their homes, and collect, store, and drain storm water from land within the MUD's boundaries. This includes a water plant, a wastewater treatment plant, and drainage ditches, all located within Eagle Springs. In addition, the MUD provides trash collection service for our residents, and we also own and operate two public parks within the Eagle Springs community.
Swan:	MUDs are political subdivisions of the State of Franklin, right?
Hastings:	Correct. MUDs operate independently of county government. I've heard them described as being one of the most fundamental forms of local government

	because they provide municipal-level services, have elected officials who live in the MUD, and are authorized to charge fees to their residents, assess and collect taxes, and sell bonds in order to pay the costs of constructing and operating the facilities that provide services to their residents.
Swan:	Can you tell me more about the MUD board of directors election process? Are your elections handled by Marin County?
Hastings:	No. Under state law, MUDs conduct their own elections, which are held in May. MUDs also appoint their own election judges for the MUD elections. The partisan or political elections, like those for governor and state assembly, are held in November, and those are the ones the Marin County election judges oversee.
Swan:	So if you were appointed as a county election judge for your precinct, you wouldn't be involved in overseeing any MUD elections?
Hastings:	Right, MUD elections are totally separate. MUD boards really aren't all that political in the party sense—they're nonpartisan. Nobody runs for a MUD position as a "Democrat" or "Republican." They run for the MUD board because they live in the MUD, they care about the basic services that are being provided, and they want to be involved in their community and make a difference.
Swan:	How long have you served on the MUD 12 board?
Hastings:	This is my second four-year term on the board. Our last election was in May 2016, so I am midway through my current term. I want to remain on the MUD board for at least another term or two.
Swan:	Okay, I think I have enough basic information to start looking into this issue. I should have answers for you within a week or two, which will give you plenty of time to weigh your options.
Hastings:	Great. Thanks.

Printout of
Marin County Board of Elections
Position Descriptions

Source: www.marincountyfranklin.gov

COUNTY ELECTION JUDGE [Summary prepared based on state election law]

What is a county election judge?

County election judges conduct the city, county, state, and federal elections in a precinct during the year. Election judges are the head officials in charge of election-day activities.

What does an election judge do?

County election judges administer the election procedures set forth in the Franklin Election Code to help ensure that elections are secure, accurate, fair, and accessible to all voters. Responsibilities include handling and securing election equipment and ballots, locating and retaining election clerks to work at their polling location, organizing the setup of the election equipment and the operation of the election, handing out and collecting ballots, setting up and closing down the polling site, and certifying the polling site results.

Election judges also serve on a panel to resolve any voting-related challenges that may arise. Election judges are responsible for following the Franklin Election Code and conducting a fair election. Although each judge is nominated by his or her political party, no display of any party affiliation is allowed during the election.

How do you get to be an election judge?

Election judges are nominated by their respective parties and are appointed by the Marin County Board of Commissioners to two-year terms. If possible, election judges reside in the precinct.

What is a chief election judge?

Two judges, one from each major political party, are appointed for each precinct. The chief election judge is from the party that received more votes in the last governor's election. The second judge works closely with the chief election judge and is responsible for conducting the election in the chief judge's absence. Both judges are required to attend training.

Is election judge a paid position?

Election judges are volunteers. They are reimbursed for the cost of any training, supplies purchased, or other expenses incurred, but are otherwise not compensated.

PRECINCT CHAIR [Summary prepared based on party bylaws]

What is a precinct chair?

A precinct is the smallest political subdivision in Franklin. Franklin counties are divided into individual precincts, each consisting of a collection of adjacent neighborhoods. Precinct chairs are political positions created by their political parties and not by statute. They are the primary political agents for the Democratic and Republican parties in their precincts. They are responsible for contacting, guiding, and organizing voters from their respective political parties in their precincts. Precinct chairs also represent their home precincts on their party's Executive Committee (EC), which conducts the local business of that political party.

What does a precinct chair do?

In addition to serving on his or her party's EC, each precinct chair is the contact person for his or her respective political party in his or her precinct. Organizing and campaigning are important duties of a precinct chair. Precinct chairs are responsible for working with others to mobilize and organize voters and get them to the polls, bridging the gap between voters and elected officials, and promoting their party's candidates and events. This includes organizing phone banks to place telephone calls to voters, organizing block walks (going door-to-door) to distribute campaign materials, and encouraging neighbors to vote in upcoming primary and general elections.

What is the Executive Committee?

Marin County has two Executive Committees: a Democratic EC and a Republican EC. Each party's EC is the governing body of that political party in Marin County and conducts all official party business. Each party's EC usually meets three times a year, sometimes more in election years. Precinct chairs are voting members of their ECs.

How do you get to be a precinct chair?

Candidates for precinct chair are elected to serve two-year terms by voters in their precincts in the respective Democratic or Republican primary election every two years.

Is precinct chair a paid position?

Precinct chairs are volunteers and are not compensated for their service.

February 2018
MPT-2 Library:
In re Hastings

STATE OF FRANKLIN CONSTITUTION
ARTICLE XII

§ 25. HOLDING MORE THAN ONE OFFICE; EXCEPTIONS

(a) No person shall hold or exercise, at the same time, more than one civil office of emolument, except for justices of the peace, county commissioners, and officers and enlisted men and women of the United States Armed Forces, the National Guard, and the Franklin State Guard, or unless otherwise specially provided herein.

(b) Exceptions: . . .

> (4) a public schoolteacher or retired schoolteacher may receive compensation for serving as a member of a governing body of a municipal utility district (MUD).

In re Hastings

Excerpts from the Franklin Election Code

§ 465. Appointment of Election Judges for Each Election Precinct. Election judges shall be appointed by each county for each election precinct in which an election is held.

* * *

§ 471. General Responsibility of County Election Judges.

(a) The chief judge is in charge of and responsible for the management and conduct of the election at the polling place of the election precinct that the judge serves.

(b) The chief judge for each election precinct shall appoint election clerks to assist the judge in the conduct of an election at the polling place served by the judge.

(c) The chief judge shall designate the working hours of and assign the duties to be performed by the election clerks serving under the judge.

. . .

(f) The chief judge shall preserve order and prevent breaches of the peace and violations of this code in the polling place and in the area within which electioneering and loitering are prohibited. In performing duties under this subsection, the chief judge may appoint one or more licensed persons to act as special peace officers for the polling place.

. . .

(h) An election judge may administer any oath required to be made at a polling place.

* * *

§ 480. Ineligibility of Candidate for Office. A person who is a candidate in an election for a contested public or party office is ineligible to serve, in an election to be held on the same day as that election, as an election judge or clerk in any precinct in which the office sought is to be voted on.

* * *

§ 492. Judges for Elections of Other Political Subdivisions. The governing body of a political subdivision other than a county shall appoint the election judges for elections ordered by the political subdivision.

ATTORNEY GENERAL OF FRANKLIN

Opinion No. 2003-9
March 17, 2003

Re: Whether Franklin Constitution article XII, section 25 prohibits a constable from simultaneously serving as a commissioner of an emergency services district

The issue presented is whether article XII, section 25 of the Franklin Constitution prohibits a constable from serving as a commissioner of an emergency services district (ESD) in the same county. We must examine each of the offices at issue.

Article XII, section 25(a) provides that "[n]o person shall hold or exercise, at the same time, more than one civil office of emolument." The constitutional dual-officeholding prohibition applies if both positions (1) qualify as "civil offices" and (2) are entitled to an "emolument."

First, we have previously determined that a constable holds a civil office of emolument. Fr. Att'y Gen. Op. No. 1999-8 (1999); *see also* Fr. Local Gov't Code § 453 (defining a constable as a "peace officer" and mandating that constables be paid on a salary basis).

Next, we must examine whether the position of ESD commissioner is also a civil office of emolument subject to article XII, section 25. The determinative factor distinguishing an officer from an employee is "whether any sovereign function of the government is conferred upon the individual to be exercised by the individual for the benefit of the general public largely independent of the control of others." *Morris Indep. Sch. Dist. v. Lehigh* (Fr. Sup. Ct. 1965).

ESDs independently exercise various governmental powers for the benefit of the public, including the power to appoint agents and employees, enter into contracts, purchase and sell property, borrow money, sue and be sued, impose and collect taxes, and perform other necessary acts relevant to providing emergency services. Fr. Local Gov't Code § 752. ESD commissioners serve as the ESD's governing board. Based on the broad, independent authority granted to ESDs, we conclude that ESD commissioners meet the *Morris* test and are thus civil officers.

Next we determine whether an ESD commissioner holds an office of "emolument." An emolument is "a pecuniary profit, gain or advantage." *State v. Babcock* (Fr. Ct. App. 1998). If an officeholder is entitled to compensation, his or her office is an "office of emolument" even if the

In re Hastings

person refuses to accept any compensation. However, the term "emolument" does not include the legitimate reimbursement of expenses. While the reimbursement of actual expenses does not constitute an emolument, any amount received in excess of actual expenses is an emolument. *Id.* Likewise, an amount received as compensation for each meeting (e.g., a fixed per diem amount) is also an emolument. *Id.*

By statute, an ESD commissioner "is entitled to receive compensation of $50 for each day the commissioner attends a commission meeting," and additionally "may be reimbursed for reasonable and necessary expenses incurred in performing official duties." Fr. Local Gov't Code § 775. The $50 per diem compensation qualifies as an emolument.

Because an ESD commissioner receives compensation for his or her services and holds a civil office of emolument, he or she cannot hold another civil office of emolument—here, constable.

SUMMARY

Article XII, section 25 of the Franklin Constitution prohibits a person from simultaneously serving as a constable and an ESD commissioner. Because we conclude that article XII, section 25 prohibits dual service in this circumstance, we need not consider whether simultaneously holding the positions of constable and ESD commissioner would implicate the common law doctrine of incompatibility.

ATTORNEY GENERAL OF FRANKLIN

Opinion No. 2008-12
February 6, 2008

Re: Whether an individual may simultaneously serve as director of a municipal utility district and member of the city zoning commission

The issue presented is whether an individual who serves as a member of the board of directors for Montgomery County Municipal Utility District No. 6 (MUD 6) may also serve as a member of the Planning and Zoning Commission (PZC) for the City of Waterford. We conclude that one person is barred from holding both offices by the common law doctrine of incompatibility.

Civil office of emolument

Article XII, section 25(a) of the Franklin Constitution provides that "[n]o person shall hold or exercise, at the same time, more than one civil office of emolument," subject to exceptions that are not relevant in this situation. MUD directors are entitled to receive compensation for serving on the MUD board—specifically, a $150 per diem payment as compensation for attending MUD board meetings or engaging in other MUD-related activities. Fr. Water Code § 46. In contrast, members of the PZC serve without compensation. Because PZC commissioners do not receive compensation, they are not civil officers of emolument. Therefore, article XII, section 25 of the Franklin Constitution does not bar a person from serving on the PZC and holding another office.

Common law doctrine of incompatibility

The common law doctrine of incompatibility may, however, prevent this dual service, whether or not a member of the PZC receives compensation for that position, because compensation is not relevant to determining whether offices are incompatible. The common law doctrine of incompatibility bars one person from holding two civil offices if the offices' duties conflict. *Spencer v. Lafayette Indep. Sch. Dist.* (Fr. Ct. App. 1947). The doctrine has three aspects: self-appointment, self-employment, and conflicting loyalties. Self-appointment and

In re Hastings

self-employment are only implicated if the responsibilities of one position include appointing or employing the second position. Here, the MUD does not appoint or employ members of the PZC and vice versa. Therefore, the only inquiry is whether the two positions involve conflicting loyalties.

The opinion in *Spencer* held that the offices of school trustee and city council member were incompatible because the boundaries of the school district's and city's jurisdictions overlapped, and the city council had authority over health, quarantine, sanitary, and fire prevention regulations applicable to school property. The court reasoned that if a person could be a school trustee and a member of the city council at the same time, school policies could be influenced or even controlled by the city council instead of the school trustees. *Id.*

As a threshold matter, in order for the conflicting-loyalties prong to apply, each position must constitute a "civil office." Therefore, we must first consider whether directors of MUDs and members of the PZC are civil officers. The Franklin Supreme Court has articulated the following test for determining whether an individual holds a civil office: "The determining factor which distinguishes a civil officer from an employee is whether any sovereign function of the government is conferred upon the individual to be exercised by the individual for the benefit of the general public largely independent of the control of others." *Morris Indep. Sch. Dist. v. Lehigh* (Fr. Sup. Ct. 1965).

Municipal utility districts provide water, sewer, drainage, and other services to suburban communities. They are local (as opposed to state or county) government entities authorized under the Franklin Constitution and are subject to the Fr. Water Code. They are governed by a board of directors, who are elected to four-year terms. Fr. Water Code § 35. A MUD board is responsible for "the management of all the affairs of the district" (*id.* § 37) and may levy and collect a tax for operation and maintenance purposes, charge fees for provision of district services, issue bonds or other financial obligations to borrow money for its purposes, and exercise various other powers set out in the Franklin Water Code (*id.* § 39). A director of a MUD is a civil officer within the test stated by the Franklin Supreme Court in *Morris* based on the number of independent functions delegated to MUD boards under the Water Code, several of which are discussed above.

We next consider whether members of the Waterford PZC are civil officers. Cities such as Waterford have zoning authority and are authorized to appoint a zoning commission. If the

Waterford PZC exercises governmental powers delegated by the city council, its members will be civil officers.

The Waterford PZC consists of nine citizens of Waterford who are appointed by the city council for a term of two years. The Waterford PZC is responsible for final approval of plats for residential development in the City. In our opinion, members of the Waterford PZC exercise a sovereign function of the government "for the benefit of the general public largely independent of the control of others" within the *Morris* test and are therefore civil officers.

Our next consideration is whether members of the Waterford PZC have powers and duties that are incompatible with the powers and duties of a MUD director. During the plat approval process, the PZC requires submission of preliminary utility plans identifying the nature and location of water and sewer services such as water and sewer plants. A PZC member who is also a director of a MUD may have divided loyalties when the proposed development is located within the MUD on whose board the PZC member serves. In this situation, the PZC is able to control and impose its policies on the MUD by determining the manner and placement of the MUD's facilities.

We conclude that the two civil offices are incompatible, and that a member of the PZC who also serves on a MUD would have divided loyalties in facing decisions that affected his or her MUD. We conclude that the common law doctrine of incompatibility prevents a member of the Waterford PZC from serving simultaneously as a director of a MUD with territory within the zoning authority boundaries of Waterford.

SUMMARY

A MUD director holds a civil office, as does a member of the PZC of the City of Waterford. Because the duties of those two offices are in conflict where the offices have overlapping jurisdictions, the common law doctrine of incompatibility bars one person from simultaneously holding both offices.

ATTORNEY GENERAL OF FRANKLIN

Opinion No. 2010-7
September 5, 2010

Re: Whether a member of a school district board of trustees may simultaneously hold the office of county treasurer

The issue presented is whether a trustee of an independent school district may simultaneously hold the office of county treasurer. For the reasons explained below, we conclude that she may do so. In the situation presented, the individual was elected for a three-year term on the board of trustees of Winfield Independent School District. Subsequently, she was appointed by the Board of Commissioners of Winfield County to fill the balance of a four-year term as the Winfield County Treasurer.

Civil office of emolument

When we consider article XII, section 25 of the Franklin Constitution and our Opinion No. 2003-9, we conclude that an individual is not barred by article XII, section 25 from simultaneously holding the offices of school trustee and county treasurer. Section 384 of the Franklin Education Code requires that trustees of an independent school district "serve without compensation." Because the office of school trustee is therefore not an "office of emolument," it follows that an individual is not barred by article XII, section 25 from simultaneously holding the offices of school trustee and county treasurer.

That does not end our inquiry, however.

Common law doctrine of incompatibility

Common law incompatibility is independent of article XII, section 25. The three aspects of the doctrine are self-appointment, self-employment, and conflicting loyalties. Self-appointment and self-employment are not implicated here because the county treasurer neither appoints nor employs members of the school board of trustees. Nor does the school board of trustees appoint or employ the county treasurer.

The third aspect of common law incompatibility, conflicting loyalties, bars the holding of simultaneous civil offices that would prevent a person from exercising independent and disinterested judgment in either or both positions. It most often arises when one person seeks to be a member of two governing boards with overlapping jurisdictions. If, for example, two governmental bodies are authorized to contract with each other, one person may not serve as a member of both.

Conflicting loyalties

Based on these principles, we must determine whether there are any duties ascribed to the office of county treasurer that would render its holding incompatible with that of school district trustee. The county treasurer is the chief custodian of county funds and is responsible for accounting for and managing all money belonging to the county, including depositing funds received by the county and disbursing county funds to pay county debts as required by law. Fr. Local Gov't Code § 411.

A number of statutes peripherally relate to the duties of the county treasurer with respect to school funds, but all of these appear to prescribe purely ministerial duties or duties that do not apply in this circumstance, such as collecting debts and maintaining the original financing records for schools in counties that do not have any independent school district. In this case, Winfield County has its own independent school district (i.e., Winfield Independent School District). The school district is a separate, distinct governmental entity with separate authority to acquire and hold real and personal property, sue and be sued, and maintain its own funds. Fr. Educ. Code § 1251.

Conceivably, a county treasurer could initiate actions to recover funds owed to Winfield County by the Winfield Independent School District. However, the county treasurer's authority is not exclusive. The Board of Commissioners, as the executive head of the county, is vested with authority to determine when suits or other actions should be instituted to recover funds belonging to the county and can separately sue to collect debts owed to the county. If it were determined that funds were owed to Winfield County by the Winfield Independent School District, the Board of Commissioners would be the proper party to sue to recover those funds. Therefore, in our opinion, the county treasurer's non-exclusive authority to sue to recover funds owed by the school district to the county does not rise to the level of incompatibility contemplated by the common law doctrine of incompatibility.

Because a county treasurer's authority to sue an independent school district is limited to the recovery of funds owed by the school district to the county, and because even that limited authority is not exclusive, we conclude that conflicting-loyalties incompatibility is not, as a matter of law, a bar to an individual's simultaneously holding the offices of county treasurer and trustee of an independent school district located within his or her county.

SUMMARY

A county treasurer is not, as a matter of law, barred either by article XII, section 25 of the Franklin Constitution or by the common law doctrine of incompatibility from simultaneously holding the office of trustee of an independent school district located within her county.

July 2017 MPTs
Peek et al. v. Doris Stern and Allied
Behavioral Health Services
In re Zimmer Farm

July 2017
MPTs

www.ncbex.org

National Conference of Bar Examiners
302 South Bedford Street | Madison, WI 53703-3622
Phone: 608-280-8550 | Fax: 608-280-8552 | TDD: 608-661-1275
e-mail: contact@ncbex.org

Contents

MPT-1: *Peek et al. v. Doris Stern and Allied Behavioral Health Services*

FILE

LIBRARY

MPT-2: *In re Zimmer Farm*

FILE

LIBRARY

Preface

The Multistate Performance Test (MPT) is developed by the National Conference of Bar Examiners (NCBE). This publication includes the items and Point Sheets from the July 2017 MPT. The instructions for the test appear on page iii.

The MPT Point Sheets describe the factual and legal points encompassed within the lawyering tasks to be completed. They outline the possible issues and points that might be addressed by an examinee. They are provided to the user jurisdictions to assist graders in grading the examination by identifying the issues and suggesting the resolution of the problems contemplated by the drafters.

For more information about the MPT, including a list of skills tested, visit the NCBE website at www.ncbex.org.

Description of the MPT

The MPT consists of two 90-minute items and is a component of the Uniform Bar Examination (UBE). It is administered by user jurisdictions as part of the bar examination on the Tuesday before the last Wednesday in February and July of each year. User jurisdictions may select one or both items to include as part of their bar examinations. (Jurisdictions that administer the UBE use two MPTs.)

The materials for each MPT include a File and a Library. The File consists of source documents containing all the facts of the case. The specific assignment the examinee is to complete is described in a memorandum from a supervising attorney. The File might also include transcripts of interviews, depositions, hearings or trials, pleadings, correspondence, client documents, contracts, newspaper articles, medical records, police reports, or lawyer's notes. Relevant as well as irrelevant facts are included. Facts are sometimes ambiguous, incomplete, or even conflicting. As in practice, a client's or a supervising attorney's version of events may be incomplete or unreliable. Examinees are expected to recognize when facts are inconsistent or missing and are expected to identify potential sources of additional facts.

The Library may contain cases, statutes, regulations, or rules, some of which may not be relevant to the assigned lawyering task. The examinee is expected to extract from the Library the legal principles necessary to analyze the problem and perform the task. The MPT is not a test of substantive law; the Library materials provide sufficient substantive information to complete the task.

The MPT is designed to test an examinee's ability to use fundamental lawyering skills in a realistic situation and complete a task that a beginning lawyer should be able to accomplish. The MPT is not a test of substantive knowledge. Rather, it is designed to evaluate six fundamental skills lawyers are expected to demonstrate regardless of the area of law in which the skills are applied. The MPT requires examinees to (1) sort detailed factual materials and separate relevant from irrelevant facts; (2) analyze statutory, case, and administrative materials for applicable principles of law; (3) apply the relevant law to the relevant facts in a manner likely to resolve a client's problem; (4) identify and resolve ethical dilemmas, when present; (5) communicate effectively in writing; and (6) complete a lawyering task within time constraints. These skills are tested by requiring examinees to perform one or more of a variety of lawyering tasks. For example, examinees might be instructed to complete any of the following: a memorandum to a supervising attorney, a letter to a client, a persuasive memorandum or brief, a statement of facts, a contract provision, a will, a counseling plan, a proposal for settlement or agreement, a discovery plan, a witness examination plan, or a closing argument.

Instructions

The back cover of each test booklet contains the following instructions:

You will be instructed when to begin and when to stop this test. Do not break the seal on this booklet until you are told to begin. This test is designed to evaluate your ability to handle a select number of legal authorities in the context of a factual problem involving a client.

The problem is set in the fictitious state of Franklin, in the fictitious Fifteenth Circuit of the United States. Columbia and Olympia are also fictitious states in the Fifteenth Circuit. In Franklin, the trial court of general jurisdiction is the District Court, the intermediate appellate court is the Court of Appeal, and the highest court is the Supreme Court.

You will have two kinds of materials with which to work: a File and a Library. The first document in the File is a memorandum containing the instructions for the task you are to complete. The other documents in the File contain factual information about your case and may include some facts that are not relevant.

The Library contains the legal authorities needed to complete the task and may also include some authorities that are not relevant. Any cases may be real, modified, or written solely for the purpose of this examination. If the cases appear familiar to you, do not assume that they are precisely the same as you have read before. Read them thoroughly, as if they all were new to you. You should assume that the cases were decided in the jurisdictions and on the dates shown. In citing cases from the Library, you may use abbreviations and omit page references.

Your response must be written in the answer book provided. If you are using a laptop computer to answer the questions, your jurisdiction will provide you with specific instructions. In answering this performance test, you should concentrate on the materials in the File and Library. What you have learned in law school and elsewhere provides the general background for analyzing the problem; the File and Library provide the specific materials with which you must work.

Although there are no restrictions on how you apportion your time, you should allocate approximately half your time to reading and digesting the materials and to organizing your answer before you begin writing it. You may make notes anywhere in the test materials; blank pages are provided at the end of the booklet. You may not tear pages from the question booklet.

Do not include your actual name anywhere in the work product required by the task memorandum.

This performance test will be graded on your responsiveness to the instructions regarding the task you are to complete, which are given to you in the first memorandum in the File, and on the content, thoroughness, and organization of your response.

July 2017
MPT-1 File:
Peek et al. v. Doris Stern
and Allied Behavioral
Health Services

Peek et al. v. Stern and Allied

ROBINSON & HOUSE LLC
Attorneys at Law
44 Court Drive Fairview

Heights, Franklin 33705

MEMORANDUM

TO: Examinee
FROM: Jean Robinson
DATE: July 25, 2017
RE: Peek et al. v. Doris Stern and Allied Behavioral Health Services

We represent a class of Union County women probationers in a lawsuit filed in federal court under 42 U.S.C. § 1983 of the Civil Rights Act. All probationers convicted of misdemeanors in Union County receive probation services through Allied Behavioral Health Services. Our complaint alleges that the defendants Allied and Doris Stern, in her capacity as executive director of Allied, are discriminating against women probationers based on gender.

The named plaintiff in our class action, Rita Peek, was sentenced to 18 months' probation by the Union County court in May 2016. (See attached sentencing order.) A condition of her probation was that she receive mental health counseling. To date, Peek has met all the requirements of her probation except for mental health counseling because Allied has failed to provide that counseling.

We filed suit in the U.S. District Court for the District of Franklin against Allied and Doris Stern alleging that they have developed a plan of services that disproportionately denies probation services to female probationers. Thus far, we have deposed Allied's Probation Services Unit director. During a recent case-management conference, the U.S. District Court judge raised the issue of whether the defendants are state actors and, therefore, subject to 42 U.S.C. § 1983. The judge ordered the parties to file simultaneous briefs on that issue alone.

Please prepare the argument section of our brief in support of our position that Stern and Allied are acting under color of state law and are subject to suit under 42 U.S.C. § 1983, relying on all available tests employed by the courts to determine whether parties are state actors. Follow our office guidelines in drafting your argument. Because the court ordered simultaneous briefs, you should anticipate the defendants' arguments and respond to them. Do not draft a separate statement of facts, but incorporate all relevant facts into your argument.

ROBINSON & HOUSE LLC

OFFICE MEMORANDUM

TO: All lawyers
FROM: Litigation supervisor
DATE: April 14, 2011
RE: Simultaneously filed persuasive briefs

All simultaneously filed persuasive briefs shall conform to the following guidelines:

Statement of the Case [omitted]

Statement of Facts [omitted]

Body of the Argument

The body of each argument should analyze applicable legal authority and persuasively argue how both the facts and the law support our client's position. Be sure to cite both the law and the evidence. Emphasize supporting authority but address contrary authority as well; explain or distinguish contrary authority in the argument. Because the court ordered simultaneous briefing, anticipate the other party's arguments and respond to them; do not reserve arguments for reply or supplemental briefing. Be mindful that courts are not persuaded by exaggerated, unsupported arguments.

Organize the argument into its major components. Present all the arguments for each component separately.

With regard to each separate component, write carefully crafted subject headings that illustrate the arguments they address. The argument headings should succinctly summarize the reasons the tribunal should take the position you are advocating. A heading should be a specific application of a rule of law to the facts of the case and not a bare legal or factual conclusion or a statement of an abstract principle. For example: <u>Improper</u>: Plaintiff has satisfied the exhaustion of administrative remedies requirement. <u>Proper</u>: Where Plaintiff requested an administrative hearing by timely completing Form 3B, but the prison has refused to schedule a hearing, Plaintiff has satisfied the exhaustion of remedies requirement.

STATE OF FRANKLIN
UNION COUNTY DISTRICT COURT

State of Franklin	)	
	)	
v.	)	**Case No. 2016-3098**
	)	
Rita Peek, Defendant	)	

SENTENCING ORDER

Rita Peek, the above-named Defendant, having been found guilty of misdemeanor battery, a violation of § 35-87 of the Franklin Criminal Code, is hereby sentenced to 10 months in jail, but that jail sentence is stayed on the condition that the Defendant successfully complete a probation term of 18 months beginning on this date and subject to the conditions listed below.

During the term of probation, the Defendant must successfully satisfy the following conditions:

1. Immediately report to the Union County Probation Officer to register as a probationer, and follow any rules or regulations established by the County Probation Officer.

2. When ordered by the County Probation Officer, report to Allied Behavioral Health Services, 806 W. Main St., Fairview Heights, Franklin, for those services ordered by this Court and any services ordered by the County Probation Officer.

3. Meet monthly with a counselor assigned by Allied Behavioral Health Services to review compliance with this Order; Allied Behavioral Health Services to inform Court of any violations of this Order.

4. Be evaluated for and undergo mental health counseling by Allied Behavioral Health Services.

5. Not consume any drugs or alcohol and submit samples of blood, urine, or both for tests to determine the presence of any prohibited substances.

6. Not violate any criminal statute of any jurisdiction.

7. Not leave the State of Franklin without the consent of this Court.

8. Pay to Allied Behavioral Health Services a fee of $50 per month.

In the event that the Defendant fails to satisfy these conditions during the probationary term, probation may be revoked and the Defendant be subject to one or more of the following: (1) reinstatement of the original 10-month jail sentence, (2) extension of probation for a term of up to three years on any conditions the Court deems appropriate, or (3) other relief that the Court deems just and proper.

Entered: May 31, 2016.

James Finch
_____
Honorable James Finch
Union County District Court

ROBINSON & HOUSE LLC

MEMORANDUM TO FILE

FROM: Jean Robinson
DATE: June 4, 2017
RE: Peek et al. v. Doris Stern and Allied Behavioral Health Services

Ever since 2014, when Union County began contracting with Allied Behavioral Health Services to provide misdemeanor probation services in the County, Allied has in effect given male probationers priority in receiving mental health counseling. As a result, Allied typically fails to provide female probationers with counseling. It is typical that when a woman's probation term ends without her completing counseling, Allied informs the sentencing court of the failure to complete counseling. The court then usually extends the term of probation, although the court does have the power to revoke probation and impose the original jail sentence.

Rita Peek, our named plaintiff, has experienced such a delay in undergoing counseling. She was sentenced to 18 months' probation on May 31, 2016, and ordered to undergo mental health counseling. Allied has failed to initiate that counseling. Peek is now over a year into her 18-month probation term. If Allied does not provide counseling services very soon, Peek will face an extension of her probation (with additional costs assessed to her). The sentencing court also has the power to reinstate her 10-month jail sentence if she does not complete the counseling within the probationary period.

Peek's criminal defense attorney filed a motion with the Union County court in March of this year, asking it to order Allied to immediately offer counseling to Peek. The court denied that motion. Peek's criminal defense attorney then contacted us.

In April, we filed a class action lawsuit (the class has been certified) in federal court alleging that Allied and Doris Stern, in her capacity as executive director of Allied, have violated female probationers' civil rights by disproportionately denying services to women, in violation of 42 U.S.C. § 1983, which entitles them to a civil remedy for the deprivation of their constitutional rights.

Later this month we are scheduled to depose James Simmons, the director of Allied's Probation Services Unit.

Excerpts from Deposition of James Simmons
June 26, 2017

Examination by Plaintiff's Attorney Jean Robinson

Q: Please state your name and position.

A: James Simmons, director of the Probation Services Unit of Allied Behavioral Health Services.

Q: Explain the organization of Allied Behavioral Health Services.

A: Allied is a nonprofit organization formed in 1975 to provide mental health counseling and other services to residents of Union and neighboring counties. We have a board of directors that hires the executive director, who is currently Doris Stern. The board determines what services we offer, approves our entering into contracts, and sets policies, including personnel policies. Each year, Ms. Stern presents a plan detailing our program goals and means of accomplishing those goals, and the board approves it. Allied is a private entity, like any nonprofit.

Q: Who is on the board of directors of Allied Behavioral Health Services?

A: We have 11 board members. One of the county judges and the county director of public health services became members when we started offering probation services and expanded the board. Before that we had just nine board members, and those nine have always included community and business leaders, religious leaders, and active citizens.

Q: What influence do the two public officials have over the board?

A: They are simply 2 of 11 board members. The board requires a majority vote to act.

Q: How is Allied organized regarding the services it provides?

A: We have two units—the Family Services Unit and the Probation Services Unit, which I direct.

Q: To whom do you report?

A: To Doris Stern and through her to Allied's board of directors.

Q: Who pays you?

A: Allied.

Q: Who evaluates you?

A: Ms. Stern.

Q: Who evaluates the counselors who provide probation services?

A: I do, and Ms. Stern reviews those evaluations.

Q: Explain the relationship between Allied and Union County's Probation Office.

A: In 2013, the State of Franklin decided that counties could contract with private entities for probation services for those defendants convicted of misdemeanors. A year later, the Union County Probation Office asked us to contract with them for probation services. Most of what Union County wanted for those on probation for misdemeanors were counseling-related services that we already provided. So we prepared all the documents the county wanted and began providing probation services. The Probation Services Unit is the part of our agency that I direct. We carry out sentencing orders of the court. How we do so is up to us, as long as we follow court orders. We submit an annual plan and quarterly and annual reports to the county. Day to day, we do not deal with the county.

Q: How is Allied funded?

A: We are funded from several sources. The county pays for most of the probation services, with the probationers' fees making up the rest. And we get grants and funds from the community—fund-raisers, corporate donors, that sort of thing. Much of the funding for our counseling for persons not on probation comes from insurance; some comes from individual clients who pay for their own services. Altogether, Allied gets 40% of its funding from public sources and 60% from private sources.

Q: I need to clarify. Consider only the funding for the Union County probation program. How much of that is funded by a combination of funds from the county itself and fees paid by the probationers?

A: One hundred percent.

Q: Union County is a unit of local government, subject to the laws of Franklin, isn't that correct?

A: I am not a lawyer, but I believe that is correct.

Q: When operating probation services for the county, Allied must meet the requirements set by state law, isn't that true?

A: Yes.

Q: State law sets out minimum qualifications for the employees of entities like Allied which provide probation services, correct?

A: Yes.

Peek et al. v. Stern and Allied

Q: Isn't it true that Allied must set out an annual plan for providing probation services and have it approved by the County Probation Officer?

A: Yes.

Q: Each probationer served by Allied has been convicted of a misdemeanor crime in a Union County District Court in the State of Franklin, isn't that right?

A: Yes, each probationer served by us has been referred to us by the courts, but our other departments offer services that are not court-referred.

Q: Isn't it true that in each case when a person is convicted of a misdemeanor and placed on probation, the judge determines the conditions of probation?

A: Yes.

Q: Allied cannot deviate from those conditions, can it—that is, you cannot add or remove conditions?

A: We carry out whatever the judge orders.

Q: Who determines what kind of counseling services you provide to probationers?

A: Again, the sentencing court. We typically evaluate probationers to determine the extent of mental health counseling needed and decide when and how they receive those services.

Q: Are you familiar with my client, Rita Peek, the named plaintiff in this case?

A: Yes, ma'am. She is a Union County probationer and under our supervision.

Q: Isn't it true that the court ordered that Ms. Peek receive mental health counseling?

A: Yes. Among other things, the court ordered mental health counseling for her. We evaluated her during her second meeting with us, back in June 2016. The result was that she needed what we call "Level Two Counseling"—both group and individual therapy sessions. We put her on our list for mental health counseling.

Q: Have you provided such counseling to her?

A: Not yet.

Q: Ms. Peek is still on a waiting list for that counseling, 13 months after she was sentenced to probation, correct?

A: Correct.

[Testimony regarding Allied's approach to providing counseling to women probationers is omitted.]

***

Q: Each quarter you report to the County Probation Officer on those probationers being served and what services were provided, correct?

A: Yes.

Q: As part of that report, the counseling waiting list is reported to, and approved by, the County Probation Officer each calendar quarter, correct?

A: Correct.

Q: During the last three quarters, at least, you have included Ms. Peek on the waiting list as needing mental health counseling and not yet served, correct?

A: I don't have the reports in front of me, but that is probably true.

Q: And the County Probation Officer has approved those quarterly reports, right?

A: Yes.

Q: I refer you to the reports Allied filed with the County Probation Officer. These show that 90% of the female probationers you serve do not even start, let alone complete, counseling within the probation term, isn't that correct?

A: If that is what the reports say, it must be true.

Q: In fact, 70% of the female probationers are given an extension of their probation term in order to complete counseling, isn't that true?

A: I believe that is true.

Q: These same reports show that, by contrast, 75% of male probationers receive and complete counseling within the period of their probation, isn't that correct?

A: If that is what the report says, then that is correct.

Q: In addition to providing mental health counseling to Ms. Peek, Allied is supposed to oversee her as a probationer, isn't that true?

A: Yes.

Q: Overseeing her means, among other things, ensuring that she reports to Allied monthly and complies with any required drug and alcohol testing, right?

A: Yes.

Q: Has Ms. Peek met all the conditions of probation imposed on her, other than receiving mental health counseling?

A: Yes, she has been a model probationer.

Q: If a probationer were to violate a condition of probation, you would report that to the court, wouldn't you?

A: Yes.

Q: If a probationer, such as Ms. Peek, failed to complete the conditions of probation, her probation could be revoked and she could be sent to jail, correct?

A: Yes.

Q: Or her probation could be extended, correct?

A: Yes.

Q: Probation is a restriction on a person's liberty, isn't it?

A: Yes.

Q: In that regard, being on probation is a restriction sort of like being in jail?

A: Well, it's a lot better than being in jail, but it is a restriction. Probationers have to comply with conditions of probation, they must meet with us in person each month, they cannot leave the state, and so on.

Q: And isn't it true that only the State of Franklin has the power to sentence someone to probation, set conditions of probation, revoke probation, and send someone to jail?

A: I am not a lawyer, but I believe that is so.

Robinson: No further questions.

July 2017
MPT-1 Library:
Peek et al. v. Doris Stern
and Allied Behavioral
Health Services

EXCERPTS FROM FRANKLIN CRIMINAL CODE

§ 35-210 Misdemeanor Sentencing; Probation

For a person convicted of a misdemeanor, the court may impose a jail sentence not to exceed 12 months. The court may suspend the jail sentence and place the person on probation for a term not to exceed three years. When placing a person on probation, the court shall determine the conditions of probation.

§ 35-211 Probation Services

(a) Each county shall appoint a County Probation Officer who shall be an employee of the county and shall provide probation services to the county as required by the Criminal Code, either directly or through other entities as provided by law.

(b) Any county may elect to provide probation services for those convicted of misdemeanors by contracting with a private entity, provided that the private entity:

1. Shall be a nonprofit entity.

2. Shall receive approval from the County Probation Officer of an annual Plan of Services which must include

    (i)   oversight of those on probation;

    (ii) monthly meetings with those on probation unless otherwise ordered;

    (iii) drug and alcohol testing; and

    (iv) drug and alcohol counseling, anger management counseling, vocational and mental health counseling, and referral to educational programs.

3. Shall require that each individual providing such services possess at least a bachelor's degree in the relevant professional field or its equivalent as determined by the County Probation Officer.

4. Shall submit to the County Probation Officer quarterly reports listing the names of probationers served during that quarter, the services provided to those probationers, and any other information required by the County Probation Officer, and shall receive approval of those reports from the County Probation Officer.

5. Shall submit to the County Probation Office an annual report of services provided and all expenses incurred and receive approval of that report from the County.

Peek et al. v. Stern and Allied

Lake v. Mega Lottery Group
United States Court of Appeals (15th Cir. 2009)

Olivia Lake sued the Mega Lottery Group pursuant to 42 U.S.C. § 1983, claiming that it fired her without due process. Mega moved to dismiss the complaint, arguing that as a private actor, it cannot be sued under 42 U.S.C. § 1983. The district court dismissed the complaint. Lake appealed. The sole issue on appeal is whether Mega acted as a state actor when it fired Lake. We affirm.

42 U.S.C. § 1983 provides for a cause of action against persons acting under color of state law who have violated rights guaranteed by the United States Constitution. *Buckley v. City of Redding*, 66 F.3d 190 (9th Cir. 1995). The Constitution's due process clause applies to states but not to private actors. However, private actors are not always free from suit for violating the Constitution. Constitutional standards protect those harmed by private actors when it is fair to say that the state is responsible for the offending conduct. To succeed on a § 1983 civil rights claim against a private actor, a claimant must prove that the private actor was a state actor.

To determine if an apparently private actor may still be a state actor, no one set of circumstances or criteria is sufficient. Rather, courts typically consider the range of circumstances when characterizing a private actor as a state actor for § 1983 purposes. Each set of factual circumstances must be examined in light of the critical question: whether "the State is responsible for the specific conduct of which the plaintiff complains." *Brentwood Acad. v. Tennessee Secondary Sch. Athletic Ass'n,* 531 U.S. 288 (2001).

There are two tests of those circumstances creating state action that are pertinent to Lake's claims. First, state action exists where the private actor was engaged in a public function delegated by the state. If the private actor exercises a function that has traditionally been a public or sovereign function, the private actor is not free from constitutional limits when performing that function. Second, a private actor engages in state action when the state exercises its coercive or influential power over the private actor or when there are pervasive entanglements between the private actor and the state. Under this test, "a state normally can be held responsible for a private decision only when it has exercised coercive power or has provided such significant encouragement . . . that the choice must in law be deemed to be that of the state." *Rendell-Baker v. Kohn*, 457 U.S. 830 (1982).

Under either of these two tests, there is a further requirement to find state action: there must be such a "close nexus between the State and the challenged action that seemingly private behavior may be fairly treated as that of the state itself." *Brentwood.*

Public function

Lake claims that Mega is engaged in a public function, relying on *West v. Atkins,* 487 U.S. 42 (1988), and on *Camp v. Airport Festival* (15th Cir. 2001). In *West,* a privately employed doctor was a state actor when he was employed to provide medical care to inmates in a state prison. The state is required to provide medical care to those it imprisons, and when the doctor contracted with the state to provide that care, he became a state actor.

In *Camp,* the plaintiff sued Airport Festival, a private nonprofit entity created to organize an aviation festival, for violating his First Amendment rights when he was arrested for leafleting during the festival. The city's police department had been directed to follow the instructions of festival organizers regarding security and arrests. Only the state has the power to deprive persons of their freedom by arresting them. When festival organizers accepted the authority to instruct the police regarding arrests, festival organizers became state actors.

Other examples of activities found to be public functions constituting state action include operating a local primary election, operating a post office, and providing for public safety through fire protection and animal control. Courts have narrowly construed the public function test to require that the action be one that is exclusively within the state's powers. Thus, courts have rejected claims that those who operate hospitals, privately owned public utilities, or schools, or provide foster care are performing public functions. While the state sometimes performs these functions, they are not traditionally the *exclusive* prerogative of the state. Over the years, private organizations have often initiated and performed these functions.

Here, the State of Franklin established a state-operated lottery in 1985. In 2005, due to the financial costs of operating a lottery, Franklin entered into a contract with Mega to operate the lottery, with the profits reverting to the state. Operating a lottery is not a traditional function of state government. Many private entities operate similar activities through racetracks, casinos, sweepstakes, and other activities. Thus, Mega is not engaged in a public function.

State coercion or influence, or pervasive entanglement

Lake next argues that there is state action because the state has coerced or influenced Mega to act. Lake argues that because Franklin contracts with Mega to operate the lottery, with the profits from the lottery becoming state proceeds, its influence over Mega is significant, if not coercive. She also argues that Franklin coerces Mega through its extensive regulation of the lottery, making Mega an agent of the state.

Lake's argument fails in light of the U.S. Supreme Court's ruling in *Rendell-Baker*. That case involved employees who claimed that their First Amendment rights were violated when they were discharged by a private school. The plaintiffs argued that the state's extensive regulation of education made the school a state actor. The Court rejected this argument because the state did not regulate, encourage, or compel the private board of trustees to fire the employees. Any government regulation was directed to education of the children, and did not compel the board to follow any particular personnel policies.

The state's exercise of its coercive power or influence must be such that the private choice can be said to be that of the state. Lake has failed to show any evidence that the State of Franklin required, recommended, or even knew about this, or any, personnel action. What the state regulates is the operation of the lottery, not the hiring and firing of Mega's employees.

Lake also argues that even if the state did not coerce Mega, there are additional pervasive state-private entanglements. She relies on *Brentwood,* 531 U.S. at 288. There, the U.S. Supreme Court ruled that the "nominally private character of the Association" could not overcome the pervasive entanglement with public institutions. Lake maintains that Franklin and Mega are entangled because of Franklin's heavy regulation of the lottery.

In *Brentwood*, the defendant Association regulated interscholastic athletic competition among public and private high schools in Tennessee. The Association's board found that Brentwood, one of the Association's member schools, had violated a rule prohibiting "undue influence" in recruiting athletes and, among other things, declared Brentwood's teams ineligible to compete in playoffs for two years. Brentwood sued the Association, alleging violation of its First and Fourteenth Amendment rights when the school was penalized for violating Association rules. The Association argued that it was not a state actor. The Court found that the Association's board of directors was composed primarily of representatives of public schools. The board effectively operated the sports program for the state's public high schools. The State Department of Education formally adopted the Association's rules as the rules for public school sports programs. Based on these findings, the Court rejected the Association's claim, concluding that the relationship of the public schools and the Association constituted a pervasive entanglement that made the Association a state actor.

Lake also points to the pervasive entanglements in *Camp* as analogous to the State's control here over the lottery. In *Camp*, although the festival was organized by a nonprofit entity, the city permitted the festival to use the airport grounds at no cost; the city's personnel were extensively involved in planning for the festival while on city time and at city expense; the city promoted the festival through its tourism bureau; and the city's airport personnel controlled access of airplanes during the festival's air show. As noted *supra*, the city's police and first responders were effectively turned over to the festival organizers for the duration of the festival. These entanglements were extensive.

In contrast, the primary relationship between the State of Franklin and Mega is a contract, no different from that between the state and any other contractor. The State of Franklin contracts with private entities to build its buildings, deliver food for its prisoners, and furnish office supplies to state legislators, to name but a few contracts. These contracts do not constitute the sort of pervasive entanglement necessary to constitute state action. When the state enters into a contract to build a state building, the contract demands compliance with many regulations, yet it is left to the contractor to execute the contract. Franklin does not involve itself in the governance of Mega. It does not endorse Mega's personnel policies as the state had in *Brentwood* when the state Department of Education approved the Association's rules. Nor does Franklin involve itself directly in the operation of Mega as the city did in running the airport festival at issue in *Camp*.

Connection to offending conduct: nexus

Even if Lake had met one or both of the tests discussed above, Lake has failed to meet the further requirement of *Rendell-Baker* that there be a nexus, meaning a connection, between the state and the challenged action. That is, Lake has not shown that the offending conduct—her being discharged without due process—was somehow connected to the state's influence over Mega. Lake was discharged by Mega in the same way that any private corporation fires any employee. The state played no role in the discharge, so Lake cannot show the required nexus. Lake offers no facts that rise to the level of the circumstances where the state and private parties have acted in concert to engage in denial of a party's civil rights. Mega's only participation with the state is to contract with the state to operate the lottery. Mega did not involve the state in any way in its decision to fire Lake.

Affirmed.

July 2017
MPT-2 File:
In re Zimmer Farm

In re Zimmer Farm

State of Franklin
County of Hartford
Office of the County Attorney
92 Oak Street
Glenview, Franklin 33705

MEMORANDUM

TO:	Examinee
FROM:	Carl S. Burns, County Attorney
DATE:	July 25, 2017
RE:	Complaints about Zimmer Farm

The county board president, Nina Ortiz, is concerned about activities at the John and Edward Zimmer farm on Prairie Road, and specifically about the bird rescue operation and bird festivals they operate on their farm. Ms. Ortiz has received numerous complaints from local residents about the activities at the farm. While she supports the concept of a bird rescue operation, Ms. Ortiz would like the bird operation moved to a location far away from any residential subdivisions. She also wants the festivals stopped. She has asked me to research whether the county's zoning ordinance can limit the Zimmers' operations. Further, she wants to know whether the Franklin Right to Farm Act (FRFA), which protects certain farms and farming activities, applies here.

In addition to the bird rescue operation and the festivals, the Zimmer farm produces apples and strawberries for local sale. The Zimmers' apple and strawberry cultivation and sales are permitted under the applicable county zoning ordinance. I want you to focus on the bird rescue operation and the festivals—the activities the neighbors are complaining about. Please prepare an objective memorandum for me analyzing these questions:

1. Is the Zimmers' bird rescue operation permitted under the county zoning ordinance?

2. Are the Zimmers' festivals permitted under the county zoning ordinance?

3. How, if at all, does FRFA affect the county's ability to enforce its zoning ordinance with respect to the bird rescue operation and the festivals?

In your analysis, address any counter arguments the Zimmers may make in support of the bird rescue operation and the festivals. Address only the questions I have raised above. Do not draft a separate statement of facts, but be sure to incorporate the relevant facts, analyze the applicable legal authorities, and explain how the facts and law affect your analysis.

Email to County Board President

TO: Nina Ortiz, County Board President (ctybdpres@Hartford.gov)
FROM: Sally Wendell (swendell@cmail.com)
DATE: May 8, 2017
SUBJECT: Zimmer farm complaints

I am writing on behalf of homeowners living in Country Manors and Orchard Estates, near the Zimmer farm. For the past two years, the Zimmers have run a bird rescue operation. The birds create noise and offensive smells and attract flies, all of which bother us. We cannot sit or eat outside or use our outdoor grills because of the bird noise, odors, and bugs. We did not have this problem before the Zimmers began their bird rescue operation. Just come out some evening and see for yourself how bad it is!

Last year, the Zimmers also hosted several bird festivals with music and food. People who came to these festivals parked on the streets in our subdivisions and walked to and from the farm, littering our streets and yards. Plus the music got pretty loud and we could hear it whether we wanted to or not. The Zimmers are planning more festivals, maybe even every month.

We paid good money for our homes because we wanted some quiet country living—that's why we moved here. Now our neighborhood is becoming like a downtown entertainment center. We taxpayers and homeowners want you to shut down the Zimmers' bird rescue operation and stop these festivals.

A taxpaying citizen,
Sally Wendell

MEMORANDUM

TO: Carl S. Burns, County Attorney
FROM: Judy Abernathy, Investigator
DATE: June 19, 2017
RE: Zimmer farm complaints

On June 14, 2017, I interviewed John Zimmer and his son Edward regarding neighbors' complaints about the Zimmers' farming activities.

As soon as I arrived at the Zimmer farm, Edward Zimmer said, "I know why you are here— just tell those neighbors 'Right to Farm.' They knew they were moving to a farm area— what did they expect?"

John Zimmer provided some background. When his parents, Gus and Ann Zimmer, purchased the property in 1951, it consisted of an apple orchard and a strawberry field. Gus and Ann continued that operation and began growing vegetables after purchasing additional land in 1960. They sold the fruit and vegetables to local grocery stores. In 1985, John and his wife, Darlene, took over the operation and expanded their produce sales to three farmers' markets.

In 1988, the Zimmers began a tradition of holding a one-day annual apple festival for their children's school. School families arrived by bus with their children and picked apples, which were for sale. The families played games and listened to music. There were approximately 100 persons in attendance.

In 2007, the Zimmers suffered several losses—a late spring freeze that ruined the strawberry crop, tough financial times, and some serious health setbacks for Darlene. In 2009, their son Edward moved to the farm to help. Darlene died in 2010. John and Edward continue to produce apples and strawberries for sale locally, but they discontinued the vegetable operation.

In 2015, Edward, who is trained as a veterinary assistant, began taking in wounded ducks, geese, owls, quail, pheasants, hawks—pretty much any fowl or bird that had been hurt. People from miles around bring him wounded birds. Edward made improvements in some of the outbuildings and now cares for as many as 100 birds at a time. I inspected the buildings where the birds are kept and did not observe any obvious threats to public health.

Edward's goal is to care for the birds until they can be released back to the wild, but those that cannot be rehabilitated stay on the farm. Edward does not sell the birds, does not make any profit from the operation, and does not intend to do so. He loves to rescue birds.

In re Zimmer Farm

Last year, Edward and John said they took a clue from agritourism, a development in the last 20 years that uses entertainment and public educational activities to market and sell agricultural products. The Zimmers held four weekend festivals at their farm in 2016. They showed me a flyer used to advertise the fall festivals. It was titled "Fall Bird Festival" and said "Support injured birds, listen to music, have a good time. Buy apples and discover the best recipes for baking with fruit." The flyer listed details such as hours of the festival, directions, etc.

As many as 200 people attended the festivals each day. To attract people to the festivals, the Zimmers had vendors provide food and drinks, and local musicians offered musical entertainment. A local chef offered two sessions on cooking and baking with fruit; the Zimmers also sold apples or strawberries, depending on the season, and cookbooks.

Each day of the festival, Edward gave a one-hour program about birds. To raise funds for his bird rescue operation, Edward sold bird-related souvenirs, including T-shirts, caps, and books. Guests were encouraged to "adopt" a wounded bird by donating to its care and upkeep. Profits from the bird-related souvenirs, along with the donations, were used to underwrite the bird rescue operation. The Zimmers plan more bird festivals this year.

I also visited the two adjoining subdivisions, both of which were developed in the 1990s. Before that residential development, the land on both sides of the 30-acre Zimmer property was farmland for over 100 years. Presently, all lots in both subdivisions have been sold and developed. Country Manors, which lies to the east of the Zimmer farm, consists of upscale homes. Orchard Estates, which lies to the west of the farm, consists of moderately priced homes very attractive to families due to a number of playgrounds and park areas within the subdivision. About 20 of the homes in Country Manors border the Zimmer Farm, and about 30 of the Orchard Estates properties border the farm. Both subdivisions are zoned R-1, single-family residential.

On June 15, I reviewed public records and confirmed that Zimmer Farms Inc. has owned the property in question since 1951. The Zimmer farm is zoned Agricultural A-1. As you know, Hartford County has countywide zoning. Most property is either single- or multi-family residential, light industrial, or agricultural. The permitted uses for A-1 zoned areas are specified in the zoning ordinance. Growing apples and strawberries for commercial sale, as the Zimmers have done, is permitted in an A-1 zone.

July 2017
MPT-2 Library:
In re Zimmer Farm

In re Zimmer Farm

EXCERPTS FROM HARTFORD COUNTY ZONING CODE

Title 15. ZONING

§ 22. Agricultural A-1 District Permitted Uses

(a) Within an A-1 district, the following uses are permitted:

(1) any agricultural use;

(2) incidental processing, packaging, storage, transportation, distribution, sale, or agricultural accessory use intended to add value to agricultural products produced on the premises or to ready such products for market;

. . .

(b) Definitions

. . .

(2) "Agricultural use" means any activities conducted for the purpose of producing an income or livelihood from one or more of the following agricultural products:

(a) crops or forage (such as corn, soybeans, fruits, vegetables, wheat, hay, alfalfa)

(b) livestock (such as cattle, swine, sheep, and goats)

(c) beehives

(d) poultry (such as chickens, geese, ducks, and turkeys)

(e) nursery plants, sod, or Christmas trees

. . .

An agricultural use does not lose its character as such because it involves noise, dust, odors, heavy equipment, spraying of chemicals, or long hours of operation.

(3) "Agricultural accessory use" means one of the following activities:

(a) a seasonal farm stand, provided that it is operated for less than six months per year and is used for the sale of one or more agricultural products produced on the premises;

(b) special events, provided that they are three or fewer per year and are directly related to the sale or marketing of one or more agricultural products produced on the premises.

EXCERPTS FROM FRANKLIN AGRICULTURE CODE
Ch. 75 Franklin Right to Farm Act

§ 2. Definitions

(a) "Farm" means the land, plants, animals, buildings, structures (including ponds used for agricultural or aquacultural activities), machinery, equipment, and other appurtenances used in the commercial production of farm products.

(b) "Farm operation" means the operation and management of a farm or an activity that occurs on a farm in connection with the commercial production, harvesting, and storage of farm products.

§ 3. Farm not nuisance

(a) A farm or farm operation shall not be found to be a public or private nuisance and shall be protected under section 4 of this Act if the farm or farm operation existed before a change in the land use or occupancy of land that borders the farmland, and if, before that change in land use or occupancy of land, the farm or farm operation would not have been a nuisance.

(b) A farm or farm operation that is protected under subsection (a) shall not be found to be a public or private nuisance as a result of any of the following:

      (i) a change in ownership;

      (ii) temporary cessation or interruption of farming;

      (iii) enrollment in a governmental program; or

      (iv) adoption of new technology.

§ 4. Local units of government

Except as otherwise provided in this section, a local unit of government shall not enact, maintain, or enforce an ordinance, regulation, or resolution that conflicts with this Act and undermines the purpose of this Act.

Effective July 1, 1983.

REPORT FROM FRANKLIN SENATE COMMITTEE ON AGRICULTURE
Pertaining to S.B. 1198, May 3, 1983

S.B. 1198 will be known as the Franklin Right to Farm Act and will protect Franklin farmland. During each of the past several years, two to three million acres of U.S. farmland have been converted to nonagricultural uses. Franklin's agricultural resources play an important role in feeding the population of Franklin, the United States, and the world. Loss of farmland imperils 2.2 million agriculture-related U.S. jobs, the habitats of 75% of our wildlife, and open spaces necessary for a healthy environment. Loss of farmland creates urban sprawl with the attendant stresses on the infrastructures of Franklin's formerly rural counties and small towns.

When land that was formerly agricultural is converted to residential land, new home dwellers, not familiar with rural life, complain of odors, noise, dust, and insects caused by animals, crops, and farm machinery. Too often these new residents file nuisance suits against their farming neighbors. Additionally, local ordinances enacted in response to residents' concerns threaten farmers with fines and/or closure if they are in noncompliance with the restrictions imposed by the ordinances. These restraints and costly lawsuits by nonfarming neighbors discourage farmers from investing in their farms and remaining on them.

S.B. 1198 protects those who farm for a living. A farming operation that was not previously a nuisance does not become one when residential development moves in next to the farmland. To qualify for this protection, farmers must show that the farm operation would not have been a nuisance at the time of the changes in the area. This protection applies to those who make their living farming, whether in an agricultural area or in a residential area, not to those with gardens for personal use. Under the common law, "coming to a nuisance," such as building a home next to a cattle operation, was ordinarily a defense for the farmer. However, courts have been reluctant to afford this defense wide applicability. This reluctance adds to the uncertainty facing farmers. S.B. 1198 codifies this common law defense and protects those who farm for a living.

Accordingly, this Committee declares that it is this state's policy to conserve, protect, and encourage the development and improvement of its agricultural land for the commercial production of food and other agricultural products, by limiting the circumstances under which a farming operation may be deemed to be a nuisance.

In re Zimmer Farm

Shelby Township v. Beck
Franklin Court of Appeal (2005)

The issue on appeal is whether the Franklin Right to Farm Act (FRFA or "the Act") preempts a local zoning ordinance.

In 1995, the Becks purchased 1.75 acres of property in Shelby Township. The property had been used for raising chickens, and there were chicken coops on the property when the Becks purchased it. In 1995, the land use plan for the township allowed farming on this land. In 1996, the Becks began raising chickens for sale at local butcher shops. In 1998, Shelby Township passed Zoning Ordinance 7.0, which requires farms to have a minimum size of three acres. In 2000, several real estate developers began to build homes near the Becks' property. Neighbors began complaining to the Township Board about the smells and noise from the Becks' chickens. The neighbors filed a petition with the Township Board, asking it to close down the Becks' operation because it was a nuisance. In 2004, the Township Board decided that the best way to close down the Becks' farm was to enforce its ordinance regarding minimum farm size. The Township sued to enforce its ordinance, and the Becks moved to dismiss, claiming that FRFA preempts the ordinance. The trial court granted the motion, and the Township appealed.

State law can preempt a municipal ordinance in two ways. First, preemption occurs when a statute completely occupies the field that the ordinance attempts to regulate. FRFA does not "occupy the field," because the legislature has also authorized local governments to enact zoning laws concerning agricultural properties. Second, preemption occurs when an ordinance conflicts with a state statute and undermines its purpose. A conflict exists when the ordinance permits what the statute prohibits or vice versa. Determining whether there is a conflict requires a careful reading of the statute and the ordinance in light of the policy and purposes behind the statute and measuring the degree to which the ordinance frustrates the achievement of the state's objectives.

If Shelby Ordinance 7.0 is in effect, the Becks cannot raise chickens on their property because it is under the minimum size required for a farm. However, Section 4 of FRFA provides that a local ordinance is preempted when it conflicts with FRFA. The question then is whether there is a conflict. Section 2 of FRFA defines a "farm" as "land, plants, animals, buildings, structures . . . and other appurtenances used in the commercial production of farm products." The Act does not set a minimum acreage for farms. Here, the Becks' operation—raising chickens for sale—is protected by FRFA because it is the commercial production of farm products, even though the operation takes place on only 1.75 acres. Thus, there is a conflict between the size requirement of the ordinance, which prohibits the Becks from raising chickens, and FRFA, which does not. Thus the ordinance and FRFA are in direct conflict, as the ordinance prohibits what is permitted by the Act. The ordinance undermines the very purpose of the Act by prohibiting this farm operation.

The Township's effort to use its size ordinance to prevent what the neighbors believe is a nuisance is the very sort of enforcement action that FRFA is designed to prevent. FRFA states that a farm shall not be found to be a nuisance if it existed before the change in land use and if, before that change, it would not have been found to be a nuisance. The Becks' operation began in 1995, before the residential development neighboring it was created. In 1995, the Becks' farm operation was a permitted use and would not have been a nuisance. Accordingly, the Becks' operation is protected by FRFA.

Our conclusion that the state law preempts the local ordinance also serves the purpose of the Act, which is to conserve land for agricultural operations and protect it from the threat of extinction by regulation from local governmental units. *See* Sen. Rpt. Comm. Agric. 1983.

Affirmed.

Wilson v. Monaco Farms
Franklin Court of Appeal (2008)

Defendant Monaco Farms (Monaco) has operated a dairy farm on its property from 1940 to the present, with changes in the ownership passing from father to son in 1970, and to granddaughter in 2000. Monaco increased the number of dairy cows on the farm from 40 to 60 in 2005, and from 60 to 200 in 2007.

Plaintiff Bill Wilson has lived in the subdivision immediately to the east of Monaco since 1990. In 2007 he filed a private nuisance action against Monaco, alleging that the flies, dust, and odors from the dairy cows interfered with his enjoyment of his property. Monaco moved to dismiss, relying on the Franklin Right to Farm Act (FRFA), which it claims continues to protect a farm operation when it expands or changes its operation. In response, Wilson argued that FRFA does not protect a farm whose expansion created a nuisance not present at the time he purchased his property. The trial court granted the motion to dismiss, and Wilson appealed. We affirm.

The present situation is the very sort of farm operation the legislature intended to protect when it enacted FRFA. Monaco has existed since 1940, and it would not have been a nuisance at that time. In 1984, the land bordering Monaco was subdivided and developed into a residential area and was zoned residential.

There were no complaints about the operation of Monaco until 2007, when it expanded from 60 to 200 cows. The question is whether FRFA continues to protect Monaco after the expansion. When it enacted FRFA, the legislature understood that circumstances could change and provided that certain changes would not affect the protections of FRFA. Section 3(b)(i) of FRFA addresses the issue of change in ownership but does not address changes in size or nature of the operation.

Wilson argues that because the legislature listed four, and only four, contemplated interruptions or changes in farm operations, those are exclusive and exhaustive. If Wilson is correct, the only changes the legislature intended to protect are the four items specified in the statute, and those four do not include expansion of farm operations.

Monaco, on the other hand, argues that where the legislature provides a list, the court must determine what is common among the items on the list and then consider whether the matter at issue is sufficiently similar to the items listed as to be included. Monaco argues that the change in size of the operation is similar to a change in technology, which does not destroy the protections of FRFA. Both changes have as their purpose the opportunity to increase farm production and thus profitability.

Both parties assume that the court must look to § 3(b) of FRFA. A better approach is to examine § 3(a), which provides that a farm "shall not be found to be a public or private nuisance . . . if the farm or farm operation existed before a change in the land use or occupancy of land that borders the farmland . . . ." Thus, the statute provides a date for measuring whether a nuisance exists, namely the date when the use of the neighboring land changed. In this case, that date is 1984, the year that the neighboring land was subdivided and developed into a residential area. The legislature may have assumed that farms might expand. Indeed, it noted in § 3(b) the possibility of change in technology. Nevertheless, the legislature established only one date for measuring whether a nuisance exists.

The purpose of FRFA is "to conserve, protect, and encourage the development and improvement of [Franklin's] agricultural land for the commercial production of food and other agricultural products, by limiting the circumstances under which a farming operation may be deemed to be a nuisance." Sen. Rpt. Comm. Agric. 1983. Relying solely on the legislature's date for determining whether a nuisance exists serves the statutory purpose.

When he bought his home in 1990, Wilson knew that he was moving next to a dairy farm. It remains a dairy farm, albeit a larger one. Nothing in FRFA prohibits expansion of farm operations. Despite the expansion of Monaco's dairy operation, it is protected by the Act, and the trial court properly dismissed Wilson's nuisance action.

Affirmed.

Koster v. Presley's Fruit
Columbia Court of Appeal (2010)

In this case, the court is asked to determine the applicability of the Columbia Right to Farm Act (CRFA). The precise issue on appeal is whether the production of wooden pallets for use in harvesting peaches is an agricultural activity protected by the Act.

Defendant Presley's Fruit (Presley's) has grown and sold peaches at its location since 1960. In 2006, Presley's added a new building and began manufacturing wooden pallets for use in harvesting and transporting peaches.

In 1997, plaintiffs Matt and Kathleen Koster purchased residential property that abuts Presley's. They had no complaints about Presley's until 2006, when they began experiencing noise and dust associated with the manufacturing of the wooden pallets. The Kosters filed a nuisance suit against Presley's, claiming that the noise and dust is a nuisance that substantially and unreasonably interferes with their enjoyment of their property.

Presley's moved to dismiss, claiming the protections of CRFA. CRFA states that a farm operation which existed one year before the change in the area is not a nuisance if it would not have been a nuisance at the time of the change in the property. The trial court granted the motion.

On appeal, the Kosters argue that CRFA protects only farm activities and not manufacturing. Presley's claims that the pallets are needed to harvest and transport the peaches (a farm product) to market and that therefore the manufacturing of the pallets is protected by CRFA.

Resolving this question requires the court to interpret and apply the provisions of CRFA. Our role in construing a statute is to "ascertain and give effect to the legislative intent." *Brady v. Roberts Electrical Mfg., Inc.* (Columbia Sup. Ct. 1999).

We must examine the Columbia statute's text and give the words their natural and ordinary meaning in light of their statutory context. If the statutory language is clear and unambiguous, the court must apply the statute's plain language and not venture beyond the text to add words not there. However, when the statutory language is unclear, the court may refer to the purpose of the legislation and the legislative history of the statute, such as legislative committee reports, to aid us in interpreting the text.

In this case, an examination of the statutory language provides the answer. CRFA defines a farm product as "those plants and animals useful to human beings produced by agriculture and includes, but is not limited to, forages and sod crops; grains and feed crops; dairy and dairy products; poultry and poultry products; livestock, including breeding and grazing animals; fruits; vegetables; or any other product which incorporates the use of food, feed, or fiber." Although that is a broad definition of farm product, there is no mention of products produced from wood.

The pallets are constructed of wood and nails or staples. The wood used for the pallets originates from outside the defendant's property. The products, therefore, are not grown, raised, or bred on the farm premises, but are only assembled there from materials purchased elsewhere. The pallets do not match any of the definitions of farm products set forth in the Act, nor are they like any of those farm products defined by the statute. The manufacturing of these wooden pallets is not an activity protected by CRFA.

We reverse the trial court's order dismissing this case. If, on remand, the Kosters are successful in their nuisance action and convince the court to order Presley's to cease producing the pallets at the farm, there will be no loss of farmland. If the Kosters succeed, Presley's land will continue to be used for the production of peaches. The land will remain agricultural. Presley's would manufacture the pallets off the farm premises rather than on the premises, or purchase the pallets from some outside source. Purchasing pallets should be no more a threat to Presley's than purchasing a truck for hauling the peaches to market.

Reversed and remanded.

Themis
Bar Review

February 2017 MPTs
In re Ace Chemical
In re Guardianship of Henry King

February 2017
MPTs

www.ncbex.org

National Conference of Bar Examiners
302 South Bedford Street | Madison, WI 53703-3622
Phone: 608-280-8550 | Fax: 608-280-8552 | TDD: 608-661-1275
e-mail: contact@ncbex.org

Contents

MPT-1: *In re Ace Chemical*

FILE

LIBRARY

MPT-2: *In re Guardianship of Henry King*

FILE

LIBRARY

Preface

The Multistate Performance Test (MPT) is developed by the National Conference of Bar Examiners (NCBE). This publication includes the items and Point Sheets from the February 2017 MPT. The instructions for the test appear on page iii.

The MPT Point Sheets describe the factual and legal points encompassed within the lawyering tasks to be completed. They outline the possible issues and points that might be addressed by an examinee. They are provided to the user jurisdictions to assist graders in grading the examination by identifying the issues and suggesting the resolution of the problems contemplated by the drafters.

For more information about the MPT, including a list of skills tested, visit the NCBE website at www.ncbex.org.

Description of the MPT

The MPT consists of two 90-minute items and is a component of the Uniform Bar Examination (UBE). It is administered by user jurisdictions as part of the bar examination on the Tuesday before the last Wednesday in February and July of each year. User jurisdictions may select one or both items to include as part of their bar examinations. (Jurisdictions that administer the UBE use two MPTs.)

The materials for each MPT include a File and a Library. The File consists of source documents containing all the facts of the case. The specific assignment the examinee is to complete is described in a memorandum from a supervising attorney. The File might also include transcripts of interviews, depositions, hearings or trials, pleadings, correspondence, client documents, contracts, newspaper articles, medical records, police reports, or lawyer's notes. Relevant as well as irrelevant facts are included. Facts are sometimes ambiguous, incomplete, or even conflicting. As in practice, a client's or a supervising attorney's version of events may be incomplete or unreliable. Examinees are expected to recognize when facts are inconsistent or missing and are expected to identify potential sources of additional facts.

The Library may contain cases, statutes, regulations, or rules, some of which may not be relevant to the assigned lawyering task. The examinee is expected to extract from the Library the legal principles necessary to analyze the problem and perform the task. The MPT is not a test of substantive law; the Library materials provide sufficient substantive information to complete the task.

The MPT is designed to test an examinee's ability to use fundamental lawyering skills in a realistic situation and complete a task that a beginning lawyer should be able to accomplish. The MPT is not a test of substantive knowledge. Rather, it is designed to evaluate six fundamental skills lawyers are expected to demonstrate regardless of the area of law in which the skills are applied. The MPT requires examinees to (1) sort detailed factual materials and separate relevant from irrelevant facts; (2) analyze statutory, case, and administrative materials for applicable principles of law; (3) apply the relevant law to the relevant facts in a manner likely to resolve a client's problem; (4) identify and resolve ethical dilemmas, when present; (5) communicate effectively in writing; and (6) complete a lawyering task within time constraints. These skills are tested by requiring examinees to perform one or more of a variety of lawyering tasks. For example, examinees might be instructed to complete any of the following: a memorandum to a supervising attorney, a letter to a client, a persuasive memorandum or brief, a statement of facts, a contract provision, a will, a counseling plan, a proposal for settlement or agreement, a discovery plan, a witness examination plan, or a closing argument.

Instructions

The back cover of each test booklet contains the following instructions:

You will be instructed when to begin and when to stop this test. Do not break the seal on this booklet until you are told to begin. This test is designed to evaluate your ability to handle a select number of legal authorities in the context of a factual problem involving a client.

The problem is set in the fictitious state of Franklin, in the fictitious Fifteenth Circuit of the United States. Columbia and Olympia are also fictitious states in the Fifteenth Circuit. In Franklin, the trial court of general jurisdiction is the District Court, the intermediate appellate court is the Court of Appeal, and the highest court is the Supreme Court.

You will have two kinds of materials with which to work: a File and a Library. The first document in the File is a memorandum containing the instructions for the task you are to complete. The other documents in the File contain factual information about your case and may include some facts that are not relevant.

The Library contains the legal authorities needed to complete the task and may also include some authorities that are not relevant. Any cases may be real, modified, or written solely for the purpose of this examination. If the cases appear familiar to you, do not assume that they are precisely the same as you have read before. Read them thoroughly, as if they all were new to you. You should assume that the cases were decided in the jurisdictions and on the dates shown. In citing cases from the Library, you may use abbreviations and omit page references.

Your response must be written in the answer book provided. If you are using a laptop computer to answer the questions, your jurisdiction will provide you with specific instructions. In answering this performance test, you should concentrate on the materials in the File and Library. What you have learned in law school and elsewhere provides the general background for analyzing the problem; the File and Library provide the specific materials with which you must work.

Although there are no restrictions on how you apportion your time, you should allocate approximately half your time to reading and digesting the materials and to organizing your answer before you begin writing it. You may make notes anywhere in the test materials; blank pages are provided at the end of the booklet. You may not tear pages from the question booklet.

Do not include your actual name anywhere in the work product required by the task memorandum.

This performance test will be graded on your responsiveness to the instructions regarding the task you are to complete, which are given to you in the first memorandum in the File, and on the content, thoroughness, and organization of your response.

February 2017
MPT-1 File:
In re Ace Chemical

Montagne & Parks LLC
Attorneys at Law
760 Main Street, Suite 100
Essex, Franklin 33702

MEMORANDUM

To:	Examinee
From:	Lauren Scott, Managing Partner
Date:	February 21, 2017
Re:	Ace Chemical: potential conflicts of interest

Our law firm has been approached by Ace Chemical Inc., which wants to sue Roadsprinters Inc. for breach of a shipping contract. Ace claims that Roadsprinters failed to timely deliver Ace's goods to a customer. It is likely that Ace has a good case—the contract has a "time is of the essence" clause and delivery of the goods was significantly delayed. The work on this case would be done here at our Franklin office; I would be the lead attorney, and our partner Samuel Dawes would be the lead litigator. The law firm of Adams Bailey serves as Roadsprinters' outside counsel.

As you know, our firm has 400 lawyers in 14 different offices. Recently, we've become aware of certain circumstances that might affect our ability to represent Ace: 1) our office in the state of Columbia represents the Columbia Chamber of Commerce, and Jim Pickens, the president of Roadsprinters, was at one time chair of the Chamber's board; 2) Samuel Dawes once represented Roadsprinters in a trademark registration; and 3) our office in the state of Olympia has interviewed and would like to hire Ashley Kaplan, an attorney who currently works in Adams Bailey's Franklin office.

We will not undertake this representation if barred by the Franklin Rules of Professional Conduct, but we would very much like to take on this client in this matter if it is ethically permissible. We know that Roadsprinters will not waive any conflicts of interest.

Please prepare a memorandum to me analyzing whether any potential conflicts of interest are raised by these three circumstances. If you determine that one or more conflicts of interest exist, for each conflict you should identify the action we need to take to comply with the Rules. Do not draft a separate statement of facts, but be sure to integrate the relevant facts into your analysis. Note that Franklin's Rules of Professional Conduct are identical to the ABA's Model Rules of Professional Conduct and that Franklin Ethics Opinions are persuasive but not binding authority before courts.

Montagne & Parks LLC

MEMORANDUM TO FILE

From: Lauren Scott, Managing Partner
Date: February 17, 2017
Re: Ace Chemical: potential conflicts of interest

Montagne & Parks, through its Franklin office, would like to represent Ace Chemical Inc. in its suit against Roadsprinters Inc. Ace alleges that Roadsprinters breached its contract with Ace when Roadsprinters failed to deliver goods to Ace's customer on time. Roadsprinters is represented by the law firm of Adams Bailey.

Potential conflict: Columbia Chamber of Commerce

Through our office in the state of Columbia, our firm represents the Columbia Chamber of Commerce (Chamber); we have represented the Chamber for the last 10 years. (The Chamber is a membership organization of local businesses that promotes the general interest of the business community.) In the course of our representation of the Chamber, we have lobbied before the Columbia legislature for tax reform. For purposes of this lobbying effort, we received no confidential business information from Chamber members.

In our communications with Chamber members, we clarified that we represented the Chamber, and not the members, in lobbying, and that the content of our communications with members was not confidential. The Chamber and its members acknowledged in writing that our representation was limited to lobbying for the Chamber itself. While we received confidential information from the Chamber about legislative strategies and tactics related solely to tax issues, we received no confidential information from or about any of the Chamber's members.

Roadsprinters has been a member of the Chamber since the Chamber's inception 15 years ago. Jim Pickens has been the president of Roadsprinters for the last 20 years and was chair of the board of the Chamber in one of the years of our representation; however, throughout the lobbying effort, the firm worked primarily with the Chamber's executive director and not with the officers of the board.

Potential conflict: Samuel Dawes

Samuel Dawes, a partner in this firm, has successfully represented Ace against other adversaries in several other matters, and Ace wants him to handle this litigation.

Seven years ago, while he was in solo private practice, Mr. Dawes represented Roadsprinters in an uncontested trademark registration. Mr. Dawes has been interviewed consistent with Franklin Rule of Professional Conduct 1.6(b)(7). We have concluded that no information that he learned, or could have learned, could possibly be relevant to the litigation against Roadsprinters. Mr. Dawes reports that he has not had any contact with Mr. Pickens, the president of Roadsprinters, for the last five years.

Potential conflict: Ashley Kaplan

Our Olympia office has informed us that it recently interviewed Ashley Kaplan for a position as a senior associate in that office. The Olympia office was very impressed with Ms. Kaplan and wants to make her an offer—the office badly needs someone with her expertise. Ms. Kaplan currently works for the Franklin office of Adams Bailey. Ms. Kaplan has provided a list of the clients for which she has done work at Adams Bailey, and Roadsprinters is on that list.

FRANKLIN DAILY NEWS
Spotlight on a "Rising Star" in the Community

ESSEX—(December 20, 2010) As part of our series profiling rising stars in our business community, the *Franklin Daily News* this month shines a spotlight on young attorney Samuel Dawes.

Mr. Dawes is a graduate of the University of Franklin (B.A. in English and J.D.) and is currently in solo private practice in Essex, Franklin. He specializes in litigation and intellectual property work. Although he might one day want to work at a big firm, Mr. Dawes currently enjoys both the flexibility and the challenge of working alone. Mr. Dawes has been in solo practice for about five years, and he says he truly loves the independence and the opportunity to form close and lasting relationships. When asked for a specific example, Mr. Dawes mentioned his relationship with Jim Pickens, the president of his client Roadsprinters Inc. He stated that "Mr. Pickens taught me so much. He was so generous with his time and advice. It is people like him who make me love my job."

According to Mr. Pickens, he came to Mr. Dawes for help in registering a trademark for "Roadsprinters" and saw real promise in the young lawyer. "Sam is a great guy and a great lawyer," he said. "Although it was not at all necessary for the work on the trademark registration, I told him how to develop client relationships and I introduced him to community business leaders. I knew he was someone who was going places—and I wanted to help him get there."

According to other lawyers with whom we spoke, Mr. Dawes is a rising star in the legal profession. He combines a strong intellect, a curious mind, and a desire to help others. He listens to his clients and truly seeks to help them. We expect great things of Mr. Dawes.

February 2017
MPT-1 Library:
In re Ace Chemical

In re Ace Chemical

Excerpts from the Franklin Rules of Professional Conduct

Rule 1.6 Confidentiality of Information

(a) A lawyer shall not reveal information relating to the representation of a client unless the client gives informed consent, the disclosure is impliedly authorized in order to carry out the representation or the disclosure is permitted by paragraph (b).

(b) A lawyer may reveal information relating to the representation of a client to the extent the lawyer reasonably believes necessary:

. . .

(4) to secure legal advice about the lawyer's compliance with these Rules;

. . .

(7) to detect and resolve conflicts of interest arising from the lawyer's change of employment or from changes in the composition or ownership of a firm, but only if the revealed information would not compromise the attorney-client privilege or otherwise prejudice the client.

(c) A lawyer shall make reasonable efforts to prevent the inadvertent or unauthorized disclosure of, or unauthorized access to, information relating to the representation of a client.

Rule 1.7 Conflict of Interest: Current Clients

(a) Except as provided in paragraph (b), a lawyer shall not represent a client if the representation involves a concurrent conflict of interest. A concurrent conflict of interest exists if:

(1) the representation of one client will be directly adverse to another client; or

(2) there is a significant risk that the representation of one or more clients will be materially limited by the lawyer's responsibilities to another client, a former client or a third person or by a personal interest of the lawyer.

(b) Notwithstanding the existence of a concurrent conflict of interest under paragraph (a), a lawyer may represent a client if:

(1) the lawyer reasonably believes that the lawyer will be able to provide competent and diligent representation to each affected client;

(2) the representation is not prohibited by law;

(3) the representation does not involve the assertion of a claim by one client against another client represented by the lawyer in the same litigation or other proceeding before a tribunal; and

(4) each affected client gives informed consent, confirmed in writing.

***

Rule 1.9 Duties to Former Clients

(a) A lawyer who has formerly represented a client in a matter shall not thereafter represent another person in the same or a substantially related matter in which that person's interests are materially adverse to the interests of the former client unless the former client gives informed consent, confirmed in writing.

(b) A lawyer shall not knowingly represent a person in the same or a substantially related matter in which a firm with which the lawyer formerly was associated had previously represented a client:

(1) whose interests are materially adverse to that person; and

(2) about whom the lawyer had acquired information protected by Rule 1.6 . . . that is material to the matter; unless the former client gives informed consent, confirmed in writing.

***

Rule 1.10 Imputation of Conflicts of Interest: General Rule

(a) While lawyers are associated in a firm, none of them shall knowingly represent a client when any one of them practicing alone would be prohibited from doing so by Rules 1.7 or 1.9, unless

(1) the prohibition is based on a personal interest of the disqualified lawyer and does not present a significant risk of materially limiting the representation of the client by the remaining lawyers in the firm; or

(2) the prohibition is based upon Rule 1.9(a) or (b) and arises out of the disqualified lawyer's association with a prior firm, and

(i) the disqualified lawyer is timely screened from any participation in the matter and is apportioned no part of the fee therefrom;

(ii) written notice is promptly given to any affected former client to enable the former client to ascertain compliance with the provisions of this Rule, which shall include a description of the screening procedures employed; a statement of the firm's and of the screened lawyer's compliance with these Rules; a statement that review may be available before a tribunal; and an agreement by the firm to respond promptly to any written inquiries or objections by the former client about the screening procedures; and

(iii) certifications of compliance with these Rules and with the screening procedures are provided to the former client by the screened lawyer and by a partner of the firm, at reasonable intervals upon the former client's written request and upon termination of the screening procedures.

Franklin Ethics Opinion 2015-212

Ten lawyers are forming a new law firm in the state of Franklin. Each of the lawyers has, until recently, been a partner at a major law firm. All of them were at different firms, and many of those firms had several offices. In establishing the new firm, the lawyers want to properly assess potential conflicts of interest and thus determine their obligations regarding clients of their former firms. Specifically, they ask the following three questions:

1) Under Rule 1.9(a) of the Franklin Rules of Professional Conduct, how does a lawyer determine whether a matter is "substantially related" to another matter?

2) How do the Rules of Professional Conduct deal with lawyers who move from one firm to another firm?

3) How do the Rules of Professional Conduct treat a law firm with offices in multiple states?

Question One. Under Rule 1.9(a) of the Franklin Rules of Professional Conduct, how does a lawyer determine whether a matter is "substantially related" to another matter?

A lawyer has always been prohibited from using confidential information that he or she has obtained from a client against that client. But because this prohibition has not seemed enough by itself to make clients feel secure about reposing confidences in lawyers, the Rules have added a further prohibition: a lawyer may not represent an adversary of his or her former client if the subject matter of the two representations is "substantially related." A substantial relationship exists when the lawyer *could* have obtained confidential information in the first representation that would be relevant in the second representation. It is immaterial whether the lawyer actually obtained such information and used it against the former client, or whether—if the lawyer is a firm rather than an individual practitioner—different people in the firm handled the two matters and scrupulously avoided discussing them. The reason that the disqualification occurs regardless of whether the lawyer actually obtained confidential information is practical: conducting a detailed factual inquiry into whether confidences had actually been revealed would likely compromise the confidences themselves.

In addition, the "substantial relationship" test is in keeping with the profession's aspiration to avoid the appearance of impropriety. For a law firm to represent one client today, and the client's adversary tomorrow in a closely related matter, creates an unsavory appearance of conflict of interest that is difficult to dispel in the eyes of the lay public—or for that matter the bench and bar. Clients will not share confidences with lawyers whom they distrust and will not trust firms that switch sides.

Question Two. How do the Rules of Professional Conduct deal with lawyers who move from one firm to another firm?

Rule 1.9 itself removes some of the harshness of the "substantial relationship" test when a lawyer moves from one firm to another. "A lawyer shall not knowingly represent a person in the same or a substantially related matter in which a firm with which the lawyer formerly was associated had previously represented a client: (1) whose interests are materially adverse to that person; and (2) about whom the lawyer had acquired information protected by Rule 1.6 . . . that is material to the matter." Thus the new firm may represent a client with materially adverse interests to the client of the moving lawyer's old firm so long as the lawyer did not *actually* acquire confidential information. Even if the lawyer acquired confidential information, Rule 1.10 allows the law firm to continue representation of the client so long as the moving lawyer is screened from all contact with the matter. In order to properly screen, the lawyer must be denied access to all digital and physical files relating to the client and/or the matter. All digital files must be password protected and the screened lawyer must not have the password. All physical files must be under lock and the screened lawyer must not have the key. In addition, all lawyers in the firm must be admonished that they cannot speak with or communicate in any way with the screened lawyer about the matter. Finally the lawyer cannot receive any compensation resulting from representation in the matter from which she or he is being screened. Screening must take place as soon as possible, but in no case may it occur after the screened lawyer has had any contact with information about the matter from which he or she is being screened.

In addition, Rule 1.10 requires that the law firm promptly give written notice to any affected former client in order to enable the former client to ascertain compliance with the provisions of the Rule. This notice shall include a description of the screening procedures employed; a statement of the firm's and of the screened lawyer's compliance with these Rules; a

In re Ace Chemical

statement that review may be available before a tribunal; and an agreement by the firm to respond promptly to any written inquiries or objections by the former client about the screening procedures.

Question Three. How do the Rules of Professional Conduct treat a law firm with offices in multiple states?

A confidence is defined by Rule 1.6 as "information relating to the representation." This is intended to be applied broadly. It includes anything that the lawyer learns that has any bearing on the matter in which the lawyer is representing the client. Even information that is publicly available is confidential if it meets the definition in Rule 1.6. The Franklin Rules of Professional Conduct presume that confidences are shared by members of a law firm. This is why Rule 1.10 presumptively imputes a conflict of one member of a firm to the entire firm. Especially in these days of telecommuting, electronic files, and multi-state transactions, the imputation of Rule 1.10 applies to all members of the law firm, regardless of the office in which they work. Thus the conflict of one member of the firm is imputed to the entire firm—every office of that firm, regardless of the number of offices the firm maintains.

Hooper Manufacturing, Inc. v. Carlisle Flooring, Inc.
Franklin Supreme Court (2002)

In this action, Carlisle Flooring, Inc., has filed a complaint alleging that Hooper Manufacturing, Inc., has interfered with Carlisle's ability to contract with other manufacturers that produce the wax necessary for the creation of Carlisle's hardwood floors. Carlisle has a contract with Hooper, and for the last 10 years, Carlisle has bought all of its wax from Hooper. In its complaint, Carlisle alleges that Hooper has recently raised its prices for wax to the point that Carlisle can no longer produce hardwoods at a competitive price. In addition, Carlisle alleges that it sought out other wax producers but was told by each of them that Hooper would not allow them to sell to Carlisle.

The case is in the early stages of discovery, and Carlisle has filed a motion to disqualify Hooper's counsel, the venerable law firm of Klein and Wallace (K&W). The trial court denied the motion to disqualify, and Carlisle filed an interlocutory appeal to the Franklin Court of Appeal. The Court of Appeal reversed the trial court, and Hooper appeals.

According to affidavits filed by Carlisle, attorneys from K&W work as lobbyists for the professional trade association to which Carlisle belongs. Hooper counters that the lobbying organization is distinct from its members. Thus, according to Hooper, K&W should not be disqualified as its counsel.

Lobbying is an activity in which attorneys often engage. For purposes of determining whether a lawyer previously represented or is currently representing a client, we will take for granted that lobbying constitutes representation by an attorney. The harder question here is whether K&W's representation of the trade association is tantamount to representation of a member of that trade association.

The first issue we must address is what law to apply to this case. Both parties have cited the Franklin Rules of Professional Conduct. We acknowledge that the Rules of Professional Conduct are only intended to govern the regulation of lawyers. They are thus not binding on courts when faced with questions other than attorney discipline. Nonetheless, it would be foolish for courts to ignore those Rules when they are applicable to a lawyer's conduct. In the absence of any overriding policy considerations, courts in this state will be guided by the Rules of Professional Conduct, in addition to any other applicable law, in determining motions for disqualification based on conflicts of interest.

In re Ace Chemical

Since this case involves a concurrent conflict of interest, we look to Rule 1.7 of the Franklin Rules of Professional Conduct.

K&W is representing Hooper in direct opposition to Carlisle. The question thus posed is whether the representation of the trade association to which Carlisle belongs is equivalent to the representation of Carlisle itself.

In making this determination, the Court must be guided by the facts of the particular situation. The critical question one must ask is whether the trade association member provided confidential information to the lawyer that was necessary for the lawyer's representation of the trade association. If the answer is "yes," then the representation of the trade association is equivalent to representation of the member. However, even if the answer to that question is "no," the representation might still be deemed equivalent if the lawyer advised the member of the trade association that any and all information provided to the lawyer would be treated as confidential.

Confidential information is any information related to the representation of the client and learned during the course of the representation. Franklin Rule of Professional Conduct 1.6. The definition is very broad and includes all information, even publicly available information, that the lawyer discovers or gleans while representing the client. The information must, however, be related to the representation. A client cannot protect extraneous information simply by telling his or her lawyer. A client may have many conversations with the lawyer about any number of matters which have no relevance to the representation for which the lawyer was retained. These conversations cannot later be used by the client to prevent the lawyer from representing a party who is adverse to the client.

In this case, Carlisle, as a member of the trade association, provided only publicly available information to K&W lawyers for their work of lobbying on behalf of the trade association. While information related to the representation is normally treated as confidential if it meets the other requirements of Rule 1.6, we hold that a member's provision of publicly available information to counsel for the trade association does not, in and of itself, disqualify counsel for the trade association from representing a client who is adverse to the member.

We must then ask whether the lawyers for the trade association (here K&W) advised the member (here Carlisle) that information provided to the lawyers for the trade association would be treated as confidential. Affidavits submitted by attorneys from K&W state that they informed the members of the trade association, including Carlisle, that the information provided to K&W and in support of the representation of the trade association would not be kept confidential.

Based on the fact that Carlisle provided only publicly available information to K&W in its representation of the trade association and that K&W told Carlisle that any information provided to K&W would not be kept confidential, we hold that representation of the trade association is not equivalent to representation of Carlisle. Thus, K&W's representation of Hooper is not directly adverse to a former client (i.e., the trade association).

But our analysis does not end there. Under Rule 1.7(a)(2), we must next ask whether representation of both Hooper and the trade association will materially limit the firm's ability to represent either client.

The critical factual inquiry is whether an employee of Carlisle had an important position in the trade association and, in that position, worked closely with the lawyers for the trade association. The affidavits filed by Carlisle state that Carlisle's chief executive officer, Nina Carlisle, serves as one of three members of the trade association's legislative and policy committee. In this capacity, Nina Carlisle works closely with K&W attorneys, developing legislative strategy and directing K&W lawyers on legislative tactics. The affidavit notes that Nina Carlisle meets with these attorneys in person and communicates with them via email every day during the legislative session, and an average of every two weeks during the rest of the year.

Under Rule 1.7(a)(2), this contact between K&W attorneys and Carlisle's chief executive officer materially limits K&W's ability to represent both Hooper and the trade association. The language of Rule 1.7(a)(2) refers to the "personal interest of the lawyer." This standard requires us to focus on the nature and extent of the relationship between the attorneys and Carlisle's representatives. The closer and more frequent the contact and the more active the role of the member representative in directing the lawyer, the greater the risk that the lawyer's ability to engage in concurrent representation is "materially limited." In this case, Carlisle's CEO plays an active role in directing K&W's attorneys and has frequent contact with them. This creates a substantial risk that the K&W attorneys' personal interests would materially limit the concurrent representation.

Carlisle's motion to disqualify Hooper's counsel should have been granted. The order of the Court of Appeal is AFFIRMED and the matter remanded to the trial court.

February 2017
MPT-2 File:
In re Guardianship of Henry King

Sibley and Wallace Law Office, P.C.
232 Cable Car Road
Dry Creek, Franklin 33808

MEMORANDUM

To: Examinee
From: Eleanor Wallace
Date: February 21, 2017
Re: Guardianship of Henry King

We represent Ruth King Maxwell in an adult guardianship case in which she seeks to be named as the guardian for her father, Henry King. Ruth's brother, Noah King, opposes Ruth's petition to become guardian. Noah is asking the court to appoint him as guardian instead.

In 2013, Henry King learned that he had a condition that might leave him incompetent to manage his affairs. At that time, Henry executed an advance health-care directive naming Noah as his health-care agent and a durable power of attorney giving Noah the power to make financial decisions for him. Those documents also nominated Noah to become Henry's guardian if that later proved necessary.

Since then, Ruth has become increasingly concerned about Noah's handling of his authority over their father's finances and medical care. Her concerns came to a head after a series of events which led to conflict with her brother and caused her to seek our representation.

We filed a petition to have Ruth named as guardian for Henry. There was an evidentiary hearing on Ruth's petition last week; relevant portions of the transcript are attached. The court ruled that Henry's nomination of Noah as prospective guardian in 2013 was valid at the time it was made. It also ruled that Henry is now incompetent, cannot manage his affairs, and needs a guardian. All counsel (Henry's court-appointed attorney, Noah's attorney, and our office on behalf of Ruth) have been instructed to submit proposed Findings of Fact and Conclusions of Law. Our proposed Findings and Conclusions should persuade the court that (1) it has authority to override the nomination, and (2) Ruth should be appointed guardian.

Please draft our proposed Findings of Fact and Conclusions of Law to submit to the court. Be sure to review and follow our office guidelines on drafting proposed Findings of Fact and Conclusions of Law so that the court will be more likely to adopt them and rule in our favor.

Sibley and Wallace Law Office, P.C.

OFFICE MEMORANDUM

To:	All attorneys
From:	Managing partner
Date:	March 4, 2016
Re:	Preparation of proposed Findings of Fact and Conclusions of Law

In bench trials, trial courts usually require the parties to file proposed Findings of Fact and Conclusions of Law. Findings of Fact are the court's final factual determinations based on the evidence presented. Conclusions of Law are the court's legal determinations when it applies the law to its factual findings. A judge will often adopt one party's proposed Findings of Fact and Conclusions of Law. It is thus critical that we draft our proposed Findings and Conclusions so that the court will adopt them. This memo states our firm's conventions for this kind of filing.

All proposed Findings of Fact on all issues are grouped together in one section under the heading "Findings of Fact." They are then followed by all Conclusions of Law on all issues grouped together under the heading "Conclusions of Law."

Each section should consist of separate, sequentially numbered paragraphs. In general, each "Finding" or "Conclusion" should consist of one sentence stating a single fact or legal conclusion. Use the following conventions:

(1) *Proposed Findings of Fact:* Set forth those facts that the testimony and other evidence support and that are necessary to our claim or defense. Think about how to sequence and structure your Findings to lead to the legal conclusions that you would like the court to reach. This will help you to identify the facts that support your legal conclusions and to put them in the most persuasive order. Be sure that the Findings accurately reflect the record. (Our paralegal will add citations to the record as appropriate.)

The Findings should cover all the relevant facts, including those *not* favorable to our position. For those Findings that are unfavorable to our client's position, frame them in a way that minimizes their effect.

Omit any facts not relevant to the Conclusions of Law.

(2) *Proposed Conclusions of Law:* Concisely state the legal conclusions necessary to support our claim or defense. Organize this section by first stating general rules and then applying these rules to specific facts from the Findings of Fact. Include citations to the legal authorities that support the relevant conclusions.

Your proposed Findings of Fact and Conclusions of Law, while drafted to favor your client, should not be explicitly argumentative. *In re Guardianship of Martinez* (Fr. Ct. App. 2009) contains a trial court's Findings of Fact and Conclusions of Law that the appellate court approved as an example of how to effectively write proposed Findings and Conclusions.

Contrast the example in *Martinez* with the example below, which states too many facts in one paragraph and does not present them in a coherent or persuasive sequence:

1. Testator died on July 3, 2015, and Petitioner submitted Testator's will for probate on July 10, 2015. Testator executed a will on May 6, 2003. The will submitted on July 10, 2015, is identical to the one executed on May 6, 2003. This will contained signature lines for Testator and for two witnesses; Testator signed on the line designated for his signature. One of the witness lines was empty.

The following represents a more appropriate draft of these Findings of Fact:

1. Testator executed a will on May 6, 2003.

2. The will contained a signature line for Testator, signed by him.

3. The will contained two signature lines for witnesses, only one of which contained a signature.

4. Testator died on July 3, 2015.

5. Petitioner submitted this will for probate on July 10, 2015.

Transcript of Testimony of Ruth King Maxwell
February 13, 2017

Att'y Wallace: Could you state your name?

Ruth Maxwell: Ruth King Maxwell.

Wallace: Your address?

Maxwell: 4465 East Canyon Avenue, Dry Creek, Franklin.

Wallace: What is your relationship to Henry King?

Maxwell: I am his daughter.

Wallace: Could you tell the court why you brought this case?

Maxwell: I want to be named guardian for my father and to keep my brother from becoming guardian. I'm worried about how my brother has treated my father.

Wallace: Your brother already has authority to act for your father, is that right?

Maxwell: Yes. He has my father's power of attorney for financial matters and is his health-care agent.

Wallace: Tell the court how that came about.

Maxwell: My father is 74 years old now. Our mother died in 2012; a year after that, he started to have trouble with his memory and began to lose his attention span. He consulted his doctor, who referred him to a neurologist and a psychiatrist. He was told that he had early signs of dementia.

When that happened, Dad set up arrangements for his health care and finances if he did become incompetent. At that time, I lived in a different state. My brother, Noah, lived here in Dry Creek. We all talked it over and agreed that it made sense for my father to give Noah the authority to make health-care and financial decisions for him and to nominate Noah as his prospective guardian. Noah was closer and could respond more quickly.

So Dad signed an advance directive and a power of attorney and in both documents nominated Noah as his prospective guardian. Dad was doing well then.

Wallace: Your honor, we have stipulated to the validity of those documents that were signed May 20, 2013. Ms. Maxwell, what happened then?

Maxwell: For a while, my father was fine. Then, about two years ago, he began to get worse. Eventually, he wouldn't go out of the house; he would sit in his favorite chair and stare out the window or at a book or at the TV. Sometimes he would talk with one of us, but he made less and less sense. He wasn't upset, but he was very different from the way he had been before. Not as sharp or funny. It has been like that for nearly two years. His doctor tells us that his condition is permanent. I know that he can't take care of himself, and I'm worried about my brother's ability to take care of Dad.

Wallace: Why are you worried about your brother?

Maxwell: About a year and a half ago, I came back to Dry Creek to visit my father. When I talked with him, I saw that he was favoring his right arm, leaning away from that side in his chair. I asked him what had happened, and he said, "Nothing." I insisted, and he eventually said that he had fallen in the shower, but that everything was okay. I asked him to show me his arm, and he finally did. It was bruised up and down the back of his arm.

I talked with Noah, and he said that he knew about the fall, but that Dad hadn't really complained that much about it, so he didn't think it was much of a problem. He agreed to take Dad to the doctor, and I went with him. The arm was just bruised, badly, but there were no broken bones, thank God.

Wallace: What did you do next?

Maxwell: I had it out with my brother a few days later. He said that I shouldn't worry, that he knew how to take care of Dad, and that I should just stay out of it. He got pretty angry. I couldn't figure out why, so I let it go.

Wallace: What happened after that?

Maxwell: In August 2016, I was able to transfer to a nearby office for my company. I started to spend two or three evenings a week with my father. This is when I found out that my father had broken his wrist in June when he tripped over a rug in his bedroom. Noah did not tell me about this until I confronted him about it after I had moved back to Dry Creek.

Wallace: What else did you notice about your father's condition?

Maxwell: I began to notice that Noah wasn't buying any food for him. The refrigerator was always nearly empty, just skim milk and a little bread, and there was only canned soup in the cupboards. I started buying food and cooking for him, whenever I could. Eventually, I hired someone to shop and cook for him.

Wallace:	What did you learn about the state of your father's finances?
Maxwell:	One day I arrived at Dad's house and found an overdue notice from the electric company. I called the company, and they said that they would only deal with Noah. So I called Noah, and he said that he had missed a few months' payments but not to worry about it.
Wallace:	What did you do then?
Maxwell:	I decided to look through Dad's bank statements and his bills. Noah kept all of that at Dad's house. It turns out that Noah had not been paying a lot of different bills. Nothing was too far behind, but the electric bill wasn't the only one where he had received threatening letters. Some were from Dad's doctor, who was about to send his account to collection.
	I also saw that Dad had been spending a lot of money. His checking account statement showed a lot of charges from Amazon and other online retailers, but I didn't see anything new around the house. When I asked Dad, he said that he wanted to give his friends gifts, to make sure that they came to visit him. All told, for the two months that I reviewed that day, he had spent roughly $2,200 online. Dad only gets about $2,500 a month between his pension and his Social Security.
Wallace:	Did you talk with your brother?
Maxwell:	I confronted Noah the same day. He got very angry and told me to let it go . . . not so nicely, I'm afraid. He said that he had known about the online purchases and that it was hard to keep Dad from doing what he wanted. He said that it was those purchases that made it hard to keep up with the bills. Noah said that he had all of these other bills under control and that nothing would get shut off. I said that wasn't good enough. We had a bad argument.
Wallace:	No further questions.

Transcript of Testimony of Noah King
February 13, 2017

Att'y Wallace:	Could you state your name?
King:	Noah King.
Wallace:	What is your relationship to the proposed ward Henry King?
King:	I am his son. I am also his health-care agent and have his durable power of attorney.

. . .

Wallace:	I have here several bank statements. These are your father's, aren't they?
King:	Yes, these are my father's bank statements for the last 12 months.
Wallace:	How do you know about them?
King:	I manage my father's finances, so I see these every month.
Wallace:	Don't these statements show a series of purchases from Amazon and eBay?
King:	Yes, they do. About a year ago, I saw that my father had started to buy things online. I checked his accounts and saw that he had asked to ship these items to various friends. When I asked my father about it, he said that he wanted to make those gifts because he felt that he owed his friends favors and because he wanted them to come visit him. I didn't feel comfortable calling his friends to ask for these things back. I also didn't have the heart to tell him to stop. So I just let it go on.
Wallace:	Your father is on a fixed income, isn't he?
King:	Yes, he is. He gets $2,515 per month, between his Social Security and his pension.
Wallace:	These charges total about $9,000 over the past 12 months, isn't that correct?
King:	Yes, it is.
Wallace:	In some months, he charged as much as $1,200, isn't that so?
King:	Yes, that's right. After that month, I did ask him to stop it and tried to explain how it was hurting him. But he didn't seem to understand.
Wallace:	You didn't take any other steps to stop the spending, did you?
King:	No, I didn't. Like I said, I didn't think it was my place to keep him from spending his money the way he wanted. And he has enough money.

. . .

In re Guardianship of Henry King

Wallace:	I'm showing you medical records concerning your father's treatment over the last year. You're not familiar with these, are you?
King:	Not with these records, no.
Wallace:	Are you familiar with your father's medical condition over the past year?
King:	Of course I am.
Wallace:	I want to ask you about his condition on June 22, 2016. Your father broke a bone in his wrist, isn't that so?
King:	Yes, but it was an accident. I went by one evening to check on Dad, and he complained of being a little stiff, but he didn't seem in all that much pain. The next day at lunch, a neighbor called me and said that I should come look at him, that his wrist was swollen. I came over, and she was right. I took him to the emergency room right away. I watched them put on a cast. They discharged him that night.
Wallace:	You don't know how this happened, do you?
King:	I wasn't there and he wouldn't tell me at the time. I think he was embarrassed. I later learned that he had tripped on a rug. His wrist is completely healed now.
Wallace:	You didn't tell your sister about it at the time, did you?
King:	No, I didn't. I just didn't think she needed to know. I knew she would get upset with me and blame me for it.

. . .

February 2017
MPT-2 Library:
In re Guardianship of Henry King

In re Guardianship of Henry King

Excerpts from Franklin Guardianship Code

§ 400 Definition of Guardian

"Guardian" means an individual appointed by a court to manage the income and assets and provide for the essential requirements for health and safety and personal needs of someone found incompetent.

§ 401 Order of Preferences for Appointment of Guardian for an Adult

(a) The court shall appoint as guardian that individual who will best serve the interest of the adult, considering the order of preferences set forth in this Code section. The court may disregard an individual who has preference and appoint an individual who has a lower preference or no preference, provided, however, that the court may disregard the preference listed in paragraph (1) of subsection (b) of this Code section only upon good cause shown.

(b) Individuals who are eligible have preference in the following order:

(1) The individual last nominated by the adult in accordance with the provisions of subsection (c) of this Code section;

(2) The spouse of the adult;

(3) An adult child of the adult;

. . .

(c) At any time prior to the appointment of a guardian, an adult may nominate in writing an individual to serve as that adult's guardian should the adult be judicially determined to be in need of a guardian, and that nomination shall be given preference as described in this Code, provided:

(1) it expressly identifies the individual who shall serve as guardian; and

(2) it is signed and acknowledged by the adult in the presence of two witnesses who sign in the adult's presence.

§ 402 Revocation or Suspension of Guardian

Upon petition of an interested party or upon its own motion, whenever it appears to the court that good cause may exist to revoke or suspend the guardian or to impose sanctions, the court shall investigate the allegations and may require such accounting as the court deems appropriate. After investigation, the court may, in the court's discretion, revoke or suspend the guardian, impose any other sanction or sanctions as the court deems appropriate, or issue any other order as in the court's judgment is appropriate under the circumstances of the case.

In re Guardianship of Henry King

Matter of Selena J.
Franklin Court of Appeal (2011)

This appeal presents an all-too-familiar scenario in guardianship cases, in which one sibling claims a breach of fiduciary duty by another sibling who has been nominated as the proposed guardian of a parent.

The proposed ward, Selena J., is 81 years old and lives with her daughter Naomi (a registered nurse). In 2008, Selena executed an advance directive naming Naomi as her health- care agent, and a durable financial power of attorney naming Naomi as her agent to manage her finances. Both documents nominated Naomi as Selena's guardian in the event of a later guardianship.

The petitioner, Michael, is Selena's son. In 2010, he petitioned to become his mother's guardian. He claimed that Naomi had failed to use the power of attorney to manage their mother's assets after Selena's mental decline became apparent. He also claimed that Naomi had failed to provide care for their mother, ignoring signs of mental decline and failing to seek medical care for various illnesses that their mother had suffered.

Naomi responded and asked the trial court to name her as guardian. She requested that the court give priority to Selena's expressed wishes, as required by Franklin Guardianship Code § 401(b)(1).

After discovery, Naomi moved for summary judgment, which the trial court granted. The court noted that neither party contested Selena's competency at the time that she nominated Naomi, and found that the nominations had complied with the formalities laid out in Franklin Guardianship Code § 401(c). Both parties conceded that Selena presently needed a guardian. The trial court ruled as a matter of law that it had to honor Selena's wishes. It appointed Naomi as guardian. Michael appealed.

We begin with the proposition that the law recognizes and protects an individual's right to make decisions about her medical and financial affairs. An advance directive permits the individual to specify the medical care she would prefer to receive and to name a "health-care agent" to make those decisions when she lacks the competency to do so. A durable financial power of attorney gives the individual the right to name an agent to handle financial matters when she lacks the competency to do so. Both documents create a fiduciary relationship. Both a health-care agent and the holder of a durable financial power have a legal obligation to act in the principal's best interest and to avoid self-dealing.

These documents can raise difficult questions when someone later petitions for the appointment of a guardian. Franklin law has long held that a later guardianship overrides an earlier grant of authority through either an advance directive or a power of attorney. The authority granted to the guardian supersedes any conflicting authority granted to the agent under either document. *Matter of Collins* (Fr. Sup. Ct. 2002).

At the same time, the law also permits an individual to nominate a person (including the individual's agent) as a possible future guardian, provided that the nomination is in writing and complies with certain formal requirements. Franklin Guardianship Code § 401(c). Should this happen, the statute accords the person so nominated the highest preference for appointment as guardian. *Id.* § 401(b)(1).

The trial court correctly relied on these statutes in concluding that Selena had named Naomi as her preferred guardian. However, the trial court erred in appointing Naomi as a matter of law.

The statute does not make the nomination of a preferred guardian binding in a later guardianship proceeding. The statute states that a court in a guardianship proceeding "may disregard an individual who has preference and appoint an individual who has a lower preference or no preference." *Id.* § 401(a). The statute makes clear that a court may disregard an advance nomination of a guardian, but "only upon good cause shown." *Id.* This language creates a preference in favor of the nominated person. But this preference may be overcome with a sufficient factual showing of good cause.

In this case, the trial court erred in failing to consider Michael's evidence that good cause existed not to appoint his sister as guardian. Michael's affidavits indicate evidence that Naomi had neglected her mother's financial affairs and that she had also neglected to arrange for needed medical care for her mother. Without assessing the persuasive effect of this evidence, at the very least it creates an issue of fact on whether "good cause" exists to override Selena's nomination of Naomi.

No Franklin case has yet ruled on the "good cause" standard as it relates to overturning a *proposed* ward's previously stated preference for a guardian. As noted, the trial court failed to discuss the available evidence as it related to good cause.

In re Guardianship of Henry King

The trial court on remand should apply a good cause standard to determine whether Selena's nomination of Naomi should be honored. This court has previously analyzed good cause in the context of the *removal* of a court-appointed guardian. Franklin Guardianship Code § 402; *In re Guardianship of Martinez* (Fr. Ct. App. 2009). The same good cause standard applies in this context: a court may refuse to appoint a proposed guardian when that person's previous actions would have constituted a breach of a fiduciary duty had the person been serving as a guardian. Such conduct is of special concern when that person has actually served as a fiduciary for the proposed ward under an advance directive or power of attorney.

For these reasons, we reverse the trial court's judgment and remand the case for proceedings consistent with this opinion.

In re Guardianship of Martinez
Franklin Court of Appeal (2009)

Evelyn Waters appeals from a judgment against her in connection with expenditures that she made while guardian of her niece, Marlena Martinez, who is an incapacitated adult. Evelyn also appeals from an order removing her as Marlena's guardian.

A trial court has authority to remove a guardian for good cause pursuant to Franklin Guardianship Code § 402. That statute gives the trial court discretion to determine whether the available information establishes good cause. *Id.* That statute also permits the trial court to "issue any other order as in the court's judgment is appropriate under the circumstances of the case."

We will affirm the trial court's exercise of discretion unless its decision is clearly erroneous. In this case, the trial court issued written Findings of Fact and Conclusions of Law that specified the basis for its decision. These Findings and Conclusions, which we adopt, state as follows:

FINDINGS OF FACT:

1. Evelyn Waters has served as guardian of her niece, Marlena Martinez, since November 2005.

2. Marlena was born in May 1984 and suffered significant injuries at birth that left her profoundly disabled.

3. In 1988, a medical malpractice action arising from complications during Marlena's birth led to a substantial settlement that resulted in an annuity to Marlena of over $8,000 per month.

4. In 2005, Marlena's last surviving parent died, after which a trial court appointed Evelyn as Marlena's guardian.

5. Since Evelyn's appointment, Marlena has lived with Evelyn, who has served as Marlena's primary caregiver.

6. In July 2006, Evelyn purchased a house for herself in her own name, using $25,000 in funds from Marlena's estate for the down payment.

7. In August 2006, Marlena moved into the house with Evelyn.

In re Guardianship of Henry King

8. In November 2006, Evelyn submitted her first annual report as guardian, which described the home purchase and mentioned several other expenditures without providing a detailed accounting.

9. This first annual report included expenditures during the previous year for an automobile, for mortgage payments, and for $2,500 per month to Evelyn as "caregiver's salary."

10. Despite repeated requests from this court, Evelyn did not submit more detailed reports or any statement justifying these expenses.

11. In May 2007, this court appointed counsel to represent Marlena.

12. In June 2007, Marlena's counsel petitioned this court to remove Evelyn as guardian and to require her to reimburse Marlena's estate for any expenses not specifically used to provide for Marlena's care.

13. This court granted the motion and appointed Marlena's uncle, Joseph Sears, as guardian to succeed Evelyn.

14. On July 30, 2007, Evelyn filed her final accounting about Marlena's estate. Both Marlena's counsel and the new guardian objected to that accounting.

15. This court has reviewed both of the reports filed by Evelyn, covering the period from December 2005 to June 2007. During this period, Evelyn spent over $137,000 from Marlena's monthly annuity payments.

16. Evelyn has sufficiently documented that $55,000 in expenditures, including the salary paid to Evelyn, was necessary for Marlena's individual needs, and that an additional $35,000 reflected Marlena's prorated share of household outlays (such as mortgage payments, real estate taxes, moving expenses, groceries, utilities, and car payments).

17. Evelyn has provided no documentation to justify the remaining $47,000 expended from Marlena's monthly annuity.

18. The $25,000 down payment for the house purchased in Evelyn's name (*see* ¶ 6) was cash from the sale of investments in Marlena's estate.

CONCLUSIONS OF LAW:

1. A guardian has the responsibility to apply the income and principal of the ward's estate "so far as necessary for the comfort and suitable support of the ward." *Nonnio v. George* (Fr. Sup. Ct. 1932).

2. A guardian acts in a fiduciary capacity toward the ward, which requires the guardian not to expend the ward's funds so as to benefit the guardian. *See In Re Samuels* (Fr. Sup. Ct. 2002).

3. The law does not require approval of expenditures in advance, but a trial court may disapprove of expenditures after they have been made. *Id.*

4. Good cause exists to remove a guardian when a guardian breaches her fiduciary duty by using the ward's funds to benefit the guardian. *Nonnio v. George.*

5. As guardian for Marlena, Evelyn had a fiduciary duty to use Marlena's funds for Marlena's comfort and suitable support and not to benefit herself as guardian. *Nonnio v. George; In Re Samuels.*

6. Those expenditures totaling $55,000 that directly benefitted Marlena and those totaling $35,000 for Marlena's pro rata share of household expenses did not breach Evelyn's fiduciary obligations as guardian. *Nonnio v. George.*

7. All other expenditures benefitted Evelyn personally and breached her fiduciary obligations as guardian. *Id.*

8. The use of $25,000 from the sale of investments from Marlena's estate to purchase a house in Evelyn's name also breached Evelyn's fiduciary obligations as guardian. *Id.*

9. These breaches constitute good cause for revoking Evelyn's authority as guardian for Marlena. *Id.*

DISCUSSION

On appeal from this order, Evelyn claims that the trial court abused its discretion in removing her as guardian of Marlena. She insists that in managing Marlena's estate, her "primary goal" was to make Marlena's life "as comfortable and pleasurable as possible." Evelyn contends that the trial court's requirement that she repay Marlena's estate for all undocumented expenses punished her for insignificant errors in reporting.

A guardian owes a fiduciary duty to her ward. This duty obligates the guardian to act in the best interest of the ward and not to use her decision-making authority to benefit the guardian. A guardian can breach this duty by action or neglect, if the action or neglect harms the ward. A fiduciary can harm the ward through mismanagement of finances, neglect of the ward's physical well-being, or similar actions. A fiduciary can also be held accountable if she uses her decision-making authority to benefit the guardian at the ward's expense.

The Findings of Fact belie Evelyn's argument that the trial court punished her for reporting errors. The Findings demonstrate that, even if Marlena received excellent care, Evelyn almost completely disregarded her fiduciary obligation to preserve and manage the estate to provide for Marlena's needs. Instead, Evelyn drew upon estate funds for her own support and comfort. Far from an abuse of discretion, the trial court's order carefully distinguishes between those funds used for Marlena's needs, those funds used for her fair share of common expenses, and those funds for the use of which no justification existed. "No abuse of discretion exists where a trial court identifies clearly and specifically those facts which support its Conclusions of Law." *Nonnio.*

The trial court's decision fully accords with the applicable principles of guardianship law. It does not punish Evelyn for minor failures in accounting. Instead, it uses the court's statutory authority to "issue any other order as in the court's judgment is appropriate under the circumstances of the case." Franklin Guardianship Code § 402.

This court acknowledges that caring for Marlena at home may have been an exceptionally expensive undertaking. But that expense did not relieve Evelyn of the obligation of establishing which expenses were necessary and related to Marlena's individual needs. The trial court's Findings of Fact established that Evelyn treated the estate not as Marlena's separate funds to be used for Marlena's needs, but as a personal asset available to pay for Evelyn's food, housing, and other personal expenses.

Judgment affirmed.

July 2016 MPTs
In re Whirley
Nash v. Franklin Department of Revenue

July 2016
MPTs

www.ncbex.org

National Conference of Bar Examiners
302 South Bedford Street | Madison, WI 53703-3622
Phone: 608-280-8550 | Fax: 608-280-8552 | TDD: 608-661-1275
e-mail: contact@ncbex.org

Contents

Preface

The Multistate Performance Test (MPT) is developed by the National Conference of Bar Examiners (NCBE). This publication includes the items and Point Sheets from the July 2016 MPT. The instructions for the test appear on page iii.

The MPT Point Sheets describe the factual and legal points encompassed within the lawyering tasks to be completed. They outline the possible issues and points that might be addressed by an examinee. They are provided to the user jurisdictions to assist graders in grading the examination by identifying the issues and suggesting the resolution of the problem contemplated by the drafters.

For more information about the MPT, including a list of skills tested, visit the NCBE website at www.ncbex.org.

Description of the MPT

The MPT consists of two 90-minute items and is a component of the Uniform Bar Examination (UBE). It is administered by user jurisdictions as part of the bar examination on the Tuesday before the last Wednesday in February and July of each year. User jurisdictions may select one or both items to include as part of their bar examinations. (Jurisdictions that administer the UBE use two MPTs.)

The materials for each MPT include a File and a Library. The File consists of source documents containing all the facts of the case. The specific assignment the examinee is to complete is described in a memorandum from a supervising attorney. The File might also include transcripts of interviews, depositions, hearings or trials, pleadings, correspondence, client documents, contracts, newspaper articles, medical records, police reports, or lawyer's notes. Relevant as well as irrelevant facts are included. Facts are sometimes ambiguous, incomplete, or even conflicting. As in practice, a client's or a supervising attorney's version of events may be incomplete or unreliable. Examinees are expected to recognize when facts are inconsistent or missing and are expected to identify potential sources of additional facts.

The Library may contain cases, statutes, regulations, or rules, some of which may not be relevant to the assigned lawyering task. The examinee is expected to extract from the Library the legal principles necessary to analyze the problem and perform the task. The MPT is not a test of substantive law; the Library materials provide sufficient substantive information to complete the task.

The MPT is designed to test an examinee's ability to use fundamental lawyering skills in a realistic situation and complete a task that a beginning lawyer should be able to accomplish. The MPT is not a test of substantive knowledge. Rather, it is designed to evaluate six fundamental skills lawyers are expected to demonstrate regardless of the area of law in which the skills are applied. The MPT requires examinees to (1) sort detailed factual materials and separate relevant from irrelevant facts; (2) analyze statutory, case, and administrative materials for applicable principles of law; (3) apply the relevant law to the relevant facts in a manner likely to resolve a client's problem; (4) identify and resolve ethical dilemmas, when present; (5) communicate effectively in writing; and (6) complete a lawyering task within time constraints. These skills are tested by requiring examinees to perform one or more of a variety of lawyering tasks. For example, examinees might be instructed to complete any of the following: a memorandum to a supervising attorney, a letter to a client, a persuasive memorandum or brief, a statement of facts, a contract provision, a will, a counseling plan, a proposal for settlement or agreement, a discovery plan, a witness examination plan, or a closing argument.

The back cover of each test booklet contains the following instructions:

You will be instructed when to begin and when to stop this test. Do not break the seal on this booklet until you are told to begin. This test is designed to evaluate your ability to handle a select number of legal authorities in the context of a factual problem involving a client.

The problem is set in the fictitious state of Franklin, in the fictitious Fifteenth Circuit of the United States. Columbia and Olympia are also fictitious states in the Fifteenth Circuit. In Franklin, the trial court of general jurisdiction is the District Court, the intermediate appellate court is the Court of Appeal, and the highest court is the Supreme Court.

You will have two kinds of materials with which to work: a File and a Library. The first document in the File is a memorandum containing the instructions for the task you are to complete. The other documents in the File contain factual information about your case and may include some facts that are not relevant.

The Library contains the legal authorities needed to complete the task and may also include some authorities that are not relevant. Any cases may be real, modified, or written solely for the purpose of this examination. If the cases appear familiar to you, do not assume that they are precisely the same as you have read before. Read them thoroughly, as if they all were new to you. You should assume that the cases were decided in the jurisdictions and on the dates shown. In citing cases from the Library, you may use abbreviations and omit page references.

Your response must be written in the answer book provided. If you are using a laptop computer to answer the questions, your jurisdiction will provide you with specific instructions. In answering this performance test, you should concentrate on the materials in the File and Library. What you have learned in law school and elsewhere provides the general background for analyzing the problem; the File and Library provide the specific materials with which you must work.

Although there are no restrictions on how you apportion your time, you should allocate approximately half your time to reading and digesting the materials and to organizing your answer before you begin writing it. You may make notes anywhere in the test materials; blank pages are provided at the end of the booklet. You may not tear pages from the question booklet.

Do not include your actual name anywhere in the work product required by the task memorandum.

This performance test will be graded on your responsiveness to the instructions regarding the task you are to complete, which are given to you in the first memorandum in the File, and on the content, thoroughness, and organization of your response.

.

July 2016
MPT-1 File:
In re Whirley

HUMPHRIES & ASSOCIATES, LLP
ATTORNEYS AT LAW
2700 MADISON AVE., SUITE 120
FRANKLIN CITY, FRANKLIN 33017

MEMORANDUM

TO: Examinee
FROM: Della Gregson, Partner
DATE: July 26, 2016
RE: Barbara Whirley matter

Our client, Barbara Whirley, is renting a house. She is a little over halfway through a one-year residential lease and has encountered several problems with the house. Ms. Whirley would prefer not to move and wants the conditions repaired. She needs to know her options under Franklin law to remedy each condition.

In Franklin, specific statutes govern the landlord-tenant relationship. *See* Franklin Civil Code § 540 *et seq.* Both landlords and tenants have certain statutory duties, in addition to any duties they may have under a written lease.

Please draft a memorandum to me analyzing and evaluating Ms. Whirley's options with regard to each of the unrepaired conditions, which are described in the attached client interview summary. If more than one option is available with regard to a specific condition, explain the potential advantages and disadvantages of each option. If an option is *not* available to Ms. Whirley with respect to a particular condition, briefly explain why. Do not include a separate statement of facts, but be sure to incorporate the relevant facts, analyze the applicable legal authorities, and explain how the facts and law affect your analysis.

HUMPHRIES & ASSOCIATES, LLP
ATTORNEYS AT LAW
2700 MADISON AVE., SUITE 120
FRANKLIN CITY, FRANKLIN 33017

MEMORANDUM TO FILE

FROM: Della Gregson, Partner
DATE: July 25, 2016
RE: Summary of interview of Barbara Whirley

Today I met with Barbara Whirley regarding her dispute with her landlord over repairs needed to the rental house where she resides. This memorandum summarizes the interview:

- In January of this year, Whirley rented a three-bedroom, two-bathroom house from Sean Spears. See attached lease.

- Whirley is the only occupant of the home, and she has a dog, Bentley. She and Spears agreed in a separate "Pet Addendum" to the lease that she was allowed to have a dog. Whirley will provide a copy of the Pet Addendum at our next meeting.

- The house has eight rooms: a kitchen, a living room, a master bedroom with bathroom, two additional bedrooms, one additional bathroom, and a laundry room. The master bathroom is accessible through the master bedroom. The second bathroom is in the hallway between the second and third bedrooms. She uses one spare bedroom as her home office and the other as a guest room for family and friends when they visit her (one or two visits per month).

- Whirley is experiencing a number of problems with the residence.

- About two months after she moved in, the toilet in the second bathroom began leaking.

- In late March, she began having problems with the outdoor sprinkler system not functioning.

- In May, she noticed a smell in the guest bedroom. The smell is coming from the carpet near the sliding glass door leading from the bedroom to the backyard. The carpet is damp, and there is a half-inch gap between the bottom of the door and the door frame. Whirley isn't sure whether the door is off its track or whether the door is too small for the door frame. She has not opened the door since she moved in. The door is currently in the closed position, but she isn't sure whether any of her houseguests may have used the door. When she discovered the gap between the door and door frame and tried to open the door, the door wouldn't budge. She has placed plastic along the door frame to try to keep outside moisture from coming in, to no avail. The carpet near the sliding door is increasingly discolored and smelly, and she has noticed mold growing around the door. The smell is so bad now that no one can use the room.

- Whirley keeps Bentley in the laundry room on weekdays while she is at work, because the laundry room door exits to the backyard and has a "doggy door" that allows Bentley to go in and out of the laundry room throughout the day. Bentley is a golden retriever, and sometimes he gets bored when Whirley is at work and chews on things. Five days ago, Whirley realized that Bentley had sneaked along the side of the washing machine next to the wall and chewed away a two-foot strip of the baseboard and areas of the wall above the baseboard. She has since moved the washing machine closer to the wall to prevent Bentley from having access to the chewed area. Since Spears allowed Whirley to have a dog at the house, she would like to have him take care of the repairs to the wall and baseboard if possible.

- Whirley has notified Spears about the toilet, sprinkler system, and guest bedroom sliding door and carpet, but he has not made any repairs. See attached emails.

- Whirley is now considering making arrangements herself to have the repairs completed. She has obtained an estimate from a handyman, a copy of which is attached.

- Whirley has paid her rent ($1,200) on time every month.

- The average cost to rent a two-bedroom house in the same area is $1,000. The average cost to rent a three-bedroom house in the area is $1,200 (what Whirley is currently paying).

- Whirley does not want to leave her home because it is close to her workplace in a desirable neighborhood with limited rental options.

RESIDENTIAL LEASE AGREEMENT

THIS AGREEMENT (the "Agreement") is made and entered into this __1st__ day of January 2016 by and between Sean Spears ("Landlord") and _Barbara Whirley_ ("Tenant"). For and in consideration of the covenants and obligations contained herein and other good and valuable consideration, the receipt and sufficiency of which is hereby acknowledged, the parties hereby agree as follows:

1. PROPERTY. Landlord owns certain real property and improvements located at 1254 Longwood Drive, Franklin City, Franklin 33015 (the "Premises"). Landlord desires to lease the Premises to Tenant for use as a private residence upon the terms and conditions contained herein. Tenant desires to lease the Premises from Landlord for use as a private residence upon the terms and conditions contained herein.

2. TERM. This Agreement shall commence on _January 1, 2016_, and shall continue until December 31, 2016, as a term lease.

3. RENT. Tenant agrees to pay $ 1,200 per month by no later than the 3rd day of each month during the lease term . . . .

* * *

8. PETS. No animals are allowed on the Premises, even temporarily, unless authorized by a separate written Pet Addendum to this Agreement. Tenant will pay Landlord $ 25.00 per day per animal as additional rent for each day Tenant violates the animal restrictions by keeping an unauthorized animal. Landlord may remove or cause to be removed any unauthorized animal and shall not be liable for any harm, injury, death, or sickness to unauthorized animals. Tenant is responsible and liable for any damage or required cleaning to the Premises caused by any unauthorized animal . . . .

9. SECURITY DEPOSIT. On or before execution of this Agreement, Tenant will pay a security deposit to Landlord of $ 1,200 . . . . At the end of the lease, Landlord may deduct reasonable charges from the security deposit for damage to the Premises, excluding normal wear and tear, and all reasonable costs associated with repairing the Premises.

* * *

11. DESTRUCTION OF PREMISES. If the Premises become totally or partially destroyed during the term of this Agreement such that Tenant's use is seriously impaired, Landlord or Tenant may terminate this Agreement immediately upon three days' written notice to the other.

* * *

14. PROPERTY MAINTENANCE.

A. <u>Tenant's General Responsibilities</u>. Tenant, at Tenant's expense, shall

    (1) keep the property clean;

    (2) promptly dispose of all garbage in appropriate receptacles;

    . . .

    (11) not leave windows or doors in an open position during any inclement weather;

    (12) promptly notify Landlord, in writing, of all needed repairs.

B. <u>Yard Maintenance</u>. Unless prohibited by ordinance or other law, Tenant will water the yard at reasonable and appropriate times and will, at Tenant's expense, maintain the yard.

* * *

16. EARLY DEPARTURE FROM PREMISES. If Tenant vacates the Premises before the end of the lease term, Landlord may hold Tenant responsible for all rent payments due for the balance of the lease term, subject to any remedies available to Tenant under Franklin law.

Dated this __1st__ day of __January, 2016__

Tenant's Signature __Barbara Whirley__

Landlord's Signature __Sean Spear__

Email Correspondence between Barbara Whirley and Sean Spears

From: Barbara Whirley<bwhirl@cmail.com>
To: Sean Spears<sspears65@cmail.com>
Subject: Repair request
Date: February 19, 2016

Hi, Sean. Last weekend I noticed some water on the floor of the hall bathroom between the toilet and the shower. I think the toilet may have a leak. Can you please stop by in the next couple of days to see if the toilet is leaking? I'll put a towel down and make sure to keep the area dry in the meantime. Thanks!

From: Sean Spears<sspears65@cmail.com>
To: Barbara Whirley<bwhirl@cmail.com>
Subject: Repair request
Date: February 27, 2016

Hi, Barbara. I'm sorry it's taken me a while to get back to you. I've been out of town—my oldest son just got married! I'm back in town now, but I'm absolutely snowed under at work this week. I should be able to swing by this weekend—would Saturday morning work for you?

From: Barbara Whirley<bwhirl@cmail.com>
To: Sean Spears<sspears65@cmail.com>
Subject: Leaking toilet
Date: March 4, 2016

Sean, I left two phone messages that last Saturday morning was good for me, and I waited at the house until almost 2 p.m. that day, but you never showed up. The leak in the toilet is getting worse. I've put a plastic bucket behind the toilet to catch the dripping water. Please stop by as soon as you can. I am home most weeknights by 6 p.m. and should be around this weekend. Thanks!

From: Barbara Whirley<bwhirl@cmail.com>
To: Sean Spears<sspears65@cmail.com>
Subject: Needed repairs
Date: March 31, 2016

Sean, I've tried calling you several times over the last few weeks and left voicemail messages about the leaking toilet, but you haven't called me back. The toilet really needs to be fixed. The leak is so bad now that I have to empty the plastic bucket twice a day and sometimes the toilet doesn't flush. In addition, the automatic sprinkler system for the front yard just stopped working, so I have to water the front flower beds by hand two or three times a week. This takes 15–20 minutes and is a real hassle—especially in this hot weather. I do not see any leaks, so I think the sprinkler box has malfunctioned. Can you please figure out what is wrong and get it fixed? Please call or email me about both of these problems ASAP. Thanks!

From: Sean Spears<sspears65@cmail.com>
To: Barbara Whirley<bwhirl@cmail.com>
Subject: Needed repairs
Date: April 6, 2016

Barbara, I'm sorry for the delay, but I've got a lot on my plate right now. I promise I will get by the house to check on everything as soon as I can. Please hold down the fort in the meantime! Thanks!

From: Barbara Whirley<bwhirl@cmail.com>
To: Sean Spears<sspears65@cmail.com>
Subject: Needed repairs
Date: April 27, 2016

Sean, I just got your voicemail message saying you wanted to stop by this weekend. I will be out of town Friday and Saturday, but anytime on Sunday would work for me. See you Sunday!

From: Barbara Whirley<bwhirl@cmail.com>
To: Sean Spears<sspears65@cmail.com>
Subject: Needed repairs
Date: May 4, 2016

Sean, what happened Sunday?! I thought you were going to stop by.... If you can't make it, then please at least have the courtesy to call and let me know! When can you come by?

From: Barbara Whirley<bwhirl@cmail.com>
To: Sean Spears<sspears65@cmail.com>
Subject: Problem with sliding door and other repairs
Date: May 26, 2016

Sean, I have been very patient. The toilet in the hall bathroom has been leaking for the past three months, and the automatic sprinkler system is still not working. These problems are very troubling, but now there's an even bigger problem—the sliding glass door in the guest bedroom is leaking and the carpet is wet and smelly. The smell is so bad that I can't even use the guest bedroom! Plus, mold is growing around the door, and I know that mold can cause health problems, so I have stopped using this room. I think the door <u>and </u>the carpet need to be replaced! Maybe you didn't take seriously the other problems I reported and that's why you haven't made any of the other repairs I've requested. But now a whole room in the house is completely unusable! Why should I pay rent for a 3-bedroom house when all I'm really getting is a 2-bedroom house and my guests have to sleep on the living room couch? If you don't make arrangements to get everything fixed, then I'm going to look into making the repairs myself and take appropriate legal action. I really like living here, but I can't continue to "hold down the fort" any longer!

JB Handyman Services
You Break It, We Fix It!

Estimate 000347
DATE: June 23, 2016

98 Meadow Lane
Franklin City, Franklin 33019
Phone 111-555-4500

TO:

Barbara Whirley
1254 Longwood Drive
Franklin City, Franklin 33015

Description	Amount
Replace toilet water supply valve and hose; Reseal toilet tank	$200
Replace automatic sprinkler control box (6 zones)	$300
Replace sliding glass door, door frame, and insulation; Replace 10 X 12 square-foot carpet and pad adjacent to door	$1,800
Replace 2-foot section of baseboard in laundry room; Patch and repair drywall above damaged baseboard; Retexture and repaint damaged wall to match existing wall	$300

Total Estimate $2,600

THANK YOU FOR YOUR BUSINESS!

July 2016
MPT-1 Library:
In re Whirley

Excerpts from Franklin Civil Code

Franklin Civil Code § 540 – Requirement of Tenantability

The lessor of a building intended for human occupation must put it into a condition fit for such occupation and repair all subsequent conditions that render it untenantable.

Franklin Civil Code § 541 – Untenantable Dwellings

A dwelling shall be deemed untenantable for purposes of Section 540 if it lacks any of the following:

(1) Effective waterproofing and weather protection of roof and exterior walls, including unbroken windows and doors.

(2) Plumbing or gas facilities . . . maintained in good working order.

(3) Heating facilities . . . maintained in good working order.

. . .

(7) Electrical lighting, wiring, and equipment . . . maintained in good working order.

(8) Floors, stairways, and railings maintained in good repair.

(9) Interior spaces free from insect or vermin infestation.

Franklin Civil Code § 542 – Tenant's Remedies for Untenantable Dwellings

(a) If a landlord neglects to repair conditions that render a premises untenantable within a reasonable time after receiving written notice from the tenant of the conditions, for each condition, the tenant may:

(1) if the cost of such repairs does not exceed one month's rent of the premises, make repairs and deduct the cost of repairs from the rent when due;

(2) if the cost of repairs exceeds one month's rent, make repairs and sue the landlord for the cost of repairs;

(3) vacate the premises, in which case the tenant shall be discharged from further payment of rent or performance of other conditions as of the date of vacating the premises; or

(4) withhold a portion or all of the rent until the landlord makes the relevant repairs, except that the tenant may only withhold an appropriate portion of the rent if the conditions substantially threaten the tenant's health and safety.

In re Whirley

(b) If the exercise of any of these remedies leads to an eviction action, a justified use of the remedies provided in (a)(1)–(4) in this section is an affirmative defense and may shape the tenant's relief in the event it is determined that the landlord has breached Section 540.

(c) For the purposes of this section, if a tenant makes repairs more than 30 days after giving notice to the landlord, the tenant is presumed to have acted after a reasonable time. A tenant may make repairs after shorter notice if the circumstances require shorter notice.

(d) The tenant's remedies under subsection (a) shall not be available if the condition was caused by the violation of Section 543.

(e) The remedies provided by this section are in addition to any other remedy provided by this chapter, the rental agreement, or other applicable statutory or common law.

Franklin Civil Code § 543 – Tenant's Affirmative Obligations

No duty on the part of the landlord to repair shall arise under Section 540 or 541 if the tenant is in violation of any of the following affirmative obligations, provided the tenant's violation contributes materially to the existence of the condition or interferes materially with the landlord's obligation under Section 540 to effect the necessary repairs:

(1) To keep that part of the premises which the tenant occupies and uses clean and sanitary as the condition of the premises permits.

(2) To properly use and operate all electrical, gas, and plumbing fixtures and keep them as clean and sanitary as their condition permits.

(3) Not to permit any person or animal on the premises to destroy, deface, damage, impair, or remove any part of the dwelling unit or the facilities, equipment, or appurtenances thereto.

* * *

Franklin Civil Code § 550 – Eviction Proceedings

(a) In an eviction action involving residential premises in which the tenant has raised as an affirmative defense a breach of the landlord's obligation under Section 540, the court shall determine whether a substantial breach of this obligation has occurred.

(b) If the court finds that a substantial breach of Section 540 has occurred, the court shall (i) order the landlord to make repairs and correct the conditions which constitute the breach, (ii) order that the monthly rent be reduced by an appropriate amount until repairs are completed, and (iii) award the tenant possession of the premises.

(c) If the court determines that there has been no substantial breach of Section 540 by the landlord, then judgment shall be entered in favor of the landlord.

(d) As used in this section, "substantial breach" means the failure of the landlord to maintain the premises with respect to those conditions that materially affect a tenant's health and safety.

Burk v. Harris

Franklin Court of Appeal (2002)

Defendant Ashley Harris (Tenant) appeals the judgment entered in favor of plaintiff Roger Burk (Landlord) in this eviction action. The issue on appeal is whether the trial court misapplied the law when it found that the conditions proved to exist were nonsubstantial and therefore not a breach of the warranty of tenantability.

Landlord sought possession of the premises, forfeiture of the lease agreement, and past-due rent. Tenant asserted the defense of breach of the warranty of tenantability, set forth in Franklin Civil Code § 540, and the right to withhold rent under § 542(a)(4).

At trial, Tenant testified that the roof and windows of the premises had leaked during the entire term of her tenancy and, as a result, had caused water damage to the walls and floors and had damaged her personal property. Tenant also testified that the thermostat was broken and that the shower leaked. Tenant offered into evidence several letters she sent to Landlord complaining about the leaking roof and other conditions in the apartment, as well as photographs documenting the problems. Landlord denied receiving any such letters, asserted that he had not been inside the premises since Tenant moved in and did not have a key to the residence, and introduced before-and-after photos of repairs he had made upon learning of Tenant's complaints.

The trial court found that the conditions were not "substantial" as defined in Franklin Civil Code § 550. Accordingly, it entered judgment for Landlord for possession of the premises and past-due rent.

In *Gordon v. Centralia Properties Inc.* (Fr. Sup. Ct. 1975), the Franklin Supreme Court held that in every residential lease, there is an implied warranty of tenantability. In *Gordon*, the Franklin Supreme Court further held that a tenant who proves that the landlord has breached the warranty of tenantability is entitled not only to maintain possession of the premises but also to an appropriate reduction of rent corresponding to the reduced value of the premises. The *Gordon* court further held that a tenant is not entitled to a reduction in rent for minor violations that do not materially affect a tenant's health and safety. *Id.*

The *Gordon* decision is codified in the Franklin Civil Code. Under this statutory scheme, when a tenant raises breach of the warranty of tenantability as a defense in an eviction case, the trial court is required to determine whether a substantial breach has occurred. *See* §§ 542(b) and 550(a). If the court finds that there has been a substantial breach, it shall order the landlord to make the repairs and correct the conditions caused by the breach, order that monthly rent be reduced by an appropriate amount, and award the tenant possession of the premises. § 550(b).

Section 540 requires that the landlord of a building intended for human occupation "put it into a condition fit for such occupation and repair all subsequent conditions that render it untenantable." Under § 541, a dwelling is untenantable for human occupancy if it lacks effective waterproofing and weather protection of roof and exterior walls, plumbing maintained in good working order, heating facilities maintained in good working order, and floors maintained in good repair.

Here, the trial court found that the premises were not properly waterproofed from the outside elements, the thermostat did not work, and the shower leaked. The trial court erred when it concluded that these conditions were nonsubstantial. These conditions are not merely cosmetic defects or matters of convenience but affect Tenant's health and safety.

Accordingly, Tenant is entitled to judgment on the defense of breach of the warranty of tenantability, to possession of the premises, and to an appropriately reduced rent. *See* §§ 542(a)(4) and 550(b).

To determine the appropriate reduction in rent, a trial court may either (i) measure the difference between the fair rental value of the premises if they had been as warranted and the fair rental value as they were during occupancy in unsafe or unsanitary condition, or (ii) reduce a tenant's rental obligation by the percentage corresponding to the relative reduction of use of the leased premises caused by the landlord's breach.

Additionally, the trial court must order Landlord to make the repairs necessary under the statute. These are issues for the trial court to determine on remand. Reversed and remanded.

Shea v. Willowbrook Properties LP
Franklin Court of Appeal (2012)

After suffering through two separate bedbug infestations in his apartment, plaintiff Jordan Shea moved out and filed a complaint against his landlord, Willowbrook Properties LP, seeking to recover rent he had paid for the apartment ($1,000/month for 16 months) and out-of-pocket expenses relating to the infestation ($2,000). After a bench trial, the trial court found Willowbrook responsible for the first infestation, but not the second. It awarded Shea a fraction of the damages he sought ($400), limiting his recovery to his documented out-of-pocket expenses and declining to award any rent recovery. Shea appeals.

The facts are as follows: within a few days of entering into a six-month lease with Willowbrook on July 1, 2010, Shea began to suffer from insect bites, which he discovered were the result of bedbugs. He reported this to Willowbrook, which sprayed his apartment, replaced his carpeting, and cleaned his apartment thoroughly to remove the bugs. While this work was being done, Shea stayed at a nearby motel. For several months after Willowbrook cleaned his apartment, Shea experienced no bedbug problems, so he believed that the problem had been corrected. In January 2011, he renewed his lease for an additional year; he then departed for a three-week study-abroad program. Upon his return, he started to get bedbug bites again; the bedbug problem continued throughout the renewal period, but Shea failed to report the second infestation to Willowbrook. He finally moved out of the apartment in October 2011, two months before the end of his lease.

A. Rent

The trial court denied Shea's claim that he was entitled to a full refund of all the rent he had paid over the course of his tenancy. When a landlord breaches the warranty of tenantability and creates an untenantable property, as is alleged here, a tenant has several options: (1) repair and deduct the cost of repairs if the cost of the repairs is less than one month's rent; (2) repair and sue, if the cost of the repairs exceeds one month's rent; (3) vacate the premises and be discharged of paying further rent; or (4) withhold some or all of the rent if the landlord does not make the repairs, provided the conditions substantially threaten the tenant's health and safety. Franklin Civil Code §§ 540, 542. In his lawsuit, Shea sought to recover all the rent he had paid ($16,000) pursuant to the initial and renewed leases.

We believe that the trial court correctly declined to award Shea the rent requested. First, the evidence supports the conclusion that Willowbrook's efforts to address the first infestation (spraying, replacing carpet, and cleaning the apartment) were successful. Shea even renewed his lease for another 12 months, from which the trial court concluded that the apartment was free of the infestation when he renewed and was therefore not untenantable as he claimed. Thus there is no factual basis to support awarding Shea damages for rent paid in 2010 under the first lease.

Nor is there a basis to award damages with respect to the second bedbug infestation, which arose in 2011 after Shea returned from abroad. Shea failed to demonstrate that the 2011 prolonged bedbug infestation occurred through Willowbrook's fault and through no fault of his own. If Shea were responsible, he would have been obligated to resolve the issue himself. *See* Franklin Civil Code § 543 (landlord has no duty to repair under § 540 or 541 if tenant has breached his affirmative obligation to keep premises as clean and sanitary as the condition of premises permits). If Shea believed that his landlord was responsible for the bedbug infestation, he had an obligation to mitigate his damages by promptly notifying Willowbrook to give it an opportunity to resolve the problem. *See Burk v. Harris* (Fr. Ct. App. 2002). Since this did not occur, the trial court declined to find Willowbrook responsible for the second infestation and concluded that Shea was not entitled to vacate the premises under § 542(a)(3). Because Shea retained possession of the apartment and reaped the benefit of staying, he could have been held responsible for the remaining two months of rent under the lease had Willowbrook sought it.

The trial court correctly declined to award Shea any damages related to rent already paid. We affirm the denial of the $16,000 rent reimbursement claim.

B. Out-of-pocket expenses

Shea also requested a total of $2,000 for motel and medication costs he incurred while living in the apartment. However, Shea submitted a receipt only for $400 for the motel room he rented while his apartment was being sprayed for bedbugs during the initial infestation in 2010. He provided no further documentation of his claimed expenses. Therefore, the trial court properly awarded him $400 but appropriately declined to award $1,600 for medication because Shea provided no documentation or explanation of how he came to that number.

Affirmed.

July 2016
MPT-2 File:
Nash v. Franklin Department
of Revenue

The Carter Law Firm LLC
1891 Virginia Way
Bristol, Franklin 33800

MEMORANDUM

TO: Examinee
FROM: Sara Carter
DATE: July 26, 2016
RE: Tax Appeal of Joseph and Ellen Nash

Our clients Joseph and Ellen Nash own property in Knox Hollow, on which they raise Christmas trees for sale. For many years, they sold only to friends and neighbors. Five years ago, they started a commercial tree-farming operation and put a lot more money into the farm.

Starting that same year, they began to claim tax deductions for expenses from a trade or business. They had a huge start-up loss to report in the first year. Since then, their income from the farm has gone up, but their expenses have varied. For each of the past five years, they reported a loss on their joint tax return.

Since the Nashes' last tax filing, as the law allows, the Franklin Department of Revenue (FDR) reviewed the Nashes' returns for the years 2011–2015 and denied their claim of full deductions for the farm expenses for those years. The FDR said that the Nashes could only take deductions to offset income they earned from the farm in each of those five years. The Nashes want the full deductions so that they can offset the business losses against their other income.

The FDR also denied the Nashes' claim for a home office deduction.

The FDR assessed the Nashes with additional tax for all five years. To avoid interest and penalties, the Nashes paid the additional tax. Representing themselves, they filed an internal administrative review with the FDR, which was unsuccessful. (See attached Notice of Decision.)

The Nashes then retained us and we filed an appeal to the Franklin Tax Court, which went to hearing last week. We stipulated to the dollar amounts in question, and Mr. Nash testified. I have attached a transcript. The Tax Court has requested post-hearing briefing.

Please draft the legal argument portion of our brief to the Tax Court, following the attached guidelines for drafting persuasive briefs. You should argue that Mr. Nash's testimony establishes the Nashes' right under Franklin law to the full deductions that they claimed. Franklin law uses the federal Internal Revenue Code and regulations to calculate Franklin tax liability.

The Carter Law Firm LLC
1891 Virginia Way
Bristol, Franklin 33800

OFFICE MEMORANDUM

TO: Attorneys
FROM: Sara Carter
DATE: August 18, 2014
RE: Format for Persuasive Briefs

The following guidelines apply to persuasive briefs filed in the Franklin Tax Court.

[Other sections omitted]

. . .

III. Legal Argument

Your legal argument should be brief and to the point. Make your points clearly and succinctly, citing relevant authority for each legal proposition.

Do not restate the facts as a whole at the beginning of your legal argument. Instead, integrate the facts into your legal argument in a way that makes the strongest case for our client.

Use headings to separate the sections of your argument, and follow the same rule as your argument: do not state abstract conclusions, but integrate factual detail into legal propositions to make them more persuasive. An ineffective heading states only: "The deduction should be allowed." An effective heading states: "Under the Internal Revenue Code, the appellant may deduct the amount by which the value of the gift exceeds the value of the concert ticket he received."

The body of your argument should analyze applicable legal authority and persuasively argue how both the facts and the law support our client's position. Supporting authority should be emphasized, but contrary authority should also be cited, addressed in the argument, and explained or distinguished.

Finally, anticipate and accommodate any weaknesses in your case in the body of your argument. If possible, structure your argument in such a way as to highlight your argument's strengths and minimize its weaknesses. If necessary, make concessions, but only on points that do not concede essential elements of your claim or defense.

FRANKLIN DEPARTMENT OF REVENUE
NOTICE OF DECISION — ADMINISTRATIVE REVIEW

Taxpayers: Joseph Nash and Ellen Nash   **Type:** Joint Filing
Tax Years: 2011–2015   **Date Issued:** May 16, 2016

The taxpayers claim that the Franklin Department of Revenue incorrectly denied their claims for (1) deductions for expenses paid or incurred during the taxable year in carrying on a trade or business and (2) deductions related to the business use of their home.

(1) The taxpayers claim certain deductions related to the carrying on of a "Christmas tree farming" business as follows:

	2011	*2012*	*2013*	*2014*	*2015*
Income	$1,500	$2,000	$2,000	$3,500	$5,000
Deductions	$35,000	$9,500	$7,000	$9,000	$12,500
Gain/(Loss)	($33,500)	($7,500)	($5,000)	($5,500)	($7,500)

The Department determines that the taxpayers are not engaged in the tree-farming business for profit, due to the lack of a profit motive. Therefore, the taxpayers cannot take full deductions in each year. Instead, they may only deduct annual expenses up to the amount of income earned from the tree-farming activity: $1,500 in 2011; $2,000 in 2012; $2,000 in 2013; $3,500 in 2014; $5,000 in 2015. Of the nine factors identified in federal regulation 26 C.F.R. § 1.183–2(b)(1–9), which is controlling in Franklin tax cases, these factors support our conclusion: no profit in the tax years in question; a regular history of losses; no plan to recoup those losses; a history of similar activity without any deductions; and no evidence of operations in a businesslike manner.

(2) The taxpayers may take no deduction attributable to the use of a room in their home because the room was not used exclusively for business purposes. Internal Revenue Code § 280A(c)(1).

The assessment of tax for the years in question is affirmed. The taxpayers have exhausted their internal administrative remedies. They have the right to appeal to the Franklin Tax Court.

Ann Miller

Ann Miller, Commissioner of Franklin Department of Revenue

FRANKLIN TAX COURT, SIXTH DISTRICT
Transcript of Testimony of Joseph Nash
July 21, 2016

DIRECT EXAMINATION BY ATTORNEY CARTER

Att'y Carter: State your name for the record.

Joseph Nash: Joseph Nash.

Carter: Where do you live?

Nash: 3150 Old Sawmill Road in Knox Hollow, Franklin.

Carter: How long have you lived there?

Nash: Since we bought it in 1997.

Carter: Describe the land, please.

Nash: It's 13 acres: an acre for the house and sheds, and another two acres of fields. The rest is forested.

Carter: You started claiming tax deductions in 2011. Please tell the court how you used the land before then.

Nash: Originally, about two acres of the land had Leland cypress, spruce, and pine on it, good for Christmas trees. Soon after we bought it, our daughter and her friends would cut down trees for their own use. After a while, we put up a sign on the road each November and put out a garbage can with saws and twine in it. We charged $15 for the cypress, $20 for the pine, and $25 for the spruce.

Carter: What happened next?

Nash: At some point, we realized that most of the good trees would be gone in a few years. So I researched how to raise Christmas trees in a more orderly way.

Carter: What did you do?

Nash: I read a lot of books on raising trees, Christmas trees in particular. I took a whole series of classes on forest management. Finally, I met a nearby Christmas tree farmer and spent a whole vacation on that farm. I got really interested in it.

Carter: What did you do next?

Nash: First we set apart some of the acreage, cut everything down, and replanted in organized rows, leaving space to plant new seedlings in rotation. When the new trees came in, we'd sell them off, same as before.

Carter:	How much did you make?
Nash:	Up until five years ago, never more than $1,000 in any one year.
Carter:	Did you report this as income on your tax returns during this period?
Nash:	Yes. And up until that point, we claimed no deductions.
Carter:	What happened then?
Nash:	About five years ago, in 2011, the tree farmer I'd worked with let me know that he was planning to go out of business. And my wife retired from her job with the county. So we had to decide whether to step it up or not. We both liked working in the fields and selling the trees, so we said, "Why not?"
Carter:	Then what happened?
Nash:	That same year we contacted the farmer's commercial customers, as a target for expansion. Then we invited the farmer over to walk us through what a bigger operation would look like. He showed us how to keep records about the trees and to keep good books. We did exactly what he told us . . . still do.
Carter:	You couldn't have sold that many more trees right away.
Nash:	No, we didn't. 2011 was a hard year, because we cut down several acres of forest for additional fields and bought new equipment to deal with the additional planting. We couldn't do it by hand, the way we had before. So we bought specialized equipment to trim and shape the trees.
Carter:	How do you manage things?
Nash:	Starting in 2011, we set aside a room in the house just for this business. We keep the records there, and catalogues and books that we consult. We have a computer that we use just for the business and nothing else. The room has a desk and two chairs, and that's it. Nothing happens there but the business.
Carter:	How did things go from then on?
Nash:	Well, that first year, we made only $1,500, including sales to some retailers in the city. We made more each year after that, up until last year when we made $5,000.
Carter:	How much of that was profit?
Nash:	None of it. We had a huge loss in 2011. After that, we had to maintain the equipment, and we had to increase the size of each year's planting to

increase our sales five to six years later. For the past two years, we have had to hire people to help us during the harvest; it was just too much for us. And of course, the economy has been bad, and sales haven't been what we thought they would be. It's coming back, though.

Carter: How much time have you and your wife put into this?

Nash: Since 2011, my wife has spent pretty much full time year-round on this. I spend summers and weekends, when I can . . . a lot more time during the harvest. We love it; it's hard work, but it's outdoors and it's satisfying.

Carter: Just to be clear, you've never made a profit?

Nash: That's right.

Carter: Do you plan to make a profit?

Nash: Yes, we will make a profit, once the trees we started planting five years ago are big enough for harvesting. We have reliable customers who want our trees, and we've learned a lot in the past few years about how to keep costs down.

Carter: No further questions.

CROSS-EXAMINATION BY Franklin Dep't of Revenue ATTORNEY SHEPARD

Att'y Shepard: Mr. Nash, you work full-time at Knox County High School as an associate principal, correct?

Joseph Nash: Yes, that's right.

Shepard: Since your wife retired, hasn't she received a pension from the county?

Nash: Yes.

Shepard: You've lived off your salary and her pension the last five years, correct?

Nash: Yes.

Shepard: You've never run a business of your own, have you?

Att'y Carter: Objection. Argumentative.

Shepard: I'll rephrase. Other than this activity on your land, you and your wife have never run a business of your own, have you?

Nash: No.

Shepard: You've never taken a salary for either of you from this activity, have you?

Nash: No.

Shepard:	You don't insure your trees, do you?
Nash:	No. We do insure the farm equipment.
Shepard:	You don't advertise, do you?
Nash:	No, not commercially. Our local business is by word of mouth, and we have good connections with our commercial customers.
Shepard:	You testified that you set a room aside only for this activity.
Nash:	Yes.
Shepard:	How did you use the room before?
Nash:	We used it as a spare bedroom.
Shepard:	You said that there is nothing in that room but a desk and two chairs?
Nash:	Yes—we took out the bed.
Shepard:	One of those two chairs is a recliner, isn't it? And you have a radio and TV there too, correct?
Nash:	Yes. I keep the TV on the Weather Channel, for business reasons.
Shepard:	The computer is connected to the Internet.
Nash:	By wireless, yes.
Shepard:	Your dogs will lie in that room with you while you're there?
Nash:	Yes, they will.
Shepard:	There's a fireplace in that room too, isn't there?
Nash:	Yes.
Shepard:	You testified that you love tree farming and are fascinated by it?
Nash:	Yes.
Shepard:	You enjoy working on the land and making things grow.
Nash:	I do.
Shepard:	It doesn't really matter to you if this activity makes a profit, does it?
Nash:	Maybe not; but we mean to make one anyway. That's part of the fun.
Shepard:	No further questions.

July 2016
MPT-2 Library:
Nash v. Franklin Department
of Revenue

Excerpts from Internal Revenue Code

Internal Revenue Code § 162. Trade or business expenses

(a) **In general.** There shall be allowed as a deduction all the ordinary and necessary expenses paid or incurred during the taxable year in carrying on any trade or business . . .

Internal Revenue Code § 183. Activities not engaged in for profit

(a) **General rule.** In the case of an activity engaged in by an individual . . . , if such activity is not engaged in for profit, no deduction attributable to such activity shall be allowed under this chapter except as provided in this section.

(b) [deductions for activity not engaged in for profit limited to the amount of income earned by that activity] [text omitted]

(c) **Activity not engaged in for profit defined.** For purposes of this section, the term "activity not engaged in for profit" means any activity other than one with respect to which deductions are allowable for the taxable year under section 162. . . .

Internal Revenue Code § 280A. Disallowance of certain expenses in connection with business use of home, rental of vacation homes, etc.

(a) **General rule.** Except as otherwise provided in this section, in the case of a taxpayer who is an individual . . . , no deduction otherwise allowable under this chapter shall be allowed with respect to the use of a dwelling unit which is used by the taxpayer during the taxable year as a residence.

. . .

(c) **Exceptions for certain business or rental use . . .**

(1) **Certain business use.** Subsection (a) shall not apply to any item to the extent such item is allocable to a portion of the dwelling unit which is exclusively used on a regular basis—

(A) as the principal place of business for any trade or business of the taxpayer.

Nash v. Franklin Dep't of Revenue

Excerpts from Code of Federal Regulations
Title 26. Internal Revenue

26 C.F.R. § 1.183–2. Activity not engaged in for profit defined.

   (a) In general. [Except as otherwise provided . . . ,] no deductions are allowable for expenses incurred in connection with activities which are not engaged in for profit. . . . The determination whether an activity is engaged in for profit is to be made by reference to objective standards, taking into account all of the facts and circumstances of each case. Although a reasonable expectation of profit is not required, the facts and circumstances must indicate that the taxpayer entered into the activity, or continued the activity, with the objective of making a profit. . . . In determining whether an activity is engaged in for profit, greater weight is given to objective facts than to the taxpayer's mere statement of his intent.

   (b) Relevant factors. In determining whether an activity is engaged in for profit, all facts and circumstances with respect to the activity are to be taken into account. No one factor is determinative in making this determination. In addition, it is not intended that only the factors described in this paragraph are to be taken into account in making the determination, or that a determination is to be made on the basis that the number of factors (whether or not listed in this paragraph) indicating a lack of profit objective exceeds the number of factors indicating a profit objective, or vice versa. Among the factors which should normally be taken into account are the following:

   (1) Manner in which the taxpayer carries on the activity. The fact that the taxpayer carries on the activity in a businesslike manner and maintains complete and accurate books and records may indicate that the activity is engaged in for profit. Similarly, where an activity is carried on in a manner substantially similar to other activities of the same nature which are profitable, a profit motive may be indicated. A change of operating methods, adoption of new techniques or abandonment of unprofitable methods in a manner consistent with an intent to improve profitability may also indicate a profit motive.

   (2) The expertise of the taxpayer or his advisors. Preparation for the activity by extensive study of its accepted business, economic, and scientific practices, or consultation with those who are expert therein, may indicate that the taxpayer has a profit motive where the taxpayer carries on the activity in accordance with such practices. . . .

(3) The time and effort expended by the taxpayer in carrying on the activity. The fact that the taxpayer devotes much of his personal time and effort to carrying on an activity, particularly if the activity does not have substantial personal or recreational aspects, may indicate an intention to derive a profit. A taxpayer's withdrawal from another occupation to devote most of his energies to the activity may also be evidence that the activity is engaged in for profit. . . .

(4) Expectation that assets used in activity may appreciate in value. The term profit encompasses appreciation in the value of assets, such as land, used in the activity. . . .

(5) The success of the taxpayer in carrying on other similar or dissimilar activities. The fact that the taxpayer has engaged in similar activities in the past and converted them from unprofitable to profitable enterprises may indicate that he is engaged in the present activity for profit, even though the activity is presently unprofitable.

(6) The taxpayer's history of income or losses with respect to the activity. A series of losses during the initial or start-up stage of an activity may not necessarily be an indication that the activity is not engaged in for profit. However, where losses continue to be sustained beyond the period which customarily is necessary to bring the operation to profitable status, such continued losses, if not explainable as due to customary business risks or reverses, may be indicative that the activity is not being engaged in for profit. If losses are sustained because of unforeseen or fortuitous circumstances which are beyond the control of the taxpayer, such as drought, disease, fire, theft, weather damages, other involuntary conversions, or depressed market conditions, such losses would not be an indication that the activity is not engaged in for profit. A series of years in which net income was realized would of course be strong evidence that the activity is engaged in for profit.

(7) The amount of occasional profits, if any, which are earned. The amount of profits in relation to the amount of losses incurred, and in relation to the amount of the taxpayer's investment and the value of the assets used in the activity, may provide useful criteria in determining the taxpayer's intent. An occasional small profit from an activity generating large losses, or from an activity in which the taxpayer has made a large investment, would not generally be determinative that the activity is engaged in for profit. However, substantial profit, though only occasional, would generally be indicative that an

activity is engaged in for profit, where the investment or losses are comparatively small.
. . .

(8) The financial status of the taxpayer. The fact that the taxpayer does not have substantial income or capital from sources other than the activity may indicate that an activity is engaged in for profit. Substantial income from sources other than the activity (particularly if the losses from the activity generate substantial tax benefits) may indicate that the activity is not engaged in for profit especially if there are personal or recreational elements involved.

(9) Elements of personal pleasure or recreation. The presence of personal motives in carrying on of an activity may indicate that the activity is not engaged in for profit, especially where there are recreational or personal elements involved. On the other hand, a profit motivation may be indicated where an activity lacks any appeal other than profit. It is not, however, necessary that an activity be engaged in with the exclusive intention of deriving a profit or with the intention of maximizing profits. . . . An activity will not be treated as not engaged in for profit merely because the taxpayer has purposes or motivations other than solely to make a profit. Also, the fact that the taxpayer derives personal pleasure from engaging in the activity is not sufficient to cause the activity to be classified as not engaged in for profit if the activity is in fact engaged in for profit as evidenced by other factors whether or not listed in this paragraph.

Stone v. Franklin Department of Revenue

Franklin Tax Court (2008)

In this appeal, we review and affirm a decision of the Franklin Department of Revenue denying deductions to taxpayers Jim and Maxine Stone related to the operation of a horse- breeding business. Orders of the Department of Revenue are presumed correct and valid; the taxpayer bears the burden of demonstrating that the challenged order is incorrect. *Nelson v. Franklin Dep't of Revenue* (Franklin Tax Ct. 1998). The Franklin legislature intended to incorporate the federal Internal Revenue Code (IRC) and the Code of Federal Regulations (CFR) for the purpose of determining Franklin taxable income.

The Stones claimed deductions for expenses relating to the operations of an alleged trade or business: a horse-breeding business operated under the name "Irontree." The FDR limited their deductions to the amount of income that they earned from horse breeding in each of the last seven tax years, because the Stones lacked a profit motive. The Stones appeal, seeking full deductions.

26 C.F.R. § 1.183–2 outlines the activities that may be considered "for profit" in order to allow income tax deductions. The regulation requires an objective standard and delineates nine factors used to assess whether the taxpayer "entered into the activity, or continued the activity, with the objective of making a profit." 26 C.F.R. § 1.183–2(a) & (b). These factors are not exclusive, nor is one factor or combination of factors determinative on the issue of profit motive. *Morton v. Franklin Dep't of Revenue* (Franklin Sup. Ct. 1984).

1) *Manner of Carrying Out Activity:* The Stones operated Irontree for nearly 20 years, and began to claim deductions for the last seven. The Stones offered slight evidence of businesslike operations. They produced no records of business activities. Mr. Stone knew little about when horses were purchased or sold, the prices paid, or what training occurred. They lacked a business plan and had no plan to recoup their losses. Such plans can suggest a motive to earn a profit. *Jennings v. Franklin Dep't of Revenue* (Franklin Tax Ct. 2001).

The Stones bought horse semen from a national champion. The Stones contend that this purchase reflected an effort to stem their losses, an effort that failed. The Stones never paid or received a salary from Irontree. Only for a hobby does one work for nothing for 20 years. The Stones advertised only by attending horse shows, an insufficient effort to advertise a horse

Nash v. Franklin Dep't of Revenue

breeding business. The Stones did not insure the assets of Irontree. Thus, when a horse slipped on some ice and eventually died, Irontree received nothing for its loss.

2) *Taxpayer Expertise:* The Stones have no formal education in breeding horses or the business of horse breeding. They have only recreational experience. They contend that they consulted with others on issues such as crossbreeding, animal care, and fence construction. But nothing shows that the Stones got or took advice on how to make Irontree profitable.

3) *Time and Effort Invested:* Mr. Stone claimed that he and his wife worked 30 to 40 hours per week on the farm, but did not show how he spent this time. The Stones kept full-time jobs. At best, we find this factor to be neutral.

4) *Appreciation of Assets:* Irontree consists of 20 acres, including the Stones' residence; barns for storage of hay, equipment, and tack; horse stalls; and wash stalls. Mr. Stone conceded that none of these assets appreciated.

5) *Success in Similar Activities:* Irontree was the Stones' first attempt at operating a horse-breeding operation or any business.

6) *History of Income and Losses:* The Stones own six horses. A seventh, Shiloh, was born and sold in 2005. During the years in question, Irontree accumulated losses of $132,751, compared to income of $4,000 from the sale of Shiloh. That $4,000 compared to losses of $33,901 in the same year. This history of losses over the entire existence of Irontree shows neither a history of profitability nor the potential for income to match losses.

7) *Amount of Profits:* Irontree made no profit in any of the years in question, or in any two consecutive years of its entire history. It seems unlikely that Irontree ever had the opportunity to generate a profit, let alone a profit substantial enough to justify the significant losses incurred.

8) *Financial Status of Taxpayer:* Mr. Stone worked for a bank during all the years in question, and Ms. Stone worked for an insurance agency. The Stones' income averaged $163,000. The Stones never received a salary or relied upon income from Irontree.

9) *Recreational Nature of Activity:* Mr. Stone engaged in rodeo events as part of his work with Irontree. He has been riding horses since he was a child, and rode horses in games and trail rides. Despite the hours and difficult work required to maintain the farm, the Stones' activities, including the pleasure in riding and caring for horses, indicate recreation, rather than operation of a business for profit.

Conclusion

For all of the foregoing reasons, we find that the factors outlined in 26 C.F.R. § 1.183–2(b)(1–9), except perhaps for factor three, weigh in favor of the Department. Therefore, we find that the Stones did not enter into the activity, or continue the activity, with the objective of making a profit. 26 C.F.R. § 1.183–2(a). The Department's assessment is affirmed.

Lynn v. Franklin Department of Revenue

Franklin Tax Court (2013)

Lorenzo Lynn claimed deductions for $2,307 in expenses attributable to the business use of his homes. The Franklin Department of Revenue denied those deductions and assessed additional tax due. Lynn paid the tax and then filed a claim for a refund. After an administrative review affirmed the Department's decision, Lynn timely appealed to this court. We affirm in part and reverse in part.

Lynn claimed that he operated his law practice first out of his house in Chatsworth, Franklin, and then out of his apartment in Athens, Franklin (to which he moved in May 2006). He claimed that the first floor of the Chatsworth house (25% of the total area of the house) and one of the eight rooms of the Athens apartment (the "computer office room") were used exclusively for his law practice. The Department argues that Lynn did not use any portion of either his house or his apartment exclusively as a principal place of business and that he is not entitled to any deduction for the business use of either residence.

We note that the Franklin legislature intended to make Franklin personal income tax law identical to the Internal Revenue Code (IRC) for purposes of determining Franklin taxable income, subject to adjustments and modifications specified by Franklin law. IRC § 280A provides that, generally, no deduction is allowed with respect to the personal residence of a taxpayer. However, under § 280A(c)(1)(A), this prohibition does not apply to expenses allocable to a portion of the taxpayer's residence that is used exclusively and on a regular basis as the principal place of business for any trade or business of the taxpayer. The exclusive use requirement is an "all-or-nothing" standard. *McBride v. Franklin Dep't of Revenue* (Franklin Tax Ct. 1990). The legislative history explains:

> Exclusive use of a portion of a taxpayer's dwelling unit means that the taxpayer must use a specific part of a dwelling unit solely for the purpose of carrying on his trade or business. The use of a portion of a dwelling unit for both personal purposes and for the carrying on of a trade or business does not meet the exclusive use test.

S. Rept. No. 94–938, at 48 (1976).

We first consider the Chatsworth house. We find that Lynn used the first floor of the premises—25% of the total area of the home—exclusively and on a regular basis as the principal place of business of his law practice. The area's physical separation from the living areas of the home, its physical conversion from a residential-type "mother-in-law suite" to an office, and the fact that it had a separate entrance with an awning all inform our finding.

We next consider the "computer office room" of the Athens apartment. We find that Lynn did not prove that he used the "computer office room" exclusively as the principal place of business of his law practice. Lynn testified cursorily that he used the room exclusively for his law practice and that he stored files and law books there. But he offered almost no details about what was in the room and how the room was used. His reference to the room as the "computer office room" suggests that his computer was in the room, but we believe that he used his computer for both personal and business tasks. Moreover, he testified that he would occasionally watch his infant daughter in that room, while his wife attended to personal business, and that he would do so by having his daughter watch television at a low volume. The presence of a television in the room, coupled with his cursory testimony about business use, leads us to conclude that Lynn has not met his burden of proving that he used the "computer office room" exclusively as his principal place of business.

Accordingly, we reverse the determination of the Department as it relates to the business use of the Chatsworth home and affirm its determination as it relates to the Athens apartment.

February 2016 MPTs

In re Anderson

Miller v. Trapp

THE MPT®

MULTISTATE PERFORMANCE TEST

February 2016
MPTs

www.ncbex.org

National Conference of Bar Examiners
302 South Bedford Street | Madison, WI 53703-3622
Phone: 608-280-8550 | Fax: 608-280-8552 | TDD: 608-661-1275
e-mail: contact@ncbex.org

Contents

Preface

The Multistate Performance Test (MPT) is developed by the National Conference of Bar Examiners (NCBE). This publication includes the items and Point Sheets from the February 2016 MPT. The instructions for the test appear on page iii.

The MPT Point Sheets describe the factual and legal points encompassed within the lawyering tasks to be completed. They outline the possible issues and points that might be addressed by an examinee. They are provided to the user jurisdictions to assist graders in grading the examination by identifying the issues and suggesting the resolution of the problem contemplated by the drafters.

For more information about the MPT, including a list of skills tested, visit the NCBE website at www .ncbex.org.

Description of the MPT

The MPT consists of two 90-minute items and is a component of the Uniform Bar Examination (UBE). It is administered by user jurisdictions as part of the bar examination on the Tuesday before the last Wednesday in February and July of each year. User jurisdictions may select one or both items to include as part of their bar examinations. (Jurisdictions that administer the UBE use two MPTs.)

The materials for each MPT include a File and a Library. The File consists of source documents containing all the facts of the case. The specific assignment the examinee is to complete is described in a memorandum from a supervising attorney. The File might also include transcripts of interviews, depositions, hearings or trials, pleadings, correspondence, client documents, contracts, newspaper articles, medical records, police reports, or lawyer's notes. Relevant as well as irrelevant facts are included. Facts are sometimes ambiguous, incomplete, or even conflicting. As in practice, a client's or a supervising attorney's version of events may be incomplete or unreliable. Examinees are expected to recognize when facts are inconsistent or missing and are expected to identify potential sources of additional facts.

The Library may contain cases, statutes, regulations, or rules, some of which may not be relevant to the assigned lawyering task. The examinee is expected to extract from the Library the legal principles necessary to analyze the problem and perform the task. The MPT is not a test of substantive law; the Library materials provide sufficient substantive information to complete the task.

The MPT is designed to test an examinee's ability to use fundamental lawyering skills in a realistic situation and complete a task that a beginning lawyer should be able to accomplish. The MPT is not a test of substantive knowledge. Rather, it is designed to evaluate six fundamental skills lawyers are expected to demonstrate regardless of the area of law in which the skills arise. The MPT requires examinees to (1) sort detailed factual materials and separate relevant from irrelevant facts; (2) analyze statutory, case, and administrative materials for applicable principles of law; (3) apply the relevant law to the relevant facts in a manner likely to resolve a client's problem; (4) identify and resolve ethical dilemmas, when present; (5) communicate effectively in writing; and (6) complete a lawyering task within time constraints. These skills are tested by requiring examinees to perform one or more of a variety of lawyering tasks. For example, examinees might be instructed to complete any of the following: a memorandum to a supervising attorney, a letter to a client, a persuasive memorandum or brief, a statement of facts, a contract provision, a will, a counseling plan, a proposal for settlement or agreement, a discovery plan, a witness examination plan, or a closing argument.

Instructions

The back cover of each test booklet contains the following instructions:

You will be instructed when to begin and when to stop this test. Do not break the seal on this booklet until you are told to begin. This test is designed to evaluate your ability to handle a select number of legal authorities in the context of a factual problem involving a client.

The problem is set in the fictitious state of Franklin, in the fictitious Fifteenth Circuit of the United States. Columbia and Olympia are also fictitious states in the Fifteenth Circuit. In Franklin, the trial court of general jurisdiction is the District Court, the intermediate appellate court is the Court of Appeal, and the highest court is the Supreme Court.

You will have two kinds of materials with which to work: a File and a Library. The first document in the File is a memorandum containing the instructions for the task you are to complete. The other documents in the File contain factual information about your case and may include some facts that are not relevant.

The Library contains the legal authorities needed to complete the task and may also include some authorities that are not relevant. Any cases may be real, modified, or written solely for the purpose of this examination. If the cases appear familiar to you, do not assume that they are precisely the same as you have read before. Read them thoroughly, as if they all were new to you. You should assume that the cases were decided in the jurisdictions and on the dates shown. In citing cases from the Library, you may use abbreviations and omit page references.

Your response must be written in the answer book provided. If you are using a laptop computer to answer the questions, your jurisdiction will provide you with specific instructions. In answering this performance test, you should concentrate on the materials in the File and Library. What you have learned in law school and elsewhere provides the general background for analyzing the problem; the File and Library provide the specific materials with which you must work.

Although there are no restrictions on how you apportion your time, you should allocate approximately half your time to reading and digesting the materials and to organizing your answer before you begin writing it. You may make notes anywhere in the test materials; blank pages are provided at the end of the booklet. You may not tear pages from the question booklet.

Do not include your actual name anywhere in the work product required by the task memorandum.

This performance test will be graded on your responsiveness to the instructions regarding the task you are to complete, which are given to you in the first memorandum in the File, and on the content, thoroughness, and organization of your response.

February 2016
MPT-1 File:
In re Anderson

CALVETTI, LAWRENCE & MASTERSON
Attorneys at Law
84 Richmond Avenue, Suite 1300
Lafayette, Franklin 33526

MEMORANDUM

To:	Examinee
From:	David Lawrence
Date:	February 23, 2016
Re:	Workers' Compensation Claim

Our client Nicole Anderson seeks legal advice regarding a workers' compensation claim that is being filed against her by Rick Greer, a handyman hired by Anderson to perform general maintenance and repair work for her residential rental properties. Greer was injured while painting the exterior of one of Anderson's rental houses.

Under the Franklin Workers' Compensation Act, codified in the Franklin Labor Code § 200 *et seq.*, employers are required to maintain insurance coverage for employees who may sustain injuries arising out of and in the course of their employment. When employees are injured on the job, they can submit workers' compensation claims and be paid for their lost wages during the period in which their injuries prevent them from returning to work, as well as their medical costs.

Workers' compensation applies only to employees; it does not apply to independent contractors. Anderson did not maintain workers' compensation insurance coverage because she did not believe she was required to insure Greer against injury. If Greer is found to be Anderson's employee, Anderson could face substantial personal liability as well as penalties under the Workers' Compensation Act for failing to provide this coverage.

Please draft a memorandum to me in which you analyze whether Greer would be considered an employee of Anderson under the applicable statutory provisions and case law. Do not include a separate statement of facts, but be sure to incorporate the relevant facts, analyze the applicable legal authorities, and explain how the facts and law affect your analysis and conclusion.

Transcript of client interview: Nicole Anderson
February 19, 2016

Attorney Lawrence: Ms. Anderson, it's a pleasure to meet you. I understand that you're seeking our assistance with regard to a workers' compensation claim that is being asserted against you. Why don't you tell me a little more about your business and then we can talk about the claim.

Nicole Anderson: Well, about five years ago, I got involved in the rental property business when I couldn't sell the house that I owned and lived in. I couldn't afford two mortgages, so I ended up renting out my old house. I had such a positive experience as a first-time landlord that I decided to invest in additional rental properties. Over the past five years, my rental property business has steadily grown, and I now own 11 rental properties, all of them single-family houses, here in Lafayette.

    Initially, when I had only a couple of rental properties, I personally handled most of the basic maintenance work like painting and replacing trim, basic plumbing problems, and the like. If a particular project was too complicated or time-consuming, I'd recruit family members to help me or hire out the work to various handymen as needed. About three years ago, I reached the point where I had too many rental properties to keep up with as far as basic maintenance and repair work, and I was tired of dealing with different handymen, some of whom were less reliable than others. So I decided to find someone who could perform all of the maintenance and repair work on my rental properties. That's when I found Rick Greer.

Atty: And is Mr. Greer the person who was injured and who is attempting to assert a workers' compensation claim against you?

Client: Yes, I just received this claim form. [Workers' compensation claim form attached.]

Atty: How did you come to find him?

Client: I saw an ad in the online Yellow Pages for "Greer's Fix-Its." After speaking with him and checking his references, I felt confident that he would do a good job at a reasonable price.

Atty: How long has Mr. Greer provided handyman services for you?

Client: Since June of 2013.

Atty: Did the two of you enter into any kind of written agreement?

Client: Not anything formal, but we did discuss the parameters of his work by email. I've brought a copy of the emails in which we discussed what he was going to do, how he was going to be paid, and what the general arrangement would be.

Atty: Great. Let me take a look at it . . . . The email says Mr. Greer was going to perform general maintenance and repair work. What specific kinds of services has he provided?

Client: He does a lot of stuff—everything from cleaning and repairing rental houses between occupancies to minor renovations and upgrades, in addition to basic maintenance and general upkeep such as painting, cleaning gutters, simple plumbing and electrical work, hauling debris to the dump, and other odds and ends. I also require him to inspect the exterior of each of the properties monthly, using a checklist that I've provided to him.

Atty: And how is he paid?

Client: We negotiate the payment amount for each project. I always pay him by check when the work is done. Sometimes I pay him on an hourly basis at a rate of $25 per hour, and other times I pay him a flat rate by the project. For instance, I pay him a flat fee of $200 per room to paint standard interior rooms. If a room is large or the ceiling or trim needs to be painted in addition to the walls, then we negotiate a higher fee. For plumbing and electrical projects, I pay him by the hour. I also reimburse him for any materials that he may need to purchase in connection with each project, such as paint, wiring, and lumber. I've agreed to pay him a minimum of $250 per month, even if he doesn't do 10 hours of work in that month, to be sure that he is always available to me.

Atty: Do you withhold any taxes from the money you pay him?

Client: No, I always thought he was responsible for paying his own taxes.

Atty: How often does he perform handyman services for your rental properties, and how many hours a week or a month would you say that it works out to?

Client: Typically, he handles around five projects a month, sometimes more, sometimes less. Each project is different, and some take more time than others, but I'd estimate that on average he spends about 10 hours a month working on projects at my rental properties. When a tenant moves out, which happens about once every 18 months or so, he can spend as little as 5 hours or as much as 15 to 20 hours getting the place ready to re-rent, depending on how well the tenant took care of the house. With 11 rental properties, there's a pretty steady flow of necessary maintenance and repair work. When something comes up, I call him and then he works me into his schedule and gets the project done.

Atty: What was Mr. Greer doing on the day he was injured?

Client: He was painting the front exterior of my rental house on Clover Circle.

Atty: What happened that day?

Client: Well, on February 11, I was at the rental house on Clover, telling him what I wanted him to do. I told him to be sure to mask the windows, that I didn't want rollers but a narrow brush to paint the trim, and to apply three coats of paint.

Atty: Do you always give him detailed directions like that?

Client: Not always, but I'm pretty particular. I want my properties to look nice, so I want the job done right. This was an expensive rental, and I wanted it to look really nice.

Atty: Okay, what happened next?

Client: I walked around the corner of the house, and a few minutes later I heard Rick yell. I ran back and found that he had fallen off a ladder and was hurt. He had broken his right arm and was in a lot of pain. I got him into my car and drove him to the hospital. The hospital took him into the emergency room right away.

Atty: What happened next?

Client: I called his wife from the hospital, and when I knew she was coming, I went home. Later on I tried to reach Rick and his wife by phone. They never answered and didn't return the messages I left. The next day, I called Jim, a friend of mine who owns an eight-unit apartment complex and uses Rick on repair and maintenance projects for that complex. Jim told me that he had spoken with Rick, who had said that his arm would be in a cast for at least four weeks and that he probably wouldn't be able to work for another two to four weeks after the cast came off, while he underwent physical therapy.

Atty: Who owns the ladder?

Client: As far as I know, Rick does.

Atty: Do you ever provide him with any tools for the work he performs for your rental houses?

Client: Sometimes on paint jobs, when there's a particular color that I want Rick to use, I've bought the paint from the hardware store to make sure that it's the right color, instead of having Rick buy it and then reimbursing him. I've also picked out ceiling fans, faucets, and other fixtures for rental properties on occasion, but that's about it. Rick usually provides everything else. He has one of those big built-in toolboxes on the bed of his pickup truck with all kinds of tools, everything from power drills and big saws to wrenches and screwdrivers. I think he keeps a lot of tools on hand for bigger projects that come up, like the remodel that he completed at Jim's apartment complex last year.

Atty: You mentioned that you sometimes select the paint color and fixtures such as ceiling fans and faucets on some of Mr. Greer's projects. Do you also get involved in other aspects of his work?

Client: It really depends. When it comes to paint color, the installation of a ceiling fan, or the way I want something to look when it's finished, I usually get involved in the process to make sure the project turns out the way I want it to, but I don't micromanage him or anything like that. He's very good at what he does and he knows what he's doing. If I tell him that a toilet is leaking, he figures out what the problem is and then fixes it. I work full-time as an accountant, and my job keeps me very busy, so most of the time I just swing by the property after Rick's done to make sure the work got done right before paying him for the work.

Atty: When did you find out that he was going to file a workers' comp claim against you?

Client: Not until yesterday, when he faxed over a workers' compensation claim form and asked me to fill out the "Employer" section. I was really shocked when I received the form because it never occurred to me that Rick might consider himself to be an employee of mine. I haven't withheld taxes or obtained any insurance coverage for Rick, and I don't even want to think about what it would cost to pay his medical bills or lost wages.

Atty: I understand your concerns. I think I have a pretty good idea of the professional arrangement between you and Mr. Greer. I'm going to need to research the legal issues surrounding his workers' compensation claim. I will give you a call next week to let you know what I think the next steps are.

Client: Okay. I look forward to hearing from you. And thanks so much for your help with this.

Email Correspondence Between Anderson and Greer

From: Nicole Anderson<nicorentals@cmail.com>
Date: 17 June 2013, 9:00 a.m.
To: Rick Greer <Rick@Greersfixits.com>
Subject: Handyman Work

Hi, Rick. Great talking with you earlier this week! I called your references, and they had nothing but good things to say about you. So I'd like to go ahead and have you help me with general repair and maintenance projects at my rental properties. I think I already told you this, but all are single-family houses with the usual ongoing maintenance and repair needs. I'm not sure how often I'll need your help, but I look forward to working with you.

Nicole

From: Rick Greer <Rick@Greersfixits.com>
Date: 17 June 2013, 11:15 a.m.
To: Nicole Anderson<nicorentals@cmail.com>
Subject: Handyman Work

Sounds good. Just let me know when you need my services, and I will make sure to get out to the property and get the problem handled. As I told you, I charge all my customers $25/hour for electrical and plumbing work and routine maintenance and repairs. We can discuss the price of other projects as they come up.

Rick

From: Nicole Anderson<nicorentals@cmail.com>
Date: 18 June 2013 8:15 a.m.
To: Rick Greer <Rick@Greersfixits.com>
Subject: Handyman Work

Okay. If you need to do any work on the inside of a rental house, I'll need to coordinate with my tenant to make sure that someone is there to let you in and that it's a convenient time for the tenant and for you. Exterior projects like gutter work can be done basically at your convenience. If the tenant has a dog, I just need to give the tenant a heads-up so that we can make sure the dog is secured before you show up. Will call you as soon as I need your help. Thanks!

Nicole

STATE OF FRANKLIN
DEPARTMENT OF LABOR RELATIONS
DIVISION OF WORKERS' COMPENSATION

WORKERS' COMPENSATION CLAIM FORM (DWC 1)

Employee: Complete the **"Employee"** section and give the form to your employer. Keep a copy and mark it **"Employee's Temporary Receipt"** until you receive the signed and dated copy from your employer.

Employee—complete this section and see note above.

1. Name ____ Rick Greer _____ Today's date February 18, 2016 _____
2. Home address ____ 13269 Cabot Road, Lafayette, Franklin 33527 _____
3. Date of injury ____ February 11, 2016 ____ Time of injury 9:00 __ a.m. _____ p.m.
4. Address and description of where injury happened ____ I fell from a ladder at 3025 Clover Circle, Lafayette, Franklin 33529, while painting a house for my employer, Nicole Anderson. _____
5. Describe injury and part of body affected broken right arm _____

6. Signature of employee ____ *Rick Greer* _____

Employer—complete this section and see note below.

7. Name and address of employer _____
_____
8. Date employer first knew of injury _____
9. Date claim form was provided to employee _____
10. Date employer received claim form _____
11. Name and address of insurance carrier_____
12. Insurance policy number _____
13. Signature of employer representative _____
14. Title_____ 15. Telephone _____

Employer: You are required to date this form and provide copies to your insurer or claims administrator and to the employee, dependent, or representative who filed the claim within **five working days** of receipt of the form from the employee.

SIGNING THIS FORM IS NOT AN ADMISSION OF LIABILITY.

o Employer copy   o Employee copy   o Claims administrator   o Temporary receipt

In re Anderson

February 2016
MPT-1 Library:
In re Anderson

In re Anderson

Excerpts from the Franklin Workers' Compensation Act
Franklin Labor Code § 200 *et seq.*

Article 2. Employers and Employees

***

§ 251. "Employee" means every person in the service of an employer under any appointment or contract of hire, whether express or implied, oral or written . . . .

***

§ 253. "Independent contractor" means any person who renders service for a specified recompense for a specified result, under the control of his principal as to the result of his work only and not as to the means by which such result is accomplished.

***

§ 257. Any person rendering service for another, other than as an independent contractor, or unless expressly excluded herein, is presumed to be an employee.

***

§ 280. The provisions of this statute shall be liberally construed by the courts with the purpose of extending their benefits for the protection of persons injured in the course of their employment.

Article 7. Workers' Compensation Proceedings

***

§ 705. The following are affirmative defenses, and the burden of proof rests upon the employer to establish them: (a) That an injured person claiming to be an employee was an independent contractor or otherwise excluded from the protection of this division where there is proof that the injured person was at the time of his injury actually performing service for the alleged employer.

. . .

Robbins v. Workers' Compensation Appeals Board

Franklin Court of Appeal (2007)

This is an appeal from a decision of the Franklin District Court affirming an order of the Workers' Compensation Appeals Board. The Board held that appellant Matthew Robbins was an "independent contractor" and not an "employee" for purposes of the Franklin Workers' Compensation Act (Franklin Labor Code § 200 *et seq*.) and thus was not eligible for workers' compensation benefits. We affirm.

Background

Robbins injured his head and lower back when he fell from a roof while trimming bushes at the Maple Leaf Diner in the Town of Jefferson. Robbins filed a workers' compensation claim against the diner's owner, Alana Parker.

Parker called no witnesses at the workers' compensation hearing. Robbins testified that he has been gardening, painting, fixing pipes, and doing graffiti removal for 25 years. His clients are people who either know him or are referred to him by word of mouth. He charges by the hour, but sometimes he contracts for an entire job. He usually does the same type of work but for different people each day. Robbins does not have a roofer's license or a general contractor's license. He has no office and no employees, and he does not advertise.

Parker arranged for Robbins to trim the bushes along the roofline of the diner on two occasions. The first time was in August 2004, and the second, July 15, 2005, was the day he fell.

In 2004, Parker paid Robbins by the hour, although they did not discuss the number of hours he would work. Nor did they discuss the hourly rate until he was finished. On the 2004 visit, Parker paid Robbins $150. She did not deduct taxes from his pay. He pays his own taxes. Parker and Robbins did not discuss at that time when he would provide services in the future, agreeing only that Parker would contact him when his services were needed. On the second visit, in July 2005, Parker and Robbins did not discuss either the number of hours to be worked or the rate. As it turned out, Robbins was not paid for that visit because, after his fall, he did not complete the work and never sent a bill. Robbins had no plans to do additional work at the diner in the future, other than to trim bushes whenever Parker asked.

On the day he fell, Robbins brought all the equipment he needed to do the job, including a trimmer, a rake, a broom, a leaf blower, and a ladder. He arrived in his own truck. Parker did not tell him to bring an assistant that day, how to do the job, or how long it would take. She did not tell him to arrive at any given time, only that he should arrive before the diner opened.

Discussion

The question before us is whether Robbins was an employee or an independent contractor when he was injured. The Board's decision that Robbins was an independent contractor (and therefore not entitled to workers' compensation benefits) will be upheld if it is supported by substantial evidence in the record.

Workers' compensation laws protect individuals who are injured on the job by awarding prompt compensation, regardless of fault, for work injuries. *Raleigh v. Juneau Enterprises, Inc.* (Fr. Ct. App. 1992). The principal test of an employment relationship is whether the person to whom service is rendered has the "right to control" the manner and means of accomplishing the result desired. Franklin Labor Code § 253. The existence of such right of control, not the extent of its exercise, gives rise to the employer-employee relationship. However, this test is not exclusive. Several secondary factors, the "*Doyle* factors," *infra*, also are relevant to one's status as an employee or an independent contractor.

Franklin courts have liberally construed the Workers' Compensation Act to extend benefits to persons injured in their employment. *Id.* § 280. Because workers' compensation statutes are remedial, public policy considerations also influence the determination of whether an individual is entitled to workers' compensation protections.

Right-of-Control Test

We begin with the right-of-control test set forth in *Doyle v. Workers' Compensation Appeals Board* (Fr. Sup. Ct. 1991). *Doyle* involved unskilled harvesters who worked for the defendant grower. *Doyle* held that, because all meaningful aspects of the relationship (e.g., price, crop cultivation, fertilization and insect prevention, payment, and the right to deal with buyers) were controlled by the defendant grower, the grower exercised "pervasive control over the operation as a whole," and the unskilled harvesters were its employees. The harvesters' only decisions were which plants were ready to pick and which needed weeding. The harvesters' work was an integral component of the grower's operations, over which the grower exercised pervasive control, and the purported "independence" of the harvesters from the grower's supervision was not a result of superior skills but was rather a function of the unskilled nature of the labor, which required little supervision.

Here, Robbins was engaged to produce *the result* of trimming the bushes. Neither party presented evidence that Parker had the power to control the manner or means of accomplishing the trimming. Indeed, it is Parker's inability to control the means and manner by which Robbins provided the trimming service that puts the facts here in stark contrast to those in *Doyle*. Robbins testified that in general, no one tells him how to do his work on the jobs he accepts and that Parker did not tell him how to do the trimming at the diner. Once he accepted a job, he testified, he completed it without direction from the person for whom he was rendering the service. Thus, the lack of supervision here was not a function of the unskilled nature of the job, as in *Doyle*. Nor does the fact that Parker asked Robbins to arrive early suggest that Parker controlled any aspect of the trimming. It was Robbins who chose both the date and time to perform the service. In short, under the principal test of the employment relationship, Parker did not have the right to control Robbins's work.

Doyle Factors

In addition to the right-of-control test set forth in *Doyle*, we also must analyze the secondary factors identified in that case to determine whether Robbins was an independent contractor or an employee. These "*Doyle* factors" are derived largely from the Restatement (Second) of Agency and from other jurisdictions.

They are (1) whether the worker is engaged in a distinct occupation or an independently established business; (2) whether the worker or the principal supplies the tools or instrumentalities used in the work, other than those customarily supplied by employees; (3) the method of payment, whether by time or by the job; (4) whether the work is part of the regular business of the principal; (5) whether the worker has a substantial investment in the worker's business other than personal services; (6) whether the worker hires employees to assist him; (7) whether the parties believe they are creating an employer-employee relationship; and (8) the degree of permanence of the working relationship. The *Doyle* factors are not to be applied mechanically as separate tests but are intertwined, and their weight often depends on particular combinations of the factors. The process of distinguishing employees from independent contractors is fact-specific and qualitative rather than quantitative.

In applying the *Doyle* factors to the facts at hand, we note that, first, Robbins performed his work for Parker as part of his gardening services, which he has been doing independently for approximately 25 years. Although Robbins does not advertise, he has several different clients who telephone or email him to perform specific jobs. Not only does he have many other clients, but Parker did not ask him to perform any service other than trimming the bushes.

Second, Robbins supplied the equipment he used for the job; and they were not tools a restaurant would commonly have.

Third, he was not hired by the day or hour, or even on a regular basis. Payment was only discussed after the work was complete. Sometimes Robbins charged by the hour and sometimes by the job, and he was paid on a job-by-job basis, with no obligation on the part of either party for work in the future. Taxes were not deducted from his payment. Robbins estimates and pays his own taxes.

Fourth, in concluding that the harvesters in *Doyle* were employees, the court found that their work constituted "a regular and integrated portion of [the grower's] business operation, in that [its] entire business was the production and sale of agricultural crops." Although seasonal, the work in *Doyle* was a permanent part of the agricultural process, and many harvesters returned to work for Doyle each year—all of which led the court to conclude that the "permanent integration of the workers into the heart of Doyle's business is a strong indicator that Doyle functions as an employer." By contrast, Robbins is a gardener whose work is wholly unrelated to the restaurant business; it constitutes only occasional, discrete maintenance. Robbins, for example, was asked to work when the diner was closed so that his work would not interfere with the diner's *regular business*.

We note that Robbins has 25 years' experience in his gardening business and a substantial investment in equipment and other aspects of the business, satisfying the fifth factor.

Although Robbins did not hire employees to assist him (the sixth *Doyle* factor), this alone does not negate the overwhelming evidence satisfying the other *Doyle* factors.

Neither Robbins nor anyone else testified that the parties believed they were creating an employer-employee relationship (the seventh *Doyle* factor). This factor is neutral.

With regard to the eighth and final *Doyle* factor, the degree of permanence in the working relationship, no date for Robbins's return was specified after the first time he trimmed bushes at the diner. Robbins understood that he would be contacted only when his services were needed, with the result that he worked for a circumscribed period of time with no permanence whatsoever in his working relationship with Parker. Indeed, Robbins had done trimming work for Parker only twice in the space of nearly a year, and there were no plans for him to return to the diner. Thus, Robbins's profit or loss depended on his scheduling, the time taken to perform the services, and his investment in tools and equipment.

Altogether, six of the *Doyle* factors support the Board's conclusion that Robbins was an independent contractor because he "render[ed] service for a specified recompense for a specified result, under the control of his principal as to the result of his work only and not as to the means by which such result [was] accomplished." Franklin Labor Code § 253.

Policy Consideration

Finally, in deciding whether a worker is an employee or an independent contractor, the court must consider the remedial purpose of workers' compensation laws, the class of persons intended to be protected, and the relative bargaining positions of the parties. The policy underlying Franklin's workers' compensation law indicates that the exclusion of independent contractors from the law's benefits should apply to those situations where the worker had control over how the work was done and, in particular, had primary power over work safety and could distribute the risk and cost of injury as an expense of his own business.

Thus the *Doyle* court, in its analysis of the harvesters' employment status, considered that if the grower were not the employer, the harvesters themselves and the public at large would have to assume the entire financial burden when injuries occur. Accordingly, the harvesters were in the class of workers for which the protections of workers' compensation law were intended.

Robbins, by contrast, was in a distinctly different position from the harvesters in *Doyle*—he was free to take or reject the jobs that Parker offered. He negotiated payment with Parker and was not in a weak bargaining position. These facts support the conclusion that Robbins does not fall under the protections of the workers' compensation act but is an independent contractor.

Conclusion

Here, no amount of liberal construction can change the balance of evidence. Robbins was an independent contractor. This conclusion does not defeat the policy behind the workers' compensation system. The decision of the Board is affirmed.

Harris v. Workers' Compensation Appeals Board
Franklin Court of Appeal (2003)

This is an appeal from the Workers' Compensation Appeals Board. The Board held, and the trial court affirmed, that a golf caddie was an independent contractor rather than an employee and was not entitled to workers' compensation for injuries sustained on the job. We reverse.

Appellant Jordan Harris claimed that he sustained various orthopedic injuries in October 2001, while employed by Lamar Country Club as a golf caddie. The Club argued that Harris was an independent contractor. At the hearing before the Board, Harris testified that he had had continuous employment with the Club since May 2000, working from 7:00 a.m. to 3:00 p.m. daily. He said he was required to wear special clothing: he was issued a cap and had to buy a Club shirt. The Club maintains a caddie assignment and locker room, and has adopted rules of conduct for caddies—including one requiring them to get permission to go to other areas of the Club. According to Harris, his duties were greeting Club members, giving advice about the course, retrieving balls, carrying and cleaning golf clubs, getting carts, and changing shoe spikes. Harris received his assignments from the Club, but members would instruct him while he accompanied them on the course, which is where he was injured. There were no written contracts or tax forms, and Harris had no other caddie business.

Kim Day, the Club's office manager, testified that Harris was not on the Club's payroll, and was paid in cash through various members' accounts. She added that the Club provides caddies for its members, but that there is no set schedule and they are free to work elsewhere.

Andrew Schaefer, the Club's caddie master, testified that he considers the caddies' abilities and personalities when assigning them to members. Members can request certain caddies, but assignments can be refused and caddies may work elsewhere without repercussion. According to Schaefer, once on the course, the members supervise the caddies, although the caddies sometimes advise and serve as guides on the course. Among other things, caddies search for and clean balls and remove flags on the greens. Schaefer also testified that caddies have no set days or hours: they normally sign in and inform him when they are leaving. It is Schaefer's job to pay the caddies cash and charge the members' accounts.

On appeal, Harris notes that employment is presumed under the law when services are provided, and he argues that the Club failed to meet its burden of proving independent contractor status under the Franklin Labor Code § 705(a). Harris also contends that when the matter is analyzed under *Doyle v. Workers' Compensation Appeals Board* (Fr. Sup. Ct. 1991), the conclusion is inescapable that he was an employee.

Both sides agree that the Club and the caddie master have absolute authority over the premises, while the members direct the caddies on the golf course. But this does not mean that the Club's control does not extend to caddying. It is undisputed that the Club supervised Harris's dress, his behavior, and the types of services he rendered, and it administered the payment process.

A person who engages an independent contractor to perform a job for him or her may retain broad general power of supervision and control as to the results of the work so as to ensure satisfactory performance of the contract—including the right to inspect, to stop the work, to make suggestions or recommendations as to the details of the work, or to prescribe alterations or deviations in the work—without changing the nature of the independent contractor relationship or the duties arising from that relationship.

Under Franklin Labor Code § 253, employer/employee status exists when the employer controls the manner and means of the work and not just the results. We believe that is the case here. The Club primarily determines assignments based on caddies' abilities and personalities, and keeps track of attendance if not hours. The ability to reject assignments seems of small import considering the effect on income and the Club's clearly superior bargaining position.

The *Doyle* factors also support the conclusion that Harris was an employee. Since Day testified that the Club provides caddies for its members, it is apparent that caddying is an integral part of the Club's business. Thus, Harris provided services which also benefited the Club, and employment is presumed in such situations. Franklin Labor Code § 257. In addition, Harris did not have his own business, and the fact that the Club allows caddies to work elsewhere does not negate a finding of employment. Although some items of equipment such as golf clubs are supplied by the members, the Club provides a caddie room and lockers.

Considering the totality of circumstances, and § 280 of the Labor Code, which provides that the statute be liberally construed with the purpose of extending benefits to those injured in the course of employment, we conclude that Harris was an employee. The decision of the Workers' Compensation Appeals Board denying workers' compensation benefits is vacated, and the case is remanded for further proceedings consistent with this opinion.

February 2016
MPT-2 File:
Miller v. Trapp

Stuart, Parks & Howard LLC
Attorneys at Law
1500 Clark Street
Franklin City, Franklin 33007

MEMORANDUM

To: Examinee
From: Timothy Howard, Partner
Date: February 23, 2016
Re: Katie Miller

We have been retained by Katie Miller to pursue civil assault and battery claims against Steve Trapp, guitarist and lead vocalist for the band the Revengers, for an incident that occurred at a concert two weeks ago. I have met with Miller and reviewed the evidence. Our firm has agreed to take the case because Miller has meritorious claims for assault and battery, and because her uncle is a valued client of the firm.

Yesterday, I called Trapp's lawyer, Saul Leffler, and told him that we are preparing to sue Trapp for his assault and battery of Miller. I asked Leffler if his client would be interested in resolving the matter short of litigation. Leffler was dismissive and said that Miller does not have a case. I have attached a memo summarizing our phone conversation.

Please draft both of the following:

(1) A demand letter addressed to Attorney Leffler, written for my signature

Your letter should persuasively state the basis for Miller's assault and battery claims against Trapp and argue that Miller will be able to recover compensatory and punitive damages. Follow our firm's guidelines on drafting demand letters (attached). Leave blank the specific amounts that we will request for each category of damages. I will fill in the amounts later.

(2) A brief memo to me

Your memo should set forth your recommendation of the specific amounts along with the rationale for these amounts for each category of damages that we could reasonably expect to recover at trial. Use the attached cases and summaries of recent Franklin civil jury verdicts as guidance on what a jury might award for Miller's damages. Refer to these jury verdicts in your memo to me, but do not cite them in the demand letter. I will fill in the amounts in the demand letter after I have reviewed your memo.

Miller v. Trapp

Stuart, Parks & Howard LLC

OFFICE MEMORANDUM

To: All Attorneys
From: Managing Partner
Date: September 5, 2013
Re: Guidelines for Drafting Demand Letters

A demand letter states our client's legal claims and demands that the opposing party pay damages and/or take or cease taking a certain action. A demand letter is designed to advocate a position and to persuade the recipient.

A demand letter typically includes (1) a brief statement indicating that we represent our client in this matter; (2) a brief statement of the purpose of the letter; (3) a succinct but persuasive statement of facts; (4) a thorough analysis of the bases for our client's claims; (5) a blank space for a specific settlement demand or amount, to be filled in by the supervising partner; (6) a deadline by which the opposing party must comply (usually one or two weeks); and (7) the consequences for failing to comply by the deadline, including the risks of litigation for the opposing party.

When discussing the bases for our client's claims, you should thoroughly analyze and integrate both the facts and the applicable law and respond to arguments that have been made against the claims.

A well-written demand letter can promote a favorable settlement. It should set forth the strongest credible arguments on behalf of our client so that there is room for negotiation.

RockNation, a blog by Katie Miller
Commentary on Rock and Roll

February 3, 2016

Rock fans, I have some exciting news. Through my gig reporting for my college newspaper, I got a press pass for the Revengers concert next week at the Franklin City Arena. I am going to find Revengers guitarist and lead vocalist Steve Trapp backstage after the show and interview him. I promise I will provide the details of that interview here. Wish me luck!! I'm really psyched to talk to Steve Trapp. He's super hot and famous.

RockNation, a blog by Katie Miller
Commentary on Rock and Roll

February 16, 2016

Readers, I am very disappointed to tell you that I can't provide an account of an interview with Steve Trapp of the Revengers as promised. I had planned to interview him after the Revengers concert at the Franklin City Arena last week. Instead of giving me an interview, Steve gave me a dislocated shoulder!

After the concert, I was eagerly waiting offstage to speak to Steve. It was a long wait, rock fans, because the Revengers played two encores, which were awesome. After the final song, the band walked offstage. I was hoping to stop Steve for a quick impromptu interview. I had my smartphone out, set to record. A bunch of other photographers and journalists were waiting too. I was about half of the way back in the group. Nina Pender, a photographer from *Celebrity* magazine, was in the very front. When Steve walked offstage, Nina moved in to take a picture of him. Steve punched her in the nose, wrested the camera out of her hands, and smashed it on the ground. I stood there frozen, mouth agape. Steve continued toward us. He looked at me and yelled, "Get out of my way, you little punk, or I'll beat the hell out of you." He raised his arm as if to hit me. I was freaking out. Instead of hitting me, he grabbed my phone out of my hand and smashed it on the ground. I was holding the phone tightly because of the crowd. When he grabbed my phone, he pulled so hard that he dislocated my shoulder, and I had to go to the hospital.

I have been a wreck since this happened. The pain was unbelievable for almost four hours until the doctor popped my shoulder back in place. I have $5,000 in medical bills; I had my arm in a sling for three days; I missed a week of my part-time work in the school cafeteria, which cost me $100; and I had to pay $500 to replace my phone.

This is all devastating. Steve has been my idol since he started playing with the Revengers. I have everything the Revengers ever recorded, and I have followed every piece of news about Steve's music and personal life. I think Steve should have to pay for what he did, don't you? My blog will no longer celebrate the Revengers as the best rock-and-roll band. I now rate Palindrome as the top living rock-and-roll band!

Reeling Rock   **February 13, 2016**
The Online Magazine about Rock and Roll
Steve Trapp Allegedly Punches Photographer in Post-concert Melee

FRANKLIN CITY — Musician Steve Trapp, lead vocalist and guitarist for the Revengers, was involved in an alleged assault on a photographer last Tuesday, February 9, as he left the stage after a Revengers concert. The Franklin City Police Department is conducting a criminal investigation into the incident, which occurred at approximately 11:00 p.m.

Trapp became upset at *Celebrity* magazine photographer Nina Pender as she was trying to take his photograph. Trapp asked Pender to stop shooting. He then walked over to Pender, punched her in the face, and slammed her camera on the ground. Other photographers at the scene captured the incident. Paramedics were called, and Pender was taken to a hospital where she was treated for serious injuries.

The day after the incident, Trapp left Franklin City to stay at his 15-bedroom vacation home in Xanadu, the exclusive Franklin beach resort. Trapp could not be reached for comment.

Pender has filed a criminal complaint against the musician, and Franklin City Police Department Detective Kevin Park said that an investigation is ongoing. He said that the case will be presented to the District Attorney's office as early as today. "With the photographs and videos, it's pretty solid evidence," reported Park.

Pender's lawyer, Russ Smalls, told *Reeling Rock* that Pender intends to file a civil lawsuit against Trapp seeking $5 million in damages.

Others were injured during the incident. After Trapp assaulted Pender, the musician stormed through the crowd of dozens of paparazzi and journalists. Witnesses report that Trapp yelled obscenities and pushed individuals out of his way. One newspaper reporter was taken to the hospital with a shoulder injury.

Trapp has had previous run-ins with the law. In 2009, he was charged with possession of illegal drugs, but the charges were later dropped. In 2012, Trapp pleaded guilty to misdemeanor assault and battery after attacking his then bodyguard, Alex Peel.

The Revengers' latest album, *Jab*, has received universal acclaim. *Reeling Rock* awarded *Jab* four out of five stars. *Jab* was also named 2015 Album of the Year at the Franklin City Music Awards.

[Photographs of Trapp punching Pender and a link to amateur YouTube video of the encounter, both of which were included with the article, are omitted.]

Miller v. Trapp

Stuart, Parks & Howard LLC

MEMORANDUM TO FILE

From: Timothy Howard
Date: February 22, 2016
Re: Katie Miller matter; phone conversation with Saul Leffler

Today I spoke with Saul Leffler, Steve Trapp's lawyer. We discussed Katie Miller's claims for assault and battery against Trapp. Leffler was dismissive and said that we would be "crazy" to pursue them.

Leffler denied that Trapp had committed a battery. According to Leffler, Trapp had just finished performing a two-and-a-half-hour high-energy rock concert, and he was exhausted from the performance and eager to get to his dressing room. According to Leffler, Trapp does not recall even touching Katie Miller as he passed the crowd of journalists. Leffler also claimed that even if Trapp had made any contact with Miller, it would have been accidental. Assuming that there was some contact, Leffler said that Miller had consented to a certain amount of jostling by attending the concert and going backstage. Leffler said that Trapp did not intend to harm her, and therefore did not have the requisite intent for battery.

Leffler also said that Miller lacks a meritorious claim for assault. In response to my statement that Trapp's conduct caused Miller to have an imminent apprehension of a battery, he said, "Baloney." Leffler conceded that Trapp was annoyed that so many journalists were crowded in his path; however, Leffler stated that Trapp did nothing that would cause Miller to fear that he would harm her. Leffler denied that Trapp singled out Miller or attempted to frighten her in any way.

Leffler got very upset when I mentioned punitive damages, and he accused Miller of attempting to capitalize on Trapp's fame and fortune. Leffler insisted that a jury will never find that Trapp had any injurious intent toward Miller. He emphasized that Trapp is a famous, well-respected musician, who generously donates to a wide variety of charities, including shelters for homeless women. Leffler said that Trapp does not even know Miller, and he has no evil motives toward young women generally or Miller in particular. I responded that the last thing Trapp needed now was more bad publicity. Leffler had no comment.

Leffler concluded by saying that if our firm pursues Miller's claims, we will lose.

FRANKLIN JURY VERDICT SUMMARIES

$360,000—Cook v. Matthews Garage (March 2015)

Plaintiff went into defendant's automobile repair shop to complain about the way his wife, a customer, had been treated by one of defendant's employees. That employee then pushed plaintiff to the floor and screamed and cursed at him. Plaintiff's arm was broken. Defendant knew that the employee had been terminated from prior jobs because of his tendency to use violence to settle work-related disputes.

Medical expenses—$10,000
Pain and suffering—$50,000
Punitive damages—$300,000

$1,500,000—Alma v. Burgess (April 2015)

Defendant attacked plaintiff, a 35-year-old teacher, when plaintiff was leaving her house at night. Defendant stabbed plaintiff in the torso and upper leg. Plaintiff was taken by ambulance to the hospital, where she received treatment and remained for four days.

Medical expenses—$100,000
Pain and suffering—$400,000
Punitive damages—$1,000,000

$52,000—Little v. Franklin Chargers, Inc. (October 2015)

Plaintiff attended a professional basketball game as a spectator. During halftime, defendant's team mascot grabbed plaintiff hard and attempted to pull him onto the floor to participate in an entertainment routine. The mascot pulled plaintiff's arm with such force that plaintiff fell down, dislocating his left shoulder. Plaintiff felt that he had been humiliated in front of his fiancée and a stadium full of onlookers.

Medical expenses—$12,000
Pain and suffering—$40,000
Punitive damages of $200,000 requested but denied.

Miller v. Trapp

February 2016
MPT-2 Library:
Miller v. Trapp

Horton v. Suzuki

Franklin Court of Appeal (2009)

This is an appeal from a judgment for the plaintiff following a bench trial of a civil battery case. The defendant argues that 1) the lower court's finding of lack of consent was clearly erroneous; 2) the lower court's finding on intent was clearly erroneous; and 3) even if there was a battery, the damages award was excessive.

Plaintiff John Horton sued defendant Rikuo Suzuki, his karate instructor, for injuries suffered as a result of an alleged battery committed by Suzuki.

It is undisputed that Horton was a student in a karate class conducted by Suzuki. Horton testified that he knew he would be subjected to rough physical contact by classmates and the instructor as a necessary part of the class. A classmate testified that Horton was speaking in the locker room to another student after class when Suzuki apparently misunderstood what Horton said and struck Horton on the cheek. The classmate further testified that Suzuki appeared angry and yelled at Horton.

Suzuki argues that Horton consented to the contact by enrolling in the karate class. Several witnesses for Suzuki testified that a student of karate must expect rough treatment from his instructor and that the instructor often physically disciplines the students during class. Suzuki testified that he was attempting to discipline Horton when he struck him. However, there is no evidence that the blow had any connection with the karate instruction, and the evidence indicates that Suzuki struck Horton for some personal reason.

An actor is subject to liability to another for the tort of battery if he or she acts intending to cause a harmful or offensive contact, or an imminent apprehension of such a contact, and a harmful or offensive contact results. To prevail on a civil battery claim, the plaintiff must show that he or she did not consent to (or give apparent consent to) the defendant's contact. Consent and apparent consent are relevant to whether there was in fact a harmful or offensive contact.

Here Horton may have consented to a certain amount of harmful or offensive contact during his karate instruction. Nothing in the record, however, indicates that Horton consented to being struck on the cheek by his instructor after class had been dismissed.

Suzuki also argues that he is not liable for battery because he did not intend to harm or offend Horton. In Franklin, for a plaintiff to prevail on a battery claim, it is sufficient that the defendant intended to cause a contact that turned out to be harmful or offensive. The defendant does not have to have intended that the contact result in harm or offense.

Thus, it is irrelevant whether Suzuki intended that Horton be harmed or offended. Suzuki intended to strike Horton on the cheek, and in doing so engaged in intentional harmful and offensive contact.

Finally, Suzuki argues that even if there was a battery, the trial court erred by awarding Horton excessive damages of $7,500. For intentional torts like assault or battery, a plaintiff may seek two kinds of damages: compensatory and punitive. Compensatory damages may include medical expenses, lost wages, and pain and suffering. Pain and suffering includes physical pain as well as mental suffering such as insult and indignity, hurt feelings, and fright caused by the battery. Moreover, mental suffering may be inferred from proof of fright caused by a sudden, unprovoked, and unjustifiable battery. There is no mathematical formula for assessing the value of pain and suffering; that determination is left to the sound discretion of the trier of fact.

Horton suffered a cut on the inside of his mouth which became infected, and for which he incurred only $1,500 in medical expenses. The court properly found that Suzuki committed battery and awarded Horton $7,500 in compensatory damages: $1,500 for medical expenses and $6,000 for pain and suffering.

Although punitive damages are also available in civil assault and battery cases, the trial court denied Horton's request for punitive damages and that denial was not appealed.

We find the total award of $7,500 to be adequate and in conformity with awards in battery cases in which the injuries incurred were minimal.

Our review of the record persuades us that there is sufficient evidence to support the lower court's findings. We therefore conclude that the lower court's findings were not clearly erroneous.

Affirmed.

Polk v. Eugene

Franklin Supreme Court (2004)

This is a suit for compensatory and punitive damages growing out of an alleged battery. The plaintiff, Barrington Polk, is a physician. The defendant, John Eugene, is a member of the private Hills Club. After a jury trial, the court rendered judgment for the plaintiff, including an award of punitive damages. The Franklin Court of Appeal reversed. The questions before this Court are whether a battery was committed and, if so, whether the trial court abused its discretion in entering judgment for $3,000 in punitive damages.

Polk had been invited to a one-day medical conference at the Hills Club. The invitation included a luncheon. The luncheon was buffet style, and Polk stood in line with others. As Polk was about to be served, Eugene approached him, snatched the plate from Polk's hand, and shouted that Polk could not be served in the club because of his race. Polk was not actually touched during the incident. Polk testified that he did not fear or apprehend physical injury but that he was highly embarrassed by Eugene's conduct in the presence of his associates.

The jury found that Eugene "forcibly dispossessed plaintiff of his dinner plate" and "shouted in a loud and offensive manner" that Polk could not be served there, thus subjecting Polk to humiliation and indignity. The jury found that Eugene acted maliciously and awarded Polk $1,000 in compensatory damages for pain and suffering due to his humiliation and indignity and $3,000 in punitive damages. Eugene appealed, arguing that there was no battery but even if there was a battery, the evidence did not support an award of punitive damages.

The court of appeal held that there was no battery because there was no physical contact and therefore did not reach the issue of punitive damages. However, it has long been settled that actual physical contact is not necessary to constitute a battery, so long as there is contact with clothing or an object closely identified with the body.

Under the facts of this case, we have no difficulty in holding that the intentional grabbing of Polk's plate constituted a battery. We held that the snatching of an object from one's hand constituted a battery in *Riley v. Adams* (Franklin Sup. Ct. 1960). In *Riley*, the plaintiff bought some articles of intimate apparel from a store at which the defendant was the manager. The defendant claimed that he suspected that the plaintiff had not paid for all the articles in her shopping bag. Rather than confronting the young woman at the cash register or in the store, the defendant waited until she had walked several blocks and crossed the square to confront her. He

Miller v. Trapp

ran up and took the plaintiff's bag from her by force. He proceeded to search it and take the articles out and hold them up to the public view. The court held that the defendant's acts constituted a battery, explaining that "to constitute a battery, it is not necessary to touch the plaintiff's body or even his clothing. Knocking or snatching anything from plaintiff's hand or touching anything connected with his person, when done in an offensive manner, is sufficient to constitute an offensive touching." *Riley.*

Since the essence of the plaintiff's grievance consists in the offense to his dignity involved in the unpermitted and intentional invasion of his person and not in any physical harm done to his body, it is not necessary that the plaintiff's actual body be disturbed. Unpermitted and intentional contact with anything so connected with the body as to be customarily regarded as part of another's person is actionable as an offensive contact with his person. We hold, therefore, that the forceful dispossession of Polk's plate in an offensive manner was sufficient to constitute a battery.

Damages for mental suffering are recoverable without a showing of actual physical injury in a civil action for battery because the basis of that action is the unpermitted and intentional invasion of the plaintiff's person and not the actual harm done to the plaintiff's body. Personal indignity is the essence of an action for battery; consequently, the defendant is liable not only for contacts that do actual physical harm but also for those that are offensive. We hold, therefore, that Polk was entitled to compensatory damages for mental suffering due to the battery, even in the absence of any physical injury.

We now turn to the question of punitive damages. The jury verdict concluded with a finding that $3,000 would "reasonably compensate plaintiff for Eugene's evil act and reckless disregard of plaintiff's feelings and rights."

It has long been established in Franklin that punitive damages may be awarded for conduct that is outrageous, because of the defendant's evil motive or his reckless indifference to the rights of others. This common law rule makes sense in terms of the purposes of punitive damages. Punitive damages are awarded in the jury's discretion to punish the defendant for his outrageous conduct and to deter him and others like him from similar conduct in the future. The focus is on the character of the tortfeasor's conduct—whether it is of the sort that calls for deterrence and punishment over and above that provided by compensatory awards. In assessing punitive damages, the trier of fact can properly consider (a) the character of the defendant's act, namely whether it is of the sort that calls for deterrence and punishment; (b) the nature and extent of the harm to the plaintiff that the defendant caused or intended to cause; and (c) the wealth of the defendant.

Punitive damages are never awarded as a matter of right, no matter how egregious the defendant's conduct. Compensatory damages, by contrast, are mandatory. Once liability is found, the jury is required to award compensatory damages in an amount appropriate to compensate the plaintiff for his loss.

Eugene argues that the award of punitive damages is not supported by substantial evidence. However, the standard of review for an award of punitive damages is whether the trial court abused its discretion. The amount of punitive damages is left to the discretion of the trier of fact, based on the circumstances of each case, but should not be so unrelated to the injury and compensatory damages proven as to plainly manifest passion and prejudice rather than reason and justice. The United States Supreme Court has instructed that few awards exceeding a single-digit ratio between punitive and compensatory damages will satisfy due process. *State Farm v. Campbell*, 538 U.S. 408 (2003).

An appellate court should disturb a determination of punitive damages only in extreme cases. Here, the jury awarded $1,000 in compensatory damages and $3,000 in punitive damages. The punitive damages awarded were only three times the amount of compensatory damages and within the *State Farm v. Campbell* guideline.

The jury found that Eugene acted with an evil motive and a reckless disregard of Polk's rights and feelings. The record contains sufficient evidence to support this finding.

The court of appeal's holding that there was no battery is reversed, and the judgment of the trial court is reinstated in favor of the plaintiff.

Brown v. Orr

Franklin Court of Appeal (2000)

The plaintiff, Lydia Brown, appeals from a summary judgment for the defendant, Richard Orr, in which the trial court found that his actions did not constitute assault. For the reasons set forth below, we reverse.

Brown and Orr were both employed at Hotel Livingston in Franklin City and were members of the same labor union. During a conversation concerning the proper method of filing a grievance against the hotel with the union, Orr allegedly shook his finger in Brown's face. Brown told Orr that the last man who pointed his finger at her "was sorry that he did it." Orr then allegedly stated that he would "take [her] down anytime, anywhere." The conversation then ended, and Brown returned to work. The next day she and Orr had a second confrontation, during which Orr allegedly repeated his earlier threat. Following that second incident, Brown became "agitated and upset" and reported Orr's threats to her supervisor. Brown commenced this civil suit against Orr for assault. Orr moved for summary judgment, claiming that his conduct did not create a reasonable apprehension of physical harm in Brown. The trial court granted Orr's motion. Brown appeals. We reverse.

An actor is subject to liability for assault if he acts intending to cause a battery or imminent apprehension of a battery and the plaintiff is put in well-founded apprehension of an imminent battery. The trial court found that Orr's conduct could not have put Brown in apprehension of an imminent battery.

On appeal, Brown cites *Holmes v. Nash* (Fr. Sup. Ct. 1990) in arguing that Orr's threats, when combined with the fact that he shook his finger in her face during their first conversation, created a question for the jury on the issue of assault. She contends that Orr's actions were similar to those of the defendant in *Holmes*.

In *Holmes*, defendant Tom Nash repeatedly threatened to kill plaintiff Jenny Holmes if she sued him. When Holmes filed a legal action, Nash came to her home, beat on the door, and attempted to pry it open, while repeating his threats to kill her. There was also evidence that Nash made harassing telephone calls to Holmes. Those acts so unnerved Holmes that she changed the locks on her door, nailed her windows closed, and had friends spend the night at her home. In *Holmes*, the court held, "Words standing alone cannot constitute an assault. However, they may give meaning to an act, and when taken together, they may create a well-founded fear of a battery in the mind of the person at whom they are directed, thereby constituting an assault." The court concluded that it could not say that Nash's actions were sufficient to give rise to a well-founded apprehension of an imminent harmful or offensive contact but that it was a question for the jury.

Although the facts in this case are not as strong as those in *Holmes*, we cannot say that, as a matter of law, Orr's acts and threats could not create a reasonable or well-founded apprehension of imminent physical harm. There was evidence that after Orr's first alleged threat, Brown walked away. That evidence is not conclusive, however, as to whether she discounted the threat or whether she left to avoid the threatened harm. Brown also testified that after the second alleged assault the next day, she had to leave work because she was so frightened and upset.

Summary judgment is appropriate if there is no genuine issue of material fact and a party is entitled to judgment as a matter of law. After reviewing the evidence before the trial court in a light most favorable to the non-movant, as this court must do when reviewing a summary judgment, we conclude that Brown presented sufficient evidence that Orr's alleged threats created a well-founded fear of imminent harm and created a jury question on her claim of assault. Therefore, the summary judgment on Brown's assault claim is reversed.

Reversed and remanded.

Miller v. Trapp

Miller v. Trapp

Themis
Bar Review

July 2015 MPTs
In re Bryan Carr
In re Franklin Aces

THE MPT

MULTISTATE PERFORMANCE TEST

July 2015
MPTs

www.ncbex.org

National Conference of Bar Examiners
302 South Bedford Street | Madison, WI 53703-3622
Phone: 608-280-8550 | Fax: 608-280-8552 | TDD: 608-661-1275
e-mail: contact@ncbex.org

Contents

Preface

The Multistate Performance Test (MPT) is developed by the National Conference of Bar Examiners (NCBE). This publication includes the items and Point Sheets from the July 2015 MPT. The instructions for the test appear on page iii.

The MPT Point Sheets describe the factual and legal points encompassed within the lawyering tasks to be completed. They outline the possible issues and points that might be addressed by an examinee. They are provided to the user jurisdictions to assist graders in grading the examination by identifying the issues and suggesting the resolution of the problem contemplated by the drafters.

For more information about the MPT, including a list of skills tested, visit the NCBE website at www .ncbex.org.

Description of the MPT

The MPT consists of two 90-minute items and is a component of the Uniform Bar Examination (UBE). It is administered by user jurisdictions as part of the bar examination on the Tuesday before the last Wednesday in February and July of each year. User jurisdictions may select one or both items to include as part of their bar examinations. (Jurisdictions that administer the UBE use two MPTs.)

The materials for each MPT include a File and a Library. The File consists of source documents containing all the facts of the case. The specific assignment the examinee is to complete is described in a memorandum from a supervising attorney. The File might also include transcripts of interviews, depositions, hearings or trials, pleadings, correspondence, client documents, contracts, newspaper articles, medical records, police reports, or lawyer's notes. Relevant as well as irrelevant facts are included. Facts are sometimes ambiguous, incomplete, or even conflicting. As in practice, a client's or a supervising attorney's version of events may be incomplete or unreliable. Examinees are expected to recognize when facts are inconsistent or missing and are expected to identify potential sources of additional facts.

The Library may contain cases, statutes, regulations, or rules, some of which may not be relevant to the assigned lawyering task. The examinee is expected to extract from the Library the legal principles necessary to analyze the problem and perform the task. The MPT is not a test of substantive law; the Library materials provide sufficient substantive information to complete the task.

The MPT is designed to test an examinee's ability to use fundamental lawyering skills in a realistic situation and complete a task that a beginning lawyer should be able to accomplish. The MPT is not a test of substantive knowledge. Rather, it is designed to evaluate six fundamental skills lawyers are expected to demonstrate regardless of the area of law in which the skills arise. The MPT requires examinees to (1) sort detailed factual materials and separate relevant from irrelevant facts; (2) analyze statutory, case, and administrative materials for applicable principles of law; (3) apply the relevant law to the relevant facts in a manner likely to resolve a client's problem; (4) identify and resolve ethical dilemmas, when present; (5) communicate effectively in writing; and (6) complete a lawyering task within time constraints. These skills are tested by requiring examinees to perform one or more of a variety of lawyering tasks. For example, examinees might be instructed to complete any of the following: a memorandum to a supervising attorney, a letter to a client, a persuasive memorandum or brief, a statement of facts, a contract provision, a will, a counseling plan, a proposal for settlement or agreement, a discovery plan, a witness examination plan, or a closing argument.

Introduction

The back cover of each test booklet contains the following instructions:

You will be instructed when to begin and when to stop this test. Do not break the seal on this booklet until you are told to begin. This test is designed to evaluate your ability to handle a select number of legal authorities in the context of a factual problem involving a client.

The problem is set in the fictitious state of Franklin, in the fictitious Fifteenth Circuit of the United States. Columbia and Olympia are also fictitious states in the Fifteenth Circuit. In Franklin, the trial court of general jurisdiction is the District Court, the intermediate appellate court is the Court of Appeal, and the highest court is the Supreme Court.

You will have two kinds of materials with which to work: a File and a Library. The first document in the File is a memorandum containing the instructions for the task you are to complete. The other documents in the File contain factual information about your case and may include some facts that are not relevant.

The Library contains the legal authorities needed to complete the task and may also include some authorities that are not relevant. Any cases may be real, modified, or written solely for the purpose of this examination. If the cases appear familiar to you, do not assume that they are precisely the same as you have read before. Read them thoroughly, as if they all were new to you. You should assume that the cases were decided in the jurisdictions and on the dates shown. In citing cases from the Library, you may use abbreviations and omit page references.

Your response must be written in the answer book provided. If you are using a laptop computer to answer the questions, your jurisdiction will provide you with specific instructions. In answering this performance test, you should concentrate on the materials in the File and Library. What you have learned in law school and elsewhere provides the general background for analyzing the problem; the File and Library provide the specific materials with which you must work.

Although there are no restrictions on how you apportion your time, you should allocate approximately half your time to reading and digesting the materials and to organizing your answer before you begin writing it. You may make notes anywhere in the test materials; blank pages are provided at the end of the booklet. You may not tear pages from the question booklet.

This performance test will be graded on your responsiveness to the instructions regarding the task you are to complete, which are given to you in the first memorandum in the File, and on the content, thoroughness, and organization of your response.

July 2015
MPT-1 File:
In re Bryan Carr

In re Bryan Carr

Anders, Davis & Waters
Attorneys at Law
6241 Lowell Street
Franklin City, Franklin 33205

To: Examinee
From: Miles Anders
Re: Bryan Carr
Date: July 28, 2015

My friend and former college roommate Bryan Carr has consulted me about a credit card problem he is facing. I offered to help him figure out a strategy for responding.

Bryan's mother died last year. Since then his father, Henry Carr, has become more and more dependent upon Bryan. Several months ago, Henry asked Bryan if Bryan could pay the estimated $1,500 it would take to repair Henry's van. Bryan gave his credit card to Henry and told him that he could charge all the repairs but could not use the card for anything else. Bryan also gave Henry a letter that said Bryan was giving Henry permission to use the card. In the end, the total repair cost was $1,850, which was charged to Bryan's card.

Bryan forgot to get the credit card and letter back from his father, and Henry used the card to buy several things in addition to the auto repairs. Over several months, Henry charged gasoline, groceries, books, and, most recently, power tools to Bryan's account. Bryan always pays the entire balance on his credit cards each month, and he had already paid for the first three months of purchases without noticing Henry's charges. However, earlier this month, Bryan discovered the unauthorized purchases. He promptly contacted the bank that issued the card to dispute the charges. The bank has notified him that he is responsible for all charges.

Bryan would like our advice about his legal obligation to pay the bank for the charges Henry made in March, April, May, and June, as detailed in the statements for these months. Please draft an opinion letter for my signature to Bryan. This letter should advise Bryan of the extent of his liability for each of Henry's purchases. The letter should follow the attached firm guidelines for opinion letters.

Anders, Davis & Waters
Attorneys at Law
6241 Lowell Street
Franklin City, Franklin 33205

OFFICE MEMORANDUM

To:	Associates
From:	Managing partner
Re:	Opinion letters
Date:	September 5, 2013

The firm follows these guidelines in preparing opinion letters to clients:

- Identify each issue separately and present each issue in the form of a "yes or no" question. (E.g., Is the client's landlord entitled to apply the security deposit to the back rent owed?)

- Following each issue, provide a concise one- or two-sentence statement which gives a "short answer" to the question.

- Following the short answer, write a more detailed explanation and legal analysis of each issue, incorporating all important facts and providing legal citations. Explain how the relevant legal authorities combined with the facts lead to your conclusions.

- Bear in mind that, in most cases, the client is not a lawyer; avoid using legal jargon. Remember to write in a way that allows the client to follow your reasoning and the logic of your conclusions.

Transcript of telephone conversation between Miles Anders and Bryan Carr

July 24, 2015

Anders: Bryan, I heard your voicemail message. I'm sorry you are having problems, and I'd like to help. Can you tell me what happened?

Carr: Well, you know that my mom died late last year. My dad has been devastated. They were married for 40 years. My mom had always organized and maintained their household and paid all the bills. Now my dad is pretty much at a loss for how to cope. Even though this is a busy season for my landscaping business, I've tried to step in to support him as much as I can, including paying some of his bills. It's been tough keeping up with all that's going on.

Anders: Can you tell me more about your dad's situation? I'm asking because I understand that this has contributed to your current problem.

Carr: About four months ago, my dad came to me after his van broke down. He had gotten a repair estimate for $1,500, and he didn't have the money on hand to pay for the repairs. I decided to help him out and told him I would pay whatever it cost to have his van repaired. I also told my dad it was a loan, but honestly, I was never going to ask him to pay me back. I love my dad and wanted to help him in his time of need.

Anders: How did you give him the money?

Carr: I let him use one of my credit cards. It seemed the easiest thing to do at the time. I had a card that had a zero balance on it. It's with Acme State Bank. When I gave my dad the credit card, I told him that he could charge the van repairs, but I also specifically told him that that was the only purchase or charge he should make on the card.

Anders: Did you do anything else?

Carr: Yes, I wrote a letter that said that my dad was authorized to use my credit card and gave it to him. I think I also wrote the credit card account number and expiration date on the letter. I made a copy of the letter and have it in my desk. I will scan it and email it to you as soon as we get off the phone.

Anders: Did the letter say anything about restricting the purchase specifically to the van repairs?

Carr: No, it didn't.

Anders: Did your dad charge the repairs?

In re Bryan Carr

Carr: Yes, my dad used my Acme State Bank card to pay for the van repairs. The final bill was somewhat more than the original estimate. Apparently an additional part was needed, making the total repair cost $1,850. That was $350 more than the original estimate. My dad charged the total amount to my credit card.

Anders: Then what happened?

Carr: With all that was going on in my life, I forgot to get my credit card back from my dad until about six weeks ago. When I finally did, I also got back the letter I'd given him. Unfortunately, I subsequently learned that my dad had already used the card to make additional purchases without ever asking my permission or even telling me. In fact, he even used my account information after returning the card and letter.

Anders: How did you find out about the additional purchases?

Carr: When I was reviewing and preparing to pay my current credit card statement, I noticed a $1,200 charge to Franklin Hardware Store for power tools. I knew I had not made this purchase. I called my dad to see if he knew anything about the power tools purchase.

Anders: What did your dad say?

Carr: He admitted he had used my account number to buy the power tools. He told me he wanted to prove to himself and the rest of the family that he could take care of the house, and he impulsively went to buy some tools to make some household repairs. He said he had written the account information on a piece of paper before returning the credit card and my letter to me.

Because my dad had already returned the credit card and my letter to me before he purchased the tools, he said he merely presented the credit card account name, number, and expiration date to the hardware store clerk. The clerk must have been out of his mind, but he accepted the information my dad presented and charged the tools to my account. My dad feels terrible and has apologized profusely. He is so ashamed of himself.

Anders: Are these the only other charges your dad made?

Carr: I wish. He also admitted that before he returned my card, he had used it to buy gas, groceries, and books over the past few months.

Anders: What did you do after you learned of all these transactions?

Carr: I pulled out my file with my Acme State Bank credit card statements and reviewed my statements for the past several months. Sure enough, upon review, I noticed that during the past four months, in addition to the van repairs, my dad had charged gasoline on two occasions at Friendly Gas, groceries on one occasion at the Corner Market, books at Rendell's Book Store, and most recently, the power tools at the Franklin Hardware Store. I always pay the entire balance on my credit cards on the due date each month. All the gas, grocery, and book charges made by my dad have already been paid in full. I noted this fact by writing "Paid—BC" on each of the past statements. I never noticed these charges before I paid my statements. The truth is, I usually don't review the bills very carefully, and I didn't notice the gas, grocery, and book charges because he and I both shop at the same places. I probably gave each statement a quick glance, if that. However, I have not yet paid the current credit card statement for June with the $1,200 power tools charge.

Anders: Have you contacted the bank or done anything else?

Carr: I called the bank to discuss the problem. They directed me to fill out and send in their form disputing the charges. I did this right away.

Anders: What happened?

Carr: This morning I received a letter from the bank informing me that I was responsible for all the charges. That's when I called your office.

Anders: What would you like to see happen?

Carr: I know my dad did something he shouldn't have done; I told him to return the tools if he still could. But he's a senior citizen and in considerable distress. The various vendors should not have allowed him to use my credit card. I know he had the card in his possession for all but the power tools purchase, but it's still not right for the bank to say I'm responsible. I'd like to know whether the bank can hold me responsible for each of the charges my dad made.

Anders: Bryan, we'll look into this quickly. Meanwhile, please don't pay your credit card statement until you get further advice from us. I'll be back in touch before the current payment due date.

In re Bryan Carr

March 12, 2015

To Whom It May Concern:

I, Bryan Carr, give my father, Henry Carr, permission to use my Acme State Bank credit card: account number 474485AC66873641, expiration date 09/2017. If you have any questions, please feel free to call me at 555-654-8965.

Thank you,

Bryan Carr

Bryan Carr

ACME STATE BANK
P.O. Box 309
Evergreen, Franklin 33800

Billing Statement: March 2015

Bryan Carr
6226 Lake Drive
Franklin City, FR 33244

Account Number   474485AC66873641

New Charges

DATE	DESCRIPTION	AMOUNT
March 16, 2015	Schmidt Auto Repair	$1,850.00
	Total	$1,850.00

Payment Due Date	Minimum Due
April 30, 2015	$55.50

DIRECT ALL INQUIRIES TO
(800) 555-5555

MAKE ALL CHECKS PAYABLE TO
Acme State Bank
P.O. Box 309
Evergreen, FR 33800

THANK YOU FOR YOUR BUSINESS!

PAID—BC April 29, 2015

ACME STATE BANK
P.O. Box 309
Evergreen, Franklin 33800

Billing Statement: April 2015

Bryan Carr   Account Number   474485AC66873641
6226 Lake Drive
Franklin City, FR 33244

    April 30, 2015   Payment Received $1,850.00

New Charges

DATE	DESCRIPTION	AMOUNT
April 10, 2015	Friendly Gas Station	$75.00
April 16, 2015	Corner Store	$55.00
April 21, 2015	Friendly Gas Station	$76.50
	Total	$206.50

Payment Due Date	Minimum Due
May 31, 2015	$15.00

DIRECT ALL INQUIRIES TO
(800) 555-5555

MAKE ALL CHECKS PAYABLE TO
Acme State Bank
P.O. Box 309
Evergreen, FR 33800

THANK YOU FOR YOUR BUSINESS!

PAID-BC May 30, 2015

ACME STATE BANK
P.O. Box 309
Evergreen, Franklin 33800

Billing Statement: May 2015

Bryan Carr
6226 Lake Drive
Franklin City, FR 33244

Account Number   474485AC66873641

May 31, 2015   Payment Received $206.50

New Charges

DATE	DESCRIPTION	AMOUNT
May 16, 2015	Rendell's Book Store	$45.70
	Total	$45.70

Payment Due Date   Minimum Due
June 30, 2015 $15.00

DIRECT ALL INQUIRIES TO
(800) 555-5555

MAKE ALL CHECKS PAYABLE TO
Acme State Bank
P.O. Box 309
Evergreen, FR 33800

THANK YOU FOR YOUR BUSINESS!

PAID-BC June 29, 2015

In re Bryan Carr

ACME STATE BANK
P.O. Box 309
Evergreen, Franklin 33800

Billing Statement: June 2015

Bryan Carr
6226 Lake Drive
Franklin City, FR 33244

Account Number   474485AC66873641

June 30, 2015   Payment Received $45.70

New Charges

DATE	DESCRIPTION	AMOUNT
June 21, 2015	Franklin Hardware Store-power tools	$1,200.00
	Total	$1,200.00

Payment Due Date	Minimum Due
July 31, 2015	$36.00

DIRECT ALL INQUIRIES TO
(800) 555-5555

MAKE ALL CHECKS PAYABLE TO
Acme State Bank
P.O. Box 309
Evergreen, FR 33800

THANK YOU FOR YOUR BUSINESS!

July 2015
MPT-1 Library:
In re Bryan Carr

Excerpts from Federal Truth in Lending Act
15 U.S.C. §§ 1602 and 1643

§ 1602 Definitions and rules of construction

(a) The definitions and rules of construction set forth in this section are applicable for the purposes of this subchapter.

. . .

(k) The term "credit card" means any card, plate, coupon book, or other credit device existing for the purpose of obtaining money, property, labor, or services on credit.

. . .

(o) The term "unauthorized use," as used in section 1643 of this title, means a use of a credit card by a person other than the cardholder who does not have actual, implied, or apparent authority for such use and from which the cardholder receives no benefit.

*   *   *

§ 1643 Liability of holder of credit card

(a) Limits on liability

  (1) A cardholder shall be liable for the unauthorized use of a credit card only if—

    (A) the card is an accepted credit card;

    (B) the liability is not in excess of $50;

    . . .

    (E) the unauthorized use occurs before the card issuer has been notified that an unauthorized use of the credit card has occurred or may occur as a result of loss, theft, or otherwise; and

    (F) the card issuer has provided a method whereby the user of such card can be identified as the person authorized to use it.

. . .

(d) Exclusiveness of liability. Except as provided in this section, a cardholder incurs no liability from the unauthorized use of a credit card.

In re Bryan Carr

Excerpts from Restatement (Third) of Agency (2006)

§ 1.01 Agency Defined

Agency is the fiduciary relationship that arises when one person (a "principal") manifests assent to another person (an "agent") that the agent shall act on the principal's behalf and subject to the principal's control, and the agent manifests assent or otherwise consents so to act.

§ 2.01 Actual Authority

An agent acts with actual authority when, at the time of taking action that has legal consequences for the principal, the agent reasonably believes, in accordance with the principal's manifestations to the agent, that the principal wishes the agent so to act.

§ 2.03 Apparent Authority

Apparent authority is the power held by an agent or other actor to affect a principal's legal relations with third parties when a third party reasonably believes the actor has authority to act on behalf of the principal and that belief is traceable to the principal's manifestations.

§ 3.01 Creation of Actual Authority

Actual authority, as defined in § 2.01, is created by a principal's manifestation to an agent that, as reasonably understood by the agent, expresses the principal's assent that the agent take action on the principal's behalf.

§ 3.03 Creation of Apparent Authority

Apparent authority, as defined in § 2.03, is created by a person's manifestation that another has authority to act with legal consequences for the person who makes the manifestation, when a third party reasonably believes the actor to be authorized and the belief is traceable to the manifestation.

§ 3.11 Termination of Apparent Authority

(1) The termination of actual authority does not by itself end any apparent authority held by an agent.

(2) Apparent authority ends when it is no longer reasonable for the third party with whom an agent deals to believe that the agent continues to act with actual authority.

BAK Aviation Systems, Inc. v. World Airways, Inc.

Franklin Court of Appeal (2007)

In 2005, BAK Aviation Systems, Inc. (BAK), issued a credit card to World Airlines, Inc. (World), to purchase fuel for a corporate jet leased by World from BAK. World designated Ken Swenson, an independent contractor hired by World, as chief pilot of the leased jet and gave him permission to make fuel purchases with the BAK credit card but only in connection with *non-charter* flights involving World executives. However, Swenson used the credit card to charge $89,025 to World in connection with *charter* flights involving non-World customers prior to the cancellation of the credit card in 2006. When World refused to pay, BAK sought recovery in court.

The trial court entered judgment for BAK for the full amount in dispute. The court held that the federal Truth in Lending Act, which limits a cardholder's liability for "unauthorized" uses, did not apply to charges incurred by one to whom the cardholder had voluntarily allowed access for another purpose. World appeals.

The Truth in Lending Act, 15 U.S.C. § 1643(a), places a limit of $50 on the liability of a credit cardholder for charges incurred by an "unauthorized" user. This appeal concerns the applicability of this provision to a card bearer who was given permission by the cardholder to make a limited range of purchases but who subsequently made additional charges on the card. We conclude that Swenson, who incurred the charges, was not an "unauthorized" user within the meaning of § 1643(a) and therefore affirm.

Congress enacted the 1970 Amendments to the Truth in Lending Act in large measure to protect credit cardholders from unauthorized use perpetrated by those able to obtain possession of a card from its original owner. The amendments limit the liability of cardholders for all charges by third parties made without "actual, implied, or apparent authority" and "from which the cardholder receives no benefit." 15 U.S.C. §§ 1602(o), 1643. Where an unauthorized use has occurred, the cardholder can be held liable only up to a limit of $50 for the amount charged on the card, if certain conditions are satisfied. 15 U.S.C. § 1643(a)(1)(B).

17

By defining "unauthorized use" as that lacking "actual, implied, or apparent authority," Congress intended, and courts have accepted, primary reliance on principles of agency law in determining the liability of cardholders for charges incurred by third-party card bearers. Under the parameters established by Congress, the inquiry into "unauthorized use" properly focuses on whether the user acted as the cardholder's agent in incurring the debt in dispute. A cardholder, as principal, can create actual authority only through manifestations to the user of consent to the particular transactions into which the user has entered. *See* RESTATEMENT (THIRD) OF AGENCY § 3.01.

"Implied authority" has been held to mean actual authority either (1) to do what is necessary, usual, and proper to accomplish or perform an agent's express responsibilities or (2) to act in a manner in which an agent believes the principal wishes the agent to act based on the agent's reasonable interpretation of the principal's manifestations in light of the principal's objectives and other facts known to the agent. These meanings are not mutually exclusive. Both fall within the definition of actual authority. *See* RESTATEMENT (THIRD) OF AGENCY § 2.02, comment (b).

With respect to the transactions Swenson made in connection with the charter flights, we conclude that no actual or implied authority existed.

Unlike actual or implied authority, however, apparent authority exists entirely apart from the principal's manifestations of consent to the agent. Rather, the cardholder, as principal, creates apparent authority through words or actions that, reasonably interpreted by a third party from whom the card bearer makes purchases, indicate that the card bearer acts with the cardholder's consent. *See* RESTATEMENT (THIRD) OF AGENCY § 3.03.

Though a cardholder's relinquishment of possession of a credit card may create in another the appearance of authority to use the card, the statute clearly precludes a finding of apparent authority where the transfer of the card was without the cardholder's consent, as in cases involving theft, loss, or fraud. However elastic the principle of apparent authority may be in theory, the language of the 1970 Amendments demonstrates Congress's intent that charges incurred as a result of *involuntary* card transfers are to be regarded as unauthorized under §§ 1602(o) and 1643.

Because the Truth in Lending Act provides no guidance as to uses arising from the *voluntary* transfer of credit cards, the general principles of agency law, incorporated by reference in § 1602(o), govern disputes over whether a resulting use was unauthorized. These disputes frequently involve, as in this case, a cardholder's claim that the card bearer was given permission to use a card for only a limited purpose and that subsequent charges exceeded the consent originally given by the cardholder. Acknowledging the absence of actual authority for the additional charges, a majority of courts have declined to apply the Truth in Lending Act to limit the cardholder's liability, reasoning that the cardholder's voluntary relinquishment of the card for one purpose gives the bearer apparent authority to make additional charges. (Citations omitted.)

Nothing about the BAK credit card itself, or the circumstances surrounding the purchases, gave fuel sellers reason to distinguish the authorized fuel purchases Swenson made for the *non-charter* flights from the disputed purchases for the *charter* flights. It was industry custom to entrust credit cards used to make airplane-related purchases to the pilot of the plane. By designating Swenson as the pilot and subsequently giving him the BAK card, World thereby imbued him with more apparent authority than might arise from voluntary relinquishment of a credit card in other contexts. In addition, with World's blessing, Swenson had used the card, which was inscribed with the registration number of the Gulfstream jet, to purchase fuel on non-charter flights for the same plane. The only difference between those uses expressly authorized and those now claimed to be unauthorized—the identity of the passengers—was insufficient to provide notice to those who sold the fuel that Swenson lacked authority for the charter flight purchases.

Here, the disputed charges were not "unauthorized" within the meaning of 15 U.S.C. §§ 1602(o) and 1643(a)(1). Accordingly, BAK was entitled to recover the full value of the charges from World under their credit agreement. The judgment of the trial court is affirmed.

In re Bryan Carr

Transmutual Insurance Co. v. Green Oil Co.

Franklin Court of Appeal (2009)

This is an appeal from a holding of the trial court finding against defendant Green Oil Co. and in favor of plaintiff Transmutual Insurance Co. In March 2000, Transmutual obtained a Green Oil credit card for use in its business. Transmutual's office manager, Donna Smith, was responsible for requesting credit cards for Transmutual employees and paying bills. Smith did not have the authority to open new credit accounts for Transmutual; only its general manager had this authority.

On May 16, 2005, Smith made a written request to Green Oil for a GreenPlus credit card. A GreenPlus credit card may be used for purchases of goods and services other than those furnished at gasoline service stations. The GreenPlus application was signed by Smith as office manager. It also contained a signature purporting to be that of Alexander Foster as general manager and secretary-treasurer of Transmutual; however, the trial court determined that Foster's signature was forged by Smith.

During the period from May 2005 until July 2008, Smith wrongfully and fraudulently used the GreenPlus card to obtain goods and services in the amount of $26,376.53. Transmutual paid for these purchases with checks signed by Smith and an authorized officer. During this time, Transmutual employed accounting firms to perform audits, but they did not discover the fraud.

Under the federal Truth in Lending Act, 15 U.S.C. § 1643(a), a cardholder is liable only for a limited amount if certain conditions are met and if the use of the credit card was unauthorized. Accordingly, the initial determination is whether or not the use of the credit card in the case at hand was unauthorized. The federal definition of "unauthorized use" is "a use of a credit card by a person other than the cardholder who does not have actual, implied, or apparent authority for such use and from which the cardholder receives no benefit." 15 U.S.C. § 1602(o). The test for determining unauthorized use is governed by agency law, and agency law must be used to resolve this issue.

Smith did not have actual or implied authority to request a GreenPlus credit card.

The trial court correctly determined that the principle of apparent authority controls in this case.

Apparent authority is created when a third party reasonably believes the actor to be authorized and the belief is traceable to the manifestation of the principal. RESTATEMENT (THIRD) OF AGENCY § 3.03. Transmutual is bound by Smith's acts under apparent authority only to third persons who have incurred a liability in good faith and without ordinary negligence. The trial court correctly determined that Green Oil acted negligently by issuing Smith a GreenPlus credit card without independently verifying her authority. Because of Green Oil's negligence, the trial court determined that Green Oil, as the card issuer, could not rely upon Smith's ostensible authority to establish the existence of agency between Smith and Transmutual.

However, the trial court erred in not looking beyond Green Oil's negligence in issuing Smith the card. After receiving the first statement from Green Oil containing the fraudulent charges, Transmutual was negligent in not finding and reporting Smith's fraud. If the person or entity to whom a credit card is issued is careless, that

deception. Transmutual had sole power to do

person or entity may be held liable.

The federal Truth in Lending Act does not address whether cardholder negligence removes the statutory liability limit. However, we believe that Transmutual's negligence in not examining its monthly statements from Green Oil removes this case from the statutory limit on cardholder liability.

A cardholder has a duty to examine his credit card statement promptly, using reasonable care to discover unauthorized signatures or alterations. If the card issuer uses reasonable care in generating the statement and if the cardholder fails to examine his statement, the cardholder is precluded from asserting his unauthorized signature against the card issuer after a certain time.

The facts at hand are similar. Green Oil was not negligent in billing Transmutual. If someone at Transmutual other than Smith had examined its statements from Green Oil, he or she would have discovered Smith's fraud. Transmutual had the responsibility to institute internal procedures for the examination of the statements from Green Oil which would have disclosed Smith's

so. Transmutual's failure to institute such

procedures is the cause of that portion of the embezzlement that occurred following the billing from Green Oil that contained the first evidence of Smith's fraud.

Transmutual's negligence leads us to reexamine whether Smith acquired apparent authority in her use of the GreenPlus card after Transmutual became negligent. In *Farmers Bank v. Wood* (Franklin Ct. App. 1998), we set forth the test to determine whether or not apparent authority exists. The authority must be based upon a principal's conduct which, reasonably interpreted, causes a third person to believe that the agent has authority to act for the principal.

> Thus, if a principal acts or conducts his business, either intentionally or through negligence, or fails to disapprove of the agent's acts or course of action so as to lead the public to believe that his agent possesses authority to act or contract in the name of the principal, the principal is bound by the acts of the agent within the scope of his apparent authority as to persons who have reasonable grounds to believe that the agent has such authority and in good faith deal with him.

Farmers Bank, supra.

Green Oil was negligent in issuing Smith the GreenPlus card. However, during Smith's fraudulent use of the card, Green Oil was not negligent. Rather, Transmutual (the cardholder) was negligent in not requiring that someone other than Smith examine its monthly statements. Smith embezzled money from Transmutual for three years through her fraudulent use of the GreenPlus credit card. During this lengthy period of embezzlement, Transmutual always paid its monthly bill to Green Oil.

Transmutual contends that it is not proper for the court to consider the fact that Transmutual paid all the Green Oil credit card charges. That contention is without merit. As a result of Transmutual's acts of paying the charges and its failure to examine its credit card statements so that it could notify Green Oil of the fraud, Transmutual allowed Green Oil to reasonably believe that Smith was authorized to use the credit card.

We conclude under the principles of apparent authority that Transmutual is liable for all of Smith's purchases from the time the credit card was issued.

Reversed.

July 2015
MPT-2 File:
In re Franklin Aces

Franklin Arts Law Services
Pro Bono Legal Services for the Franklin Arts Community
224 Beckett Avenue
Franklin City, Franklin 33221

MEMORANDUM

TO: Examinee
FROM: Eileen Lee, Esq., Executive Director
RE: Al Gurvin
DATE: July 28, 2015

We have agreed to offer legal advice to Al Gurvin concerning a claim he may have against the Franklin Aces professional football team. The relevant materials are attached.

Our engagement by Mr. Gurvin recognizes that, as a pro bono service, we do not have the resources to represent him in litigation. Rather, we have been retained solely to provide legal advice about his potential claim. If he decides to pursue litigation, we will help him find counsel.

Mr. Gurvin has asked for 1) our evaluation of the likelihood of success should he litigate his claim against the team, 2) our assistance in seeking a settlement (we have done so and received an offer), and 3) our recommendation as to whether he should litigate or accept the settlement offer that the team has made.

Please draft a letter to Mr. Gurvin providing your recommendation as to whether he should accept the settlement offer. Your recommendation should factor in your assessment of the likely outcome of litigation, the recovery he might realize should he prevail, his goals in pressing his claim, and any other factors you think relevant. You should fully explain your reasoning as to why he should accept or reject the settlement offer.

Do not separately state the facts, but include the relevant facts in support of your legal analysis and recommendation as to the settlement offer. Remember that Mr. Gurvin is not an attorney. Your letter should explain the law and recommendation in language that, while encompassing a full legal analysis including citations to relevant legal authority, does so in terms a nonlawyer may easily understand.

FRANKLIN SPORTS GAZETTE

REJOICE, FRANKLIN FOOTBALL FANS, THE ACES ARE COMING!

By Ben Jordan   January 27, 2014

FRANKLIN CITY, Franklin—Franklin's long and unrequited longing for professional football is about to be satisfied. The Olympia Torches, after years of unsuccessful attempts to get support for a new stadium in Olympia, have announced that, starting in July of 2016, they will relocate to Franklin City.

ProBall Inc., the team owner, says that years of declining attendance in our neighboring state of Olympia—a result (in its view) of an aging, one could even say decrepit, stadium—have made a move imperative. Although many cities around the country sought to win the team, the owner chose Franklin City for several reasons, including the proximity of a good portion of the team's fan base (without a team of their own, many Franklin residents followed the Torches) and— probably more importantly—the financial support of the Franklin State and Franklin City governments to underwrite the construction of a new, state-of-the-art stadium.

That new stadium will be built in the existing Franklin City Sports Complex, run by the Franklin Sports Authority. The Sports Complex currently includes the Omnidome, where Franklin's pro basketball and hockey teams play, and Franklin Memorial Stadium, where the baseball Blue Sox play. The new stadium will be configured for soccer as well as football.

The team has also announced that it will change its name to the Franklin Aces. The new team logo and uniforms, yet to be created, will be announced in due course according to the team owner.

Transcript of Interview between Eileen Lee and Al Gurvin (June 29, 2015)

Lee: Mr. Gurvin, nice to meet you. How may we help you?

Gurvin: They've stolen my design for the new football team's logo, and I need a lawyer.

Lee: Perhaps we'd better start at the beginning. I've read your intake application, and I know you qualify for our pro bono services given your income level, but tell me about yourself and how all this got started, from the beginning.

Gurvin: Okay, sorry, let's see. I work as a janitor at the Franklin Omnidome, the hockey rink and basketball facility used by our pro teams. I got real excited last year when they announced that the Olympia pro football team was moving to Franklin City.

Lee: Why were you so excited? Are you a big football fan?

Gurvin: I'll say—more than a big fan. I'm nuts about football, and I've been rooting for the Torches for years and years. I watch every game on TV, and I'd give my eyeteeth to be able to afford tickets to see games in person.

Lee: What happened after you saw the news reports of the move?

Gurvin: Well, I'm an amateur artist—no real training, but I like to doodle. When they announced that the team was moving, they also announced that it was changing its name to the Franklin Aces. They also said that they didn't yet have a logo or uniform designs. I didn't give it a second thought. But several months later, I started to think about a design and then one day it hit me. I realized that a real good design for a logo would be a hand holding the four aces from a deck of cards, fanned out like you hold cards. So I sketched that design, and it looked pretty good. I showed the sketch to my boss, and he liked it too.

Lee: Who's your boss? What's his position?

Gurvin: Dick Kessler—he's the work crew supervisor at the Omnidome. Anyway, he suggested that I send it to Daniel Luce, the CEO of the Franklin Sports Authority. So I took a drawing of the logo and faxed it to Mr. Luce with a note.

Lee: When did that happen, and what did the note say? Do you have a copy?

Gurvin: It was 10 months ago. Here's a copy of the note, and my original sketch [see attached note and description].

Lee: What happened then?

Gurvin: Nothing—I never heard back from anyone. Then, about a month ago, the team made a big announcement with a press conference and everything at which they announced the

In re Franklin Aces

new uniforms and logo, and it was mine, exactly! Here's a copy of their logo and the press release they issued with it, which was in the local newspapers [see attached press release and logo description]. I think they stole it from me, and I should be entitled to something for it—they should pay me something like $20,000.

Lee: Have you registered the copyright in your design with the United States Copyright Office?

Gurvin: No—should I?

Lee: Well, a copyright exists from the moment a work is created, and you don't need any government action to grant it. But registration with the Copyright Office is a good idea for many reasons—for example, for our purposes, should you decide to litigate, you must have registered your claim before you can take the case to court. Even though the infringement you allege has already occurred, you can still register, but let's see what route you wish to pursue. Registration isn't expensive, and it won't hurt to wait to register for a few weeks in any event. Let me look into it. I happen to know José Alvarez, the General Counsel of ProBall Inc., the team owner—he's an old classmate and friend of mine. I'll contact him to see if we can work something out short of litigation, and get back to you.

Gurvin: Okay, great.

Lee: You should understand, Mr. Gurvin, that, while we'll be happy to evaluate your claim and help you seek a quick settlement, we're in no position to represent you if you decide to litigate it. As a pro bono service, we simply don't have the resources to undertake litigation on behalf of any client. So if litigation is ultimately the route you wish to follow, we'll try to help you find counsel, but our representation of you must end at that point.

Gurvin: Sure.

Lee: We'll draft an engagement letter for you to sign. I hope we can help you resolve this.

Copy of Fax from Al Gurvin to Daniel Luce (September 25, 2014)

Dear Mr. Luce: I'm a janitor in the Omnidome, and a big, big football fan. When I read that the Torches were moving to Franklin City, and that the team would become the Aces, I had a great idea for a logo for the team. I made a sketch, and it's attached to this note. I'd be honored if the team would consider and use my logo, and I wouldn't want anything from them if they did, except maybe some tickets to games in the new stadium. Thanks, Al Gurvin

[Actual sketch omitted]

*   *   *

[DESCRIPTION OF GURVIN SKETCH: Mr. Gurvin's sketch consists of an outline of a hand from the wrist up, without any other features, holding four cards fanned out, in order from left to right, the ace of diamonds, ace of clubs, ace of hearts, and ace of spades.]

Press Release Announcing New Franklin Aces Logo

[Franklin City, May 28, 2015] The Franklin Aces football team is delighted to announce its new logo and uniforms. After consideration of many designs, we believe this one will be most appealing to the fans and players. Later this year we will begin discussions with various merchandise manufacturers, and we expect that our fans will be able to purchase their Franklin Aces gear next year.

[Picture of Franklin Aces logo omitted.]

*   *   *

[DESCRIPTION OF NEW FRANKLIN ACES LOGO:
Although the outline of the hand is somewhat different, the Franklin Aces logo presented in the press release is otherwise identical to Mr. Gurvin's sketch.]

In re Franklin Aces

ProBall Inc.   **José Alvarez, General Counsel**
Franklin City Sports Complex, Suite 520
Franklin City, FR 33221

July 24, 2015

Eileen Lee, Esq.
Franklin Arts Law Services
224 Beckett Avenue
Franklin City, FR 33221

Dear Eileen:

Thanks for your phone call of July 7, 2015, explaining Mr. Gurvin's claim. I've looked into the matter, and our conclusion is that your client has no basis for any claim against the team.

First, the design he created, whatever its merits, is not copyrightable subject matter. The images of playing cards are familiar designs and common property containing no original authorship. That being the case, any claim he might have must fail.

Second, even if the design were copyrightable, there is no proof that those who designed the new team logo had any access to it. Thus, even if the designs were identical, there could be no copyright infringement, for without proof of access, any claim must fail. To that end, I have attached affidavits from those involved that summarize testimony that would be given in court.

Even though your client has no basis for any claim, the team's owner, in an effort to avoid unhappy publicity, makes this offer: In return for a release of any claims based on your client's design, ProBall Inc. would give Mr. Gurvin a season ticket for a single seat, in a prime location, to all home games for the team's first season. (The retail price of such a season ticket will be $5,000.) Eileen, we go back a long way, you know I'm good for my word, and I want to be forthright with you— this is the team's final, and only, settlement offer.

With kindest personal regards,

José Alvarez
José Alvarez

AFFIDAVIT OF DANIEL LUCE

STATE OF FRANKLIN   )
COUNTY OF LINCOLN   )

I, Daniel Luce, being duly sworn, depose and say:

1. I am Chief Executive Officer of the Franklin Sports Authority. The Authority is entirely separate from ProBall Inc., the owner of the Franklin Aces football team. The Authority and ProBall Inc. are not under common ownership or affiliated in any way.

2. On September 25, 2014, I received a two-page fax from Al Gurvin, a janitor at the Omnidome facility of the Franklin City Sports Complex. I do not have a copy of the fax, but I know when I received it because I checked the fax log in our office. Although I do not recall the specifics, I remember that the fax had a sketch attached to it, and that Mr. Gurvin wanted the sketch submitted as a possible logo for the Franklin Aces pro football team.

3. I knew that the team had retained ForwardDesigns, a commercial design firm, to design a logo and uniforms for the team. Hence, I did not think any input from the Authority or otherwise was needed. Although I do not remember specifically what I did with the fax, I believe I discarded it in the trash.

4. ProBall was given a suite of offices in the five-story Administrative Building of the Franklin City Sports Complex. Those offices are on the fifth floor. All the Authority's offices, including mine, are on the second floor, as is the fax machine which serves all of the Authority's departments. (The ground floor contains a museum and ticket offices; the third and fourth floors are occupied by the firms holding the parking and food concessions at our facilities.)

5. Other than occasional greetings while passing in the lobby of our building or sharing rides in the elevator, I have had no contact with anyone working for ForwardDesigns.

6. I and some of my staff meet occasionally with executives of ProBall Inc. to coordinate details concerning the construction and operation of the new football stadium. Other than that, no one from the Franklin Sports Authority has any dealings with representatives of ProBall Inc., the team owner.

Dated July 22, 2015

Daniel Luce
_____
Daniel Luce

Signed before me on this 22nd day of July, 2015

Jane Mirren
_____
Jane Mirren
Notary Public

AFFIDAVIT OF MONICA DEAN

STATE OF FRANKLIN   )
COUNTY OF LINCOLN   )

    I, Monica Dean, being duly sworn, depose and say:

    1. I am a commercial artist and designer for ForwardDesigns. Our firm was retained in August of 2014 by ProBall Inc. to design a logo and uniforms for the Franklin Aces pro football team. I was the sole designer working on the project. Our firm was paid $10,000 for its services.

    2. To facilitate my work on the project, the team gave me an office located in their suite of offices on the fifth floor of the Administrative Building of the Franklin City Sports Complex. I have had no contact with employees of the Franklin Sports Authority, other than with Julie Covington, a personal friend who works in the Authority's transportation office and with whom I occasionally have lunch. I have never met Daniel Luce, the Authority's Chief Executive Officer.

    3. As I thought about a logo for the team, one obvious choice was a hand holding the four aces from a deck of cards. I had seen many versions of that image, including many on clip art collections on the Internet, none of which were protected by copyright, and which I used for inspiration. About five months ago, I drew that design, along with about a dozen others, and submitted it to ProBall Inc., who chose it as the new team logo. I alternated the suits of the cards in the design so that they appeared as first a red suit, then a black suit, and I made the last and most visible card the ace of spades, as it is the most striking and familiar card.

    4. I do not recall ever seeing any sketch of any idea for the logo created by anyone else prior to creating my design.

    Dated July 22, 2015

                           Monica Dean
                           Monica Dean

Signed before me on this 22nd day of July, 2015

Jane Mirren
Jane Mirren
Notary Public

July 2015
MPT-2 Library:
In re Franklin Aces

Oakland Arrows Soccer Club, Inc. v. Cordova
United States District Court for the District of Columbia (1998)

The question of the boundary between copyrightable and noncopyrightable subject matter—that is, what types of works are protected by the Copyright Act, and what types of works fall outside its sphere of protection—arises in the context of this petition for a writ of mandamus against Ricardo Cordova, the Register of Copyrights. All such actions against the Register of Copyrights must be brought here in Washington, D.C., as it is the location of the Copyright Office.

The facts are simple and not in dispute: The Oakland Arrows professional soccer club developed a new logo and wished to register it with the United States Copyright Office. While registration is entirely permissive, 17 U.S.C. § 408(a), and the existence of a copyright does not depend on it, registration confers significant benefits to the copyright owner, not the least of which is that it is a prerequisite to bringing a suit for copyright infringement. 17 U.S.C. § 411.

The Arrows' new logo consisted of an oblique triangle, colored red, white, and blue. The Arrows' explanation for the design was threefold: 1) the triangle conjured up an image of an arrowhead; 2)

the triangle could be seen to be a stylized letter "A"; 3) the colors evoked the United States flag.

The Arrows submitted an application for copyright registration to the Copyright Office. The Office's procedure is to examine each work for which registration is sought and determine if the work qualifies, in its opinion, for copyright protection. In this case, the Office's examiner concluded that the work did not qualify for protection. There is an internal appeals mechanism within the Office, which the Arrows pursued, but without success. Hence, they bring this mandamus action, seeking to compel the Register of Copyrights to register the work.

We review the question de novo. While we do give deference to the decision of an expert administrative agency, that deference is not necessarily dispositive.

The standard for copyrightability is easily stated: copyright protects original works of authorship. 17 U.S.C. § 102. That standard, however, is not so easily applied. What constitutes authorship? What constitutes originality? The courts have wrestled with

In re Franklin Aces

these questions over the years. Justice Holmes, in *Bleistein v. Donaldson Lithographing Co.*, 188 U.S. 239, 250 (1903), stated that "[It] is the personal reaction of an individual upon nature . . . . [A] very modest grade of art has in it something irreducible, which is one man's alone. That something he may copyright . . ." More recently, Justice O'Connor, in *Feist Publications, Inc. v. Rural Telephone Service Co., Inc.*, 499 U.S. 340, 345 (1991), stated (internal references and quotations omitted):

> Original, as the term is used in copyright, means only that the work was independently created by the author (as opposed to copied from other works), and that it possesses at least some minimal degree of creativity . . . . To be sure, the requisite level of creativity is extremely low; even a slight amount will suffice. The vast majority of works will make the grade quite easily, as they possess some creative spark, no matter how crude, humble or obvious it may be.

How do we apply these tests to the work at hand? We are assisted, to some degree, by the regulations of the Copyright Office as to the types of works the Office will register. We quote the regulation—which the Office states is based on decades of court decisions—in full, from 37 C.F.R.:

§ 202.1 Material not subject to copyright.

The following are examples of works not subject to copyright and applications for registration of such works cannot be entertained:

(a) Words and short phrases such as names, titles, and slogans; familiar symbols or designs; mere variations of typographic ornamentation, lettering or coloring; mere listing of ingredients or contents;

(b) Ideas, plans, methods, systems, or devices, as distinguished from the particular manner in which they are expressed or described in a writing;

(c) Blank forms, such as time cards, graph paper, account books, diaries, bank checks, scorecards, address books, report forms, order forms and the like, which are designed for recording information and do not in themselves convey information;

(d) Works consisting entirely of information that is common property containing no original authorship, such as, for example: Standard calendars, height and weight charts, tape measures and rulers, schedules of sporting events, and lists or tables taken from public documents or other common sources;

(e) Typeface as typeface.

The Copyright Office, in defending its action, argues that the logo is simply a "familiar symbol or design," with a "mere variation in coloring," as in subsection (a) of the regulation. While the Arrows make many arguments as to the artistic value of the work, the effort that went into creating it, and the connections to the team which it conjures up, none of those arguments can carry the day. The copyright law does not reward effort—it rewards original expression of authorship. What we have here is a simple multicolored triangle. That is a "familiar symbol," with "mere variation of coloring." There is not enough originality of authorship in that design to merit copyright protection. In Justice O'Connor's words, even the "extremely low" "minimal degree of creativity"—the "creative spark"—is lacking here.

The Arrows' petition for a writ of mandamus is denied.

Savia v. Malcolm

United States District Court for the District of Franklin (2003)

In this action for copyright infringement, plaintiff Joseph Savia, the composer and copyright owner of the song "Perhaps," claims that defendant Lauren Malcolm copied the melody of his song and used it in her song "Love Tears" without authorization. After extensive discovery, the parties have filed cross-motions for summary judgment. We deny the plaintiff's motion and grant the defendant's motion.

Facts

In 1981, Savia wrote "Perhaps" and was successful in having it placed over the closing credits of the motion picture *The Duchess of Broken Hearts*. The motion picture had only a limited theatrical release, playing in a single "art house" movie theater in Franklin City for a three-week run. A dispute among the producers of the motion picture, for reasons not relevant here, has resulted in no further exploitation of the motion picture, either in theatrical release, in home video format, or on television, cable, the Internet, or otherwise. The motion picture was rated NC-17 by the Motion Picture Association of America because of its sexual content. That rating means that no one under the age of 17 will be admitted to a theater showing the motion picture. "Perhaps" was never commercially recorded, other than for the soundtrack of the

motion picture, and no recording of it has ever been released. Savia registered the work with the United States Copyright Office, and there is no dispute about the validity of the copyright in "Perhaps" or that he is the copyright owner.

In 2002, Malcolm, a lifelong resident of Franklin City and a highly successful 25-year-old songwriter, wrote "Love Tears," which was commercially recorded and released by Remnants of Emily, a well-known rock band. The recording achieved great success, ultimately making number one on the *Billboard* "Hot 100" chart for four weeks. The recording has sold over two million copies, and the song has been widely performed and has been used in commercial advertisements. Malcolm, as songwriter, has, through the end of 2002, earned approximately $1.5 million in royalties attributable to the song from these various uses.

The parties each presented expert testimony from musicologists. These expert witnesses agreed, and the court as finder of fact also finds, that the lyrics of the songs are entirely different, but that the melodies are, if not identical, virtually so.

The Standard for Infringement

It is rare that direct evidence of copyright

infringement exists. Therefore, the courts have turned to circumstantial evidence in determining whether one work infringes another. In doing so, the courts in this Circuit have uniformly applied a two-prong test for infringement: 1) Are the works "substantially similar"? 2) Did the alleged infringer have access to the copyrighted work? The reasons for these two standards should be obvious: If the works are not, at the very least, substantially similar, there can be no infringement. And if the alleged infringer had no access to the allegedly infringed work, there could be no possibility of copying. Certainly, the more similar the works, the less evidence of access need be adduced. But plausible evidence of access must always be found.

Two cases are instructive. In *Fred Fisher, Inc. v. Dillingham*, 298 F. 145 (S.D.N.Y. 1924), the legendary songwriter Jerome Kern was accused of plagiarizing the bass line from a wildly popular earlier work. Although Kern testified that he did not consciously use the earlier work, the court concluded that Kern, a working songwriter who kept up with current popular music, must have heard it and so had access to it. Kern also argued that the bass line could be found in earlier works which were not protected by copyright; if he had copied from those works, he would not be infringing. But, as Kern could not prove that he was even aware

of those works before the lawsuit, his argument failed, and he was found liable for infringement.

In *Bright Tunes Music Corp. v. Harrisongs Music, Ltd.*, 420 F. Supp. 177 (S.D.N.Y. 1976), *aff'd sub nom ABKCO Music Inc. v. Harrisongs Music, Ltd.*, 722 F.2d 988 (2d Cir. 1983), George Harrison (of the Beatles) was accused of plagiarizing the melody of an earlier popular rock and roll song. He testified that he did not consciously copy the earlier song, and the court believed him. Nevertheless, the court concluded that he had access to the earlier song and so had "unconsciously" copied it; he was found liable for infringement.

Analysis

Here, there is no question that the works are virtually identical. Substantial similarity—indeed, striking similarity—of the melodies is proven. The question is whether Malcolm had access to Savia's song. Can access be plausibly inferred from the evidence? We conclude that it cannot.

As noted, Savia's song was released to the public only in the form of the closing credits of a motion picture, one that had only a limited run in Franklin City. Further, the motion picture had been rated NC-17, meaning that no

41

one under the age of 17 would be admitted to the theater. At the time the motion picture was released, Malcolm was four years old. While we can take judicial notice of the fact that the ratings code is sometimes more honored in the breach than in the observance, we think it implausible that a four-year-old child would be admitted to a theater showing an NC-17– rated movie.

Savia argues that, even so, Malcolm might have had access to "Perhaps" by hearing someone who had seen the motion picture play or sing the song. Without a scintilla of evidence to justify that conclusion, we cannot credit such mere speculation.

Conclusion

We conclude that there is no plausible evidence that Malcolm had access to Savia's work. For that reason, notwithstanding the virtual identity of the melodies of the two songs, we conclude that Malcolm's song was original with her and was not copied from Savia's. We deny Savia's motion for summary judgment and grant Malcolm's motion for summary judgment.

Herman v. Nova, Inc.
United States District Court for the District of Franklin (2009)

In our previous opinion, [citation omitted], Nova, Inc., a motion picture producer, was found liable to Herman for copyright infringement of Herman's unpublished screenplay. We now address the question of damages.

Herman, an amateur author, had, unsolicited, submitted the screenplay to Nova. Nova then used the screenplay as the basis for its own screenplay, from which, it announced, it was going to make a motion picture. It issued a press release announcing its intention to make a motion picture based on its own screenplay; the press release included a synopsis of the screenplay. Herman saw the press release and, before Nova took any further action, successfully sued Nova for copyright infringement.

Because Herman had not registered his copyright in his unpublished screenplay with the United States Copyright Office before the act of infringement occurred, his damages are limited to his actual damages and the infringer's profits. 17 U.S.C. §§ 412, 504(b). Had Herman registered before the infringement, he would have been entitled to statutory damages in lieu of actual damages and profits, and, in the court's discretion, costs, including attorney's fees. Here, as Nova, the infringer, took no action after appropriating Herman's work and realized no gain, direct or indirect, thereafter, there are no profits resulting from the infringement which can be awarded. (The result would be different if, for example, the motion picture had been made and released, but such is not the case here.) The question, then, is what are Herman's actual damages?

As Herman was an amateur author, he had no track record of payments for his work and hence can submit no evidence of his own as to his screenplay's worth. The evidence adduced in discovery, from Nova's records and from third-party witnesses, shows that the range of payment which a motion picture producer like Nova would make for a screenplay of this sort would be between $15,000 and $50,000.

Given the unquestioned infringement that took place, we are disposed to award damages at the upper end of that range. Hence, judgment will be entered in Herman's favor for $50,000.

February 2015 MPTs

In re Harrison

In re Community General Hospital

February 2015

MPTs

www.ncbex.org

National Conference of Bar Examiners
302 South Bedford Street | Madison, WI 53703-3622
Phone: 608-280-8550 | Fax: 608-280-8552 | TDD: 608-661-1275
e-mail: contact@ncbex.org

Contents

Preface

The Multistate Performance Test (MPT) is developed by the National Conference of Bar Examiners (NCBE). This publication includes the items and Point Sheets from the February 2015 MPT. The instructions for the test appear on page iii.

The MPT Point Sheets describe the factual and legal points encompassed within the lawyering tasks to be completed. They outline the possible issues and points that might be addressed by an examinee. They are provided to the user jurisdictions to assist graders in grading the examination by identifying the issues and suggesting the resolution of the problem contemplated by the drafters.

For more information about the MPT, including a list of skills tested, visit the NCBE website at www .ncbex.org.

Description of the MPT

The MPT consists of two 90-minute items and is a component of the Uniform Bar Examination (UBE). It is administered by user jurisdictions as part of the bar examination on the Tuesday before the last Wednesday in February and July of each year. User jurisdictions may select one or both items to include as part of their bar examinations. (Jurisdictions that administer the UBE use two MPTs.)

The materials for each MPT include a File and a Library. The File consists of source documents containing all the facts of the case. The specific assignment the examinee is to complete is described in a memorandum from a supervising attorney. The File might also include transcripts of interviews, depositions, hearings or trials, pleadings, correspondence, client documents, contracts, newspaper articles, medical records, police reports, or lawyer's notes. Relevant as well as irrelevant facts are included. Facts are sometimes ambiguous, incomplete, or even conflicting. As in practice, a client's or a supervising attorney's version of events may be incomplete or unreliable. Examinees are expected to recognize when facts are inconsistent or missing and are expected to identify potential sources of additional facts.

The Library may contain cases, statutes, regulations, or rules, some of which may not be relevant to the assigned lawyering task. The examinee is expected to extract from the Library the legal principles necessary to analyze the problem and perform the task. The MPT is not a test of substantive law; the Library materials provide sufficient substantive information to complete the task.

The MPT is designed to test an examinee's ability to use fundamental lawyering skills in a realistic situation and complete a task that a beginning lawyer should be able to accomplish. The MPT is not a test of substantive knowledge. Rather, it is designed to evaluate six fundamental skills lawyers are expected to demonstrate regardless of the area of law in which the skills arise. The MPT requires examinees to (1) sort detailed factual materials and separate relevant from irrelevant facts; (2) analyze statutory, case, and administrative materials for applicable principles of law; (3) apply the relevant law to the relevant facts in a manner likely to resolve a client's problem; (4) identify and resolve ethical dilemmas, when present; communicate effectively in writing; and (6) complete a lawyering task within time constraints. These skills are tested by requiring examinees to perform one or more of a variety of lawyering tasks. For example, examinees might be instructed to complete any of the following: a memorandum to a super- vising attorney, a letter to a client, a persuasive memorandum or brief, a statement of facts, a contract provision, a will, a counseling plan, a proposal for settlement or agreement, a discovery plan, a witness examination plan, or a closing argument.

Instructions

The back cover of each test booklet contains the following instructions:

You will be instructed when to begin and when to stop this test. Do not break the seal on this booklet until you are told to begin. This test is designed to evaluate your ability to handle a select number of legal authorities in the context of a factual problem involving a client.

The problem is set in the fictitious state of Franklin, in the fictitious Fifteenth Circuit of the United States. Columbia and Olympia are also fictitious states in the Fifteenth Circuit. In Franklin, the trial court of general jurisdiction is the District Court, the intermediate appellate court is the Court of Appeal, and the highest court is the Supreme Court.

You will have two kinds of materials with which to work: a File and a Library. The first document in the File is a memorandum containing the instructions for the task you are to complete. The other documents in the File contain factual information about your case and may include some facts that are not relevant.

The Library contains the legal authorities needed to complete the task and may also include some authorities that are not relevant. Any cases may be real, modified, or written solely for the purpose of this examination. If the cases appear familiar to you, do not assume that they are precisely the same as you have read before. Read them thoroughly, as if they all were new to you. You should assume that the cases were decided in the jurisdictions and on the dates shown. In citing cases from the Library, you may use abbreviations and omit page references.

Your response must be written in the answer book provided. If you are using a laptop computer to answer the questions, your jurisdiction will provide you with specific instructions. In answering this performance test, you should concentrate on the materials in the File and Library. What you have learned in law school and elsewhere provides the general background for analyzing the problem; the File and Library provide the specific materials with which you must work.

Although there are no restrictions on how you apportion your time, you should allocate approximately half your time to reading and digesting the materials and to organizing your answer before you begin writing it. You may make notes anywhere in the test materials; blank pages are provided at the end of the booklet. You may not tear pages from the question booklet.

This performance test will be graded on your responsiveness to the instructions regarding the task you are to complete, which are given to you in the first memorandum in the File, and on the content, thoroughness, and organization of your response.

February 2015
MPT-1 File:
In re Harrison

In re Harrison

Barbour, Lopez & Whirley
Attorneys at Law
788 Washington Blvd.
Abbeville, Franklin 33017

MEMORANDUM

To: Examinee
From: Esther Barbour
Date: February 24, 2015
Re: Daniel Harrison matter

Last year, our client Daniel Harrison bought a 10-acre tract (the Tract) of land in the City of Abbeville from the federal government, which had used the property as an armory and vehicle storage facility. The Tract is currently zoned for single-family residential development. Harrison applied for a rezoning of the property for use as a truck-driving training facility, but the City has denied the application.

Harrison wants to know whether he can pursue an inverse condemnation case seeking compensation from the City based on the denial of his rezoning application. Inverse condemnation is a legal proceeding in which a private property owner seeks compensation from a governmental entity based on the governmental entity's use or regulation of the owner's property.

Please draft a memorandum to me identifying each of the inverse condemnation theories available under Franklin and federal law and analyzing whether Harrison might succeed against the City under each of those theories. Note that there has been no physical taking, so do not address that issue. Do not prepare a separate statement of facts, but be sure to incorporate the relevant facts, analyze the applicable legal authorities, and explain how the facts and law affect your analysis.

In re Harrison

Barbour, Lopez & Whirley

MEMORANDUM TO FILE

From: Esther Barbour
Date: February 23, 2015
Re: Summary of interview of Daniel Harrison

Today I met with Daniel Harrison regarding a 10-acre Tract he bought from the federal government. He provided the following background information about the Tract's zoning, its prior use, and his plans for development.

- From 1978 to 2014, the Franklin National Guard operated an armory and vehicle storage building on the Tract. The buildings and parking lot are located on approximately three acres, and the remaining seven acres are undeveloped, heavily sloped, and wooded.

- In 1994, the City of Abbeville enacted an R–1 (single-family residential) zoning ordinance, restricting development to single-family housing and prohibiting all commercial and industrial uses on the Tract.

- The Guard operated the armory and storage building without objection from the City until March 2014, when the property was decommissioned and the Guard began looking for buyers. The buildings were (and still are) in good shape, but they contain levels of asbestos and lead paint that may pose environmental hazards if the buildings are renovated or demolished.

- The Tract borders a City park and baseball field and is near the municipal airport. The area surrounding the Tract has had very little residential growth since the 1960s.

- In June 2014, Harrison purchased the Tract from the Guard through a bid process for $100,000 (about $10,000 per acre), intending to use the existing Guard buildings for commercial purposes. He believed that the Tract was "grandfathered in" and not subject to the 1994 residential zoning ordinance.

- There were several other bids on the Tract, ranging from $20,000 to $88,800. Harrison anticipates that the City will point to his winning bid and the other bids submitted as proof of the Tract's value. However, the other bids were made before the City rejected Harrison's proposed non-residential use of the Tract, and Harrison believes that the other bidders bid on the Tract believing (as he did) that the zoning ordinance would not be enforced.

- Harrison also believes that it is not feasible to develop the Tract for residential use (see attached emails).

- In August 2014, Harrison negotiated a lease of the Tract to a truck-driving school. After negotiating the lease, Harrison contacted the City and was informed that the City intended to enforce the residential zoning ordinance.

- He then submitted an application to the City's Planning and Zoning Board requesting that the zoning of the Tract be changed from R–1 (single-family residential) to C–1 (general commercial/industrial) to allow the Tract to be used as a truck-driving school.

- The Board recommended approval of the rezoning application, but the Abbeville City Council voted unanimously to deny it.

- At the Council meeting, some Council members were concerned about the proximity of the Tract to a park; one suggested that with a special-use permit, the property could be used for a church, medical or dental clinic, business office, or day-care center. Harrison believes that these other uses are not feasible because the Tract is in a remote area of the City with little traffic and no growth, and because of the prohibitive cost of renovating the existing structures for such non-industrial uses.

- Harrison wants to keep the Tract, but he's very concerned about losing money on it. The Tract would be worth $200,000 if used for industrial purposes (see attached appraisal). But because the City denied his rezoning application, the Tract is not producing and will not produce any income. Harrison estimates that if the Tract is not rezoned, he will lose between $10,000 and $15,000 per year due to maintenance, taxes, insurance, and deterioration.

MASTER APPRAISALS LLP
3200 Barker Road
Abbeville, Franklin 33020

Mr. Daniel Harrison   January 9, 2015
1829 Timber Forest Drive
Abbeville, Franklin 33027

SUBJECT: Market Value Appraisal for Harrison Tract

Dear Mr. Harrison:

Master Appraisals LLP submits the accompanying appraisal of the referenced property. The purpose of the appraisal is to develop an opinion of the market value of the fee simple interest in the property based on the highest and best use value of the property, if zoned for general commercial/industrial use. The appraisal is intended to conform to the Uniform Standards of Professional Appraisal Practice and applicable state appraisal regulations.

The subject is a parcel of improved land containing two buildings and a parking lot and consisting of an area of 10.0 acres or 435,600 square feet. The property is zoned R–1 (single-family residential) but has been used as a military armory and vehicle storage facility. The existing structures appear to be perfect for conversion to an industrial or training facility of some kind. That appears to be the highest and best use of the property, in its "as-improved" state. Thus, the appraisal assumes that the property will be used for industrial or training purposes.

VALUE CONCLUSION

Appraisal Premise: Market Value   **Date of Value:** January 6, 2015

Interest Appraised: Fee Simple   **Value Conclusion:** $200,000 total ($20,000/acre)

If you have any questions or comments regarding the information contained in this letter or the attached report, please contact the undersigned. Thank you for the opportunity to be of service.

Respectfully submitted,

MASTER APPRAISALS LLP

Margaret Jane Charleston

Margaret Jane Charleston
Certified General Real Estate Appraiser
Franklin Certificate # FR-053010

[Balance of APPRAISAL REPORT omitted]

January 19, 2015, Email Correspondence Between Harrison and Real Estate Agent

From: Daniel Harrison<dharr@cmail.com>
To: Amy Conner<amyc@abbevillerealty.com>
Subject: Development options for my land

Hi, Amy. Remember the 10-acre tract of land that I bought last year? I've been trying to get the tract rezoned as C-1 commercial so that I can lease it to a truck-driving school that wants to open a new training facility in Abbeville. The City Council denied my rezoning application and told me that the only development it will allow is single-family residential. Frankly, I just don't think anyone would want to live way down there. You've been a real estate agent for 15 years. What do you think?

From: Amy Conner<amyc@abbevillerealty.com>
To: Daniel Harrison<dharr@cmail.com>

I agree. I don't think the land is suitable for residential development. Assume that you could build three houses per acre—that would be 30 homes on the 10-acre tract. Typically, it costs between $15,000 and $20,000 per lot to develop land for single-family housing, including grading the land and installing utilities and drainage systems. That's a reasonable Investment if the land is near a business district because people will pay a premium to live close to work.

But your land is almost 45 minutes southeast of the business district. There are several single-family lots a few miles from your tract, priced at $4,500 each, and they aren't selling. I think you'd be lucky to get $5,000 per lot if you developed the land, assuming you could sell the lots.

From: Daniel Harrison<dharr@cmail.com>
To: Amy Conner<amyc@abbevillerealty.com>

That's what I thought. I wasn't sure about the numbers, but I didn't think it was doable.... You've seen the tract — do you have any idea what it would cost to tear down the existing buildings and parking lot and clear the wooded areas of the tract?

In re Harrison

From: Amy Conner<amyc@abbevillerealty.com>
To: Daniel Harrison<dharr@cmail.com>

In other deals I've worked on, I've seen it cost $25,000 or more to demolish a building or parking lot. Here, the property has two buildings with likely environmental issues, and a parking lot and shrubs and trees to remove. You're probably looking at a minimum expense of $75,000.

From: Daniel Harrison<dharr@cmail.com>
To: Amy Conner<amyc@abbevillerealty.com>

I just don't have that kind of money.... If I can't lease the land to the truck-driving school and I can't develop it for residential housing, what do you think it's worth in its current condition?

From: Amy Conner<amyc@abbevillerealty.com>
To: Daniel Harrison<dharr@cmail.com>

Not much. Maybe a few hundred dollars an acre. But that's about it.

February 2015
MPT-1 Library:
In re Harrison

Franklin Constitution, Article I, Section 13

No person's property shall be taken, damaged, or destroyed for or applied to public use without adequate compensation being made, unless by the consent of such person . . . .

United States Constitution, Fifth Amendment ("Takings Clause")

No person shall . . . be deprived of life, liberty, or property, without due process of law; nor shall private property be taken for public use, without just compensation.

In re Harrison

Newpark Ltd. v. City of Plymouth
Franklin Court of Appeal (2007)

This appeal involves an inverse condemnation claim in which a developer (Newpark Ltd.) contends that the City of Plymouth's denial of its rezoning application effected an unconstitutional regulatory taking of property. We affirm the trial court's judgment against the developer.

The property at the center of this dispute consists of 93 acres of land acquired by Newpark for $930,000 ($10,000 per acre). The tract is located in an area zoned "SF–E" (single-family residential development). The area has been zoned for one-acre-minimum lots since 1967. The tract was used primarily for pastureland at the time of purchase. While Newpark was unaware that the tract was zoned for one-acre-minimum lots when it signed the purchase contract, it was aware of the zoning by the time of closing.

In August 2000, after closing on the tract, Newpark applied for a zoning change to allow the development of 325 single-family lots on the 93 acres with a density of approximately 3.5 units per acre. The City Council considered and denied the application. Newpark then sued the City, seeking damages for inverse condemnation.[1] The trial court found in favor of the City, and this appeal followed.

At the outset, we note that the fact that the zoning restriction had already been enacted when Newpark bought the tract does not bar it from bringing a takings action against the City, regardless of whether Newpark had notice of the restriction. Unreasonable zoning regulations do not become less so through the passage of time or title. *See Palazzolo v. Rhode Island,* 533 U.S. 606 (2001) (rejecting argument that post-zoning purchasers cannot challenge a regulation under the Takings Clause).

The Takings Clause of the Fifth Amendment to the United States Constitution, as applied to the states through the Fourteenth Amendment, prohibits the government from taking private property for public use

---

[1] Inverse condemnation occurs when the government takes private property for public use without paying the property owner, and the property owner sues the government to recover compensation for the taking. Because the property owner in such situations is the plaintiff, the action is called *inverse* condemnation because the order of the parties is reversed as compared to a direct condemnation action where the government is the plaintiff who sues a defendant landowner to take the owner's property.

without just compensation. *Id.* A taking can be physical (e.g., land seizure, continued possession of land after a lease to the government has expired, or deprivation of access to the property owner), or it can be a regulatory taking (where the regulation is so onerous that it makes the regulated property unusable by its owner). *See Soundpool Inv. v. Town of Avon* (Franklin Sup. Ct. 2003). The constitutionality of a regulatory taking involves the consideration of a number of factual issues, but whether a zoning ordinance is a compensable taking is a question of law.

The state of Franklin's prohibition against taking without just compensation is set forth in Article I, Section 13, of the Franklin Constitution and is comparable to the Takings Clause of the United States Constitution, despite minor differences in wording. *See Sheffield Dev. Co. v. City of Hill Heights* (Franklin Sup. Ct. 2006). Therefore, Franklin courts look to federal cases for guidance in these situations.

The United States Supreme Court recently clarified the types of regulatory taking: (1) a total regulatory taking, where the regulation deprives the property of all economic value; (2) a partial regulatory taking, where the

challenged regulation goes "too far"; and (3) a land-use exaction, which occurs when governmental approval is conditioned upon a requirement that the property owner take some action that is not proportionate to the projected impact of the proposed development (e.g., a developer is required to rebuild a road but the improvements are not necessary to accommodate the additional traffic from the proposed development). *Lingle v. Chevron,* 544 U.S. 528 (2005).[2]

Here, Newpark does not argue that the City has physically taken its property, nor does it assert a partial regulatory taking or a land-use exaction. Thus, we need only consider the first type of regulatory taking: whether the City ordinance restricting development of Newpark's land to one-acre-minimum lots constitutes a total regulatory taking.

A total regulatory taking occurs when a property owner is called upon to sacrifice *all* economically beneficial uses in the name of

---

[2]The Franklin Supreme Court recognizes a fourth type of regulatory taking in situations where a regulation does not "substantially advance" a legitimate governmental interest. In *Lingle,* the United States Supreme Court rejected the "substantially advances" formula under federal constitutional law. Its continuing validity is still an issue under Franklin law, but the parties have not raised it. Thus, we need not determine whether the "substantially advances" test remains valid in a regulatory takings case under the Franklin state constitution.

In re Harrison

the common good. This type of regulatory taking was first articulated by the United States Supreme Court in *Lucas v. South Carolina Coastal Council*, 505 U.S. 1003 (1992). A *Lucas*-type total regulatory taking is limited to the extraordinary circumstance when no productive or economically beneficial use of the land is permitted and the owner is left with only a token interest.

Newpark contends that the only way to achieve an economically productive use of the property is for the City to allow single-family development of some type. This argument not only mischaracterizes the zoning ordinance but also misapplies the *Lucas* test upon which the argument is premised. The SF–E zoning *does* permit the development of a single-family residential subdivision, albeit in one-acre-minimum lots. The appraisal experts for both parties testified that, due to market conditions and the current zoning, the cost to develop one-acre lots would exceed the potential for revenue. The City's appraiser testified that the highest and best use of the property is to hold the property for the future.

Although the testimony established that the development would not be profitable under current conditions, the absence of profit

potential does not equate with impossibility of development. To the contrary, the takings clause does not require the government to guarantee the profitability of every piece of land subject to its authority, although lost profits are a relevant factor to consider in assessing the value of property and the severity of the economic impact of rezoning on a landowner.

The City's expert testified that the property's value is approximately $5,000 per acre. Newpark's expert testified that the property is worth $2,000 per acre. Both experts testified that Newpark paid more for the property ($10,000 per acre) than it is worth. The court reasonably concluded that Newpark had assumed certain risks attendant to real estate investment. But such risks have no place in a total takings analysis because the government has no duty to underwrite the risk of developing and purchasing real estate. Although investment-backed expectations are relevant to a *partial* regulatory taking analysis rather than a total taking analysis, we note that when such expectations are measured, the historical uses of the property are critically important. Here, the zoning always required one-acre-minimum lots, and the historical use of the property was farmland.

Newpark's expert testified that the value of the property, if capable of being developed, is $25,000 per acre. Expert testimony on both sides provides a range of value for the property in an undeveloped state from $2,000 to $5,000 per acre. Newpark claims that the $2,000 constitutes no value at all.

We do not read *Lucas* to hold that the value of land is a function of whether it can be profitably developed. To the contrary, the economic viability test "entails a relatively simple analysis of whether value remains in the property after governmental action." *Sheffield*. The appropriate *Lucas* inquiry is whether the value of the property has been completely eliminated. The deprivation of value must be such that it is tantamount to depriving the owner of the land itself. *Id.*

Newpark also argues that the property is valueless because if it cannot be developed as a residential subdivision, it will remain vacant, with a value equivalent to that of parkland. The fallacy of this approach is that it equates the lack of availability of a property for its most economically valuable use with the condition of being "valueless." Although the regulation in *Lucas* precluded the development of oceanfront property, the property still had value. The owner could enjoy other attributes of the property: he could picnic, camp, or live on the land in a mobile trailer. The owner also retained other valuable property rights—the right to exclude others and to alienate the land. *Id.* (Blackmun, J., dissenting); *see also Wynn v. Drake* (Fr. Sup. Ct. 2003) (no taking when zoning left owner with only recreational and horticultural uses). Here, the court could reasonably conclude that the property retains residual uses and therefore some value.

Newpark's insistence that it is virtually impossible to find a tract of land without value is instructive. The fact that a piece of land will rarely be deemed utterly lacking in economic viability is consistent with the *Lucas* limitation of such claims to extraordinary circumstances. Here, because the property has a value of at least $2,000 per acre, we conclude that those extraordinary circumstances are not present. Because the ordinance does not completely eliminate the property's value, there has been no unconstitutional taking.[3]

Affirmed.

---

[3] We note that a necessary result of a taking under these circumstances—had Newpark prevailed— would be that upon payment of adequate compensation, the City would own the property. Thus, had Newpark prevailed in its claim for inverse condemnation, Newpark would have been required to transfer title of the property to the City.

In re Harrison

Venture Homes Ltd. v. City of Red Bluff
Franklin Court of Appeal (2010)

Appellant Venture Homes Ltd. owns two apartment buildings in the City of Red Bluff. After the City rezoned adjacent land, Venture sued the City, alleging that the rezoning had reduced the value of its property. The trial court granted the City's summary judgment motion. We affirm.

Background

In 1999, upon application of developer Austin Inc., the City created Planned Unit Development No. 12 (PUD 12). (A PUD is an alternative to traditional zoning containing a mix of residential, commercial, and public uses.) PUD 12 is a 195-acre mixed-use development, consisting of multi-family housing, shopping centers, and office buildings. The original development plan allowed a maximum of 900 apartment units to be built on the site. Austin built two apartment buildings, containing 800 units, which Venture subsequently purchased in 2002. Austin retained ownership of the remaining land in PUD 12.

When Venture bought the 800-unit apartment complex, it assumed that only 100 additional apartment units could be built in PUD 12. Because Venture thought that a 100-unit apartment building would be too small to be commercially viable, and because Venture believed that the City needed Venture's consent to allow additional apartment units in PUD 12, Venture assumed that it effectively had 100 additional units in reserve for future expansion of the two apartment buildings that it had purchased.

However, in April 2006, at Austin's request, the City carved out an area from PUD 12 and rezoned it. Austin then filed an application for creation of a new PUD within the boundaries of PUD 12. After public hearings, the City passed an ordinance creating PUD 30, an eight-acre tract zoned for 350 additional multi-family units.

Discussion

Venture alleges that creation of PUD 30 gives rise to a claim for inverse condemnation under the Franklin Constitution. Venture does not claim that its property was physically invaded or that the City's zoning regulations eliminated all economically beneficial uses of its property. Rather, Venture argues that the City's creation of PUD 30 amounted to a partial regulatory taking for which Venture should be compensated.

A. Partial Regulatory Takings Test

A partial regulatory taking may arise where there is not a complete taking, either physically or by regulation, but the regulation goes "too far," causing an unreasonable interference with the landowner's right to use and enjoy the property. *See Penn Central Transp. Co. v. New York City*, 438 U.S. 104 (1978). Because the Franklin Constitution's takings clause is similar to the Takings Clause of the Fifth Amendment to the United States Constitution, we look to federal law to analyze Venture's takings claims. *See Newpark Ltd. v. City of Plymouth* (Franklin Ct. App. 2007).

For a partial regulatory taking to occur, the governmental regulation must, at a minimum, diminish the value of an owner's property. Not every regulation that diminishes the value of property, however, is a taking.

There is no bright-line test for determining whether a partial, *Penn Central*–type regulatory taking has occurred. Whether a regulation goes "too far" requires a factual inquiry using the following guiding factors: (1) the economic impact of the regulation, (2) the extent to which the regulation interferes with the property owner's reasonable investment-backed expectations, and (3) the character of the governmental action. *Sheffield Dev. Co. v. City of Hill Heights* (Franklin Sup. Ct. 2006) (citing *Penn Central*).

Our goal is to determine, after analyzing and balancing all relevant evidence, whether a regulatory action is the functional equivalent of a classic taking in which the government directly appropriates private property, such that fairness and justice demand that the burden of the regulation be borne by the public rather than by the private landowner.

Our analysis must not be merely mathematical. Rather, while applying the balancing test, we must remember that purchasing and developing real estate carries with it certain financial risks, and it is not the government's duty to underwrite those risks.

(1) Economic Impact of the Regulation

The first *Penn Central* factor, the regulation's economic impact on the property owner, is undisputed for the purpose of this appeal. Venture presented expert testimony that the value of its apartment properties was reduced from $65.6 million to $62.9 million. The City stipulated to Venture's figure for purposes of this appeal. While significant in absolute terms, this diminution in value of $2.7 million reflects a loss of only about 4%.

The City cites several cases that suggest that such a small diminution in value is rarely if ever held to be a taking. The City claims that because Venture's loss was a small part of its property's value, Venture failed to show that creation of the new PUD unreasonably interfered with its use of the property. Although this one factor is not dispositive, the City is correct when it asserts that the small relative amount of Venture's loss weighs heavily against Venture's claims.

(2) Interference with Reasonable Investment-Backed Expectations

The second *Penn Central* factor requires us to consider the extent to which the regulation has interfered with Venture's reasonable investment-backed expectations.

The record shows that the ordinance at issue caused minimal interference with Venture's *reasonable* investment-backed expectations.

Venture concedes that the only harm it has suffered is increased competition and a resulting diminution in the value of its property. The City has not rezoned Venture's property to prohibit a current or proposed use, nor has the City substantially altered the character of the surrounding land use. The City simply increased the number of multi-family units permitted within the original boundaries of PUD 12, which already included a significant number of multi-family units.

In *Sheffield*, the Franklin Supreme Court held that the existing and permitted uses of the property constitute the "primary expectation" of an affected landowner for purposes of determining whether a regulation interferes with the landowner's reasonable investment-backed expectations.

In creating PUD 30, the City has not altered the existing or permitted uses of Venture's property and therefore has not interfered with Venture's "primary expectation." Venture can continue to operate its 800-unit complex and can build an additional 100 units on its property, should it decide to do so.

(3) Character of the Governmental Action

The third Penn Central factor is the character of the governmental action. This factor is the least concrete and carries the least weight. This factor's purpose, when viewed in light of the goal of the takings test (to determine if the Constitution requires the burden of the regulation to be borne by the public or by the landowner) is to elicit consideration of whether a regulation disproportionately harms a particular property. If the rezoning was general in character, that weighs against the property owner, whereas if the rezoning impacted the owner's property disproportionately harshly, that weighs in the owner's favor that a taking did occur.

Venture asserts that the governmental action in this case targeted a small subsection of an otherwise cohesive PUD, thereby increasing competition for its apartment complex. Venture claims that the City created PUD 30 solely to satisfy Austin. The City disputes this and responds by citing language from the ordinance creating PUD 30 and public meeting minutes that suggest that the new

PUD was crafted to "create a more modern pedestrian-friendly and urban environment."

The issue is whether the City created PUD 30 for the public welfare or did so to benefit the private interests of Austin. Venture presented evidence that could lead a reasonable fact finder to conclude that one of the City's purposes, or perhaps even its primary purpose, for enacting the ordinance was to benefit Austin. That evidence does not preclude summary judgment for the City, however, because the other two *Penn Central* factors—particularly the first (the economic impact of the regulation)—weigh so heavily against Venture that, as a matter of law, there is no taking here.

B. The "Substantial Advancement" Takings Test

Venture also argues that the City's ordinance creating PUD 30 effects a taking of its property because the ordinance does not "substantially advance legitimate state interests." The United States Supreme Court rejected this test in *Lingle v. Chevron*, 544 U.S. 528 (2005). Prior to *Lingle*, the Franklin Supreme Court applied the "substantial advancement" test to state regulatory-takings claims, but it has not yet addressed whether the test still applies in light of *Lingle*. Assuming that the test is still valid in Franklin, there was no taking under the "substantial advancement" test.

The "substantial advancement" test examines the nexus between the effect of the ordinance and the legitimate state interest it is supposed to advance. This requirement is not, however, equivalent to the "rational basis" standard applied to due process and equal protection claims. The standard requires that the ordinance "substantially advance" the legitimate state interest sought to be achieved rather than merely analyzing whether the government could rationally have decided that the measure achieved a legitimate objective.

The City asserts that the new PUD promotes a mixed-use, pedestrian-friendly, urban development that will enhance the quality of life of its citizens. Venture contends that the City's stated goal is a pretext—that its real goal was only to benefit Austin by making Austin's land more valuable. Even if that were true, however, we are not required to consider the City's *actual* purpose. Instead, we look for a nexus between the effect of the ordinance and the legitimate state interest it is *supposed* to advance. The City could reasonably have concluded that increasing housing density in a PUD already zoned for multi-family housing, shopping centers, and office space would advance the legitimate state interest of enhancing the quality of life of citizens by decreasing traffic, lowering commuting times, and encouraging citizens to walk. Accordingly, the creation of PUD 30 is not a taking under the "substantial advancement" test.

Affirmed.

February 2015
MPT-2 File:
In re Community
General Hospital

Jackson, Gerard, and Burton LLP
Attorneys at Law
222 St. Germaine Ave.
Lafayette, Franklin 33065

MEMORANDUM

To: Examinee
From: Hank Jackson, Partner
Date: February 24, 2015
Re: Community General Hospital; Response to OCR Audit

Our client, Community General Hospital, is subject to the Health Insurance Portability and Accountability Act of 1996, commonly called "HIPAA," and its related regulations. Frances Paquette, the hospital CEO, sent me the attached letter from the Office of Civil Rights (OCR) of the U.S. Department of Health and Human Services outlining three cases in which allegations have been made of improper disclosures of patient health information. She is very concerned about the inquiry and fears that the government may file an enforcement action resulting in penalties and adverse publicity. She needs our assistance in responding.

Please review the accompanying materials and draft a letter responding to the OCR and persuading it that no enforcement action under HIPAA is warranted. The OCR has discretion as to whether it brings an enforcement action. Take that into account in drafting your letter: be persuasive but not confrontational. Your response should cite the specific applicable regulations and apply them to the facts of each case.

An investigative report from the hospital's medical records director is attached. To help orient you, I have also attached a short memorandum I wrote to the CEO when the federal HIPAA regulations, known as the "Privacy Rule," were put into final form in 2002. While there have been updates to the HIPAA regulations since this 2002 memorandum was drafted, I have reviewed its content in light of those changes and have confirmed that the content is unaffected by subsequent additions or clarifications to the HIPAA regulations.

U.S. Department of Health and Human Services

Office of Civil Rights
1717 Federal Way
Lafayette, Franklin 33065

February 9, 2015

Community General Hospital
600 Freemont Blvd.
Lafayette, Franklin 33065

Re: Results of Audit for Compliance with HIPAA Regulations

Dear Community General Hospital:

As a result of complaints received and a recent audit of patient health care records at your facility, we preliminarily find that disclosures of protected health information may have been made in violation of the provisions of 45 C.F.R. § 164.500 *et seq.* We found no written authorization for disclosure of the protected health information in the medical charts of three patients: Patient #1 (reporting a wound to police over the patient's objection); Patient #2 (disclosing to police suspicions about arsenic poisoning of a decedent and then releasing the decedent's entire medical record); and Patient #3 (disclosing information relating to a patient's treatment which later resulted in the patient's arrest).

You are hereby notified that unless we receive a response justifying the disclosures within 20 days of your receipt of this letter, this office will consider pursuing an enforcement action and seeking appropriate civil penalties.

Please direct your response to the undersigned at the address noted above. Thank you.

Sincerely,

Robert Fields

Robert Fields
Investigator

COMMUNITY GENERAL HOSPITAL
INTRAOFFICE MEMORANDUM

TO: Frances Paquette, CEO
FROM: Megan Larson, Medical Records Director
DATE: February 13, 2015
RE: Your request relating to Office of Civil Rights letter

As requested, I investigated the facts and circumstances relating to the patients identified in the Office of Civil Rights letter of February 9, 2015. I also reviewed the relevant health care records and interviewed hospital personnel. In each instance, the disclosure of the patient's health information was duly noted in the patient's chart. In no case does the chart contain a signed authorization from the patient or the patient's representative for release of protected health information on our usual form. My investigation discovered information beyond that which appears in the medical charts, information that would not have been available to the OCR when it conducted its audit of the charts.

Patient #1

Patient #1, an 18-year-old male, was brought to the Emergency Department on September 20, 2014, with a gunshot wound to his right calf. Patient #1 said that he was the victim of a gang dispute. The treating physician told Patient #1 that the physician would have to report the gunshot wound to the police. Patient #1 vehemently objected, saying that any report would further endanger him because a police inquiry would certainly prompt retribution from gang members.

After treating the wound, and despite the patient's objection, the treating physician called the Lafayette Police Department and reported the wound. The next day, the physician sent a written report by first-class mail to the police department. See Attachment A. The report contained no additional records.

I was told that the patient's family had filed a complaint with the OCR.

Patient #2

Patient #2, a 67-year-old man, was admitted to the hospital on November 7, 2014, and died at the hospital on November 9, 2014. On admission, the patient complained of severe headaches and diarrhea, confusion, and drowsiness. Soon after admission, the patient began vomiting, complained of stomach pain, and experienced severe convulsions. Nursing staff observed leukonychia (white fingernail pigmentation). After death, an autopsy was conducted. The pathologist concluded that the cause of death was multi-system organ failure caused by arsenic poisoning. See Attachment B, pathology report.

Our executive vice president knows the decedent's family, which owns a large-scale manufacturing business in Lafayette. She was also aware of considerable strife between the decedent and members of the family over ownership of the business. She reviewed the pathology report the day after the decedent's death. That same day, she invited a police detective to lunch and informed him of the patient's death, of the conclusion of the pathology report, and of her awareness of the serious conflict between the patient and other members of his family. Later that day, she told the Medical Records Department to give to the detective the entirety of the records of the patient's last two hospital stays (the most recent stay and one six months before his death), including the admission records, his progress notes, and the pathology report. The hospital provided the earlier records because the pathologist had used those records to rule out other causes for the fatal illness.

A family member learned of the disclosure to the police and is quite upset. He has filed a complaint about the disclosure to the OCR.

Patient #3

Patient #3, a 35-year-old male, was admitted to the Emergency Department on December 17, 2014, accompanied by his sister. The sister said that a neighbor had called her to the patient's apartment after hearing loud noises. The sister had found the patient emptying his cupboards and throwing plates and glassware against the wall. The sister persuaded the patient to come to the hospital with her.

An interview with the patient eventually established that he had taken PCP ("angel dust"), together with alcohol. Throughout the interview, the patient became increasingly agitated and belligerent. His speech was rapid, and his thoughts were disorganized and chaotic. He reported being threatened by persons who his sister later stated had died years ago. By the end of the interview, the patient had focused his agitation on his employer, saying that he was angry about work conditions and constantly felt belittled and undermined at his workplace.

The patient wanted to leave the hospital. The treating physician advised him not to leave, but the patient insisted. The patient began shouting, "I hate my boss and I hate what she's done. I'm going to get her . . ." He then ran out of the hospital. The patient's sister then told the hospital staff that she thought the patient had a gun at home.

Shortly thereafter, a Franklin state trooper came into the Emergency Department on an unrelated matter. Because of a concern for the safety of others, the treating physician reported to the trooper Patient #3's name, his combative demeanor, and the threat to his employer, but not a specific cause of the patient's combative behavior. Patient #3 was later arrested on the street two blocks from his workplace, but was unarmed. The County Jail released him shortly thereafter. Patient #3's lawyer has complained to the OCR about the treating physician's disclosure of protected health information to the trooper.

COMMUNITY GENERAL HOSPITAL
EMERGENCY DEPARTMENT

Luke Ridley, M.D.
600 Freemont Blvd.
Lafayette, Franklin 33065

September 21, 2014

Via First-Class Mail, USPS

Chief of Police Alexander Mason
Lafayette Police Department
Municipal Building
1102 Third Avenue
Lafayette, Franklin 33065

Re: Report of gunshot wound

Dear Chief Mason:

Following up on my telephone call to you yesterday, this is to report that on September 20, 2014, I treated David Meyers of 55 Baker Street, Lafayette, Franklin 33065, at Community General Hospital in Lafayette, Franklin, for a gunshot wound to his right calf.

Sincerely,

Luke Ridley
Luke Ridley, M.D.

Community General Hospital Pathology Report		
Patient Name: Stewart Weller DOB: 1/16/1947 Sex: Male MRN: 51552435 Provider: Blue Cross / Blue Shield	Case No.: CGH-0-03-13231 Collected: 11/9/2014 Received: 11/10/2014 Deliver to: File	
POST-MORTEM PATHOLOGY REPORT		
Diagnosis: Tests:	Arsenic poisoning Admission and Emergency Department records Physical examination Stomach wash Blood (10 ml), hair, urine, feces	

Admission and ER records:
On admission on 11/7/2014, patient complained of headaches, diarrhea, confusion, drowsiness. In the Emergency Department, patient vomited, suffered severe convulsions, and complained of stomach pain. Patient pronounced dead on 11/9/2014 at 20:43.

Physical examination (post-mortem):
Observable white fingernail pigmentation (leukonychia), including transverse white lines across fingernails (Mee's lines). Faint garlic odor around mouth. Irritation of nasal mucosa, pharynx, larynx, and bronchi. Fatty yellow liver. Lungs display excessive accumulation of serous fluid. Degenerative changes to liver. Heart displays excessive accumulation of serous fluid.

Blood, hair, urine, feces:
Toxic levels of arsenic compounds, more than 12 times expected from normal environmental exposure, and most likely ingested as arsenic trioxide.

Conclusion:	Death resulting from multi-organ system failure caused by acute arsenic poisoning.

Charlotte Maxsimic, M.D.
CGH Pathology

November 10, 2014

Jackson, Gerard, and Burton LLP
Attorneys at Law
222 St. Germaine Ave.
Lafayette, Franklin 33065

MEMORANDUM

To: Frances Paquette, CEO, Community General Hospital
From: Hank Jackson, Partner
Date: August 30, 2002
Re: Federal HIPAA Regulations, or the "Privacy Rule"

You asked me to review the new federal HIPAA regulations and to provide you with an introduction to them as they relate to the privacy of health information held by Community General Hospital. This memo is a very brief summary of what is known as the "Privacy Rule" and what can happen if the Hospital does not comply with the Privacy Rule's provisions.

The Health Insurance Portability and Accountability Act of 1996 (HIPAA), 42 U.S.C. § 201 et seq., required creation of published standards and regulations for the exchange, privacy, and security of patient health information. The regulations were published in final form on August 14, 2002. Community General Hospital is a "covered entity" under the regulations.

The regulations govern the circumstances under which a covered entity may disclose to others information in any form or medium, whether electronic, paper, or oral, that can be individually identifiable with a patient. "Individually identifiable" health information means that the information identifies the individual or provides a reasonable basis to believe that it can be used to identify the individual. The Privacy Rule refers to such information as "protected health information" (PHI).

A covered entity may not disclose PHI, except either (1) as permitted or required by the Privacy Rule or (2) as authorized by the identified individual (or personal representative) in writing. PHI includes information, including demographic data, that relates to

- the individual's past, present, or future physical or mental health or condition;
- the provision of health care to the individual; or
- the past, present, or future payment for the provision of health care to the individual.

As a general proposition, Community General should not disclose PHI to outside persons unless permitted by the regulations or upon a patient's written authorization. Community General may, of course, disclose PHI internally to the individual. Community General may also use and disclose PHI internally without written authorization for purposes of its own treatment, payment, and health care operations. Other permitted disclosures include certain public interest and benefit activities and certain carefully defined research, public health, and health care operations.

The Privacy Rule also permits use and disclosure of PHI without an individual's authorization for several national priority purposes. Some of these national priority purposes permit disclosures to public health authorities responsible for protecting public health and safety, or to agencies responsible for auditing and investigating the health care system and public benefits programs. Still others relate to disclosures required in judicial or administrative proceedings, or to disclosures concerning decedents to coroners, pathologists, medical examiners, and funeral home directors.

Finally, several of these national priority purposes relate to disclosures required by law or for purposes of law enforcement or public safety. They permit a covered entity to disclose PHI without individual authorization under the following circumstances:

- As required by law (including by statute, regulation, or court order).
- For law enforcement purposes, in six carefully defined circumstances, including:

  (1) as required by law or by administrative requests;

  (2) to identify or locate a suspect, fugitive, material witness, or missing person;

  (3) to respond to a law enforcement official's request for information about a victim or suspected victim of a crime;

  (4) to alert law enforcement to a person's death, if the covered entity suspects that criminal activity caused the death;

  (5) when a covered entity believes that PHI is evidence of a crime that occurred on its premises; and

  (6) in a medical emergency not occurring on its premises, when necessary to inform law enforcement about the commission and nature of a crime, the location of the crime or crime victims, and the perpetrator of the crime.

In re Community General Hospital

- Where the covered entity believes that disclosure is necessary to prevent or lessen a serious and imminent threat to a person or the public, when such disclosure is made to someone it believes can prevent or lessen the threat (including the target of the threat).

In most cases, when the Privacy Rule *permits* Community General to disclose PHI, it requires Community General to make reasonable efforts to limit the information that it discloses to the "minimum necessary" to accomplish the intended purpose of the disclosure. While the "minimum necessary" standard applies to many uses and disclosures, there are situations (specified in the HIPAA regulations) in which covered entities are not subject to this "minimum necessary" limitation.

The U.S. Department of Health and Human Services Office for Civil Rights (OCR) is responsible for administering and enforcing compliance with the Privacy Rule and may conduct complaint investigations, review compliance, and impose substantial civil money penalties for violations of the Privacy Rule.

February 2015
MPT-2 Library:
In re Community
General Hospital

Excerpt from Franklin Statutes
Chapter 607. Professions and Occupations, Mandatory Reporting

§ 607.29 Gunshot or stab wounds to be reported. The physician, nurse, or other person licensed to practice a health care profession treating the victim of a gunshot wound or stabbing shall make a report to the chief of police of the city or the sheriff of the county in which treatment is rendered by the fastest possible means. In addition, within 24 hours after initial treatment or first observation of the wound, a written report shall be submitted, including a brief description of the wound and the name and address of the victim, if known, and shall be sent by first-class U.S. mail to the chief of police of the city or the sheriff of the county in which treatment was rendered.

Excerpts from Health Insurance Portability and Accountability Act (HIPAA) regulations, 45 C.F.R. §§ 164.502 and 164.512

45 C.F.R. § 164.502 Uses and disclosures of protected health information: general rules.

(a) **Standard.** A covered entity may not use or disclose protected health information, except as permitted or required by this subpart . . . .

> (1) **Covered entities: Permitted uses and disclosures.** A covered entity is permitted to use or disclose protected health information as follows:
>
> > (i) To the individual;
> >
> > . . . and
> >
> > (vi) As permitted by and in compliance with this section, [or] § 164.512 . . . .

* * *

(b) **Standard: Minimum necessary**

> (1) **Minimum necessary applies.** When using or disclosing protected health information or when requesting protected health information from another covered entity . . . , a covered entity must make reasonable efforts to limit protected health information to the minimum necessary to accomplish the intended purpose of the use, disclosure, or request.
>
> (2) **Minimum necessary does not apply.** This requirement does not apply to:
>
> > (i) Disclosures to or requests by a health care provider for treatment;
> > * * *
> >
> > (v) Uses or disclosures that are required by law, as described by § 164.512(a); and
> >
> > (vi) Uses or disclosures that are required for compliance with applicable requirements of this subchapter.

* * *

(f) **Standard: Deceased individuals.** A covered entity must comply with the requirements of this subpart with respect to the protected health information of a deceased individual.

(g) (1) **Standard: Personal representatives.** As specified in this paragraph, a covered entity must . . . treat a personal representative as the individual for purposes of this subchapter.

> * * *

(4) **Implementation specification: Deceased individuals.** If under applicable law an executor, administrator, or other person has authority to act on behalf of a deceased individual or of the individual's estate, a covered entity must treat such person as a personal representative under this subchapter, with respect to protected health information relevant to such personal representation.

* * * *

45 C.F.R. § 164.512 Uses and disclosures for which an authorization or opportunity to agree or object is not required.

A covered entity may use or disclose protected health information without the written authorization of the individual . . . in the situations covered by this section, subject to the applicable requirements of this section. When the covered entity is required by this section to inform the individual of, or when the individual may agree to, a use or disclosure permitted by this section, the covered entity's information and the individual's agreement may be given orally.

(a) **Standard: Uses and disclosures required by law.**

> (1) A covered entity may use or disclose protected health information to the extent that such use or disclosure is required by law and the use or disclosure complies with and is limited to the relevant requirements of such law.

> (2) A covered entity must meet the requirements described in paragraph . . . (f) of this section for uses or disclosures required by law.

* * *

(f) **Standard: Disclosures for law enforcement purposes.** A covered entity may disclose protected health information for a law enforcement purpose to a law enforcement official if [any of] the conditions in paragraphs (f)(1) through (f)(6) of this section are met, as applicable.

> (1) **Permitted disclosures: Pursuant to process [or] as otherwise required by law.**
> A covered entity may disclose protected health information:
>> (i) As required by law including laws that require the reporting of certain types of wounds or other physical injuries . . . .

* * *

In re Community General Hospital

(3) **Permitted disclosure: Victims of a crime.** Except for disclosures required by law as permitted by paragraph (f)(1) of this section, a covered entity may disclose protected health information in response to a law enforcement official's request for such information about an individual who is or is suspected to be a victim of a crime . . . if:

  (i) The individual agrees to the disclosure; or

  (ii) The covered entity is unable to obtain the individual's agreement because of incapacity or other emergency circumstance, provided that:

   (A) The law enforcement official represents that such information is needed to determine whether a violation of law by a person other than the victim has occurred, and such information is not intended to be used against the victim;

   (B) The law enforcement official represents that immediate law enforcement activity that depends upon the disclosure would be materially and adversely affected by waiting until the individual is able to agree to the disclosure; and

   (C) The disclosure is in the best interests of the individual as determined by the covered entity, in the exercise of professional judgment.

(4) **Permitted disclosure: Decedents.** A covered entity may disclose protected health information about an individual who has died to a law enforcement official for the purpose of alerting law enforcement of the death of the individual if the covered entity has a suspicion that such death may have resulted from criminal conduct.

* * *

(j) **Standard: Uses and disclosures to avert a serious threat to health or safety.**

  (1) **Permitted disclosures.** A covered entity may, consistent with applicable law and standards of ethical conduct, use or disclose protected health information, if the covered entity, in good faith, believes the use or disclosure:

   (i) (A) Is necessary to prevent or lessen a serious and imminent threat to the health or safety of a person or the public; and

   (B) Is to a person or persons reasonably able to prevent or lessen the threat, including the target of the threat;

  * * *

(4) **Presumption of good faith belief.** A covered entity that uses or discloses protected health information pursuant to paragraph (j)(1) of this section is presumed to have acted in good faith with regard to a belief described in paragraph (j)(1)(i) . . . of this section, if the belief is based upon the covered entity's actual knowledge or in reliance on a credible representation by a person with apparent knowledge or authority.

* * *

In re Community General Hospital

July 2014 MPTs
In re Kay Struckman
In re Linda Duram

July 2014
MPTs

www.ncbex.org

National Conference of Bar Examiners
302 South Bedford Street | Madison, WI 53703-3622
Phone: 608-280-8550 | Fax: 608-280-8552 | TDD: 608-661-1275
e-mail: contact@ncbex.org

Contents

Preface

The Multistate Performance Test (MPT) is developed by the National Conference of Bar Examiners (NCBE). This publication includes the items and Point Sheets from the July 2014 MPT. The instructions for the test appear on page iii.

The MPT Point Sheets describe the factual and legal points encompassed within the lawyering tasks to be completed. They outline the possible issues and points that might be addressed by an examinee. They are provided to the user jurisdictions to assist graders in grading the examination by identifying the issues and suggesting the resolution of the problem contemplated by the drafters.

For more information about the MPT, including a list of skills tested, visit the NCBE website at www.ncbex.org.

Description of the MPT

The MPT consists of two 90-minute items and is a component of the Uniform Bar Examination (UBE). It is administered by user jurisdictions as part of the bar examination on the Tuesday before the last Wednesday in February and July of each year. User jurisdictions may select one or both items to include as part of their bar examinations. (Jurisdictions that administer the UBE use two MPTs.)

The materials for each MPT include a File and a Library. The File consists of source documents containing all the facts of the case. The specific assignment the examinee is to complete is described in a memorandum from a supervising attorney. The File might also include transcripts of interviews, depositions, hearings or trials, pleadings, correspondence, client documents, contracts, newspaper articles, medical records, police reports, or lawyer's notes. Relevant as well as irrelevant facts are included. Facts are sometimes ambiguous, incomplete, or even conflicting. As in practice, a client's or a supervising attorney's version of events may be incomplete or unreliable. Examinees are expected to recognize when facts are inconsistent or missing and are expected to identify potential sources of additional facts.

The Library may contain cases, statutes, regulations, or rules, some of which may not be relevant to the assigned lawyering task. The examinee is expected to extract from the Library the legal principles necessary to analyze the problem and perform the task. The MPT is not a test of substantive law; the Library materials provide sufficient substantive information to complete the task.

The MPT is designed to test an examinee's ability to use fundamental lawyering skills in a realistic situation and complete a task that a beginning lawyer should be able to accomplish. The MPT is not a test of substantive knowledge. Rather, it is designed to evaluate six fundamental skills lawyers are expected to demonstrate regardless of the area of law in which the skills arise. The MPT requires examinees to (1) sort detailed factual materials and separate relevant from irrelevant facts; (2) analyze statutory, case, and administrative materials for applicable principles of law; (3) apply the relevant law to the relevant facts in a manner likely to resolve a client's problem; (4) identify and resolve ethical dilemmas, when present; (5) communicate effectively in writing; and (6) complete a lawyering task within time constraints. These skills are tested by requiring examinees to perform one or more of a variety of lawyering tasks. For example, examinees might be instructed to complete any of the following: a memorandum to a supervising attorney, a letter to a client, a persuasive memorandum or brief, a statement of facts, a contract provision, a will, a counseling plan, a proposal for settlement or agreement, a discovery plan, a witness examination plan, or a closing argument.

Instructions

The back cover of each test booklet contains the following instructions:

You will be instructed when to begin and when to stop this test. Do not break the seal on this booklet until you are told to begin. This test is designed to evaluate your ability to handle a select number of legal authorities in the context of a factual problem involving a client.

The problem is set in the fictitious state of Franklin, in the fictitious Fifteenth Circuit of the United States. Columbia and Olympia are also fictitious states in the Fifteenth Circuit. In Franklin, the trial court of general jurisdiction is the District Court, the intermediate appellate court is the Court of Appeal, and the highest court is the Supreme Court.

You will have two kinds of materials with which to work: a File and a Library. The first document in the File is a memorandum containing the instructions for the task you are to complete. The other documents in the File contain factual information about your case and may include some facts that are not relevant.

The Library contains the legal authorities needed to complete the task and may also include some authorities that are not relevant. Any cases may be real, modified, or written solely for the purpose of this examination. If the cases appear familiar to you, do not assume that they are precisely the same as you have read before. Read them thoroughly, as if they all were new to you. You should assume that the cases were decided in the jurisdictions and on the dates shown. In citing cases from the Library, you may use abbreviations and omit page references.

Your response must be written in the answer book provided. If you are using a laptop computer to answer the questions, your jurisdiction will provide you with specific instructions. In answering this performance test, you should concentrate on the materials in the File and Library. What you have learned in law school and elsewhere provides the general background for analyzing the problem; the File and Library provide the specific materials with which you must work.

Although there are no restrictions on how you apportion your time, you should allocate approximately half your time to reading and digesting the materials and to organizing your answer before you begin writing it. You may make notes anywhere in the test materials; blank pages are provided at the end of the booklet. You may not tear pages from the question booklet.

This performance test will be graded on your responsiveness to the instructions regarding the task you are to complete, which are given to you in the first memorandum in the File, and on the content, thoroughness, and organization of your response.

July 2014 MPT

 *FILE*

MPT-1: *In re Kay Struckman*

In re Kay Struckman

Attorneys at Law
610 E. Broadway
Windsor, Franklin 33073

M E M O R A N D U M

TO: Examinee
FROM: Steve Ramirez
DATE: July 29, 2014
RE: Kay Struckman consultation

I have been retained by Kay Struckman, a local attorney. As you will see from her letter, Ms. Struckman wishes to modify her current retainer agreement to require arbitration of fee disputes. She wants to be sure that the modification of her retainer agreements with existing clients is ethical and that the arbitration provision would be legally enforceable.

I have attached some materials that bear on Ms. Struckman's question, including a judicial decision and a formal ethics opinion, both from outside of Franklin, that deal with similar issues. Franklin, Columbia, and Olympia have all adopted identical versions of Rule 1.8 of the Model Rules of Professional Conduct of the American Bar Association. There is no Franklin ethics opinion that has addressed the specific issues raised by Ms. Struckman, but there are two Franklin Court of Appeal cases that may be relevant.

I am scheduled to meet with Ms. Struckman this week to advise her on the goals set forth in her letter. To help me prepare for the meeting, please draft a memorandum to me responding to her request for advice as communicated in her letter. Your memorandum should include support for your conclusions with citation to legal authority, taking care to distinguish contrary authority, where appropriate.

I think it is possible—from both an ethics and a legal enforceability perspective—to modify her retainer agreements to require arbitration of fee disputes, but only if certain conditions are met. Be sure to set forth those conditions in your memorandum.

KAY STRUCKMAN
Attorney at Law
9300 Wisteria Boulevard, Suite 301
Brule, Franklin 33036

July 22, 2014

Steve Ramirez
Ramirez & Jay LLP
610 E. Broadway
Windsor, Franklin 33073

Re: Modification of Retainer Agreements

Dear Steve:

I am pleased that you found time to talk with me earlier today and even more pleased that you have agreed to advise me in this matter. I write to confirm the scope of advice I seek and confirm what I said during our meeting.

As I told you, the question on which I need legal advice is whether I may ethically modify retainer agreements with existing clients to include a provision requiring binding arbitration to resolve future fee disputes, and, if so, what is necessary to ensure that any resulting modification would be legally enforceable.

By way of background, I am a sole practitioner who represents small businesses and individuals. Most of my clients seek advice on small business matters including government regulation, licensing, incorporating, and related matters; family matters including adoption, divorce, custody, and guardianship; and estate planning. I do litigation as well as transactional work related to these matters. Many clients have asked me to insert arbitration clauses in the contracts I draft for their businesses. Although I haven't had any fee disputes, I've been considering adding an arbitration clause to my retainer agreements to be proactive.

My current retainer agreement allows annual increases in my fees. I would like to modify my retainer agreements with existing clients to include a provision requiring binding arbitration of

4

future fee disputes in exchange for forgoing annual increases in my fees for two years. The provision I would like to include is as follows:

> Any claim or controversy arising out of, or relating to, Lawyer's representation of Client shall be settled by arbitration, and binding judgment on the arbitration award may be entered by any court having jurisdiction thereof.

I request your advice on these particular issues:

First, would it be ethical for me to modify my retainer agreements with existing clients using the above language to cover future fee disputes? Is the language I've proposed above sufficient, and if not, why? What else do I need to add to make the provision comport with my ethical obligations to my clients? What process, if any, must I provide to my clients to modify their retainer agreements? In short, what steps do I need to take to ensure compliance with the Franklin Rules of Professional Conduct?

Second, assuming that it is ethical to modify my retainer agreements, would the language I propose to cover future fee disputes be legally enforceable? If not, what revisions to the language would I need to make? Is there anything else that I would need to do to ensure legal enforceability?

Although I want to do right by my clients, I do not want to impose undue burdens on myself. Fee disputes are not complicated. I would like to see fee disputes resolved quickly and with a minimum of costs to me—and to my clients.

I look forward to meeting with you to discuss these matters.

Very truly yours,

Kay Struckman

Kay Struckman

In re Kay Struckman

July 2014 MPT

 ## LIBRARY

MPT-1: *In re Kay Struckman*

In re Kay Struckman

FRANKLIN RULE OF PROFESSIONAL CONDUCT 1.8

[Franklin Rule 1.8 is identical to Rule 1.8 of the ABA Model Rules of Professional Conduct; however, the Franklin Supreme Court has added its own comments.]

Rule 1.8 Conflict of Interest: Current Clients: Specific Rules

(a) A lawyer shall not enter into a business transaction with a client or knowingly acquire an ownership, possessory, security or other pecuniary interest adverse to a client unless:

(1) the transaction and terms on which the lawyer acquires the interest are fair and reasonable to the client and are fully disclosed and transmitted in writing in a manner that can be reasonably understood by the client;

(2) the client is advised in writing of the desirability of seeking and is given a reasonable opportunity to seek the advice of independent legal counsel on the transaction; and

(3) the client gives informed consent, in a writing signed by the client, to the essential terms of the transaction and the lawyer's role in the transaction, including whether the lawyer is representing the client in the transaction.

. . .

(h) A lawyer shall not:

(1) make an agreement prospectively limiting the lawyer's liability to a client for malpractice unless the client is independently represented in making the agreement . . . .

*　　*　　*

Comments

(i) The Franklin Supreme Court has ruled that although modifying a retainer agreement with an existing client amounts to a business transaction within the meaning of Rule 1.8, entering into a retainer agreement with a new client does not. *Rice v. Gravier Co.* (Fr. Sup. Ct. 1992).

*　　*　　*

In re Kay Struckman

COLUMBIA STATE BAR ETHICS COMMITTEE
ETHICS OPINION 2011-91

Question Presented and Brief Answer

May a lawyer modify a retainer agreement with an existing client to include a provision requiring binding arbitration of any future malpractice claim?

No. We do not believe that the lawyer can meet the requirements of Rule 1.8 of the Columbia Rules of Professional Conduct in making such a modification.

Discussion

Nothing in the Columbia Rules of Professional Conduct prohibits agreements requiring binding arbitration of existing malpractice claims. An agreement to modify a retainer agreement is governed by Rule 1.8 as well as by other principles discussed herein. We have a number of concerns.

First, Rule 1.8 requires that the lawyer inform the client in writing of the essential terms of the agreement. We assume that lawyers will make a sincere effort to explain the arbitration process, but we question whether the client will understand the advantages and disadvantages of arbitration as well as the tactical considerations of arbitration versus litigation. We are most concerned about those small business and individual clients who lack the benefit of in-house counsel or other resources to advise them about arbitration. It is not enough to explain that arbitration differs from litigation. Clients must be told the major implications of arbitration, such as lack of formal discovery and lack of a jury or judge trial. Because the proposed agreement covers *future* malpractice claims, the client is asked to enter into the agreement without consideration of the particular facts and circumstances of a dispute that might arise at some   later time.

Second, lawyers are in a fiduciary relationship with their clients. Lawyers bear the burden of demonstrating the reasonableness and good faith of the agreements they enter into with their clients. Should a client challenge the agreement requiring binding arbitration of future malpractice claims, the court will be called upon to scrutinize the agreement carefully. The standard of good

10

faith and reasonableness implies a heightened obligation of lawyers to be fair and frank in specifying the terms of the attorney-client relationship. Most clients will be less sophisticated than lawyers in understanding how arbitration differs from litigation. It will be very difficult for lawyers to meet their obligations as fiduciaries under these circumstances.

Third, we are concerned that a few lawyers might use mandatory binding arbitration of future malpractice claims to avoid investigations into misconduct. By doing so, a lawyer would in effect deprive the Columbia Supreme Court, and its Disciplinary Commission, of its jurisdiction to investigate and discipline lawyers who engage in misconduct. We cannot condone a tactic that undermines the authority of the Supreme Court to oversee the conduct of lawyers.

Although some courts have approved agreements requiring binding arbitration of future fee disputes, they have imposed certain conditions. A common condition is that the lawyer must urge the client to seek the advice of independent legal counsel concerning the agreement. Such a condition is consistent with our Rule 1.8(a), which requires that the lawyer advise the client to seek the advice of independent legal counsel and give the client a reasonable opportunity to do so. We are not convinced that lawyers can meet this condition with respect to an agreement requiring binding arbitration of future *malpractice* claims. It is unrealistic to expect a client to seek and pay for independent counsel in the midst of the lawyer's representation. Moreover, the client is being told not to trust the client's own lawyer.

Another common condition is that the lawyer must advise the client that certain legal rights, including the right to trial, may be affected. The lawyer must also explain the implications of that forfeiture of the right to a jury trial.

An agreement requiring binding arbitration of malpractice claims may be appropriate once the claim has arisen and the client is represented by new counsel who can adequately inform and advise the client about arbitration. However, we conclude that a lawyer may not modify a retainer agreement with an existing client to require binding arbitration of future malpractice claims.

Lawrence v. Walker

Franklin Court of Appeal (2006)

Gina Lawrence filed a claim for malpractice against Robert Walker, whom she had retained as her attorney in a divorce matter. Walker responded that the retainer agreement signed by Lawrence at the inception of the representation requires binding arbitration of malpractice claims. The district court denied Walker's motion to compel arbitration, and this interlocutory appeal followed.

Because arbitration is a matter of contract, the threshold issue here is whether attorney and client agreed to mandatory binding arbitration of the malpractice claim. But because clients as a class are particularly dependent on, and vulnerable to, their attorneys and therefore deserve safeguards to protect their interests, an agreement requiring binding arbitration must have been entered into openly and fairly to be legally enforceable. *Cf. Johnson v. LM Corp.* (Fr. Ct. App. 2004) (so holding as to employees vis-à-vis employers).

The retainer agreement that Lawrence signed requires the parties to submit to binding arbitration "disputes regarding legal fees and any other aspect of our attorney-client relationship." The agreement does not specify that malpractice claims are one of the matters to be arbitrated.

An agreement requiring binding arbitration effects a waiver of several rights. In rendering an award, arbitrators, unlike judges, are not required to follow the law. Awards based on an erroneous interpretation of the law or evidence cannot be overturned by the courts except in very limited instances. Because of limited judicial review, the choice of arbitrator is critical.

Further, parties may or may not have certain procedural rights in arbitration, such as the right to subpoena witnesses, to cross-examine them, or even to participate in an in-person hearing. Arbitration proceedings are often confidential. There is no reporting system that provides convenient public access to these proceedings. Therefore, it is unlikely that a client could know what to expect from an arbitration.

Because of the implications of an agreement to arbitration, courts enforce an agreement requiring binding arbitration only where the

12

client has been explicitly made aware of the existence of the arbitration provision and its implications. Absent notification and at least some explanation, the client cannot be said to have exercised a "real choice" in entering into the agreement.

The arbitration provision in the present case was part of a retainer agreement drafted by the attorney and presented to the client for her signature. It was not the product of negotiation.

It is undisputed that the term "malpractice" does not appear in the retainer agreement. The critical sentence reads "disputes regarding legal fees and any other aspect of our attorney-client relationship." It is more likely that Lawrence, the client, understood only that she was agreeing to mandatory binding arbitration of future fee disputes, not that her agreement also affected malpractice claims.

The language of an agreement should be interpreted most strongly against the party who created the uncertainty. This ambiguity in the language might alone be reason to conclude that Lawrence did not voluntarily agree to arbitrate malpractice claims. Moreover, where a fiduciary duty exists, as here between an attorney and a client, the attorney bears the burden of proving the good faith of any agreement the attorney enters into with the client. In such a case, the attorney is well advised to draft the agreement clearly.

We do not mean to express an opinion against arbitration of disputes between lawyers and clients. Where parties enter into an agreement openly and with complete information, arbitration represents an appropriate and even desirable approach to resolving such disputes. Arbitration affords both parties a speedier and often less costly method to reach a resolution of a dispute. It employs more flexible rules of evidence and procedure.

Having said this, we repeat that agreements requiring binding arbitration involve a waiver of significant rights, and should be entered into only after full disclosure of their consequences. Moreover, the court must carefully scrutinize agreements between clients and attorneys to determine that their terms are fair and reasonable. In *Johnson v. LM Corp.*, we examined the terms of an arbitration program for employees. We articulated the minimum requirements for the enforceability of an agreement requiring binding arbitration in a context involving

13

employers and employees and the latter's statutory rights. We believe that the context here, involving attorneys and clients and the former's fiduciary duties, is analogous.

In this case, the attorney has failed in his burden to show that the client knowingly entered into the agreement requiring binding arbitration of malpractice claims. Therefore, we need not consider the protections we discussed in *Johnson*.

Accordingly, we conclude that the client did not enter into an agreement requiring binding arbitration of malpractice claims that was legally enforceable. In light of that holding, we need not address the question of whether the agreement was ethically compliant.

Affirmed.

Johnson v. LM Corporation

Franklin Court of Appeal (2004)

Claire Johnson and other employees brought an action seeking a declaration that the LM Mandatory Employee Arbitration Program is contrary to public policy and therefore unlawful. The LM program requires company employees to submit employment disputes to binding arbitration, including those claims based on statutes such as the Equal Pay Act and the Human Rights Act. The district court declared the program lawful, and the employees appealed.

By agreeing to mandatory binding arbitration of a statutory claim, the parties do not forgo the substantive rights afforded by the statute. Rather, the parties submit the dispute to an arbitral, rather than a judicial, forum. The employees argue, however, that the arbitration process contains a number of shortcomings that prevent the vindication of their statutory rights.

Our Supreme Court has held that employees as a class are particularly dependent on, and vulnerable to, their employers and therefore deserve safeguards to protect their interests. *Lafayette v. Armstrong* (Fr. Sup. Ct. 1999). On the basis of that holding, the Court formulated five minimum requirements for a legally enforceable employment agreement requiring binding arbitration of statutory claims. Such an arbitration agreement must (1) provide for a neutral arbitrator, (2) provide for more than minimal discovery, (3) require a written, reasoned decision, (4) provide for all of the types of relief that would otherwise be available in court, and (5) not require employees to pay unreasonable fees or costs as a condition of access to the arbitration forum. *Id.*

Because of the limited review of arbitration decisions, the choice of arbitrator may be crucial. There is variety in how arbitrators are selected and variety in the number of arbitrators used in an arbitration. Regardless of the choices available, what is critical is that every arbitrator be neutral. To ensure neutrality, an arbitrator must disclose any grounds that might exist for a conflict between the arbitrator's interests and parties' interests. According to the LM program, the arbitrators are to be selected from the Franklin Arbitration Association (FAA), a long-standing and well-respected private nonprofit provider of arbitrators. To maintain

15

its reputation, the FAA requires its arbitrators to disclose any conflicts of interest that could compromise their neutrality. Assuming that the program in place requires that the arbitrators provide information about potential conflicts of interest so that the parties have the information necessary to determine whether to challenge any arbitrator assigned, the LM program passes muster as providing for neutral arbitrators.

The employees claim that the limit on the number of depositions permitted in the LM program, namely three depositions by each party, frustrates their ability to conduct discovery and thus fails to meet *Lafayette*'s second requirement that there be more than minimal discovery. While due process may not require the same degree of discovery that our courts permit, due process does require that there be a fair opportunity to be heard. Arguably, some discovery may be necessary if parties are to have a fair hearing. However, in this case, the employees' argument has no merit. Even our state rules of civil procedure limit the number of depositions that may be taken without a showing that additional discovery is needed. Depositions are not the only means of discovery useful to the parties in preparing for hearings. Often, a simple exchange of documents will assist the parties in trial preparation. We presume, because there is no evidence to the contrary, that an arbitrator would permit additional discovery if a proper showing were made.

The employees argue that the LM program provides no assurance that arbitrators will issue a written decision stating the reasons for their decisions, and no assurance that arbitrators will be aware that they may award all the relief available under the statute. The employees further argue that because review is limited, they will have no means of determining whether the arbitrators followed the law unless they issue written decisions giving reasons for the decision. Our Supreme Court has already ruled on the necessity of a written decision giving reasons for the decision in arbitration proceedings. *Lake v. Whiteside* (Fr. Sup. Ct. 1994). While the procedures in the case at bar do not require a written, reasoned decision, this court must assume that the arbitrators will follow the law and produce such a decision. By reviewing the reasons given for the arbitrators' written decisions, the employees will be able to determine whether the arbitrators considered all the remedies available.

Finally, the employees argue that the LM program violates the requirement that the parties not be required to pay unreasonable

16

fees or costs as a condition of accessing the arbitral forum. They point to provisions in the LM program that each party to the arbitration shall pay a pro rata share of the fees of the arbitrators, together with other costs of the arbitration incurred or approved by the arbitrators.

Unfortunately, in this case, the record is unclear as to what the fees and costs are. The parties are in dispute as to how the arbitration expenses will be divided between the employees and the employer. It is possible that exorbitant fees and costs will frustrate the employees' ability to pursue their statutory claims. If so, the program may be unlawful. Because the record here is unclear, we vacate the judgment of the district court and remand for further proceedings.

Vacated and remanded.

Sloane v. Davis

Olympia Supreme Court (2009)

Attorney Margit Davis and her client, Liam Sloane, entered into a retainer agreement that provided that the parties would use binding arbitration to resolve any disputes concerning Davis's representation. Sloane later sued Davis for negligence in representing him in a business matter. Davis moved to compel arbitration, which the trial court granted. The court of appeals affirmed.

Sloane concedes that he voluntarily agreed to the arbitration clause in the retainer agreement, concedes that the arbitration process was generally fair, and concedes that if this agreement applied to any issue other than attorney malpractice, it would be legally enforceable. He simply argues that, as a matter of public policy, attorneys should not be permitted to use arbitration to avoid litigation of an attorney malpractice matter.

This court has previously found that attorneys must adhere to certain standards when entering into business transactions with their clients. These standards include ensuring that the terms of the transaction are fair and are fully disclosed in writing and in a manner reasonably understandable to the client. The attorney must also advise the client in writing of the desirability of seeking independent legal advice about the transaction. The client must then give informed consent in writing. *Olympia Rule of Professional Conduct 1.8*

Davis more than met her obligations under Rule 1.8. First, the terms of the business transaction, here the arbitration process, were fair. Since Sloane concedes that the arbitration process Davis uses is fair, we need not further consider that issue.

Second, Davis made a full disclosure in writing in a manner that was easily understandable to the client. When Davis met with Sloane, she orally explained the retainer agreement, including the arbitration clause. Davis then mailed a copy of the retainer agreement to Sloane along with a brochure explaining arbitration. The brochure explained that by agreeing to arbitrate, Sloane would waive his right to a jury trial. The brochure explained the types of matters that might be arbitrated, including malpractice claims, and also provided examples of arbitration procedures that might be different from those Sloane would experience in litigation. It also explained that

18

the arbitrators would be required to disclose any conflicts of interest, follow the law, award appropriate remedies available under the law, and issue a written decision explaining the basis for the decision.

Further, the brochure sent to Sloane explained that Sloane could and should seek the advice of another attorney before signing the retainer agreement. The accompanying letter asked Sloane to sign and return the retainer agreement within one week, if Sloane agreed to it. In fact, Sloane did not seek independent legal advice but signed the retainer agreement and returned it to Davis on the same day he received it.

Sloane's argument that Davis failed to meet her obligations under Rule 1.8 is without merit. Likewise, Sloane's argument that he was unaware of the ramifications of the arbitration process is without merit.

Sloane also argues that, as a matter of public policy, even if the requirements of Rule 1.8 were met and even if the agreement to arbitrate was legally enforceable, attorneys should not be permitted to use arbitration to avoid litigation of a dispute with a client. We disagree.

By agreeing to use arbitration rather than litigation to resolve an attorney malpractice claim, the client does not give up the right to sue. The client simply shifts determination of the dispute from the courtroom to an arbitral forum. In doing so, the client and the attorney often benefit from a process that can be speedier and more cost-effective than litigation. The arbitration process can offer a more informal means of resolution and provides a private forum, often more attractive to client and attorney alike.

Sloane is correct that the attorney cannot prospectively limit liability to the client. But this retainer agreement contains no limit on liability. Rather, where the arbitrator is bound to follow the law and to award remedies, if any, consistent with the law, there does not appear to be any limit.

Sloane also argues that the attorney cannot limit the ability of the Olympia Supreme Court to discipline attorneys who violate the norms of practice. But nothing in this retainer agreement prevents Sloane or anyone from filing a charge with the Board of Attorney Discipline.

Affirmed.

19

July 2014 MPT

 *FILE*

MPT-2: *In re Linda Duram*

In re Linda Duram

BURTON AND FINES LLC
Attorneys at Law
963 N. Oak Street
Swansea, Franklin 33594

MEMORANDUM

TO:	Examinee
FROM:	Henry Fines
DATE:	July 29, 2014
RE:	Linda Duram FMLA matter

Our client, Linda Duram, is a graphic artist employed by Signs Inc. She applied for leave under the Family and Medical Leave Act (FMLA) from her employer; this was her first request for FMLA leave. The employer denied her request. Despite the denial, Linda traveled with her grandmother, Emma Baston, to attend the funeral of Emma's sister. Because Linda left town without an approved leave, Signs Inc. placed her on probation and threatened termination should another incident occur. Linda is particularly concerned about a threat of termination because she will almost certainly need to take additional leave in the future to care for her grandmother.

We have been retained to persuade Signs Inc. to reverse its earlier decision denying FMLA leave and retract the threat of termination.

Please prepare a letter for my signature addressed to Mr. Steven Glenn, Vice President of Human Resources for Signs Inc., arguing that Linda is entitled to leave under the FMLA. Follow the firm's attached guidelines for demand letters. Signs Inc.'s legal department will be reviewing the letter, so we need to provide a persuasive legal argument, including citing relevant authority. Your letter should also respond to the arguments raised by Mr. Glenn. I will submit the letter along with the medical evidence I have just received from Ms. Baston's doctor and Linda's affidavit describing her relationship with her grandmother.

There is no dispute that Signs Inc. is a covered employer under the FMLA. Nor is there a dispute that Linda, a full-time employee for the required number of weeks, is a covered employee. Do not address those issues.

BURTON AND FINES LLC
Attorneys at Law
963 N. Oak Street
Swansea, Franklin 33594

OFFICE MEMORANDUM

TO: All Attorneys
FROM: Managing Partner
DATE: November 3, 2012
RE: Guide for Drafting Demand Letters

A demand letter is a letter in which an attorney or party states a legal claim and demands that the recipient take or cease taking a certain action. Demand letters are designed to advocate a position and persuade the reader. A well-written demand letter can promote a favorable resolution of the claim without the time or costs involved in litigation.

A demand letter typically includes (1) a brief statement identifying the sender and, if appropriate, identifying the attorney-client relationship; (2) a brief statement of the purpose of the letter; (3) a brief description of the situation; (4) a thorough analysis of the basis for the client's claim, including a response to arguments raised against the claim; and (5) a specific settlement demand.

When discussing the basis for the client's claim, you should thoroughly analyze and integrate both the facts and applicable law in making your arguments, with appropriate citations to the law. You should respond to arguments that have been made against our client's position.

Use language appropriate to the recipient, but assume that the letter will be read by an attorney. Use a tone that is convincing but not insulting. Do not overstate or exaggerate the facts or the law, because doing so can undermine the strength of our client's position.

Email Correspondence

From: Linda Duram, Art Department
To: Steven Glenn, Vice President, Human Resources
Re: Request for Family and Medical Leave
Date: July 7, 2014, 9:15 a.m.

I request five days' leave under the Family and Medical Leave Act to accompany my grandmother to her sister's funeral. She died yesterday, and the funeral is Wednesday, July 9th. My grandmother has only a few months to live because of her heart disease. My grandmother raised me; she cannot travel by herself. She needs me to care for her and to give her medications and therapies. She has been depressed because of her health, and now with losing her only sister, she is very distraught. So am I. I just learned of her sister's death yesterday and I could not sleep last night. Please approve this request as soon as possible—we have to leave tomorrow.

From: Steven Glenn, Vice President, Human Resources
To: Linda Duram, Art Department
Re: Your request for Family and Medical Leave
Date: July 7, 2014, 3:30 p.m.

Dear Ms. Duram,

Signs Inc. denies your request for FMLA leave because (1) the Act does not apply to care for grandparents; (2) even if it did, the Act only applies to care provided in a home, hospital, or similar facility, not to travel; (3) the Act does not apply to funerals; and (4) you failed to give the requisite 30 days' notice.

I am sorry to learn of the death of a family member. You may take the two days of vacation time that you have accrued. Absence without approved vacation time or other leave is grounds for discipline up to and including discharge.

Steven Glenn

Vice President of Human Resources, Signs Inc.

In re Linda Duram

From: Steven Glenn, Vice President, Human Resources
To: Linda Duram, Art Department
Re: Your request for Family and Medical Leave
Date: July 16, 2014, 8:30 a.m.

Dear Ms. Duram,

As you know, we denied your request for leave under the FMLA for reasons previously stated in my email of July 7, 2014. Despite that denial, you left the office for five days. You had two days accrued vacation time, so we have allowed two days as vacation time. However, there was no approval for the remaining three days, and you will not be paid for these three days. Therefore, you were absent from your position without approved leave for three days.

In accordance with our Employee Policy 12.7, you are placed on probation. Any future unapproved absence will be grounds for immediate termination.

Steven Glenn

Vice President of Human Resources, Signs Inc.

In re Linda Duram

Affidavit of Linda Duram

Upon first being duly sworn, I, Linda Duram, residing in the County of Vilas, Franklin, do state:

1. My maternal grandparents, Emma and Bill Baston, raised me for many years since I was six years old, due to my parents having drug abuse problems.

2. When I was in grade school, one of my parents was usually in jail, so my brother and I lived with our grandparents off and on for months at a time. When I was 12, our parents were sent to prison, so my brother and I moved in with our grandparents for 18 months.

3. When our parents got out of prison, they moved into an apartment and took us back. Six months later they entered rehab and we stayed with our grandparents for three months. When they got out of rehab, they lived with us in our grandparents' home until I was in high school. In my junior year of high school, our parents went to prison again for three more years.

4. Grandpa Bill and Grandma Emma never adopted us because our parents were gone only for short terms. Our parents were afraid to sign any legal papers giving our grandparents custody because they did not know how that would affect their other legal problems.

5. When our parents were gone, our grandparents took care of us, fed us, clothed us, gave us gifts at holidays and birthdays, took us to school and the doctor, things like that. Even when one or both of our parents were living with us, it was our grandparents who fed us and saw that we got to school and did homework, that sort of thing. They came to our games and band performances, even when our parents were back home. Our grandparents paid for summer baseball and soccer camps. When we went to college, our parents were home and getting "clean" from drugs, but our grandparents loaned us the money to get a car to go to school.

6. Grandpa Bill died a few years ago, and Grandma has been steadily declining in health. My parents—they moved to their own home a few years ago—are too caught up in their own problems to help care for Grandma. There is now a team of people who care for her in her

In re Linda Duram

home. I take care of her every Sunday. Grandma told me that I was the only one who could care for her on this difficult trip to her sister's funeral.

Signed and sworn this 22nd day of July, 2014.

Linda Duram

Linda Duram

Signed before me this 22nd day of July, 2014.

Jane Mirren

Jane Mirren

Notary Public, State of Franklin

SWANSEA CARDIOLOGY CENTER
43 Hospital Drive, Suite 403
Swansea, Franklin 33596

July 24, 2014

To whom it may concern:

I have treated Emma Baston for the past 10 years for issues related to her cardiac condition and high blood pressure. Two months ago, I diagnosed Ms. Baston with end-stage congestive heart failure which will lead to her death, likely in a few months. Ms. Baston cannot walk, bathe herself, take her medications, feed herself, dress, or perform similar functions of daily life without assistance. She uses a wheelchair and oxygen. She needs to have fluids pumped from her heart. I have prescribed medication and therapies to be provided for Ms. Baston at home. These will not cure her but will relieve her suffering and make her comfortable as she lives her final months. Ms. Baston also suffers from depression. I ordered Home Health Services and chore services to assist her with daily functioning. I monitor her condition weekly.

Ms. Baston was able to travel to Franklin City to attend the funeral of her sister, which I understand required her to be gone a week. Ms. Baston had to be accompanied by someone familiar with her condition and her personal needs and able to attend to her and assist her as outlined above.

Her granddaughter, Linda Duram, has the power of attorney over her health care decisions and attends to Ms. Baston along with other family members and home health care workers. Linda has cared for her grandmother for the past two months. Linda has learned how to transport Ms. Baston into and out of the wheelchair, administer oxygen, operate the heart pump, administer the medications, and provide the personal care Ms. Baston requires. Ms. Duram needed to be absent from work for five days to make this trip.

If you need any further information, please do not hesitate to contact me.

Maria Oliver, M.D.

Maria A. Oliver, M.D.

In re Linda Duram

July 2014 MPT

▶ *LIBRARY*

MPT-2: *In re Linda Duram*

In re Linda Duram

The Family and Medical Leave Act of 1993, 29 U.S.C. § 2601 *et seq.*

29 U.S.C. § 2611 Definitions

. . .

(7) Parent. The term "parent" means the biological parent of an employee or an individual who stood in loco parentis to an employee when the employee was a son or daughter.

. . .

(11) Serious health condition. The term "serious health condition" means an illness, injury, impairment, or physical or mental condition that involves—

> (A) inpatient care in a hospital, hospice, or residential medical care facility; or

> (B) continuing treatment by a health care provider.

29 U.S.C. § 2612 Leave requirement

(a) In general

(1) Entitlement to leave. . . . [A]n eligible employee shall be entitled to a total of 12 workweeks of leave during any 12-month period for one or more of the following:

> (A) Because of the birth of a son or daughter of the employee and in order to care for such son or daughter.

> (B) Because of the placement of a son or daughter with the employee for adoption or foster care.

> (C) In order to care for the spouse, or a son, daughter, or parent, of the employee, if such spouse, son, daughter, or parent has a serious health condition.

> (D) Because of a serious health condition that makes the employee unable to perform the functions of the position of such employee.

. . .

(e) Foreseeable leave

(1) Requirement of notice. In any case in which the necessity for leave under subparagraph (A) or (B) of subsection (a)(1) of this section is foreseeable based on an expected birth or placement, the employee shall provide the employer with not less than 30 days' notice, before the date the leave is to begin, of the employee's intention to take leave under such subparagraph, except that if the date of the birth or placement requires leave to begin in less than 30 days, the employee shall provide such notice as is practicable.

In re Linda Duram

Code of Federal Regulations
Title 29. Labor

§ 825.112 Qualifying reasons for leave, general rule.

(a) Circumstances qualifying for leave. Employers covered by FMLA are required to grant leave to eligible employees: . . .

> (3) To care for the employee's spouse, son, daughter, or parent with a serious health condition . . . ;

§ 825.113 Serious health condition.

(a) For purposes of FMLA, "serious health condition" entitling an employee to FMLA leave means an illness, injury, impairment or physical or mental condition that involves inpatient care . . . or continuing treatment by a health care provider as defined in § 825.115.

. . .

(c) The term "treatment" includes (but is not limited to) examinations to determine if a serious health condition exists and evaluations of the condition. Treatment does not include routine physical examinations, eye examinations, or dental examinations. A regimen of continuing treatment includes, for example, a course of prescription medication (e.g., an antibiotic) or therapy requiring special equipment to resolve or alleviate the health condition (e.g., oxygen). A regimen of continuing treatment that includes the taking of over-the-counter medications such as aspirin, antihistamines, or salves; or bed-rest, drinking fluids, exercise, and other similar activities that can be initiated without a visit to a health care provider, is not, by itself, sufficient to constitute a regimen of continuing treatment for purposes of FMLA leave.

(d) . . . Ordinarily, unless complications arise, the common cold, the flu, ear aches, upset stomach, minor ulcers, headaches other than migraine, routine dental or orthodontia problems, periodontal disease, etc., are examples of conditions that do not meet the definition of a serious health condition and do not qualify for FMLA leave. . . .

*　　*　　*

§ 825.115 Continuing treatment.

A serious health condition involving continuing treatment by a health care provider includes any one or more of the following:

> . . .

34

(c) Chronic conditions. Any period of incapacity or treatment for such incapacity due to a chronic serious health condition. A chronic serious health condition is one which:

(1) Requires periodic visits (defined as at least twice a year) for treatment by a health care provider, or by a nurse under direct supervision of a health care provider;

(2) Continues over an extended period of time (including recurring episodes of a single underlying condition); and

(3) May cause episodic rather than a continuing period of incapacity (e.g., asthma, diabetes, epilepsy, etc.).

* * *

§ 825.302 Employee notice requirements for foreseeable FMLA leave.

(a) Timing of notice. An employee must provide the employer at least 30 days advance notice before FMLA leave is to begin if the need for the leave is foreseeable based on an expected birth, placement for adoption or foster care, planned medical treatment for a serious health condition of the employee or of a family member, . . . If 30 days' notice is not practicable, such as because of a lack of knowledge of approximately when leave will be required to begin, a change in circumstances, or a medical emergency, notice must be given as soon as practicable . . . .

§ 825.303 Employee notice requirements for unforeseeable FMLA leave.

(a) Timing of notice. When the approximate timing of the need for leave is not foreseeable, an employee must provide notice to the employer as soon as practicable under the facts and circumstances of the particular case. . . .

(b) Content of notice. An employee shall provide sufficient information for an employer to reasonably determine whether the FMLA may apply to the leave request. Depending on the situation, such information may include that a condition renders the employee unable to perform the functions of the job; that the employee is pregnant or has been hospitalized overnight; whether the employee or the employee's family member is under the continuing care of a health care provider; . . . .

Shaw v. BG Enterprises

United States Court of Appeals (15th Cir. 2011)

Gus Shaw requested leave under the Family and Medical Leave Act (FMLA), 29 U.S.C. § 2601 *et seq.,* from BG Enterprises. When that leave was denied, Shaw sued, alleging interference with FMLA leave. The district court entered judgment for BG Enterprises after a bench trial. Shaw appeals. We affirm.

Congress enacted the FMLA to balance the demands of the workplace with the needs of families, to promote the stability and economic security of families, to promote national interests in preserving family integrity, and to entitle employees to take reasonable leave to care for the serious health conditions of specified family members. 29 U.S.C. § 2601(b). The FMLA entitles eligible employees of covered employers to take unpaid, job-protected leave for specified family and medical reasons, such as a serious health condition, the birth or adoption of a child, or the care of a child, spouse, or parent who has a serious health condition. *Id.* § 2612.

To succeed on a claim of interference with FMLA leave, a plaintiff must show that he was eligible for FMLA protections, that his employer was covered by the FMLA, that he was entitled to take leave under the Act, that

he provided sufficient notice of his intent to take leave, and that his employer denied the FMLA benefits to which the employee was entitled. The only issue here is whether the employee was entitled to take leave.

Shaw, a managerial employee for BG Enterprises, sought leave to care for his daughter, who was seriously injured in an auto accident and subsequently died. On Saturday, May 10, 2008, Shaw learned that his daughter Janet had been seriously injured in a car accident in Franklin City, where she attended Franklin State University. Shaw and his wife immediately left for the hospital where Janet was being treated, some 200 miles away. On Monday, May 12, Shaw informed BG that he would not be at work because of his daughter's accident.

On May 19, Shaw submitted written documentation supporting his prior request under the FMLA for leave to care for his daughter and also to attend her funeral. He attached a medical certification from the hospital stating that Janet had suffered traumatic injuries as a result of the accident, was in a coma, and was unable to care for herself. Shaw stated that he had spent the initial weekend by Janet's bedside and had

36

then returned to his home in High Ridge while his wife stayed at the hospital. While at home, he arranged for Janet to be transferred to a rehabilitation facility, regularly called the hospital and talked with his wife about Janet, and spent the remainder of the time performing repairs to the Shaw home so that Janet could be cared for at home. He also attached a copy of the death certificate indicating that Janet had died on May 16, while still hospitalized.

BG denied Shaw's request for FMLA leave, arguing that the FMLA's use of the term "care for" does not include hospital visits, doing home repairs, arranging for transfer to another facility, or attending the funeral. Shaw asked BG to reconsider its denial of FMLA leave. BG refused and Shaw sued.

The critical issue here is what is meant by FMLA's use of the term "care for." We have not faced this issue until now. Neither the Act nor the regulations promulgated pursuant to the FMLA define the term "care for." Our sister circuits have attempted to define the term.

In *Tellis v. Alaska Airlines* (9th Cir. 2005), the Ninth Circuit held that the FMLA required that there be "some actual care," some level of participation in ongoing treatment of a serious health condition. In that case, an employer terminated an airline mechanic based in Seattle after the employee used FMLA leave to fly to another state to retrieve his car rather than staying with his wife during her high-risk pregnancy. Because the employee had left his wife's side for four days, instead of participating in her ongoing treatment, the Ninth Circuit held that he was not "caring for" her as required to invoke the protections of the FMLA. The court found that the person giving the care must be in "close and continuing proximity to the ill family member."

In a Twelfth Circuit case, *Roberts v. Ten Pen Bowl* (12th Cir. 2006), Sara Roberts sought FMLA leave to relocate her son to another state to live with an uncle. Roberts claimed that her son had a psychological condition that caused him to be easy prey for bullying by other students, and she wanted to move him to a safer location. She claimed that the relocation was treatment for his psychological condition. The Twelfth Circuit court upheld the denial of leave under the FMLA. The court found that relocating a child to a safer location, however admirable that may be, was in no way analogous to treatment for a serious health condition, a necessary requirement under the FMLA.

Roberts also argued that the FMLA allows leave to provide comfort or reassurance to a family member, citing its legislative history:

> The phrase "to care for," in [§ 2612(a)(1)(C)], is intended to be read broadly to include both physical and psychological care. Parents provide far greater psychological comfort and reassurance to a seriously ill child than others not so closely tied to the child. In some cases there is no one other than the child's parents to care for the child. The same is often true for adults caring for a seriously ill parent or spouse. S. Rep. No. 103-3, at 24 (1993), U.S. Code Cong. & Admin. News 1993, pp. 3, 26.

While a parent may offer comfort and reassurance to a child who has a serious health condition, the FMLA requires that there be treatment provided for that serious health condition. Roberts failed to show that her son was receiving any treatment.

These cases are helpful in attempting to define the term "care for." They point to the need for the employee seeking leave (1) to be in close and continuing proximity to the person being cared for, and (2) to offer some actual care to the person with a serious health condition. If the employee seeks leave to offer psychological care to the person with a serious health condition, the ill person must be receiving some treatment for a physical or psychological illness.

Here, Shaw was not in close and continuing proximity to his daughter while she was in the hospital and he was at home in High Ridge. His wife may have been in proximity to Janet, but she is not the employee seeking leave. Nor was Shaw providing care to Janet or offering her psychological comfort. Arguably, he provided comfort while he was at her bedside during the May 10 weekend, but that weekend did not constitute work time for which he needed leave. His actions may have been helpful to his daughter's situation, but they are not activities within the meaning of the term "care for" under the FMLA. He is also not entitled to leave to attend his daughter's funeral. The FMLA contemplates that the care must be given to a living person.

Affirmed.

Carson v. Houser Manufacturing, Inc.

United States Court of Appeals (15th Cir. 2013)

Plaintiff Sam Carson appeals from a judgment of the district court holding that he does not meet the definition of "parent" as provided in the Family and Medical Leave Act (FMLA), 29 U.S.C. § 2601 *et seq.* We affirm.

The FMLA creates an employee's right to take unpaid leave to care for a son or daughter who has a serious health condition. *Id.* § 2612(a)(1)(C). Under the FMLA, the term "son or daughter" means "a biological . . . child . . . , or a child of a person standing in loco parentis, who is (A) under 18 years of age; or (B) 18 years of age or older and incapable of self-care because of a mental or physical disability." *Id.* § 2611(12). Here, Carson's employer denied his request for two weeks of FMLA leave to care for his grandson, who was recovering from abdominal surgery.

The plain language of the FMLA does not authorize FMLA leave for the care of grandchildren. The plaintiff can only be entitled to FMLA leave to care for his grandson if he stands *in loco parentis* to the grandson. The FMLA does not define the term *in loco parentis,* a term typically defined by state law.

Under the law of the State of Franklin where Carson resides, the term *in loco parentis* refers to a person who intends to and does put himself in the situation of a lawful parent by assuming the obligations incident to the parental relation without going through the formalities of legal process (such as guardianship, custody, or adoption). The court may consider such factors as the child's age, the child's degree of dependence, or the amount of support provided by the person claiming to be *in loco parentis*.

Carson relies on the case of *Phillips v. Franklin City Park District* (Fr. Ct. App. 2006). Phillips was the paternal grandmother of Anthony Phillips, whose father died when Anthony was three years old. Anthony's mother became depressed and unable to care for Anthony but did not relinquish parental rights over Anthony, nor did Phillips seek to adopt Anthony. From the time Anthony was four, he lived in Phillips's home, and it was

Phillips who enrolled Anthony in school, took him to medical appointments, provided for his day-to-day financial support, attended parent-teacher conferences, and even served as driver for Anthony's Boy Scout troop. That was sufficient proof to meet the *in loco parentis* standard.

The evidence in this case is not similar to that of *Phillips*. Carson is the grandfather of David Simms. David lived with his parents until his parents died in a car accident when David was 15 years old. David moved in with his older brother and lived with his brother until he left for college. During the time after his parents were deceased, David did spend some weekends and extended vacations with Carson. While in college, he returned often to his brother's home and often to Carson's home during summers and holidays. Carson claims that he provided David with financial support while he was in college, gave him financial and moral advice, and attended David's graduation from college.

While these efforts by Carson likely guided and aided David at a critical time in his life, they are not that dissimilar from what many grandparents do without assuming a parental role. The trial court was correct in finding that the proof offered by Sam Carson was insufficient to meet the standard of one who is *in loco parentis*.

Affirmed.

Themis
BarReview

February 2014 MPTs
In re Rowan
In re Peterson Engineering Consultants

THE MPT
MULTISTATE PERFORMANCE TEST

February 2014
MPTs

www.ncbex.org

National Conference of Bar Examiners
302 South Bedford Street | Madison, WI 53703-3622
Phone: 608-280-8550 | Fax: 608-280-8552 | TDD: 608-661-1275
e-mail: contact@ncbex.org

Contents

Preface

The Multistate Performance Test (MPT) is developed by the National Conference of Bar Examiners (NCBE). This publication includes the items and Point Sheets from the February 2014 MPT. The instructions for the test appear on page iii.

The MPT Point Sheets describe the factual and legal points encompassed within the lawyering tasks to be completed. They outline the possible issues and points that might be addressed by an examinee. They are provided to the user jurisdictions to assist graders in grading the examination by identifying the issues and suggesting the resolution of the problem contemplated by the drafters.

For more information about the MPT, including a list of skills tested, visit the NBCE website at www.ncbex.org.

Description of the MPT

The MPT consists of two 90-minute items and is a component of the Uniform Bar Examination (UBE). User jurisdictions may select one or both items to include as part of their bar examinations. (UBE jurisdictions use two MPTs as part of their bar examinations.) It is administered by participating jurisdictions on the Tuesday before the last Wednesday in February and July of each year.

The materials for each MPT include a File and a Library. The File consists of source documents containing all the facts of the case. The specific assignment the examinee is to complete is described in a memorandum from a supervising attorney. The File might also include transcripts of interviews, depositions, hearings or trials, pleadings, correspondence, client documents, contracts, newspaper articles, medical records, police reports, or lawyer's notes. Relevant as well as irrelevant facts are included. Facts are sometimes ambiguous, incomplete, or even conflicting. As in practice, a client's or a supervising attorney's version of events may be incomplete or unreliable. Examinees are expected to recognize when facts are inconsistent or missing and are expected to identify potential sources of additional facts.

The Library may contain cases, statutes, regulations, or rules, some of which may not be relevant to the assigned lawyering task. The examinee is expected to extract from the Library the legal principles necessary to analyze the problem and perform the task. The MPT is not a test of substantive law; the Library materials provide sufficient substantive information to complete the task.

The MPT is designed to test an examinee's ability to use fundamental lawyering skills in a realistic situation. Each test evaluates an examinee's ability to complete a task that a beginning lawyer should be able to accomplish. The MPT requires examinees to (1) sort detailed factual materials and separate relevant from irrelevant facts; (2) analyze statutory, case, and administrative materials for applicable principles of law; (3) apply the relevant law to the relevant facts in a manner likely to resolve a client's problem; (4) identify and resolve ethical dilemmas, when present; (5) communicate effectively in writing; and (6) complete a lawyering task within time constraints.

These skills are tested by requiring examinees to perform one or more of a variety of lawyering tasks. For example, examinees might be instructed to complete any of the following: a memorandum to a supervising attorney, a letter to a client, a persuasive memorandum or brief, a statement of facts, a contract provision, a will, a counseling plan, a proposal for settlement or agreement, a discovery plan, a witness examination plan, or a closing argument.

Instructions

The back cover of each test booklet contains the following instructions:

You will be instructed when to begin and when to stop this test. Do not break the seal on this booklet until you are told to begin. This test is designed to evaluate your ability to handle a select number of legal authorities in the context of a factual problem involving a client.

The problem is set in the fictitious state of Franklin, in the fictitious Fifteenth Circuit of the United States. Columbia and Olympia are also fictitious states in the Fifteenth Circuit. In Franklin, the trial court of general jurisdiction is the District Court, the intermediate appellate court is the Court of Appeal, and the highest court is the Supreme Court.

You will have two kinds of materials with which to work: a File and a Library. The first document in the File is a memorandum containing the instructions for the task you are to complete. The other documents in the File contain factual information about your case and may include some facts that are not relevant.

The Library contains the legal authorities needed to complete the task and may also include some authorities that are not relevant. Any cases may be real, modified, or written solely for the purpose of this examination. If the cases appear familiar to you, do not assume that they are precisely the same as you have read before. Read them thoroughly, as if they all were new to you. You should assume that the cases were decided in the jurisdictions and on the dates shown. In citing cases from the Library, you may use abbreviations and omit page references.

Your response must be written in the answer book provided. If you are using a laptop computer to answer the questions, your jurisdiction will provide you with specific instructions. In answering this performance test, you should concentrate on the materials in the File and Library. What you have learned in law school and elsewhere provides the general background for analyzing the problem; the File and Library provide the specific materials with which you must work.

Although there are no restrictions on how you apportion your time, you should allocate approximately half your time to reading and digesting the materials and to organizing your answer before you begin writing it. You may make notes anywhere in the test materials; blank pages are provided at the end of the booklet. You may not tear pages from the question booklet.

This performance test will be graded on your responsiveness to the instructions regarding the task you are to complete, which are given to you in the first memorandum in the File, and on the content, thoroughness, and organization of your response.

February 2014 MPT

▶ *FILE*

MPT-1: *In re Rowan*

Law Offices of Jamie Quarles
112 Charles St.
Franklin City, Franklin 33797

TO: Examinee
FROM: Jamie Quarles
DATE: February 25, 2014
RE: *Matter of William Rowan*

We represent William Rowan, a British citizen, who has lived in this country as a conditional permanent resident because of his marriage to Sarah Cole, a U.S. citizen. Mr. Rowan now seeks to remove the condition on his lawful permanent residency.

Normally, a married couple would apply together to remove the conditional status, before the end of the two years of the noncitizen's conditional residency. However, ten months ago, in April 2013, Ms. Cole and Mr. Rowan separated, and they eventually divorced. Ms. Cole actively opposes Mr. Rowan's continued residency in this country.

However, Ms. Cole's opposition does not end Mr. Rowan's chances. As the attached legal sources indicate, he can still file Form I-751 Petition to Remove Conditions on Residence, but in the petition he must ask for a waiver of the requirement that he file the petition jointly with his wife.

Acting pro se, Rowan timely filed such a Form I-751 petition. The immigration officer conducted an interview with him. Ms. Cole provided the officer with a sworn affidavit stating her belief that Rowan married her solely to obtain residency. The officer denied Rowan's petition.

Rowan then sought our representation to appeal the denial of his petition. We now have a hearing scheduled in Immigration Court to review the validity of that denial. Before the hearing, we will submit to the court the information described in the attached investigator's memo, which was not presented to the immigration officer. We do not expect Cole to testify, because she has moved out of state.

Please draft our brief to the Immigration Judge. The brief will need to argue that Mr. Rowan married Ms. Cole in good faith. Specifically, it should argue that the immigration officer's decision was not supported by substantial evidence in the record before him and that the totality of the evidence supports granting Rowan's petition.

I have attached our guidelines for drafting briefs. Draft only the legal argument portion of the brief; I will draft the caption and statement of facts.

Law Offices of Jamie Quarles
112 Charles St.
Franklin City, Franklin 33797

TO: Attorneys
FROM: Jamie Quarles
DATE: March 29, 2011
RE: Format for Persuasive Briefs

These guidelines apply to persuasive briefs filed in trial courts and administrative proceedings.

I. Caption
[omitted]

II. Statement of Facts (if applicable)
[omitted]

III. Legal Argument

Your legal argument should be brief and to the point. Assume that the judge will have little time to read and absorb your argument. Make your points clearly and succinctly, citing relevant authority for each legal proposition. Keep in mind that courts are not persuaded by exaggerated, unsupported arguments.

Use headings to separate the sections of your argument. In your headings, do not state abstract conclusions, but integrate factual detail into legal propositions to make them more persuasive. An ineffective heading states only: "The petitioner's request for asylum should be granted." An effective heading states: "The petitioner has shown a well-founded fear of persecution by reason of gender if removed to her home country."

Do not restate the facts as a whole at the beginning of your legal argument. Instead, integrate the facts into your legal argument in a way that makes the strongest case for our client. The body of your argument should analyze applicable legal authority and persuasively argue how both the facts and the law support our client's position. Supporting authority should be emphasized, but contrary authority should also be cited, addressed in the argument, and explained or distinguished.

Finally, anticipate and accommodate any weaknesses in your case in the body of your argument. If possible, structure your argument in such a way as to highlight your argument's strengths and minimize its weaknesses. If necessary, make concessions, but only on points that do not concede essential elements of your claim or defense.

Law Offices of Jamie Quarles
112 Charles St.
Franklin City, Franklin 33797

TO: File
FROM: Jamie Quarles
DATE: November 25, 2013
RE: Interview with William Rowan

I met with William Rowan today. Rowan is a British citizen and moved to the United States and to Franklin about two and a half years ago, having just married Sarah Cole. They separated in April 2013; their divorce became final about 10 days ago. In late April, after the separation, Rowan, acting pro se, petitioned to retain his permanent residency status. After that petition was denied by the immigration officer, Rowan called our office.

Rowan met Cole in Britain a little over three years ago. He had been working toward a graduate degree in library science for several years. He had begun looking for professional positions and had come to the realization that he would have better job opportunities in the United States. He had two siblings already living in the United States.

He met Cole when she was doing graduate work in cultural anthropology at the university where he was finishing his own academic training as a librarian. He says that it was love at first sight for him. He asked her out, but she refused several times before she agreed. After several weeks of courtship, he said that he felt that she shared his feelings. They moved in together about four weeks after their first meeting and lived together for the balance of her time in Britain.

Soon after they moved in together, Rowan proposed marriage to Cole. She agreed, and they married on December 27, 2010, in London, England. Cole subsequently suggested that they move to the United States together, to which he readily agreed. In fact, without telling Cole, Rowan had contacted the university library in Franklin City, just to see if there were job opportunities. That contact produced a promising lead, but no offer. He and Cole moved to Franklin City at the end of her fellowship in May of 2011.

Rowan soon obtained a job with the Franklin State University library. He and Cole jointly leased an apartment and shared living expenses. At one point, they moved into a larger space, signing a two-year lease. When Cole needed to purchase a new car, Rowan (who at that point had the more stable salary) co-signed the loan documents. Both had health insurance through the university, and each had the other named as the next of kin. They filed two joint tax returns (for 2011 and 2012), but they divorced before they could file another.

Their social life was limited; if they socialized at all, it was with his friends. Rowan consistently introduced Cole as his wife to his friends, and he was referred to by them as "that old married man." As far as Rowan could tell, Cole's colleagues at work did not appear to know that Cole was even married.

Cole's academic discipline required routine absences for field work, conferences, and colloquia. Rowan resented these absences and rarely contacted Cole when she was gone. He estimates that, out of the approximately two and a half years of cohabitation during the marriage, they lived apart for an aggregate total of seven months.

In March of 2013, Cole announced that she had received an offer for a prestigious assistant professorship at Olympia State University. She told Rowan that she intended to take the job and wanted him to move with her, unless he could give her a good reason to stay. She also had an offer from Franklin State University, but she told him that the department was not as prestigious as the Olympia department. He made as strong a case as he could that she should stay, arguing that he could not find another job in Olympia comparable to the one that he had in Franklin.

Cole chose to take the job in Olympia, and she moved there less than a month later. Rowan realized that he would always be following her, and that she would not listen to his concerns or needs. He told her that he would not move. She was furious. She told him that in that case, she would file for a divorce. She also told him that she would fight his effort to stay in the United States. Their divorce was finalized on November 15, 2013, in Franklin.

Rowan worries that without Cole's support, he will not be able to keep his job in Franklin or stay in the United States. He does not want to return to the United Kingdom and wants to maintain permanent residency here.

In re Form I-751, Petition of William Rowan to Remove Conditions on Residence

Affidavit of Sarah Cole

Upon first being duly sworn, I, Sarah Cole, residing in the County of Titan, Olympia,　do say:

1.　　I am submitting this affidavit in opposition to William Rowan's Form I-751 Petition to Remove Conditions on Residence.

2.　　I am a United States citizen. I married William Rowan in London, England, on December 27, 2010. This was the first marriage for each of us. We met while I was on a fellowship in that city. He was finishing up his own graduate studies. He told me that he had been actively looking for a position in the United States for several years. He pursued me and after about four weeks convinced me to move in with him. Shortly after this, William proposed marriage and I accepted.

3.　　We decided that we would move to the United States. I now believe that he never seriously considered the option of remaining in Britain. I later learned that William had made contacts with the university library in Franklin City, Franklin, long before he proposed.

4.　　Before entering the United States in May 2011, we obtained the necessary approvals for William to enter the country as a conditional resident. We moved to Franklin City so that I could resume my studies.

5.　　During our marriage, William expressed little interest in my work but expressed great dissatisfaction with the hours that I was working and the time that I spent traveling. My graduate work had brought me great success, including the chance at an assistant professorship at Olympia State University, whose cultural anthropology department is nationally ranked. But William resisted any idea of moving and complained about the effect a move would have on our marriage and his career.

6.　　Eventually, I took the job in Olympia and moved in April 2013. While I knew that William did not like the move, I had asked him to look into library positions in Olympia, and he had done so. I fully expected him to follow me within a few months. I was shocked and angered when, instead, he called me on April 23, 2013, and informed me that he would stay in Franklin.

7.　　I filed for divorce, which is uncontested. It is my belief that William does not really care about the divorce. I believe now that he saw our marriage primarily as a means to get U.S.

residency. I do think that his affection for me was real. But his job planning, his choice of friends, and his resistance to my career goals indicate a lack of commitment to our relationship. In addition, he has carefully evaded any long-term commitments, including children, property ownership, and similar obligations.

Signed and sworn this 2nd day of July, 2013.

_____
Sarah Cole

Signed before me this 2nd day of July, 2013.

_____
Jane Mirren
Notary Public, State of Olympia

Law Offices of Jamie Quarles
112 Charles St.
Franklin City, Franklin 33797

TO: File
FROM: Victor Lamm, investigator
DATE: February 20, 2014
RE: Preparation for Rowan Form I-751 Petition

This memorandum summarizes the results of my investigation, witness preparation, and document acquisition in advance of the immigration hearing for William Rowan.

Witnesses:

— George Miller: friend and coworker of William Rowan. Has spent time with Rowan and Cole as a couple (over 20 social occasions) and has visited their two primary residences and has observed them together. Will testify that they self-identified as husband and wife and that he has heard them discussing leasing of residential property, purchasing cars, borrowing money for car purchase, and buying real estate, all together and as part of the marriage.

— Anna Sperling: friend and coworker of William Rowan. Has spent time with both Rowan and Cole, both together and separately. Will testify to statements by Cole that she (Cole) felt gratitude toward Rowan for moving to the United States without a job, and that Cole was convinced that Rowan "did it for love."

Documents (Rowan to authenticate):

— Lease on house at 11245 Old Sachem Road, Franklin City, Franklin, with a two-year term running until January 31, 2014. Signed by both Cole and Rowan.

— Promissory note for $20,000 initially, designating Cole as debtor and Rowan as co-signer, in connection with a new car purchase.

— Printouts of joint bank account in name of Rowan and Cole, February 1, 2012, through May 31, 2013.

— Joint income tax returns for 2011 and 2012.

— Certified copy of the judgment of divorce.

In re Rowan

February 2014 MPT

 *LIBRARY*

MPT-1: *In re Rowan*

EXCERPT FROM IMMIGRATION AND NATIONALITY ACT OF 1952
TITLE 8 U.S.C., Aliens and Nationality

8 U.S.C. § 1186a. Conditional permanent resident status for certain alien spouses and sons and daughters

(a) In general

    (1) Conditional basis for status: Notwithstanding any other provision of this chapter, an alien spouse . . . shall be considered, at the time of obtaining the status of an alien lawfully admitted for permanent residence, to have obtained such status on a conditional basis subject to the provisions of this section.

    . . .

(c) Requirements of timely petition and interview for removal of condition

    (1) In general: In order for the conditional basis established under subsection (a) of this section for an alien spouse or an alien son or daughter to be removed—

        (A) the alien spouse and the petitioning spouse (if not deceased) jointly must submit to the Secretary of Homeland Security a petition which requests the removal of such conditional basis . . . .

    . . .

    (4) Hardship waiver: The Secretary . . . may remove the conditional basis of the permanent resident status for an alien who fails to meet the requirements of paragraph (1) if the alien demonstrates that—

        . . .

        (B) the qualifying marriage was entered into in good faith by the alien spouse, but the qualifying marriage has been terminated (other than through the death of the spouse) and the alien was not at fault in failing to meet the requirements of paragraph (1).

In re Rowan

EXCERPT FROM CODE OF FEDERAL REGULATIONS
TITLE 8. Aliens and Nationality

8 C.F.R. § 216.5 Waiver of requirement to file joint petition to remove conditions by alien spouse

(a) General.

    (1) A conditional resident alien who is unable to meet the requirements . . . for a joint petition for removal of the conditional basis of his or her permanent resident status may file a Petition to Remove the Conditions on Residence, if the alien requests a waiver, was not at fault in failing to meet the filing requirement, and the conditional resident alien is able to establish that:

        . . .

        (ii) The marriage upon which his or her status was based was entered into in good faith by the conditional resident alien, but the marriage was terminated other than by death . . .

. . .

(e) Adjudication of waiver application—

        . . .

    (2) Application for waiver based upon the alien's claim that the marriage was entered into in good faith. In considering whether an alien entered into a qualifying marriage in good faith, the director shall consider evidence relating to the amount of commitment by both parties to the marital relationship. Such evidence may include—

        (i) Documentation relating to the degree to which the financial assets and liabilities of the parties were combined;

        (ii) Documentation concerning the length of time during which the parties cohabited after the marriage and after the alien obtained permanent residence;

        (iii) Birth certificates of children born to the marriage; and

        (iv) Other evidence deemed pertinent by the director.

. . .

Hua v. Napolitano

United States Court of Appeals (15th Cir. 2011)

Under the Immigration and Nationality Act, an alien who marries a United States citizen is entitled to petition for permanent residency on a conditional basis. *See* 8 U.S.C. § 1186a(a)(1). Ordinarily, within the time limits provided by statute, the couple jointly petitions for removal of the condition, stating that the marriage has not ended and was not entered into for the purpose of procuring the alien spouse's admission as an immigrant. 8 U.S.C. § 1186a(c)(1)(A).

If the couple has divorced within two years of the conditional admission, however, the alien spouse may still apply to the Secretary of Homeland Security to remove the conditional nature of her admission by granting a "hardship waiver." 8 U.S.C. § 1186a(c)(4). The Secretary may remove the conditional status upon a finding, *inter alia*, that the marriage was entered into in good faith by the alien spouse. 8 U.S.C. § 1186a(c)(4)(B).

On September 15, 2003, petitioner Agnes Hua, a Chinese citizen, married a United States citizen of Chinese descent and secured conditional admission as a permanent United States resident. The couple later divorced, and Hua applied for a hardship waiver. But the Secretary, acting through a U.S. Citizenship and Immigration Services (USCIS) immigration officer, then an immigration judge, and the Board of Immigration Appeals (BIA), denied Hua's petition. Hua appeals the denial of the petition.

Hua has the burden of proving that she intended to establish a life with her spouse at the time she married him. If she meets this burden, her marriage is legitimate, even if securing an immigration benefit was one of the factors that led her to marry. Hua made a very strong showing that she married with the requisite intent to establish a life with her husband. Hua's evidence, expressly credited by the immigration judge and never questioned by the BIA, established the following:

(1) She and her future husband engaged in a nearly two-year courtship prior to marrying.

(2) She and her future husband were in frequent telephone contact whenever they lived apart, as proven by telephone records.

(3) Her future husband traveled to China in December 2002 for three weeks to meet her family, and she paid a 10-day visit to him in the United States in March 2003 to meet his family.

(4) She returned to the United States in June 2003 (on a visitor's visa which permitted her to remain in the country through late September 2003) to decide whether she would remain in the United States or whether her future husband would move with her to China.

(5) The two married in a civil ceremony on September 15, 2003, and returned to China for two weeks to hold a more formal reception (a reception that was never held).

(6) The two lived together at his parents' house from the time of her arrival in the United States in June 2003 until he asked her to move out on April 22, 2004.

Hua also proved that, during the marriage, she and her husband jointly enrolled in a health insurance policy, filed tax returns, opened bank accounts, entered into automobile financing agreements, and secured a credit card. *See* 8 C.F.R. § 216.5(e)(2)(i).

Nevertheless, the BIA cited four facts in support of its conclusion that Hua had failed to carry her burden: (1) her application to secure conditional permanent residency was submitted within two weeks of the marriage; (2) Hua and her husband married one week prior to the expiration of the visitor's visa by which she came to the United States in June 2003; (3) Hua's husband maintained an intimate relationship with another woman during the marriage; and (4) Hua moved out of the marital residence shortly after obtaining conditional residency. Hua's husband's extramarital affair led to cancellation of the reception in China and to her departure from the marital home.

We do not see how Hua's prompt submission of a conditional residency application after her marriage tends to show that Hua did not marry in good faith. As we already have stated, the visitor's visa by which Hua entered the country expired just after the marriage, so Hua had to do something to remain here lawfully.

As to the affair maintained by Hua's husband, that might offer an indication of Hua's marital intentions if Hua knew of the relationship at the time she married. However, the uncontradicted evidence establishes that Hua learned of the affair only after the marriage.

The timing of the marriage and separation appear at first glance more problematic. Ordinarily, one who marries one week prior to the expiration of her visitor's visa and then moves out of the marital home shortly after the conditional residency interview might reasonably be thought to have married solely for an immigration benefit.

But well-settled law requires us to assess the entirety of the record. A long courtship preceded this marriage. Moreover, Hua's husband, and not Hua, initiated the separation after Hua publicly shamed him by retaining counsel and detailing his affair at her conditional residency interview.

We conclude that the Secretary's decision lacks substantial evidence on the record as a whole, and thus that petitioner Hua has satisfied the "good faith" marriage requirement for eligibility under 8 U.S.C. § 1186a(c)(4)(B). Remanded for proceedings consistent with this opinion.

Connor v. Chertoff

United States Court of Appeals (15th Cir. 2007)

Ian Connor, an Irish national, petitions for review of a decision of the Board of Immigration Appeals (BIA), which denied him a statutory waiver of the joint filing requirement for removal of the conditional basis of his permanent resident status on the ground that he entered into his marriage to U.S. citizen Anne Moore in bad faith. 8 U.S.C. § 1186a(c)(4)(B).

Connor met Moore in January 2002 when they worked at the same company in Forest Hills, Olympia. After dating for about one year, they married in a civil ceremony on April 14, 2003. According to Connor, he and Moore then lived with her family until November 2003, when they moved into an apartment of their own. In January 2004, Connor left Olympia to take a temporary job in Alaska, where he spent five weeks. Connor stated that in May 2004, he confronted Moore with his suspicion that she was being unfaithful to him. After Moore suggested they divorce, the two separated in June 2004 and divorced on November 27, 2004, 19 months after their wedding.

U.S. Citizenship and Immigration Services

(USCIS) had granted Connor conditional permanent resident status on September 15, 2004. On August 16, 2005, Connor filed a Petition to Remove Conditions on Residence with a request for waiver. *See* § 1186a(c)(4)(B).

Moore voluntarily submitted an affidavit concerning Connor's request for waiver. In that affidavit, Moore stated that "Connor never spent any time with [her] during the marriage, except when he needed money." They never socialized together during the marriage, and even when they resided together, Connor spent most of his time away from the residence. Moore expressed the opinion that Connor "never took the marriage seriously" and that "he only married [her] to become a citizen." Connor's petition was denied.

At Connor's hearing, the government presented no witnesses. Connor testified to the foregoing facts and provided documentary evidence, including a jointly filed tax return, an unsigned lease for an apartment dated November 2003, eight canceled checks from a joint account, telephone bills listing Connor and Moore as residing at the same address, an application for life insurance, and an application for vehicle title. There was no evidence that certain documents, such as the applications for life insurance and automobile title, had been filed. Connor also provided a letter from a nurse who had treated him over an extended period of time stating that his wife had accompanied him on most office visits, and letters that Moore had written to him during periods of separation.

Other evidence about Connor's life before and after his marriage to Moore raised questions as to his credibility, including evidence of his children by another woman prior to his marriage to Moore. Connor stated that Moore knew about his children but that he chose not to list them on the Petition for Conditional Status and also that the attorneys who filled out his I-751 petition omitted the children due to an error. Connor testified that he did not mention his children during his interview with the USCIS officer because he thought that they were not relevant to the immigration decision as they were not U.S. citizens.

In a written opinion, the immigration judge found that Connor was not a credible witness because of his failure to list his children on the USCIS forms or mention them during his interview and because of his demeanor during cross-examination. The immigration judge commented on Connor's departure for Alaska within eight months of his marriage to Moore, and on the lack of any corroborating testimony about the bona fides of the marriage by family or friends. The immigration judge concluded that the marriage had not been entered into in good faith and denied Connor the statutory waiver. The BIA affirmed.

Under the substantial evidence standard that governs our review of § 1186a(c)(4) waiver determinations, we must affirm the BIA's order when there is such relevant evidence as reasonable minds might accept as adequate to support it, even if it is possible to reach a contrary result on the basis of the evidence. We conclude that there was substantial evidence in the record to support the BIA's adverse credibility finding and its denial of the statutory waiver.

Adverse credibility determinations must be based on "specific, cogent reasons," which

19

the BIA provided here. The immigration judge's adverse credibility finding was based on Connor's failure to inform USCIS about his children during his oral interview and on the pertinent USCIS forms. Failing to list his children from a prior relationship undercut Connor's claim that his marriage to Moore was in good faith. That important omission properly served as a basis for an adverse credibility determination.

Substantial evidence supports the determination that Connor did not meet his burden of proof by a preponderance of the evidence. To determine good faith, the proper inquiry is whether Connor and Moore intended to establish a life together at the time they were married. The immigration judge may look to the actions of the parties after the marriage to the extent that those actions bear on the subjective intent of the parties at the time they were married. Additional relevant evidence includes, but is not limited to, documentation such as lease agreements, insurance policies, income tax forms, and bank accounts, as well as testimony about the courtship and wedding. Neither the immigration judge nor the BIA may substitute personal conjecture or inference for reliable evidence.

In this case, inconsistencies in the documentary evidence and the lack of corroborating testimony further support the agency's decision. Connor provided only limited documentation of the short marriage. Unexplained inconsistencies existed in the documents, such as more addresses than residences. Connor provided no signed leases, nor any indication of any filed applications for life insurance or automobile title. No corroboration existed for Connor's version of events from family, friends, or others who knew Connor and Moore as a couple. Connor offered only a letter from a nurse, who knew him only as a patient.

Finally, Connor claims that Moore's affidavit was inadmissible hearsay, and that it amounted to unsupported opinion testimony on the ultimate issue. Connor misconstrues the relevant rules at these hearings. The Federal Rules of Evidence do not apply; evidence submitted at these hearings must only be probative and fundamentally fair. To be sure, Moore's affidavit does contain opinion testimony on Connor's intentions. However, the affidavit also contains relevant factual information drawn from firsthand observation. The immigration judge was entitled to rely on that information in reaching his conclusions.

It might be possible to reach a contrary conclusion on the basis of this record. However, under the substantial evidence standard, the evidence presented here does not compel a finding that Connor met his burden of proving that the marriage was entered into in good faith.

Affirmed.

In re Rowan

February 2014 MPT

 *FILE*

MPT-2: *In re Peterson Engineering Consultants*

Lennon, Means, and Brown LLC
Attorneys at Law
249 S. Oak Street
Franklin City, Franklin 33409

TO: Examinee
FROM: Brenda Brown
DATE: February 25, 2014
RE: Peterson Engineering Consultants

Our client, Peterson Engineering Consultants (PEC), seeks our advice regarding issues related to its employees' use of technology. PEC is a privately owned, non-union engineering consulting firm. Most of its employees work outside the office for over half of each workday. Employees need to be able to communicate with one another, the home office, and clients while they are working outside the office, and to access various information, documents, and reports available on the Internet. PEC issues its employees Internet-connected computers and other devices (such as smartphones and tablets), all for business purposes and not for personal use.

After reading the results of a national survey about computer use in the workplace, the president of PEC became concerned regarding the risk of liability for misuse of company-owned technology and loss of productivity. While the president knows that, despite PEC's policies, its employees use the company's equipment for personal purposes, the survey alerted her to problems that she had not considered.

The president wants to know what revisions to the company's employee manual will provide the greatest possible protection for the company. After discussing the issue with the president, I understand that her goals in revising the manual are (1) to clarify ownership and monitoring of technology, (2) to ensure that the company's technology is used only for business purposes, and (3) to make the policies reflected in the manual effective and enforceable.

I attach relevant excerpts of PEC's current employee manual and a summary of the survey. I also attach three cases that raise significant legal issues about PEC's policies. Please prepare a memorandum addressing these issues that I can use when meeting with the president.

Your memorandum should do the following:

(1) Explain the legal bases under which PEC could be held liable for its employees' use or misuse of Internet-connected (or any similar) technology.

(2) Recommend changes and additions to the employee manual to minimize liability exposure. Base your recommendations on the attached materials and the president's stated goals. Explain the reasons for your recommendations but do not redraft the manual's language.

PETERSON ENGINEERING CONSULTANTS

EMPLOYEE MANUAL
Issued April 13, 2003

Phone Use

Whether in the office or out of the office, and whether using office phones or company-owned phones given to employees, employees are not to incur costs for incoming or outgoing calls unless these calls are for business purposes. Employees may make calls for incidental personal use as long as they do not incur costs.

Computer Use

PEC employees given equipment for use outside the office should understand that the equipment is the property of PEC and must be returned if the employee leaves the employ of PEC, whether voluntarily or involuntarily.

Employees may not use the Internet for any of the following:

- engaging in any conduct that is illegal
- revealing non-public information about PEC
- engaging in conduct that is obscene, sexually explicit, or pornographic in nature

PEC may review any employee's use of any company-owned equipment with access to the Internet.

Email Use

PEC views electronic communication systems as an efficient and effective means of communication with colleagues and clients. Therefore, PEC encourages the use of email for business purposes. PEC also permits incidental personal use of its email system.

*   *   *

NATIONAL PERSONNEL ASSOCIATION
RESULTS OF 2013 SURVEY CONCERNING COMPUTER USE AT WORK
Executive Summary of the Survey Findings

1. Ninety percent of employees spend at least 20 minutes of each workday using some form of social media (e.g., Facebook, Twitter, LinkedIn), personal email, and/or texting. Over 50 percent spend two or more of their working hours on social media every day.

2. Twenty-eight percent of employers have fired employees for email misuse, usually for violations of company policy, inappropriate or offensive language, or excessive personal use, as well as for misconduct aimed at coworkers or the public. Employees have challenged the firings based on various theories. The results of these challenges vary, depending on the specific facts of each case.

3. Over 50 percent of all employees surveyed reported that they spend some part of the workday on websites related to sports, shopping, adult entertainment, games, or other entertainment.

4. Employers are also concerned about lost productivity due to employee use of the Internet, chat rooms, personal email, blogs, and social networking sites. Employers have begun to block access to websites as a means of controlling lost productivity and risks of other losses.

5. More than half of all employers monitor content, keystrokes, time spent at the keyboard, email, electronic usage data, transcripts of phone and pager use, and other information.

While a number of employers have developed policies concerning ownership of computers and other technology, the use thereof during work time, and the monitoring of computer use, many employers fail to revise their policies regularly to stay abreast of technological developments. Few employers have policies about the ways employees communicate with one another electronically.

February 2014 MPT

►*LIBRARY*

MPT-2: *In re Peterson Engineering Consultants*

In re Peterson Engineering Consultants

Hogan v. East Shore School

Franklin Court of Appeal (2013)

East Shore School, a private nonprofit entity, discharged Tucker Hogan, a teacher, for misuse of a computer provided to him by the school. Hogan sued, claiming that East Shore had invaded his privacy and that both the contents of the computer and any electronic records of its contents were private. The trial court granted summary judgment for East Shore on the ground that, as a matter of law, Hogan had no expectation of privacy in the computer. Hogan appeals. We affirm.

Hogan relies in great part on the United States Supreme Court opinion in *City of Ontario v. Quon*, 560 U.S. 746 (2010), which Hogan claims recognized a reasonable expectation of privacy in computer records.

We note with approval Justice Kennedy's observation in *Quon* that "rapid changes in the dynamics of communication and information transmission are evident not just in the technology itself but in what society accepts as proper behavior. As one *amici* brief notes, many employers expect or at least tolerate personal use of such equipment because it often increases worker efficiency." We also bear in mind Justice Kennedy's apt

aside that "[t]he judiciary risk error by elaborating too fully on the . . . implications of emerging technology before its role in society has become clear." *Quon*.

The *Quon* case dealt with a government employer and a claim that arose under the Fourth Amendment. But the Fourth Amendment applies only to public employers. Here, the employer is a private entity, and Hogan's claim rests on the tort of invasion of privacy, not on the Fourth Amendment.

In this case, the school provided a computer to each teacher, including Hogan. A fellow teacher reported to the principal that he had entered Hogan's classroom after school hours when no children were present and had seen what he believed to be an online gambling site on Hogan's computer screen. He noticed that Hogan immediately closed the browser. The day following the teacher's report, the principal arranged for an outside computer forensic company to inspect the computer assigned to Hogan and determine whether Hogan had been visiting online gambling sites. The computer forensic company determined that someone using the computer and Hogan's password had visited such sites on at least six occasions in the past two weeks, but that those sites had been deleted from the computer's browser history. Based on this report, East Shore discharged Hogan.

Hogan claimed that East Shore invaded his privacy when it searched the computer and when it searched records of past computer use. The tort of invasion of privacy occurs when a party intentionally intrudes, physically or otherwise, upon the solitude or seclusion of another or his private affairs or concerns, if the intrusion would be highly offensive to a reasonable person.

East Shore argued that there can be no invasion of privacy unless the matter being intruded upon is private. East Shore argued that there is no expectation of privacy in the use of a computer when the computer is owned by East Shore and is issued to the employee for school use only. East Shore pointed to its policy in its employee handbook, one issued annually to all employees, that states:

East Shore School provides computers to teachers for use in the classroom for the purpose of enhancing the educational mission of the school. The computer, the computer software, and the computer account are the property of East Shore and are to be used solely for academic purposes. Teachers and other employees may not use the computer for personal purposes at any time, before, after, or during school hours. East Shore reserves the right to monitor the use of such equipment at any time.

Hogan did not dispute that the employee policy handbook contained this provision, but he argued that it was buried on page 37 of a 45-page handbook and that he had not read it. Further, he argued that the policy regarding computer monitoring was unclear because it failed to warn the employee that East Shore might search for information that had been deleted or might use an outside entity to conduct the monitoring. Next, he argued that because he was told to choose a password known only to him, he was led to believe that websites accessed by him using that password were private. Finally, he argued that because East Shore had not conducted any monitoring to date, it had waived its right to monitor computer use and had established a practice of respect for privacy. These facts, taken together, Hogan claimed, created an expectation of privacy.

Perhaps East Shore could have written a clearer policy or could have had employees sign a statement acknowledging their understanding of school policies related to technology, but the existing policy is clear. Hogan's failure to read the entire employee handbook does not lessen the clarity of the message. Perhaps East Shore could have defined what it meant by "monitoring" or could have warned employees that deleted computer files may be searched, but Hogan's failure to appreciate that the school might search deleted files is his own failure. East Shore drafted and published to its employees a policy that clearly stated that the computer, the computer software, and the computer account were the property of East Shore, and that East Shore reserved the right to monitor the use of the computer at any time.

Hogan should not have been surprised that East Shore searched for deleted files. While past practice might create a waiver of the right to monitor, there is no reason to believe that a waiver was created here, when the handbook was re-issued annually with the same warning that East Shore reserved the right to monitor use of the computer equipment. Finally, a reasonable person would not believe that the password would create a privacy interest, when the school's policy, read as a whole, offers no reason to believe that computer use is private.

In short, Hogan's claim for invasion of privacy fails because he had no reasonable expectation of privacy in the computer equipment belonging to his employer.

Affirmed.

Fines v. Heartland, Inc.

Franklin Court of Appeal (2011)

Ann Fines sued her fellow employee, John Parr, and her employer, Heartland, Inc., for defamation and sexual harassment. Each cause of action related to electronic mail messages (emails) that Parr sent to Fines while Parr, a Heartland sales representative, used Heartland's computers and email system. After the employer learned of these messages and investigated them, it discharged Parr. At trial, the jury found for Fines and against defendants Parr and Heartland and awarded damages to Fines. Heartland appeals.

In considering Heartland's appeal, we must first review the bases of Fines's successful claims against Parr.

In emails sent to Fines, Parr stated that he knew she was promiscuous. At trial Fines testified that after receiving the second such email from Parr, she confronted him, denied that she was promiscuous, told him she had been happily married for years, and told him to stop sending her emails. She introduced copies of the emails that Parr sent to coworkers after her confrontation with him, in which Parr repeated on three more occasions the statement that she was promiscuous. He also sent Fines emails of a sexual nature, not once but at least eight times, even after she confronted him and told him to stop, and Fines found those emails highly offensive. There was sufficient evidence for the jury to find that Parr both defamed and sexually harassed Fines.

We now turn to Heartland's arguments on appeal that it did not ratify Parr's actions and that it should not be held vicariously liable for his actions.

An employer may be liable for an employee's willful and malicious actions under the principle of ratification. An employee's actions may be ratified after the fact by the employer's voluntary election to adopt the employee's conduct by, in essence, treating the conduct as its own. The failure to discharge an employee after knowledge of his or her wrongful acts may be evidence supporting ratification. Fines claims that because Heartland delayed in discharging Parr after learning of his misconduct, Heartland in effect ratified Parr's behavior. The facts as presented to the jury were that

Fines did not complain to her supervisor or any Heartland representative until the end of the fifth day of Parr's offensive behavior, when Parr sent the emails to coworkers. When her supervisor learned of Fines's complaints, he confronted Parr. Parr denied the charges, saying that someone else must have sent the emails from his account. The supervisor reported the problem to a Heartland vice president, who consulted the company's information technology (IT) department. By day eight, the IT department confirmed that the emails had been sent from Parr's computer using the password assigned to Parr during the time Parr was in the office. Heartland fired Parr.

Such conduct by Heartland does not constitute ratification. Immediately upon learning of the complaint, a Heartland supervisor confronted the alleged sender of the emails, and when the employee denied the charges, the company investigated further, coming to a decision and taking action, all within four business days.

Next, Fines asserted that Heartland should be held liable for Parr's tortious conduct under the doctrine of respondeat superior. Under this doctrine, an employer is vicariously liable for its employee's torts committed within the scope of the employment. To hold an employer vicariously liable, the plaintiff must establish that the employee's acts were committed within the scope of the employment. An employer's vicarious liability may extend to willful and malicious torts. An employee's tortious act may be within the scope of employment even if it contravenes an express company rule.

But the scope of vicarious liability is not boundless. An employer will not be held vicariously liable for an employee's malicious or tortious conduct if the employee *substantially* deviates from the employment duties for personal purposes. Thus, if the employee "inflicts an injury out of personal malice, not engendered by the employment" or acts out of "personal malice unconnected with the employment," the employee is not acting within the scope of employment. *White v. Mascoutah Printing Co.* (Fr. Ct. App. 2010); RESTATEMENT (THIRD) OF AGENCY § 2.04.

Heartland relied at trial on statements in its employee handbook that office computers were to be used only for business and not for personal purposes. The Heartland handbook also stated that use of office equipment for personal purposes during office hours

35

constituted misconduct for which the employee would be disciplined. Heartland thus argued that this provision put employees on notice that certain behavior was not only outside the scope of their employment but was an offense that could lead to being discharged, as happened here.

Parr's purpose in sending these emails was purely personal. Nothing in Parr's job description as a sales representative for Heartland would suggest that he should send such emails to coworkers. For whatever reason, Parr seemed determined to offend Fines. The mere fact that they were coworkers is insufficient to hold Heartland responsible for Parr's malicious conduct. Under either the doctrine of ratification or that of respondeat superior, we find no basis for the judgment against Heartland.

Reversed.

Lucas v. Sumner Group, Inc.

Franklin Court of Appeal (2012)

After Sumner Group, Inc., discharged Valerie Lucas for violating Sumner's policy on employee computer use, Lucas sued for wrongful termination. The trial court granted summary judgment in favor of Sumner Group. Lucas appeals. For the reasons stated below, we reverse and remand.

Sumner Group's computer-use policy stated:

Computers are a vital part of our business, and misuse of computers, the email systems, software, hardware, and all related technology can create disruptions in the work flow. All employees should know that telephones, email systems, computers, and all related technologies are company property and may be monitored 24 hours a day, 7 days a week, to ensure appropriate business use. The employee has no expectation of privacy at any time when using company property.

Unauthorized Use: Although employees have access to email and the Internet, these software applications should be viewed as company property. The employee has no expectation of privacy, meaning that these types of software should not be used to transmit, receive, or download any material or information of a personal, frivolous, sexual, or similar nature. Employees found to be in violation of this policy are subject to disciplinary action, up to and including termination, and may also be subject to civil and/or criminal penalties.

Sumner Group discovered that over a four-month period, Lucas used the company Internet connection to find stories of interest to her book club and, using the company computer, composed a monthly newsletter for the club, including summaries of the articles she had found on the Internet. She then used the company's email system to distribute the newsletter to the club members. Lucas engaged in some but not all of these activities during work time, the remainder during her lunch break. Lucas admitted engaging in these activities.

She first claimed a First Amendment right of freedom of speech to engage in these activities. The First Amendment prohibits

Congress, and by extension, federal, state, and local governments, from restricting the speech of employees. However, Lucas has failed to demonstrate any way in which the Sumner Group is a public employer. This argument fails.

Lucas also argued that the Sumner Group had abandoned whatever policy it had posted because it was common practice at Sumner Group for employees to engage in personal use of email and the Internet. In previous employment matters, this court has stated that an employer may be assumed to have abandoned or changed even a clearly written company policy if it is not enforced or if, through custom and practice, it has been effectively changed to permit the conduct forbidden in writing but permitted in practice. Whether Sumner Group has effectively abandoned its written policy by custom and practice is a matter of fact to be determined at trial.

Lucas next argued that the company policy was ambiguous. She claimed that the language of the computer-use policy did not clearly prohibit personal use. The policy said that the activities "should not" be conducted, as opposed to "shall not."[1] Therefore, she argued that the policy did not ban personal use of the Internet and email; rather, it merely recommended that those activities not occur. She argued that "should" conveys a moral goal while "shall" refers to a legal obligation or mandate.

In *Catts v. Unemployment Compensation Board* (Fr. Ct. App. 2011), the court held unclear an employee policy that read: "Madison Company has issued employees working from home laptops and mobile phones that should be used for the business of Madison Company." Catts, who had been denied unemployment benefits because she was discharged for personal use of the company-issued computer, argued that the policy was ambiguous. She argued that the policy could mean that employees were to use only Madison Company–issued laptops and phones for Madison Company business, as easily as it could mean that the employees were to use the Madison Company equipment only for business reasons. She argued that the company could prefer that employees use company equipment, rather

---

[1] This court has previously viewed with approval the suggestion from PLAIN ENGLISH FOR LAWYERS that questions about the meanings of "should," "shall," and other words can be avoided by pure use of "must" to mean "is required" and "must not" to mean "is disallowed."

than personal equipment, for company business because the company equipment had anti-virus software and other protections against "hacking." The key to the *Catts* conclusion was not merely the use of the word "should" but rather the fact that the entire sentence was unclear.

Thus the question here is whether Sumner Group's policy was unclear. When employees are to be terminated for misconduct, employers must be as unambiguous as possible in stating what is prohibited. Nevertheless, employers are not expected to state their policies with the precision of criminal law. Because this matter will be remanded to the trial court, the trial court must further consider whether the employee policy was clear enough that Lucas should have known that her conduct was prohibited.

Finally, Lucas argued that even if she did violate the policy, she was entitled to progressive discipline because the policy stated, "Employees found to be in violation of this policy are subject to disciplinary action, up to and including termination . . . ." She argued that this language meant that she should be reprimanded or counseled or even suspended *before* being terminated. Lucas

misread the policy. The policy was clear. It put the employee on notice that there would be penalties. It specified a variety of penalties, but there was no commitment or promise that there would be progressive discipline. The employer was free to determine the penalty.

Reversed and remanded for proceedings consistent with this opinion.